D1569555

A NEW

PORTUGUESE

GRAMMAR

IN FOUR PARTS,

CONTAINING

I. Rules for the modification and use of the different parts of speech.

II. The Syntax, in which are explained, after a more copious manner than hitherto attempted, the peculiar uses of the PORTUGUESE PARTICLES,

III. A Vocabulary, more particularly containing the Terms of COMMERCE, WAR, and NAVIGATION, with a variety of Phrases and familiar Dialogues, taken from common conversation, and the best authors.

IV. Various Passages extracted from the most approved modern and ancient writers, with a view to facilitate the reading of the ancient and most valuable Portuguese books.

By ANTHONY VIEYRA TRANSTAGANO,
Teacher of the Portuguese and Italian Languages.

Necesse est enim inter quos mercatura & contractuum sint, inter eos quoque sermonis esse commercia. UBERTUS FOLIETA.

LONDON,
Printed for J. NOURSE, Bookseller to His MAJESTY.
MDCCLXVIII.

TO

ROBERT ORME, Efq.

S I R,

THE beft Hiftorians and the greateft
Poet my country has produced,
have dedicated their talents to the fubject which at prefent employs your's;
and as no one is more fenfible than
yourfelf of the Geographical, Com-
mercial, and Political Knowledge, which
may be derived from an acquaintance
with their writings on Indian affairs, this
work of mine can no where be addreffed
with greater propriety than to yourfelf.

I am, SIR,

Your moft humble fervant,

ANTHONY VIEYRA.

P R E F A C E.

AS the usefulness of the Portuguese language is so well known to all English merchants, who carry on a general trade with the different parts of the known world, it will be needless to use any arguments here to prove it; and I shall reserve what I have to say on the copiousness and energy of this language for the Preface to an English and Portuguese Dictionary I am now engaged in, the First Part of which, being greatly forwarded, shall soon be sent to the press.

The reader will find in the First Part of this Grammar, what is material as a foundation of the whole.

At the end of the Second Part is a full explanation of the Particles, on which I have bestowed more time and labour, because this subject has been hitherto much neglected, although the principal ornament and elegance, not only of the Portuguese,

tuguese, but of every other language, chiefly con-
sist in the proper arrangement and judicious
intersperson of these words.

In the Third Part is a larger collection than
hitherto published of the terms of Trade, War,
Navigation, &c. which the present intercourse
between the two nations renders particularly useful.

Having found a great difficulty of procuring
Portuguese books in this country, I have been
commonly obliged to furnish with part of my pri-
vate collection those Gentlemen whom I have had
the honour of assisting in the study of this language,
during my residence here; therefore, in the
Fourth Part I have given some passages selected
out of the best Portuguese Authors; and which
will, at the same time, facilitate the reading of
their most eminent Historians, such as Goes,
Barros, Pinto, &c. whose Orthography differs
considerably from the more modern.

CONTENTS.

PART I.

6   PART

CONTETS.

PART III.

PART IV.

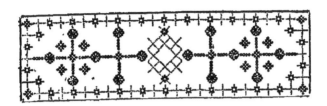

A NEW
PORTUGUESE
GRAMMAR.

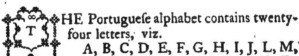

PART I.

CHAP. I.

Of the Portuguese Alphabet, and the Manner of pronouncing each separate Letter.

THE Portuguese alphabet contains twenty-four letters, viz.

A, B, C, D, E, F, G, H, I, J, L, M, N, O, P, Q, R, S, T, U, V, X, Y, Z.

The A is expressed by a sound like that of *a* in the English words *at, rat, fat,* &c.

B is expressed by a sound like that of the *be* in the first syllable of the English word *Betty.*

C is expressed by a sound like that of the first syllable of the English word *celebrated.*

D is expressed by a sound like that of the first syllable of the word *declare.*

E is

E is expressed by a sound like that we give to the English *a* when we pronounce the word *care*.

F is expressed by the same sound as in English.

G is expressed by a sound like that of the first syllable in the English word *generation*.

H is expressed by a sound like that of the English word *aghast*, if you cut off the two last letters *st*, and keep the accent upon the second *a*.

I is expressed by the sound of our *ee*.

J is called *j consoante*, i. e. the j consonant, which appellation we must read *ee consoante*, and has the same power as the *g* before *e* or *i*.

L, as in English.

M, as in English.

N, as in English.

O has nearly the same sound as in the English word *store*.

P is expressed by a sound like that of *pe* in the English word *penny*.

Q is expressed by a sound like that of the English *k*.

R is expressed by a sound like that of the English participle *erred*, if you cut off the last letter *d*.

S as in English.

T is expressed by a sound like that of *tha* in the English word *Thames*.

U is expressed by a sound like that of *oo* in the English word *poop*.

V is expressed by a sound like that of *oo*; they call it also *oo consoante*, that is, the v consonant.

X is expressed by a sound like that of our pronoun personal *she*, if you add an *s* to it, or as *shees*.

Y is expressed by a sound like that of *i* in the English word *visible*, and is called *ypsilon*.

Z is expressed by the sound of our English *zed*, leaving out the *d*, or *zea*.

Of

Of the manner of pronouncing the Portuguese Letters as combined in Syllables; and first

Of the Vowels.

A.

A in Portuguese is commonly pronounced like *a* in the following English words, *adapted, castle*, &c. It is sometimes pronounced with less strength, and closely, as in *ambos*, where the *a* is pronounced like *a* in the English word *ambition*.

E.

The letter *e* has two different sounds; the one open, like *ay* in *dayly*; the other close, like that in the English word *mellow*. Examples of the former, *fé*, faith, *pé*, foot, &c. Examples of the latter, *rede*, a net, *parede*, a wall, &c. In this consists a great part of the beauty of the Portuguese pronunciation, which, however, cannot be learned but by a long use, notwithstanding all the rules that can be given for it.

I

Is pronounced like *ee* in the English word *steel*, *aço*; or like *i* in the English words *still*, ainda ; *visible*, *visivel*.

O.

This vowel has two sounds; one open, as in the word *dó*, pity, where the *o* is pronounced like our *o* in the word *store*; the other close, as in the Portuguese article *do*, of, and the word *redondo*, round, where the *o* is to be pronounced like our *u* in *turret* or *stumble*. I is likewise in the different pronunciation of this vowel that consists the greatest part of the beauty of the Portuguese pronunciation; but it can be learned only by a long use.

U.

The vowel *u* is pronounced like *oo* in the Englifh.

Y.

Y has the fame found as the Portuguefe vowel *i*.

Of Confonants.

B

Keeps always the fame found as in Englifh.

C

Before *a*, *o*, *u*, and the confonants *l*, *r*, is properly pronounced as *k*; but before *e* and *i* it takes the hiffing found of *s*: it takes alfo the found of *s* before *a*, *o*, *u*, when there is a dafh under it thus *ç*.

☞ I could wifh the learned in Portugal would follow the refolution of the Royal Academy of Madrid, by expunging fuch dafh, and placing the s in its ftead, fince they have in both languages the fame hiffing found, which frequently occafions great confufion in the proper ufe of them.

C before *h* is pronounced like *ch* in the Englifh words *charity*, *cherry*, &c.

Double *c* itfounded only before *e* and *i*, the firft with the found of *k*, and the other with the hiffing found of *s*; as in *accidente*, accident, pronounce *ak-fidente*.

D

Is pronounced in Portuguefe as in Englifh.

F

Is pronounced always as in Englifh.

G

Before the vowels *a*, *o*, *u*, and before confonants, is pronounced as in Englifh: example, *gofto*, tafte; *gaiola*, cage; *grito*, a cry.

G be-

G before *e* and *i* denotes the found of *j* confonant.

Gua founds almoft like our *wa* : example, *guarda*, pronounce *gwarda*.

Gue, gui, are pronounced as *gue* in the word *gueft*, and *gi* in the word *gift* ; but in the verbs *arguir* and *redarguir* it is to be pronounced as if it was written *argueer*, &c.

H.

The letter *b* is never afpirated nor pronounced at the beginning of words, as *bora*, an hour ; *bomem*, a man : but, according to the modern orthography, all thofe words are written without an *b*.

H when preceded by a *c*, makes a found with it like our *cb*. See the letter C, and alfo the letters L and N.

J

Is pronounced like our *j* confonant.

K.

The Portuguefe have no fuch letter as *k*.

L

Is pronounced in Portuguefe as in Englifh.

Lb is pronounced like *g* before an *l* in the Italian words *figlio, foglio,* &c.

M

Is pronounced as in Englifh, being placed before a vowel with which it forms a fyllable ; but when it is at the end of words, and preceded by the letter *e*, caufes in Portuguefe a nafal found like that of the French words *vin,* wine ; *pain,* bread ; except *fôem, tôem,* from the verbs *foar, toar,* and fome others.

M at the end of words, preceded by an *a, o,* or *i,* has fuch a nafal obtufe found that only may be learned from a mafter's mouth.

N be-

N.

N being before a vowel with which it forms a syllable, is pronounced as in English; otherwise, it only gives a nasal found to the vowel that precedes it.

N before *b* has the same found as *gn* in Italian, or in the French words *Espagne, Allemagne.*

P.

P and *pb* are pronounced as in English.

Q

Is pronounced like *k*: example, *quero*, I am willing, pronounce *kero*.

The vowel *u* after *q* in the word *qual*, which, must be pronounced so smoothly as to render it almost imperceptible to the ear, as in the English word *quantity*, in order to distinguish it from the substantive *cal*, lime.

R.

R and double *r* are pronounced as in English.

S.

S and *ss* are pronounced as in English.

S between two vowels is pronounced like a *z*; particularly in the words ending in *oso*, as *amoroso, cuidadoso*, &c. and, as some say, in those that end in *esa*, as *mesa, defesa*, &c.

T

Is pronounced as in English.

V

Is pronounced as in English.

X

Is pronounced as *sh* in English; except *axioma*, in which, according to *Feyjo*, the *x* is to be pronounced like *c*.

X after

X after the vowel *e* is pronounced like *cs*, in the words *extençam, extenuado, expulso, excellente*, and some other words.

X between two vowels is pronounced like *gz* in the words *exactamente, exornar*; except *Alexandre, Paixão, Puxo, baxo*, and some other words, that only may be learned by use. You must take care in pronouncing the *g* so smoothly as to render it almost imperceptible to the ear.

Z

Is pronounced as in English; but at the end of words is pronounced like *s*, as *rapáz*, boy; *Francez*, French; *perdiz*, partridge; *voz*, voice; *luz*, light, &c.

The tittle, or little dash, which the Portuguese call *til*, is set by them over some letters instead of *m*; as *bē* instead of *bem*; *convē* instead of *convem*; *būa* instead of *huma*; and as it is then to be considered as an *m*, see what we have said about the pronunciation of the same letter.

They also set their *til* over the vowels *ao, aa*, in the end of words, thus, *āo, āa*. See what we have said above of *m* at the end of words preceded by an *a*.

Of Diphthongs.

The meeting of many vowels in one and the same syllable is called Diphthongs, and they are the following in the Portuguese language.

Aa, as in *maçaā*, an apple.
Ae, as in *caēs*, dogs.
Ay, as in *pay*, father.
Ai, as in *mais*, more.
Ao, as in *pao*, wood.
Au, as in *causa*, a cause.
Eo, os in *cco*, heaven.
Ey, as in *rey*, king.

Ei,

Ei, as in *amei,* I loved.

Eu, as *eu,* I.

Io, as *vio,* he saw.

Oe, as in *poēm,* they put ; *compoēm,* they compoſe ; *meloēs,* melons, &c.

Oy, as in *boy,* an ox ; *foy,* he was.

Ou, as *dou,* I give ; *fou,* I am.

Ue, as *azues,* blue.

☞ The two vowels in the following words muſt be plainly and diſtinctly pronounced.

Ai, as in *paiz,* a country, pronounce *pa-iz.*

Ea, as in *lamprea,* a lamprey, pronounce *lampre-a.*

Ia, as *clemencia,* clemency, pronounce *clemenci-a.*

Io, as in *navío,* a ſhip, pronounce *naví-o.*

Iu, as *viuva,* a widow, pronounce *vi-uva.*

Oa, as *Liſboa,* Liſbon, *proa,* a poop, pronounce, *Liſbo-a,* &c.

Oe, as *tōem, fōem,* from the verbs *tóar* and *foar,* pronounce *to-em,* &c.

Oi, as *roim,* bad, pronounce *ro-im.*

Oo, as *cooperaçam,* co-operation, pronounce *co-operaçaõ.*

Ui, as *ruina,* a ruin, pronounce *ru-ina.*

✸✸✸✸✸✸✸✸✸✸✸✸✸✸✸✸✸✸✸✸✸✸✸✸✸✸✸✸✸✸✸

C H A P. II.

Of the Articles.

THOSE particles called Articles, are properly prepoſitions, commonly put before nouns, to ſhew their gender, number, and caſe.

Theſe articles are definite or indefinite.

Of the Definite Articles.

The definite marks the gender, number, and caſe, of the nouns which it precedes.

The

The Englifh tongue has but one definite article, namely *the*, which ferves for both numbers.

The Portuguefe has two, viz. *o* for the mafculine and *a* for the feminine.

The definite articles have five cafes, the nominative, genitive, dative, accufative, and ablative; becaufe the vocative in the nouns is defigned and preceded by the particle *o*.

The Declenfion of the Mafculine Article o.

Singular.	Plural.
Nominative, *o*, the.	Nominative, *os*, the.
Genitive, *do*, of the.	Genitive, *dos*, of the.
Dative, *ao*, or *o*, to the.	Dative, *aos*, or *os*, to the.
Accufative, *ao*, or *o*, the.	Accufative, *aos*, or *os*, the.
Ablative, *do*, from *or* by the.	Ablative, *dos*, from *or* by the.

The Declenfion of the Feminine Article a.

Singular.	Plural.
Nominative, *a*, the.	Nominative, *as*, the.
Genitive, *da*, of the.	Genitive, *das*, of the.
Dative, *á*, to the.	Dative, *ás*, to the.
Accufative, *a*, the.	Accufative, *as*, the.
Ablative, *da*, from the.	Ablative, *das*, from *or* by the.

☞ Obferve, the Portuguefe have an article for each gender, both in the fingular and the plural.

Of the Indefinite Article.

The indefinite article may be put before the mafculine as well as the feminine gender, before the plural as well as the fingular number.

The indefinite article has but four cafes, the genitive, the dative, the accufative, and ablative.

One may put *de* before a noun mafculine as well as a feminine, as *huma coroa de rey*, a king's crown; the word *rey* is mafculine: *hum chapeo de palha*, a hat of ftraw; the word *palha* is of the feminine gender.

The indefinite article *de* is alfo put before the plural as well as the fingular number: example, *huma*

coroa

coroa de flores, a crown of flowers; *hum prato de arroz*, a plate of rice.

Declension of the Indefinite Article.

Genitive, *de*, of.   Accusative, *a*.
Dative, *á*, to.   Ablative, *de*, from.

☞ The accusative of this article is not expressed in English : example, *Eu conheci a seu pay*, I knew his father; *eu conheci a sua may*, I knew his mother.

The indefinite article may be also put before infinitives, and signifies *to*; as, *he tempo de fallar, de dormir, de ler*, &c. it is time to speak, to sleep, to read, &c. *eu vou a ver, a fallar*, I am going to see, to speak.

N. B. Whenever we meet *of* and *to* in English, followed by *the*, remember they are the indefinite articles, and then we must make use of the indefinite article *de*, or *a*, in Portuguese.

When the verb is in the infinitive mood, and serves as nominative to the following verb, they put the article *o* before it; as *o comer e o dormir saõ as cousas mais necessarias nesta vida*, eating and sleeping are the greatest necessaries of life.

When the preposition *in* is followed by the article *the*, or by a pronoun possessive, as *in the, in my, in thy, in his*, we must render it in Portuguese by *em o* or *no, em os* or *nos*, for the masculine; and by *em a* or *na, em as* or *nas*, for the feminine : example, in the garden, *em o jardim*, or *no jardim*; in the street, *em a rua*, or *na rua*; in thy book, *em o teu*, or *no teu livro*; in his bed, *em a sua*, or *na sua cama*, &c.

When after the preposition *with*, which in Portuguese is expressed by *com*, we find the article *the*, or a pronoun possessive, as *with the, with my*, &c. we may say *com o* or *co, com a* or *coa, com os* or *cos, com as* or *coas* : example, with the prince, *com o* or *co principe*; with the sword, *com a* or *coa espada*; with the eyes, *com os* or *cos olhos*; with my books, *com os* or *cos meus livros*, &c.

When

When the prepofition *with* is followed by a pronoun poffeffive, and thus by a noun of quality or kindred, as *with your majefty*, *with your highnefs*, *with your excellency*, *with his brother*, &c. *with* muft then be rendered by the Portuguefe *com*, as *com voffa majeftade*, *com voffa alteza*, *com o feu irmaõ*, without ufing the article.

Obferve, that the dative and accufative of the indefinite article fometimes are not expreffed in Englifh, particularly before the pronouns perfonal and proper names; example, *convem a nos*, it behoves us; *Antonio matou a Pedro*, Anthony killed Peter.

C H A P. III.

Of the Nouns.

THE Portuguefe nouns have feveral forts of terminations, as will appear below.

They have but two genders, the mafculine and feminine.

The Portuguefe nouns have no variation of cafes, like the Latin, and it is the article only that diftinguifhes the cafe.

Of Nouns ending in a.; and firft of their Declenfion.

Singular.	Plural.
Nom. *a rainha*, the queen.	Nom. *as rainhas*, the queens.
Gen. *da rainha*, of the queen.	Gen. *das rainhas*, of the queens.
Dat. *á rainha*, to the queen.	Dat. *ás rainhas*, to the queens.
Acc. *a rainha*, the queen.	Acc. *as rainhas*, the queens.
Voc. *o rainha*, O queen.	Voc. *o rainhas*, O queens.
Abl. *da* ou *pella rainha*, from	Abl. *das* ou *pellas rainhas* from
or by the queen.	or by the queens.

We have already obferved that the Portuguefe Nouns have no variation of cafes; therefore there is,

no occafion to exhibit more examples of their de-
clenfions, becaufe you have nothing to do but to
change the article according to their gender.

Of the Genders of Nouns ending in a.

Nouns ending in *a* are generally of the feminine
gender; as *rofa*, a rofe; *janella*, a window, &c.
You muft except *dia*, a day; *planeta*, a planet; and
other nouns ending in *a*, belonging to a man; as
marióla, a porter; *jefuita*, a jefuit: thofe derived
from the Greek are likewife mafculine; as *dogma*,
epigramma, *clima*; except thofe of fciences, as *mathe-
mática*, *theologia*, &c.

Except alfo from this general rule fome nouns
that have the accent upon the laft fyllable; as *alva-
rá*, a charter, or a prince's letters patent; *Pará*, one
of the captainfhips of the Portuguefe America, &c.

Obferve, that the plural of the nouns ending in *a*
is formed by adding the letter *s* to the fingular; as
likewife the plural of all nouns that terminate in
vowels.

Obferve alfo, that the nouns ending in *āa* are of
the feminine gender, and form their plural as thofe
ending in *a*.

Of the Gender of Nouns ending in e.

Nouns ending in *e* are generally of the mafculine
gender; as *dente*, a tooth; *valle*, a valley; *ventre*,
the womb, &c.

The exceptions are, *fé*, faith; *fonte*, a fountain;
chave, a key; *torre*, a tower; *ave*, a fowl; *carne*,
flefh or meat; *gente*, people; *morte*, death; *neve*,
fnow; *noite*, night; *ponte*, a bridge; *pefte*, plague;
parte, part; *ferpente*, a ferpent; *lebre*, a hare.

Except alfo all names of virtues, vices, faculties,
and paffions of the mind; as *virtude*, virtue; *fan-
tidade*, holinefs; *bondade*, goodnefs; *vaidade*, vani-
ty; *ociofidade*, idlenefs, &c.

Thirdly,

Thirdly, *idade*, age; *velhice*, oldneſs; *ruſticidade*, ruſticity; *capacidade*, capacity; *felicidade*, happineſs; *ſorte*, fortune; *arte*, art; *arvore*, a tree; *fertilidade*, fertility; *ſede*, thirſt; *ſebe*, a hedge; *couve*, cabbage; *herdade*, a farm or manor; *chaminé*, a chimney; *parede*, a wall; *ſaude*, health; *rede*, a net; *maré*, the tide; *febre*, fever; *galé*, a galley, &c.

Of the Gender of Nouns ending in i.

Nouns ending in *i* are maſculine; as *extaſi*, a rapture; *nebri*, a hawk, &c.

Of Nouns ending in o.

Nouns ending in *o* are of the maſculine gender; as *livro*, a book; *filho*, a ſon; *braço*, an arm; *veſtido*, a garment; *eſpelho*, a looking-glaſs; &c. Except, *náo*, a ſhip; *filhó*, a fritter or pancake; *eiró*, an eel.

Of Nouns ending in u.

All nouns ending in *u* are maſculine; as *perú*, a turkey; *grou*, a crane.

Of the Nouns ending in y.

Nouns ending in *y* are of the maſculine gender; as *rey*, king; *pay*, father; *boy*, ox, &c. except *ley*, a law; *māy*, a mother.

Of the other Terminations of Nouns, or of thoſe terminating in Conſonants.

1. All nouns ending in *al* are maſculine; as *final*, a ſign or token; *ſal*, ſalt. You muſt except *cal*, lime, which is feminine, and has no plural.

The plural of theſe nouns is formed by changing the letter *l* of the ſingular into *es*; as *ſinaes* from *final*; *animaes* from *animal*.

2. Nouns ending in *ar* are of the maſculine gender; as *ar*, air.

The plural of theſe nouns is formed by adding *es* to the ſingular, as *ares* from *ar*.

Some

Some nouns ending in *as* in the plural are feminine, and have no singular; as *migas, exequias,* &c.

3. Nouns ending in *az* are of the masculine gender; as *rapaz,* a boy: except *paz,* peace. The plural is found as the last.

4. Nouns ending in *el* are masculine; as *annél,* a ring; *papél,* paper, &c.

The plural of these nouns is formed by changing the *l* of the singular into *is*; as *anneis,* from *annél*; *papeis,* from *papél.*

5. Nouns ending in *em* are of the masculine gender; as *homem,* a man; *pentem,* a comb, &c. Except *ordem,* order; *viagem,* a voyage; *virgem,* a virgin, &c. but *salvagem,* a sort of beast, is common.

The plural of these nouns is formed by changing the *m* of the singular into *ns*; as *homens* from *homem,* &c.

6. Nouns ending in *er* are of the masculine gender; as *poder,* power; *prazer,* pleasure, &c. Except *colhér,* a spoon; *mulhér,* a woman.

The plural of these nouns is formed by adding *es* to the singular, as *colheres,* from *colhér.*

7. Nouns ending in *ez* are of the masculine gender; as *freguez,* a parishioner or a customer; *mez,* month; *arnez, levez, revez,* &c. Except *surdez,* deafness; *torquez, vez,* &c.

The plural of these nouns is formed by adding *es* to the singular, as *freguezes,* from *freguez*; but *tez* has no plural.

8. Nouns ending in *il* are of the masculine gender; as *fuil,* a funnel; *barríl,* a barrel.

The plural of these nouns is formed by changing the *l* of the singular into *s,* as *funis,* from *funíl,* &c. Except *aquátil, fácil, pensíl,* &c. which change the *il* into *eis* in the plural, as *fáceis* from *fácil.*

9. Nouns ending in *im* are of the masculine gender, as *espadim,* a little sword.

The

The plural of these nouns is formed by changing the *m* of the singular into *ns*, as *espadins* from *espadim*.

10. Nouns ending in *ir* or *yr* are of the masculine gender: but *martir* ou *martyr*, a martyr, is common.

The plural of these nouns is formed by adding *es* to the singular.

11. All nouns ending in *iz* are of the masculine gender; as *apprendiz*, an apprentice; *nariz*, nose; *verniz*, varnish: *matiz*, a shadowing in painting; *chafariz*, *chamariz*, &c. Except *aboiz*, *perdiz*, *raiz*, *coderniz*, *matriz*, &c.

The plural of these nouns is formed by adding *es* to the singular, as *perdizes* from *perdiz*.

12. Nouns ending in *ol* are of the masculine gender; as *anzól*, a hook; *sól*, the sun, &c.

The plural of these nouns is formed by changing the *l* of the singular into *es*, as *anzoes* from *anzól*, &c.

13. Nouns ending in *om* are of the masculine gender; as *som*, sound; *dom*, gift, &c.

The plural of these nouns is formed by changing the *m* of the singular into *ns*, as *sons* from *som*, &c.

14. Nouns ending in *or* are of the masculine gender; as *amôr*, love; *temôr*, fear, &c. except *dôr*, pain; *côr*, colour, &c.

The plural of these nouns is formed by adding *es* to the singular, as *amores* from *amor*.

Nouns ending in *os* are of the masculine gender; as *Deos*, God.

The plural of these nouns is formed by changing the *s* into *zes*, as *Deozes* from *Deos*.

15. Nouns ending in *oz* are of the masculine gender; as *albernóz*, a Moorish coat; *arróz*, rice; *algôz*, hangman, &c. Except *nóz*, a walnut; *vóz*, voice; *fóz*, the mouth of a river.

The plural of these nouns is formed by adding *es* to the singular.

7

16. Nouns

16. Nouns ending in *ul* or *um* are of the mafcu-line gender; as *ful*, the fouth; *Saúl*, Saul, a propér name of a man; *atúm*, tunny-fifh.

The plural of thofe ending in *ul*, according to the learned *Bluteau*, is formed by changing the *l* of the fingular into *es*, as *fues* from *ful*, *azues* from *azul*, blue, &c. Except *confues* from *conful*, a conful.

The plural of thofe ending in *um* is formed by changing the *m* of the fingular into *ns*, as *atuns* from *atúm*.

17. Nouns ending in *uz* are of the mafculine gender; as *arcabúz*, an arquebufs.

The plural of thefe nouns is formed by adding *es* to the fingular.

18. Nouns ending in *aō* are of the feminine gen-der; as *maō*, hand; *compofiçaō*, compofition; *ora-çaō*, oration, &c. Except *paō*, bread; *anaō*, a dwarf; *ouçaō*, a hand-worm; *trovaō*, thunder; *ef-quadraō*, a fquadron; *piaō*, a child's top; *borraō*, a blot with ink; *papelaō*, brown paper; *chaō*, the ground; *quinhaō*, a fhare.

There is no certain rule for the formation of the plural of the nouns ending in *aō*; becaufe fome change the *aō* of the fingular into *āes*, as *Alemāes*, from *Alemaō*, a German; *capitāes*, from *capitaō*, a captain; *caēs*, from *caō*, a dog; *paēs*, from *paō*, a loaf; &c. Some change the *aō* of the fingular in-to *āos*; as *cidadãos*, from *cidadaō*, a citizen; *chri-ftãos*, from *chriftão*, a chriftian; *cortezãos*, from *cor-tezão*, a coùrtier; *villaōs*, from *villaō*, a villain, &c. Some change the *aō* of the fingular into *ōes*; as *ef-quadrōes*, from *efquadraō*, a fquadron; *trovōes*, from *trovaō*, thunder; *conclusōes*, from *conclufaō*, a con-clufion or thefes fheet; *oraçōes*, from *oraçaō*, an ora-tion: and generally all the Portuguefe nouns that may be eafily made Englifh, by changing their ter-mination *çaō* into the Englifh termination *tion*, as *declinaçaō*, declenfion or declination; *confideraçaō*, con-fideration, &c. and thefe áre of the feminine gender.

19. All

19. All nouns fignifying a male muſt be of the maſculine gender; as *duque*, duke ; *marquez*, a marquis ; *conde*, count : and thoſe denoting a female are always feminine.

You may form two general rules from what has been ſaid about the formation of the plural of nouns, viz.

I. That all the nouns ending in any of the vowels have their plural formed by adding the letter *s* to the fingular.

II. That the plural of the nouns ending in *az*, *ez*, *iz*, *oz*, *uz*, is formed by adding *es* to the fingular.

Of the Augmentatives.

The Portugueſe have their augmentatives, which are formed by the increaſe of one or two ſyllables, which they add to the end of their nouns, and ſerve either to augment the fignification of nouns, or to declare a thing that is contemptible; and ſo, from *homem*, a man, they form *homemzarraõ*, a great ſtrong man ; from *tolo*, a fool, *toleiraõ*, a great fool, &c. and ſome others that only may be learned by uſe. They have alſo their augmentatives for the feminine ; as, *molherona*, a great ſtout woman ; *toleirona*, &c.

There are great many nouns that appear, by their termination, to be augmentatives, though they are not ; as, *foraõ*, a ferret ; *atafona*, an aſs or a horſe-mill, &c.

Of Diminutives.

The diminutives leſſen the fignification of their primitives.

The diminutives in the Portugueſe language are always formed by changing the laſt vowel of the primitives into *inho*; but they denote either ſmallneſs of things, or kindneſs and flattery ; as, *bichinho*, a little worm, from *bicho*, a worm ; *coitadinho*, from *coitado*, a poor little man ; *bonitinho*, a little pretty,

C from

from *bonito*, pretty. Sometimes they are formed by adding *zinho* to the primitives ; as *caõ-zinho*, a little dog, from *caõ*, a dog ; *irmaõ-zinho*, dear little brother, from *irmaõ*, &c.

The diminutives that serve for the feminine have their termination in *inha*, or *zinha* ; as *maõ-zinha*, a little hand, from *maõ*, a hand ; *cabecinha*, a little head, from *cabeça*, a head. You may see in the last example, that the diminutives serving for the feminine, and ending in *inha*, are formed by changing the last syllable *a* of the primitives into *inha*.

Observe, that many nouns appear to be diminutives without being so ; as, *moinho*, a mill ; *espinha*, a fish-bone.

Note, the diminutives in Portuguese sometimes convey a bad meaning, and denote contempt.

Of Nouns Adjective.

All adjectives ending in *o* make their feminine by changing *o* into *a* ; as, *douta*, from *douto*, learned ; but *mào*, bad, makes *mà* in the feminine.

Those that end in *aõ* have their feminine in *aã* ; as, *faã*, from *faõ*, healthy ; *louçaã*, from *louçaõ*, brisk, gay, beautiful ; *meaõ*, from *meaã*, middling, ordinary.

Those ending in *e* are common to both genders ; as, *forte*, strong, &c.

Those that end in *m* make their feminine by adding an *a* to the masculine ; as, *huma*, from *hum*, one ; *alguma*, from *algum*, some, &c. and sometimes by changing the *m* into *a* ; as, *commua*, from *commum*, common ; *boa*, from *bom*, good.

Those that end in *u* make their feminine by adding *a* to the masculine, as *nùa*, from *nù*, naked ; *crùa*, from *crù*, raw.

Those that end in *ez* are common to all the genders ; as *cortez*, civil, kind ; *capaz*, capable, &c. except some which make the feminine, by adding *a* to

the

the mafculine; as, *Franceza*, from *Francez*, French; *Portugueza*, from *Portuguez*, Portuguefe.

Efpanhol, Spanifh, makes *Efpanhola* in the feminine; but generally thofe that end in *l* are common to both genders; as, *affavel*, affable; *cruel*, cruel, &c.

Of the Comparifon of Adjectives.

The comparifon of adjectives is the way of increafing their fignification by certain degrees, which are three, viz. the pofitive, the comparative, and the fuperlative.

The pofitive lays down the natural fignification of the adjective; as, *nobre*, noble; *grande*, great.

The comparative raifes it to a higher degree, by comparing it to the pofitive, which in Portuguefe is performed by the adverbs *mais*, more; *menos*, lefs; as, *mais nobre*, nobler, *or* more noble; *menos bella*, lefs handfome.

There are fome adjectives which do not admit of *mais* or *menos* before them; as, *celefte*, *nacido*, *comprado*, *defterrado*, &c.

There are four Portuguefe comparatives which end in *or*: they may alfo be expreffed by *mais*, more, before their pofitives; as,

Mayor,	greater,	*mais grande*.
Menor,	lefs,	*mais pequeno*.
Peor,	worfe,	*mais roim*.
Melhor,	better,	*mais bom*.

To which may be added, *fuperior*, fuperior; *inferior*, inferior; *deterior*; and fome others.

Obferve, that there can be no comparifon made without the word *than*; and that this word is expreffed in Portuguefe by *que*. Ex. *Mais claro que o fol*, clearer than the fun; *mais branco que a neve*, more white than the fnow. The particle *que* is fometimes preceded by the word *do*. Ex. *Ifto he mais do que eu lhe diffe*, this is more than I told him;

be

be mais prudente do que parece, he is more wise than it appears.

N. B. The comparatives *superior*, *inferior*, and some others, do not require *que* before the second term, but the dative of the articles, viz. *á*, *ás*, *ao*, *aos:* Examp. *O outro be superior a este*, the other is superior to this.

When the Portuguese have a mind to heighten their comparisons, they make use of, *muyto mais*, a great deal, or much more ; as also of *muyto menos*, a great deal, or much less. Ex. *Cæsar be muyto mais estimado que Pompeo*, Cæsar is much more esteemed than Pompey ; *Pompeo foy muyto menos feliz que Cæsar*, Pompey was much less happy than Cæsar.

Of the Superlatives.

The Portuguese superlative is formed from the noun adjective, by changing the last letter into *issimo* for the masculine, and into *issima* for the feminine : thus, from *bello* is formed *bellissimo* and *bellissima*, most handsome. But sometimes the superlative is formed by adding *muyto*, very, to the positive ; as, *muyto alto*, very tall.

Observe, that some superlatives are differently formed; as, *frigidissimo*, from *frio*, cold ; *amicissimo*, from *amigo*, friend ; *antiquissimo*, from *antigo*, ancient ; *capacissimo*, from *capaz*, capable ; *nobilissimo*, from *nobre*, noble ; *acerrimo*, from *acre*, sharp, or acerb ; *riquissimo*, from *rico*, rich ; *fertilissimo*, from *fertil*, fruitful ; *bonissimo*, from *bom*, good ; *fidelissimo*, from *fiel*, faithful ; *sacratissimo*, from *sagrada*, sacred, &c.

The most is expressed also in Portuguese by *o mais* and *a mais* ; as, the most fair, or fairest, *o mais bello*, *a mais bella*. But you must observe, that there are some adjectives which do not admit of *muyto*, very, *o mais*, or *a mais* ; as *morto*, *desterrado*, &c.

Observe, that by changing the last letter of the superlatives into *amente*, the superlative adverbs are composed ;

compofed; as, from *doutiffimo*, learned, *doutiffima-mente*, moft learnedly, &c. But the pofitive adverbs are formed by adding *mente* to the feminine of the pofitive; as, *doutamente*, learnedly, from *douta*, the feminine of *douto*; *prudentemente*, prudently, from *prudente*, prudent.

Of numeral Nouns; and firft, of Cardinal.

The cardinal nouns are fuch as exprefs the number of things; as,

Hum, one	*Vinte e dous*, twenty-two
Dous, two	*Vinte e tres*, &c. twenty-three, &c.
Tres, three	
Quatro, four	*Trinta*, thirty
Cinco, five	*Quarenta*, forty
Seis, fix	*Cincoenta*, fifty
Sete, feven	*Seffenta*, fixty
Outo or *oito*, eight	*Setenta*, feventy
Nove, nine	*Oitenta*, eighty
Dez, ten	*Noventa*, ninety
Onze, eleven	*Cem*, a hundred
Doze, twelve	*Duzentos*, two hundred
Treze, thirteen	*Trezentos*, three hundred
Quatorze, fourteen	*Mil*, a thoufand
Quinze, fifteen	*Dous mil*, two thoufand
Dezafeis, fixteen	*Milhaõ*, or *conto*, a million
Dezafete, feventeen	*Huma dezena*, half a fcore
Dezouto, eighteen	*Huma Duzia*, a dozen
Dezanove, nineteen	*Huma Vintena*, a fcore
Vinte, twenty	*Duas Dezenas*, two fcore
Vinte e hum, twenty-one	*Tres Dezenas*, three fcore

Obferve, that all the cardinals that are adjective nouns, are not declined, being of the common gender, except *hum*, *huma*, one; *duos*, *duas*, two; and thofe compofed of *cento*, a hundred; as, *duzentos*, *duzentas*, two hundred; *quatro centos*, *quatro centas*, four hundred, &c. and when the feminine *huma* is preceded by *a*, and followed by *a outra*, then *huma* fignifies *firft*, and *a outra*, *fecondly*.

The plural, *huns*, *humas*, is taken fometimes inftead of *alguns*, *algumas*, fignifying *fome*; as *huns reys*, fome kings; *humas rainhas*, fome queens.

C 3   N. B.

N. B. *Cento* lofes *to* before a noun, either mafculine or feminine, and the *n* is changed into *m*; therefore you muft fay, *cem foldados*, not *cento foldados*. It only retains *to* and *n* when it is followed by another number, as, *cento e bum*, &c. a hundred and one, &c. and when it is fubftantive.

N. B. Sometimes *cento* is made a fubftantive; as *bum cento de caftanhas*, one hundred of chefnuts; and fo all the cardinal numbers, when preceded by an article, or by another noun of number; as, *o cinco de páos*, the five of clubs; *bum fete*, a feven.

The cardinal number is rendered into Englifh by the ordinal, when it expreffes the day of the month, or the date of any act; as, *chegou a quatro de Mayo*, he arrived the fourth day of May.

Ordinal Nouns.

Ordinal nouns are fuch as exprefs the order of things; as,

Primeyro, firft
Segundo, fecond
Terceiro, third
Quarto, fourth
Quinto, fifth
Sexto, fixth
Setimo, feventh
Oitavo, eighth
Nono, ninth
Decimo, tenth
Undecimo, or *onzeno*, eleventh
Duodecimo, twelfth
Decimo-tercio, thirteenth
Decimo-quarto, fourteenth
Decimo quinto, fifteenth
Decimo-fexto, fixteenth
Decimo-fetimo, feventeenth

Decimo-oitavo, eighteenth
Decimo-nono, nineteenth
Vigefimo, or *ventefimo*, twentieth
Vigefimo-primeyro, one and twentieth
Trigefimo, thirtieth
Quadragefimo, or *quarentefimo*, fortieth
Quinquagefimo, fiftieth
Sexagefimo, fixtieth
Septuagefimo, feventieth
Octagefimo, eightieth
Nonagefimo, ninetieth
Centefimo, the hundredth
Millefimo, the thoufandth
Ultimo, the laft

The proportional numbers are, *fimplez, duplicado* or *dobrado, triplicado* or *triplice* or *trefdobrado, quadruplicado* or *quadruplo, centuplo*; fingle, double, threefold, fourfold, a hundredfold.

The

The diftributive nouns are, *bum a bum*, one by one; *dous a dous*, two by two.

In Englifh all ordinal numbers may be formed into adverbs; but in Portuguefe they have only *primeiramente*, and *fecundariamente*, or *fegundariamente*, firft, fecondly; and to exprefs thirdly, fourthly, &c. they fay, *em terceiro lugar*, *em quarto lugar*, in the third place, in the fourth place.

A method (for thofe who underftand French) to learn a great many Portuguſe words in a fhort time.

We muft obferve, that the French fyllable *cha* is generally expreffed in Portuguefe by *ca*, rejecting the *b*. Examp. *Charbon*, *charité*, *chaftité*, *chapon*, *chapelle*, *chapitre*, &c. the Portuguefe fay, *carvaõ*, *caridade*, *caftidade*, *capaõ*, *capella*, *capitulo*, &c. Obferve alfo the following rules.

French words ending in *ance* or *ence*; as, *conftance*, *vigilance*, *clemence*, *prudence*, &c. in Portuguefe end in *ancia* or *encia*; as, *conftancia*, *vigilancia*, *clemencia*, *prudencia*, &c.

Agne makes *anha*; montagne, *montanha*; campagne, *campanha*.

Ie makes *ia*; comedie, *comedia*. Here you lean the accent upon the *a*, and not upon the *i*, as in French; *poefie*, *poefia*.

Oire makes *oria*; gloire, *gloria*; victoire, *victoria*.

Ure makes *ura*; impofture, *impoftura*; figure, *figura*.

Ifon makes *zaõ*; raifon, *razaõ*; prifon, *prizaõ*.

On makes *aõ*; charbon, *carvaõ*; baron, *baraõ*.

Ulier makes *ular*; regulier, *regular*; particulier, *particular*.

French Terminations ending in Portuguefe in e.

Ant, *ante*; vigilant, *vigilante*; amant, *amante*.

Ent, adjective, *ente*; prudent, *prudente*; diligent, *diligente*.

Te makes *dade*; pureté, *puridade*; liberalité, *liberalidade*.

French

French Terminations ending in Portuguese in vel.

Able, vel; louable, *louavel*; amiable, *amavel*.

French Terminations ending in Portuguese in ez.

Ois, names of nations, *ez*; Francois, *Francez*; Anglois, *Inglez*.

French Terminations ending in Portuguese in o.

Ain and *ien*, names of nations, *ano*; Romain, *Romano*; Italien, *Italiano*; Napolitain, *Napolitano*.
Aire, ario; salaire, *salario*; temeraire, *temerario*.
Eau, eo; chapeau; *chapeo*.
Ent, substantive, *ento*; sacrement, *sacramento*.
Eux, oso; genereux, *generoso*; gracieux, *graciofo*.
If, ivo; actif, *activo*; passif, *passivo*.
C, co; porc, *porco*; Turc, *Turco*.

French Terminations ending in Portuguese in or.

Eur, or; terreur, *terror*; humeur, *humor*; chaleur, *calor*.

Change of Terminations of the Verbs and Participles.

Er, in the infinitive mood of the first conjugation, makes *ar*; aimer, *amar*; chanter, *cantar*.
Ir makes *ir*, in the infinitive mood; as, partir, *partir*; sentir, *sentir*.
Oir makes *er* in the infinitive mood; as, concevoir, *conceber*.
The participles in *é* make *ado*; aimé, *amado*; parlé, *fallado*.
The participles in *i* make *ido*; dormi, *dormido*; menti, *mentido*.
The participles in *u* make *do*; as, conçu, *concebido*; entendu, *entendido*, &c.
There are a great many Portuguese words that have no manner of analogy with the French, which hinder these rules from being general.

C H A P.

CHAP. III.

Of the Pronouns.

THE pronouns are either perfonal, conjunctive, mixed, poffeffive, demonftrative, interrogative, relative, or improper.

Of Pronouns perfonal.

The pronouns perfonal are *eu* and *nos* for the firft perfon, and they ferve for the mafculine and feminine.

Tu and *vos* for the fecond; and thefe ferve alfo for the mafculine and feminine.

Elle for the third perfon of the mafculine gender; and it makes *elles* in the plural.

Ellà, for the third perfon of the feminine gender, forms in the plural *ellas*.

The pronouns perfonal are declined by the article indefinite, *de, a, a, da.*

The Declenfion of Pronouns perfonal.

Firft Perfon.

Singular Number.	Plural Number.
Nom. *Eu,* I	Nom. *nós,* we
Gen. *de mim,* of me	Gen. *de nós,* of us
Dat. *á mim,* to me	Dat. *à nós,* to us
Acc. *a mim,* me	Acc. *a nós,* us
Abl. *de mim,* or *por mim,* from *or* by me	Abl. *de nós,.* or *por nós,* from *or* by us.

With me is rendered by *commigo*; and fometimes they add the pronoun *mefmo* to it; *me* is expreffed by *me* in the Portuguefe; as, fpeak to me, *fallai-me*; tell me, *dizei-me*; fend me, *mandai-me*; write to me, *efcrevei-me*; elle *diffe-me,* he told me, &c.

With us is rendered in Portuguefe by *com nofco.*

Us is rendered by *nos*. Examp. tell us, *dizei-nos*; give us, *dai-nos*; fhow us, *moftrai-nos*; *elle diffe-nos*, he told us, &c. In thefe examples *us* is not a pronoun perfonal, but conjunctive, as you will fee hereafter.

Second Perfon.

Singular.	Plural.
Nom. *tu*, thou	Nom. *vós*, ye *or* you
Gen. *de ti*, of thee	Gen. *de vós*, of you
Dat. *a ti*, or *te*, to thee	Dat. *à vós*, or *vos*, to you
Acc. *a ti*, or *te*, thee	Acc. *á vós*, or *vos*, you
Abl. *de ti*, or *por ti*, from	Abl. *de vós*, ou *por vos*, from
or by thee	*or* by you

With thee is rendered by *comtigo*; and fometimes they add to it the pronoun *mefmo*. *You*, or *yourfelf*, after imperatives, are rendered by *vos*, and not *vós*; as, be you contented, *contentai-vos*; fhow yourfelf, *moftrai-vos*; hide yourfelf, *efcondei-vos*.

Thee, or *thyfelf*, are expreffed after imperatives by *te*; as, *moftraite*, fhow thyfelf.

With you is rendered in Portuguefe by *com vofca*.

Third Perfon. For the Mafculine.

Singular.	Plural.
Nom. *elle*, he *or* it	Nom. *elles*, they
Gen. *delle*, of him *or* of it	Gen. *delles*, of them
Dat. *a elle*, to him *or* to it	Dat. *a elles*, to them
Acc. *a elle*, him *or* it	Acc. *a elles*, them
Abl. *delle* ou *por elle*, from	Abl. *delles* or *por elles*, from
or by him or it.	*or* by them

The Portuguefe have no particular pronoun, as our *it*, for things that are inanimate.

Remember that the pronoun *him*, or *to him*, when joined to a verb, is always rendered in Portuguefe, by *lhe*, and *them*, or *to them*, by *lhes*.

With him is rendered in Portuguefe fometimes by *com elle*, and fometimes by *comfigo*, to which they add the pronoun *mefmo*.   3

Third

Third Perfon. Feminine.

Singular.	Plural.
Nom. *ella*, fhe *or* it	Nom. *ellas*, they
Gen. *della*, of her *or* of it	Gen. *dellas*, of them
Dat. *a ella*, to her *or* to it	Dat. *a ellas*, to them
Acc. *a ella*, her *or* it	Acc. *a ellas*, them
Abl. *della*, òr *por ella*, from *or* by her *or* it	Abl. *dellas* or *por ellas*, from *or* by them

Remember that the pronoun *her* or *to her*, when joined to a verb, is always rendered in Portuguefe by *lhe* and *them*, or *to them*, by *lhes*; as you will fee in the ponouns conjunctive.

With her is rendered in Portuguefe by *com ella* or *comfigo*.

Of the Pronoun *fi*, himfelf, *or* one's felf.

There is another pronoun perfonal that ferves indifferently for the mafculine and feminine : this is *fi*, one's felf. It has no nominative.

> Gen. *de fi*, of one's felf, himfelf, *or* herfelf.
> Dat. *a fi*, to one's felf, &c.
> Acc. *a fi*, one's felf, &c.
> Abl. *de fi* or *por fi*, from *or* by one's felf, &c.

It is often joined with the pronoun *mefmo* or *mefma*; as, *de* or *por fi mefmo*, by himfelf; *por fi mefma*, or *de fi mefma*, by herfelf; *o homem naõ ama fenaõ a fi mefmo*, man loves himfelf only; *quem naõ he bom fenaõ para fi, naõ he bem que viva*, who minds no body but himfelf only, don't deferve to live? *o vicio he abominavel de fi mefmo*, vice is hateful of itfelf; *a terra de fi*, or *de fi mefma he fertil*, the earth is fruitful of itfelf.

Obferve, that they join alfo the pronoun *mefmo* to pronouns perfonal, as the French do with their pronoun *même*, viz.

E *u*

Eu mesmo, myself	nós mesmos, ourselves
Tu mesmo, thyself	vós mesmos, yourselves
Elle mesmo, himself	elles mesmos, } themselves
Ella mesma, herself	ellas mesmas, }

o homem mesmo, man himself ; a mesma virtude, virtue itself.

1st. Obferve, that *mesmo* with the article is also an adjective, fignifying *the fame*; thus, *e mesmo, a mesma, os mesmos*, the fame, relating to fome nouns expreffed or underftood.

2dly, Note, That they join alfo the adjective *outro*, other, to the plural of the pronouns perfonal, *I* and *thou*; fo they fay, *nos outros*, we; *vos outros*, you.

3dly, *Comfigo* may be rendered in Englifh (as we have faid above) by *with him* and *with her*; but you muft obferve, that it may be rendered alfo by *with them* in the plural; and fometimes by *about him, about her*, or *about them*. Exam. *Elle*, or *ella, nunca traz dinheiro comfigo*, he, *or* fhe, never has money about him, *or* about her.

Of Pronouns conjunctive.

The pronouns conjunctive are fo called, becaufe they always come immediately before or after the verb.

The pronoums conjunctive bear a great refemblance to the pronouns perfonal: the pronouns perfonal are,

Eu, I; *tu*, thou; *elle*, he; *nos*, we; *vos*, ye; *elles*, they.

There are feven pronouns conjunctive, viz. *me*, to me, *or* me; *te*, to thee, *or* thee; *fe*, to himfelf, *or* himfelf, to herfelf, *or* herfelf; *lhe*, to him, *or* him, to her, *or* her; *nos*, to us, *or* us; *vos*, to you, *or*, you; *lhes*, to them, *or* them.

EXAMPLE.

Ifto me agrada, this pleafes me ; *he-me neceffario*, I want. *Deos te ve*, God fees thee.
Ella fe louva, fhe praifes herfelf.

4 *Eu*

Eu lhe direi, I will tell him, *or* I will tell her.
Eu lhes prometti, I promifed them : as well for the mafculine as the feminine.

The pronoun conjunctive, *lhe,* is always put after
the verb, when it is in the imperative mood ; as,
dizei-lhe, tell him ; *cortai-lhe as azas,* cut his wings ;
but when the verb is in fome other mood, it may be
put either before or after it ; as, *elle lhe cortou,* or
elle cortou-lhe a cabeça, he has cut off his head. The
fame obfervation takes place in the other pronouns
conjunctive.

The pronoun conjunctive, *fe,* is fometimes followed by *me, lhe,* &c. as, *offerece-fe-me,* it is offered
to me ; *reprefentou fe-lhe,* it was reprefented to him,
&c.

1ft, Note, that the pronouns conjunctive are
very often joined to a verb, preceded or followed by
the verb *haver.* Examp. *Dar lhe hei tanta pancada,*
or, *en lhe hei de dar tanta pancada, que,* &c. I will
cudgel him fo much, that, &c.

2dly, *Lhe* is fometimes rendered in Englifh by
you. Examp. *Que lhe parece aquillo ?* What do you
think of that ? *affente no que lhe digo,* be perfuaded,
or believe what I tell you.

Of Pronouns mixed.

There are fome pronouns in Portuguefe which are
compofed of the pronouns perfonal and conjunctive,
and which therefore are called mixed.

To clear up this matter, you muft exprefs them
as underneath, changing the letter *e* of the pronoun
conjunctive into *o* for the mafculine, and into *a* for
the feminine ; as, to fay *to me of it,* inftead of *me o,*
or *me a,* you muft fay, *mo* or *ma.* In the like manner, inftead of *lhe o* or *lhe a,* you muft fay, *lho* or
lha, &c. as you may obferve in the following pronouns mixed.

mo,

mo, m. $\begin{cases} \text{me of it,} \\ \text{or} \\ \text{it } \textit{or} \text{ him to me} \end{cases}$ *to* $\begin{cases} \text{thee of it} \\ \text{or} \\ \text{it } \textit{or} \text{ him to thee} \end{cases}$

ma, f. $\begin{cases} \text{me of it,} \\ \text{or} \\ \text{it } \textit{or} \text{ her to me} \end{cases}$ *ta* $\begin{cases} \text{thee of it} \\ \text{or} \\ \text{it } \textit{or} \text{ her to thee} \end{cases}$

mos, m. *mas*, f. $\begin{cases} \text{me of them} \\ \text{or} \\ \text{them to me} \end{cases}$ *tos*, m. *tas*, f. $\begin{cases} \text{thee of them} \\ \text{or} \\ \text{them to thee} \end{cases}$

selo, m. *sela*, f. $\Big\}$ it to himself, to herself, *or* to themselves.

selos, m. *selas*, f. $\Big\}$ them to himself, to herself, *or* to themselves
them to herself, to himself, *or* to themselves

lho, m. $\begin{cases} \text{to him, } \textit{or} \text{ to her of it} \\ \text{or} \\ \text{it to him, } \textit{or} \text{ to her} \end{cases}$

lha. f. $\begin{cases} \text{to him, } \textit{or} \text{ to her of it} \\ \text{or} \\ \text{it to him, } \textit{or} \text{ to her} \end{cases}$

lhos, m. *lhas*, f. $\Big\}$ to them of it, to him of them, *or* to her of them
to them of it, to him of them, *or* to her of them

nolo, m. *nola*, f. $\Big\}$ us of it, *or* it to us

nolos, m. p. *nolas*, f. p. $\Big\}$ them to us

volo, m. *vola*, f. $\Big\}$ you of it, *or* it to you

volos, m. p. *volas*, f. p. $\Big\}$ you of them, *or* them to you

Here you have some Examples.

Para dar-lho, to give it to him *or* to her.
Dai-mo, give it me.
Eu to darei, I'll give it you.
Entrego-to, I deliver it to you.
Dize-lho, you tell it him, *or* her.
Entrega-lhos, Deliver them to him, *or* to her.
Lá selo haja, let that to himself.
Elle nolo disse, he told us of it.
Eu volos mandarei, I'll send them to you.

If the verbs are in the infinitive, the pronouns mixed may be put either before or after the verbs; as, *para dizermo*, or *para mo dizer*, to tell me it: but if the verbs are in the gerund, the pronouns
mixed

mixed muſt be tranſpoſed; as, *dizendomo*, and not *mo dizendo*, in telling me it.

You muſt make uſe of theſe pronouns, both maſculine and feminine, according to the gender of the thing that is ſaid, ſent, delivered, &c. and not of the perſon to whom the thing is ſaid, ſent, given, &c.

Of the Pronouns poſſeſſive.

Pronouns poſſeſſive, ſo called, becauſe they ſhew that the thing ſpoken of belongs to the perſon or thing which they ſerve to denote, are of two ſorts, abſolute and relative. See the remarks hereafter.

The Engliſh have no article in the nominative before the pronouns poſſeſſive; but the Portugueſe have, as, *my, o meu, a minha*, fem. Plur. *as meus, as minhas*, fem.

The pronouns poſſeſſive in Portugueſe are the following:

Sing. *meu*, m. *minha*, f. } my
Plur. *meus*, m. *minhas*, f. } my
Sing. *teu*, m. *tua*, f. } thy
Plur. *teus*, m. *tuas*, f. } thy
Sing. *ſeu*, m. } his, *or* its
Plur. *ſeus*, m. } his, *or* its
Sing. *ſua*, f. } her *or* its
Plur. *ſuas*, f. } her *or* its
Sing. *noſſo*, m. *noſſa*, f. } our
Plur. *noſſos*, m. *noſſas*, f. } our
Sing. *voſſo*, m. *voſſa*, f. } your
Plur. *voſſos*, m. *voſſas*, f. } your

The pronouns poſſeſſive are declined by the definite article *o* for the maſculine, and by *a* for the feminine.

EXAMPLE.

Singular.

Nom. *o meu libro*, my book
Gen. *do meu livro*, of my book
Dat. *ao meu livro*, to my book
Acc. *meu livro*, my book
Abl. *do ou pello meu livro*, from *or* by my book.

Plural

Plural.

Nom. *os meu livros,* my books
Gen. *dos meus livros,* of my books
Dat. *aos meus livros,* to my books
Acc. *os meus livros,* my books
Abl. *dos* ou *pellos meus livros,* from *or* by my books

Decline all the other mafculines after the fame manner, and their feminines by the article *a*; as, my houfe, *a minha cafa*; of my houfe, *da minha cafa,* &c.

Note, you muft not ufe the definite article when the pronouns poffeffive precede nouns of quality; as well as thofe of kindred, but the indefinite article *de, a,* &c.

E X A M P L E.

Voffa mageftade, your majefty.
De voffa mageftade, of your majefty, &c.
Meu pay, my father.
De meu pay, of my father, &c.

From the above examples it appears that nouns declined by the indefinite article have no article in the nominative.

Though the definite article fometimes is ufed before nouns of kindred, yet we ought not to ufe it, according to the old proverb: *tu vivendo bonos, fcribendo fequare peritos.*

Seu is made ufe of fometimes in room of *voffo* and *voffa,* in the polite way of fpeaking: fo they fay, *tenho o feu livro,* I have your book; *falles ao feu criado,* I fpoke to your fervant; *os feus olhos faõ formofos,* your eyes are handfome.

Remarks upon the Poffeffives.

The pronouns poffeffive abfolute always come before the noun which they belong to. We have expreffed them above.

Pronouns

Pronouns poſſeſſive relative are ſo called becauſe they, not being joined to their ſubſtantive, ſuppoſe it either expreſſed before, or underſtood, and are related to it. They are the following:

	Maſc.	Fem.	
Sing.	*Meu,*	*minha,*	} mine.
Plur.	*Meus,*	*minhas,*	
Sing.	*Teu,*	*tua,*	} thine.
Plur.	*Teus,*	*tuas,*	
Sing.	*Seu,* his,	*ſua,* hers.	
Plur.	*Seus,*	*ſuas,*	theirs.
Sing.	*Noſſo,*	*noſſa,*	} ours.
Plur.	*Noſſos,*	*noſſas,*	
Sing.	*Voſſo,*	*voſſa,*	} yours.
Plur.	*Voſſos,*	*voſſas,*	

To expreſs in Portugueſe *it is mine, it is thine,* &c. we muſt ſay *he meu, he teu,* &c.

The pronouns poſſeſſive abſolute do not agree, in Portugueſe, in gender with the noun of the poſſeſſor, as in Engliſh, but with that of the thing poſſeſſed; as, *a may ama a ſeu filho,* the mother loves her ſon; *o pay ama a ſua filha,* the father loves his daughter. So you ſee that the pronoun maſculine *ſeu,* in Portugueſe, is ſometimes rendered by *her* in Engliſh, and the feminine *ſua* by *his.*

The ſame obſervation is to be made upon the poſſeſſives relative, according to the gender of the noun that is underſtood; therefore they ſay of a hat (for inſtance) belonging to a lady, *he o ſeu,* it is hers; becauſe the noun underſtood, viz. *chapeo,* hat, is of the maſculine gender.

We have already ſaid, that *ſeu* and *ſua* are ſometimes rendered in Engliſh by *your,* when they are abſolute; but you muſt alſo obſerve, that they are ſometimes rendered in Engliſh by *yours,* when they are pronouns relative, and that in the polite way of ſpeaking; and ſo they ſay, ſpeaking of any thing belonging to a gentleman or lady, *he o ſeu,* or

D *he*

be a fua, it is yours; but if the gentleman or lady are not prefent, or if they do not fpeak directly to them, though prefent, then the pronouns *feu* and *fua* muft be rendered into Englifh by *his* or *hers*.

Note, That the pronouns poffeffive abfolute, in Portuguefe, agree alfo in number with the noun of the thing poffeffed; hence it is that they fay *a fua biftoria*, its hiftory, fpeaking of a kingdom, province, &c. or, his hiftory, fpeaking of any hiftory com-pofed by a man; or, her hiftory, fpeaking of that written by a woman; or, their hiftory, fpeaking of that written by feveral hands, or of feveral people. And from this example you may learn, that the Por-tuguefe have no particular pronoun poffeffive for things that are inanimate, as we have the pronoun *its*. Hence at laft it follows, that when the Portu-guefe poffeffives *feu* and *fua* are relative, they are rendered into Englifh by *his* or *hers*, or *theirs*, ac-cording to the gender and number of the noun of the poffeffor that is underftood.

You muft alfo obferve, that they fometimes add the third pronoun perfonal, *delle*, of him, *delles*, of them, *della*, of her, *dellas*, of them; to denote more plainly whofe thing it is they fpeak of; as, *o feu li-vro delles*, their book; *as fuas palareas della*, her words, &c.

Note, That the poffeffives abfolute are left out when they are preceded by a verb, or by a pronoun conjunctive, which fufficiently denote whofe thing it is they fpeak of; the Portuguefe being then con-tented with the article: as *devo-lhe a vida*, I owe my life to him, or to it; *doe-me a barriga*, my belly akes.

When the pronouns poffeffive abfolute are before nouns of different genders in the fame fentence, and with which they are grammatically conftrued, they ought to be repeated; as *feu pay e fua may*, his fa-ther and mother; not *feu pay e may*.

Moreover,

Moreover, the Portuguese use the pronoun possessive absolute in the following case, when we use the possessive relative; a friend of mine, *hum dos meus amigos*.

The possessives *minha, tua, sua, nossa, vossa,* may be also relative, but with a different meaning. Examples: *Levarei a minha avante,* I will insist upon it, I will obtain it; *elle levará a sua avante,* he will insist upon it, he will do it; *levai a vossa avante,* go on with your resolution; *fazer das suas,* to play tricks, to dodge.

Os meu, os seus, &c. signify, my relations, or my friends, thy relations, or thy friends; as *os seus naõ o querem,* his parents or relations do not like him; *deixa-o hir com os seus,* let him go with his people, his countrymen, &c.

Take notice, that when the pronoun possessive is accompanied by a pronoun demonstrative, they do not put the article in the nominative: they do not say, *o este meu livro,* but *este meu livro,* this book of mine. But in all other cases they make use of the indefinite article; as *d'este* or *deste vosso livro,* &c.

Of the Pronouns demonstrative.

They are called pronouns demonstrative, because they serve to point out or demonstrate any thing or person; as, this book, *este livro;* that man, *aquelle homem.*

There are three principal demonstratives in Portuguese, viz. *este,* this; *esse,* that; *aquelle,* that; but observe, that *este* shews the thing or person that is just near or by us; *esse* shews the thing that is a little farther, or near the person; and *aquelle* shews what is very distant from the person who speaks, or is spoken of, and is expressed in English by *that there,* or *yonder.* You must also observe, that *esse, essa,* is used in writing to any person to express the place or town wherein he dwells; as *tenho fallado nessa cidade*

com

com muitos amigos, I have fpoken in your city with many friends.

. Thefe pronouns are declined thus :

		Mafc.	Fem.	Neut.	
Singular	Nom.	*efte*,	*efta*,	*ifto*,	this.
	Gen.	*defte*,	*defta*,	*difto*,	of this.
	Dat.	*á efte*,	*á efta*,	*á ifto*,	to this.
	Acc.	*efte*,	*efta*,	*ifto*,	.this.
	Abl.	*defte*,	*defta*,	*difto*,	from this.
				No Neut.	
Plural	Nom.	*eftes*,	*eftas*,		thefe.
	Gen.	*deftes*,	*deftas*,		of thefe.
	Dat.	*á eftes*,	*á eftas*,		to thefe.
	Acc.	*eftes*,	*eftas*,		thefe.
	Abl.	*deftes*,	*deftas*,		from thefe.

		Mafc.	Fem.	Neut.	
Singular	Nom.	*effe*,	*effa*,	*iffo*,	that *or* it.
	Gen.	*deffe*,	*deffa*,	*diffo*,	of that, &c.
	Dat.	*á effe*,	*á effo*,	*á iffo*,	to that.
	Acc.	*effe*,	*effa*,	*iffo*,	that.
	Abl.	*deffe*,	*deffa*,	*diffo*,	from that.
				No Neut.	
Plural	Nom.	*effes*,	*effas*,		thofe.
	Gen.	*deffes*,	*deffas*,		of thofe.
	Dat.	*á effes*,	*á effas*		to thofe,
	Acc.	*effes*,	*effas*,		thofe.
	Abl.	*deffes*,	*deffas*		from thofe.

		Mafc.	Fem.	Neut.	
Singular	Nom.	*aquelle*,	*aquella*,	*aquillo*,	that.
	Gen.	*daquelle*,	*daquella*,	*daquillo*,	of that.
	Dat.	*áquelle*,	*áquella*,	*áquillo*,	to that.
	Acc.	*aquelle*,	*aquella*,	*aquillo*,	that.
	Abl.	*daquelle*,	*daquella*,	*daquillo*,	from that.
				No Neut.	
Plural.	Nom.	*aquelles*,	*aquellas*,		thofe.
	Gen.	*daquelles*,	*daquellas*,		of thofe.
	Dat.	*áquelles*,	*áquellas*,		to thofe.
	Acc.	*aquelles*,	*aquellas*,		thofe.
	Abl.	*daquelles*,	*daquellas*,		from thofe.

You

You muſt obſerve, that there is an eliſion of the vowel of the indefinite article in the genitive and ablative of the pronouns *eſte* and *eſſe*, both in the ſingular and plural; and that they write and pronounce *deſte*, *deſtas*, &c. inſtead of *de eſte*, *de eſtas*; and ſo in the neuter they write *diſſo*, *diſto*, inſtead of *de iſſo*, *de iſto*. The ſame obſervation you muſt make upon the pronoun *aquelle*, wherein you will ſee another eliſion beſides, in the dative caſe.

Note, That both the Portugueſe and Spaniards have demonſtratives of the neuter gender; though they do not agree with the ſubſtantives as in Latin, becauſe they do not ſay *iſto homem*, but *eſte homem*, this man. But the word *couſa*, thing, is always underſtood, though the neuter demonſtrative does not agree with it; ſo that it is the ſame thing to ſay *iſto* or *eſta couſa*, this thing; *iſſo* or *eſſa couſa*, that thing, &c. Example, *iſſo he* or *eſſa he a couſa de que nos eſtamos fallando*, that is the thing we are ſpeaking of; *aquillo he* or *aquella he a couſa que vos déveis fazer*, that is the thing you muſt do, &c.

When the prepoſition *em*, in, comes before the pronouns demonſtratives, they make an eliſion of the vowel of it, and change the conſonant *m* into *n*; and ſo, inſtead of writing and pronouncing *em eſte*, *em eſta*, *em iſto*, *em iſſo*, *em aquillo*, they write and pronounce *neſte*, *neſta*, *niſto*, *niſſo*, &c. in this, in that, &c.

The words *outro*, *outra*, are often joined to the pronouns demonſtrative, taking off the laſt *e*; as *eſtóutro*, *eſſóutro*, *aquellóutro*. Example; *Eſtóutro homem*, this other man; *eſtóutra molher*, this other woman; *eſſóutro homem*, that other man.

They alſo join very often the pronoun *meſmo*, the ſame, to the demonſtratives; as *eſte meſmo homem*, this very ſame man; *aquillo meſmo*, that very ſame thing.

Aqui, *alî*, and *lá*, are ſometimes added to the demonſtrative, or to the noun that comes after it, in or-

der

der to specify and particularize it still more ; as *este bomem aqui*, this man ; *aquella molber lá*, that woman : *aqui* denoting a near, or present object ; and *lá*, a distant and absent one.

The pronouns *aquelle, aquella, aquelles, aquellas,* when they relate to persons, and are followed by the relative *que*, are rendered into English by *be who* or *be that, she who* or *that, they who* or *that* ; as *aquelle que ama a virtude be feliz*, he who loves virtue is happy ; *aquelles que desprezaõ a ciencia naõ conhecem o valor della*, they who despise learning know not the value of it. You must observe, that when *aquelle, aquella*, &c. are preceded by *este, esta*, &c. then *este* signifies the last thing or person spoken of, and *aquelle*, &c. the first ; as *Carlos foi grande, Frederico ambicioso, este valente, aquelle poderoso,* Charles was great, Frederic ambitious, the first powerful, the last courageous.

The pronoun possessive absolute *his, her, their,* construed in English with a noun followed by the pronoun relative *who* or *that* before a verb, is made into Portuguese by the genitive of the pronouns *aquelle, aquella, aquelles,* followed by *que*, and the possessive is left out ; as, all men blame his manners who often says that which himself does not think, *todo o mundo censura os custumes daquelle que tem por costume dizer o que naõ tem no pensamento*; Providence does not prosper their labours that slight their best friends, *a Providencia naõ abençoa o traballho daquelles que desprezaõ os seus melhores amigos.*

The English pronoun *such* followed by *as* or *that*, (but not governed of the verb substantive *to be*), is also rendered into Portuguese by *aquelles que*, or *aquelles taes que*, or *aquelle que* ; as, such as do not love virtue do not know it, *aquelles* or *aquelles taes que naõ amaõ a virtude, naõ a conhecem.*

The pronouns *isso, isto, aquillo,* before *que*, are Englished by *what* ; as *elle diz aquillo que sabe,* he says what he knows.

Aquelle

Aquelle is alfo ufed to fhew contempt; as *que quer aquelle bomem?* what does that man defire?

Of the Pronouns interrogative.

The pronouns interrogative ferve to afk queftions, and are as follow; as, who, what, which, *quem, que, qual.*

EXAMPLE.

Quem he? who is it?
Quem vos diffe iffo? who told you fo?
Que quereis? what will you have?
Com que fe fuftenta? what does he maintain him-felf with?
Que eftais fazendo? what are you doing?
De que fe faz ifto? from what is this done?
Que livro he efte? what book is this?
Que negocios tendes? what affairs have you?
Que cafa he? what houfe is it?
De qual fallaes vòs? which do you fpeak of?
Qual delles? which of them?
Quem or *qual dos dous?* which *or* whether of the two?

Thefe pronouns are thus declined.

Singular and Plural. Mafculine and Feminine.	Singular and Plural. Mafculine and Feminine.
Nom. *quem,* who.	Nom. *que,* what.
Gen. *de quem,* of whom.	Gen. *de que,* of what.
Dat. *a quem,* to whom.	Dat. *a que,* to what.
Acc. *quem,* whom.	Acc. *que,* what.
Abl. *de quem,* from whom.	Abl. *de que,* from what.

Qual is fpoken both of the perfon and of the thing, and is declined thus:

Singular. Mafculine and Feminine.
Nom. *qual,* which *or* what.
Gen. *de qual,* of which *or* what.
Dat. *á qual,* to which *or* what.
Acc. *qual,* which *or* what.
Abl. *de qual,* from which *or* what.

D 4

Plural,

Plural. Mafculine and Feminine.
Nom. *quaes*, which *or* what.
Gen. *de quaes*, of which *or* what.
Dat. *a quaes*, to which *or* what.
Acc. *quaes*, which *or* what.
Abl. *de quaes*, from which *or* what.

Obferve, that when the word *quer* is added to *quem*, or *qual*, it quite alters the meaning; *quemquer* fignifying whoever, òr any perfon, and *qualquer* any one, whether man, woman, or thing; and fometimes they add the particle *que* to them, as *quemquer que*, &c.

Of the Pronouns relative.

Pronouns relative are thofe which fhew the relation, or reference, which a noun has to what follows it. They are in Portuguefe the following : *qual*, which; *que*, that or which; *cujo*, whofe; *quem*, who.

Qual, in a fenfe of comparifon, is followed by *tal*, and then *qual* is Englifhed by *as*, and *tal* by *fo*.

N. B. When *qual* is only a relative, it is declined with the definite articles *o* or *a*.

The pronoun *que* may be relative both to perfons and things, and is common to all numbers, genders, and cafes ; as, *o livro que*, the book which ; *os livros que*, the books which ; *a carta que*, the letter which; *as cartas que*, the letters which ; *o meftre que enfina*, the mafter who teacheth ; *a molher que tenho*, the wife that I have ; *o homem que eu amo*, the man whom I love : and it is declined thus.

Singular and Plural.
Nom. *que*, which *or* who.
Gen. *de que*, of which *or* of whom.
Dat. *a que*, to which *or* to whom.
Acc. *que*, which *or* whom.
Abl. *de que*, from which *or* from whom.

Que

Que is sometimes a conjunction; as *creyo que hirei*, I believe that I shall go. See the Syntax.

The relative *quem*, who, is only relative to persons; but in the nominative case of the singular is rendered into English by *he who*, or *who*; as, *quem falla deve confiderar*, &c. he who speaks ought to confider, &c. *eu naō sei quem*, I know not who.

Obferve, that *quem* is common to all numbers, genders, and cafes; but it has no nominative in the plural.

Quem is declined thus:

Singular and Plural.

Nom. *quem*, he who, *or* fhe who, *or* whoever
Gen. *de quem*, of whom
Dat. *a quem*, to whom
Acc. *quem*, whom
Abl. *de quem*, from whom

Quem is fometimes a particle disjunctive, and then it fignifies *fome*; as, *quem canta, e quem ri*, fome fing, and fome laugh; and fometimes it ferves to exclamation; as, *quem me dera eftar em cafa!* how fain would I be at home!

Cujo, cuja, is declined thus:

	Mafc.	Fem.	
Nom.	*cujo*,	*cuja*,	whofe
Gen.	*de cuja*,	*de cuja*,	of whofe
Dat.	*a cujo*,	*a cuja*,	to whofe
Acc.	*cujo*,	*cuja*,	whofe
Abl.	*de cujo*,	*de cuja*,	from whofe

(Sing.)

The plural is formed by adding *s* to the fingular; as, *cujos, cujas*, whofe, &c.

Note, that *cujo* muft be followed by the noun or term which it refers to, and with which it agrees in gender, number, and cafe; as, *a peffoa cuja reputafam vos admira*, the perfon whofe reputation you wonder at; *o ceo cujo foccorro nunca falta*, heaven, whofe affiftance never fails; *cuja bella cara*, whofe fair vifage; *cujas bellezas*, whofe beauties; *a cujo pay*,

pay, to whofe father; *de cujos irmaõs tenho recebido*, from whofe brothers I have received. Obferve alfo that *cujo* is not to be repeated, though the terms which it refers to be of different numbers; as, *cuja valia e obras*, whofe value and deeds.

Note, that *o*, *a*, *os*, *as*, *lo*, *la*, &c. are alfo pronouns relative, when joined to verbs. See the fyntax, chap. iv.

Of the improper Pronouns.

Thefe pronouns are called *improper*, becaufe indeed they are not properly pronouns, but have a great refemblance with pronouns, as well as with adjectives. They are the following :

Hum, one
Alguem, fomebody
Algum, fome
Ninguem, nobody
Nenhum, none
Cadahum, every one, each
Cada, every
Outro, *outra*, other
Outrem, another
Qualquer, any one; whether man, or woman, or thing
Qualquer dos dous, either of the two, *or* whetherfoever of the two
Quemquer, whoever, *or* any perfon
Todo, all, *or* every
Tal, fuch, &c.

Hum has two terminations, viz. *hum*, *huma*; and in the plural it makes *huns* and *humas*. It is declinable with the indefinite article.

Alguem has only one termination, and it is only declinable in the fingular with the indefinte article.

Algum has two terminations, viz. *algum*, *alguma*; and in the plural, *alguns*, *algumas*. It is declinable with the indefinite article.

Ninguem has only one termination, and is only declinable in the fingular with the indefinite article : *ninguem o cré*, no body believes it.

Nenhum

Nenbum has two terminations. viz. *nenbum, nenbuma*, and in the plural *nenbuns, nenbumas*; and is only declinable with the indefinite article: *nenbum homem*, no man; *de nenbum effeito*, of none effect.

Cadabum has two terminations, viz. *cadabum, cadabuma*; but it has no plural, and is only declinable with the indefinite article.

Cada has but one termination. It has no plural, and is only declinable with the indefinite article: *cada dia*, every day; *cada mez*, every month.

Outro has two terminations, viz. *outro, outra*; and in the plural, *outros, outras*. It is declinable both with the definite and indefinite articles.

Outrem has only one termination. It has no plural, and is only declinable with the indefinite article.

Qualquer has only one termination. It makes *quaefquer* in the plural, and is only declined with the indefinite article. *Qualquer* is fpoken both of the perfon and of the thing.

Quemquer has but one termination. It has no plural, and is only declinable with the indefinite article. It is rendered in Englifh by *any body*: *quemquer vos dira*, any body will tell you. *Quemquer* is always fpoken of a perfon.

Todo has two terminations, viz. *todo, toda*; and in the plural, *todos, todas*. It is declinable with the indefinite article. It is fometimes taken fubftantively, and then it fignifies *the whole*; as, *o todo he mayor que a fûa parte*, the whole is bigger than its part.

Tal has only one termination. It makes *taes* in the plural, and it is declined with the indefinite article. It is common to the mafculine and to the feminine genders; and fometimes it is joined to *qual*; as, *tal qual elle he*, fuch as it is.

Tal supplies sometimes the place of the person whose name is not specified; as, *hum tal velhaco deve ser castigado,* such a rogue ought to be punished.

✱✱✱✱✱✱✱✱✱✱✱✱✱✱✱✱✱✱✱✱✱✱✱✱✱✱✱✱✱✱✱

CHAP. IV.

Of Verbs.

THE verb is a part of speech which serves to express that which is attributed to the subject in denoting the *being* or *condition* of the things and persons spoken of, the *actions* which they do, or the *impressions* they receive.

The first and the most general division of Verbs is to divide them into personal and impersonal.

A verb personal is conjugated by three persons.

EXAMPLE.

Sing.	*eu ama,*	I love
	tu amas,	thou lovest
	elle ama	he loves
Plur.	*nos amamos,*	we love
	vos amais,	ye love
	elles amaõ,	they love

A verb impersonal is conjugated by the third person of the singular number only; as, *chove,* it rains; *convem,* it behoves.

A verb, considered in regard to the syntax, is of four sorts, viz. active, passive, neuter, and reciprocal.

Some of the verbs are regular, and others irregular.

Some are also called auxiliary verbs. We shall give their definitions in their proper places.

Before

Before you begin to learn the conjugations, it will be proper to obferve, that all the verbs may be conjugated with the pronouns perfonal, *eu, tu, elle,* &c. or without them.

Of the auxiliary Verbs.

The auxiliary verbs are fo called, becaufe they help to the conjugation of other verbs. They are four in Portuguefe, viz. *haver, ter,* to have; *fer, eftar,* to be. The auxiliary verb *fer,* to be, is alfo called the verb fubftantive, becaufe it affirms what the fubject is, and is always followed by a noun that particularizes what that fubject is; as, *fer rico, prudente, douto,* &c. to be rich, wife, learned, &c.

The Conjugation of the auxiliary Verb ter, *or* haver, *to have.*

The Indicative Mood.

Prefent.

Sing. { eu tenho, ou *hey* — I have
tu tens, ou *has* — thou haft
elle tem, ou *ha* — he has *or* hath

Plur. { nos temos, ou *havemos,* ou *hemos* — we have
vos tendes, ou *haveis,* ou *heis* — you have
elles tem, ou *haõ* — they have

Preterimperfect.

Sing. { eu tinha, ou *havia,* ou *hia* — I had
tu tinhas, ou *havias,* ou *hias* — thou hadft
elle tinha, ou *havia,* ou *hia* — he had

Plur. { nos tinhamos, ou *haviamos,* ou *hiamos* — we had
vos tinheis, ou *havieis,* ou *hieis* — you had
elles tinhaõ, ou *haviaõ,* ou *hiaõ* — they had

Preterperfect definite.

Sing. { eu tive, ou *houve* — I had
tu tivefte, ou *houvefte* — thou hadft
elle teve, ou *houve* — he had

Plur. { nos tivemos, ou *houvemos* — we had
vos tiveftes, ou *houveftes* — you had
elles tiveraõ, ou *houveraõ* — they had

8 Preter-

Preterperfect.

Sing.
{
eu tenho tido — I have had
tu tens tido — thou haft had
elle tem tido — he has had
}

Plur.
{
nos temos tido — we have had
vos tendes tido — you have had
elles tem tido — they have had
}

Preterpluperfect.

Sing.
{
eu tinha tido — I had had
tu tinhas tido — thou hadſt had
elle tinha tido — he had had
}

Plur.
{
nos tinhamos tido — we had had
vos tinbeis tido — you had had
elles tinhoõ tido — they had had
}

This tenſe may alſo be conjugated thus; *tivera, tiveras, tivera, tiveramos, tivereis, tiveraõ.*

Firſt Future.

Sing.
{
eu terey, ou *haverey* — I ſhall or will have
tu terás, ou *haverás* — thou ſhalt *or* wilt have
elle terá, ou *haverá,* — he ſhall *or* will have
}

Plur.
{
nos teremos, ou *haveremos* — we ſhall *or* will have
vos tereis, ou *havereis* — ye ſhall *or* will have
elles teraõ, ou *haveraõ* — they ſhall *or* will have
}

Second Future.

Sing. *eu hey de ter,* ou *haver,* &c.   I muſt have, &c.

Third Future.

Sing. *eu haverey de ter,* ou *haver,* &c.   I ſhall be obliged to have, &c.

Fourth Future.

Sing. *eu havia de ter,* ou *haver,* &c.   I was to have, &c.

Imperative.

Sing.
{
tem tu — have thou
tenha elle, ou *hája elle* — let him have
}

Plur.
{
tenhámos, ou *hájámos nos* — let us have
tende, ou *havey vos* — have ye
tenhaõ, ou *hájaõ elles* — let them have
}

The

The imperative has no firſt perſon, becauſe it is impoſſible to command one's ſelf.

Optative and Subjunctive.

I join them together, becauſe their tenſes are ſimilar.

Preſent.

Sing.	que eu tenha, ou hája	that I have, or that I may have
	que tu tenhas, ou hájas	thou haſt, or mayeſt have
	que elle tenha, ou hája	he has, or may have
Plur.	que nos tenhâmos, ou hajâmos	we have, or may have
	que vos tenháes, ou hajáes	ye have, or may have
	que elles tenhaõ, ou hájaõ	they have, or may have

Firſt Preterimperfect.

Sing.
que eu tivéra or tivéſſe, houvera or houveſſe
que tu tivéras or tivéſſes, houvéras or houvéſſes
que elle tivera or tivéſſe bouvéra or houveſſe
} that I had, or I ſhould, would, &c. have, &c.

Plur.
que nós tivéramos or tivéſſemos, houvéramos or houvéſſemos
que vos tivéreis or tiveſſeis, houvéreis or houveſſeis
que elles tivéraõ or tiveſſem, houvéraõ or houvéſſem
} that we had, or we ſhould, would, &c. have, &c.

Second Preterimperfect.

Sing.
eu teria ou haveria
tu terias qu haverias
elle teria ou haveria
} I ſhould, would, or could have, &c.

Plur.
nos teríamos ou haveriamos
vos teríeis ou haveríeis
elles teriaõ ou haveriaõ
} we ſhould, would, or could have, &c.

Preterperfect.

Sing.	que eu tenha tido ou havido,	that I have had
	que tu tenhas tido ou havido	thou haſt had
	que elle tenha tido ou havido	he has had
Plur.	que nós tenhamos tido ou havido	we have had
	que vos tenhaes tido ou havido	you have had
	que elles tenhaõ tido ou havido	they have had

Preter-

Preterpluperfect.

It is compounded of the firſt preterimperfect ſubjunctive and the participle.

Sing. { ſe eu tivéra ou tivéſſe
{ ſe tu tivéras ou tivéſſes
{ ſe elle tivéra ou tivéſſe
Plur. { ſe nós tivéramos ou tivéſſemos
{ ſe vós tivéreis ou tivéſſeis
{ ſe elles tivéraõ ou tivéſſem

} tido { if I had had,
&c.

Second Preterpluperfect.

It is compounded of the ſecond preterimperfect
ſubjunctive and the participle.

Sing. { eu teria
{ tu terias
{ elle teria
Plur. { nos teriâmos
{ vos teriéis
{ elles teriaõ

} tido { I ſhould have had, &c.

Firſt Future.

Sing.	ſe eu tivér	if I ſhall have
	tu tivéres	thou ſhalt have
	elle tiver	he ſhall have
Plur.	ſe nos tivérmos	if we ſhall have
	vos tiverdes	you ſhall have
	elles tiverem	they ſhall have

This tenſe may be conjugated alſo thus : *bouver,*
bouvéres, bouver; bouvermos, bouverdes, bouverem.
See the Synt. of the auxiliary Verbs.

Second Future.

It is compoſed of the Firſt Future and the Participle.

Sing. { ſe eu tiver
{ tiveres
{ tiver
Plur. { tivérmos
{ tivérdes
{ tiverem

} tido { if I ſhall have had, &c.

Infinitive Mood.

Preſent.

    ter   to have

Preter-

Preterperfect.

ter tido, to have had.

Participles.

Preterit. Sing. *tido, tida,* Plur. *tidos, tidas,* had:

Future.

que ha de ter, that is to have.

Gerunds.

tendo, having *or* in having. *tendo tido*, having had.

Supine.

para ter, to have.

In like manner are conjugated its compounds, *contenho, detenho, mantenho,* &c.

Remarks upon the auxiliary verb, ter, *to have.*

The verb *ter*, to have, is an auxiliary or helping verb, which serves to conjugate other verbs: example, *ter lido*, to have read; *nos temos feito*, we have done; *elles tem visto*, they have seen, &c.

When the verb *ter* is followed by the particle *que*, before an infinitive mood, it denotes the duty, inclination, &c. of doing any thing; as, *que tendes que fazer?* what have you to do? *tenho que fazer huma visita*, I must pay a visit; *elle tem muito que dizervos*, he has a great many things to tell you.

Of the auxiliary verb haver.

This is one of the most auxiliary verbs in Portuguese, since it is not only auxiliary to itself, as *eu hei de haver*, I must have; *eu havia de haver*, I was to have, &c. but also to all sorts of verbs; as *eu hei de cantar*, I will sing, or I must sing, or I am to sing; *eu hei de hir*, I must go; *eu havia de fallar*, I was to speak; *eu hei de escrever*, I must write, &c. In which examples you may see that the verb *haver*, when auxiliary, has generally the particle *de* and the verb of the infinitive mood after it; and

E   that

that then it denotes a firm refolution, poffibility, or neceffity of doing any thing; therefore it is not to be rendered into Englifh by the verb *to have*; as you may fee in the fecond, third, and fourth future of the indicative mood.

The verb *haver*, with the particle *de*, and the verb *fer* to be after it, is an auxiliary both to the paffive verbs, and fometimes to the verb *fer* itfelf; as, *hei de fer feliz*, I fhall be happy; *O principe ha de fer refpeitado*, the prince ought to be, *or* muft be, refpected.

The fame verb *haver* is alfo auxiliary without the particle *de*; but then it is put after the verb to which it is auxiliary; and fo they fay, *darvos-hei*, I will give you; *darlhe-hei*, I will give to him, &c. In which examples you may obferve, that the auxiliary verb *haver* is put after the verb and the pronouns conjunctive, *te*, *lhe*, &c. and fometimes it is put after the verbs and the pronouns mixed; as, *mandar volo hei*, I'll fend it to you. Take notice, however, that in the foregoing examples the verb *haver* may be put before the other verb; but then it requires the particle *de*, and has a different meaning; as, in the firft example, you may fay, *hei de darvos*, I muft give to you. You muft alfo obferve, that when the indicative prefent of the auxiliary verb *haver* is auxiliary to other verbs, as in the foregoing examples, you muft cut off the laft letters *ei* from the future of the verbs; and fo you may fay, *darlhe-hei*, or *hei de dar-lhe*; but not *darei-lhe-hei*, nor *hei de darei-lhe*. Moreover, when the preterimperfect *havia* is to be auxiliary to any verb, and it is to be placed after it, you muft make ufe of *hia*, *hias*, *hia*, *hiamos*, *hieis*, *hiaõ* : and fo you may fay, *dar-lhe-hia*, *hias*, &c. but not *dar-lhe havia*, *havias*, &c. I fhould give to him, thou fhouldft, &c.

We fhall not be at a lofs how to exprefs the interrogation in Portuguefe, if only we put the pronouns perfonal after the verbs, as in Englifh, and

we

we fhall never miftake in faying, *terei eu?* fhall I have? *temos nos?* have we? *tens tu?* haft thou? *tem elle?* has he? but fometimes they do not mention the pronouns at all; as, *que faremos?* what fhall we do? *cantaremos?* fhall we fing?

Obferve, that *haver* is fometimes Englifhed by *to be*; as, *que hade fer de mim?* what is to become of me?

When we fpeak by negation, we muft ufe the word *naõ* before the verb; as, *naõ tenho*, I have not; *vos naõ conheceis*, you do not know, &c.

The conjugation of the auxiliary verb *fer*, or *eftar*, to be.

Indicative.

Prefent.

Sing.	eu *fou* or *eftou*	I am
	tu *es* or *eftás*	thou art
	elle *he* or *eftá*	he is
Plur.	nos *fomos* or *eftamos*	we are
	vos *fois* or *eftais*	you are
	elles *faõ* or *eftaõ*	they are

Preterimperfect.

Sing.	eu *era* or *eftava*	I was
	eras or *eftavas*	thou waft
	era or *eftava*	he was
Plur.	nos *éramos* or *eftávamos*	we were
	ereis or *eftaveis*	you were
	eraõ or *eftavaõ*	they were

Preterperfect definite.

Sing.	eu *fui* or *eftive*	I was
	fofte or *eftivefte*	thou waft
	foi or *efteve*	he was
Plur.	*fomos* or *eftivémos*	we were
	foftes or *eftivoftes*	you were
	foraõ or *eftiveraõ*	they were

Preter-

Preterperfect.

It is compounded of the present indicative of the auxiliary verb *ter*, to have, and its own participle, *sido*, or *estado*.

Preterpluperfect.

It is compounded of the preterimperfect indicative, and the participle *sido*, or *estado*.

Sing.	*eu tinha sido* or *estado*	I had been
	tinhas sido or *estado*	thou hadst been
	tinha sido or *estado*	he had been
Plur.	*tinhamos sido* or *estado*	we had been
	tinheis sido or *estado*	you had been
	tinhaõ sido or *estado*	they had been

This tense may also be conjugated thus; *fora*, or *estivera*; *foras*, or *estiveras*; *fora*, or *estivera*; *foramos*, or *estiveramos*; *foreis*, or *estivereis*; *foraõ*, or *estiveraõ*.

Future.

Sing.	*eu serei* or *estarei*	I shall *or* will be
	serás or *estarás*	thou shalt be
	será or *estará*	he shall be
Plur.	*seremos* or *estaremos*	we shall be
	sereis or *estareis*	you shall be
	seraõ or *estaraõ*	they shall be

Imperative.

Sing.	*se tu* or *está*	be thou
	seja or *esteja elle*	let him be
Plur.	*sejamos* or *estajamos nos*	let us be
	sede or *estai vos*	be you
	sejaõ or *estejaõ elles*	let them be

Optative and Subjunctive.

Present.

Sing.	*que eu seja* or *esteja*	that I may be, *or* that I be
	sejas or *estejas*	thou mayst be *or* be
	seja or *esteja*	he may be, &c.

Plur.

Plur. { *fejamos* or *eftejamos* we may be
fejais or *eftejais* you may be
fejaõ or *eftejaõ* they may be

First Preterimperfect.

Sing. {
que eu fora or *fosse,* } that I were *or* might
eftivera or *eftiveffe.* } be
foras or *fosses,* } thou wert
eftiveras or *eftiveffes* }
fora or *fosse,* } he were
eftivera or *eftiveffe* }

Plur. {
que nos foramos or *fossemos,* } that we were
eftiveramos or *eftiveffemos* }
foreis or *fosseis,* } you were
eftivere s or *eftiveffeis,* }
foraõ or *fossem,* } they were
eftiveraõ or *eftiveffem* }

Second Preterimperfect.

Sing. {
eu feria or *eftaria* I should *or* would be
ferias or *eftarias* thou shouldest be
feria or *eftaria* he should be

Plur. {
feriamos or *eftariamos* we should be
feries or *eftarieis* you should be
feriaõ or *eftariaõ* they should be

Preterperfect.

It is compounded of the present conjunctive of
the auxiliary verb *ter*, and its own participle *fido*,
or *eftado*.

Sing. {
que eu tenha fido or *eftado* that I have been
tenhas fido or *eftado* thou haft been
tenha fido, &c. he has been

Plur. {
tenhamos fido, &c. that we have been
tenhais fido, &c. you have been
tenhaõ fido, &c. they have been

Preterpluperfect.

It is compounded of the first preterimperfect subjunctive of the verb *ter*, and its own participle.

Sing.

Sing.	*se eu tivera or tivesse fido or eftado*	if I had been.
	tiveras, &c.	thou hadft been
	tivera, &c.	he had been
Plur.	*tiveramos, &c.*	we had been
	tiverais, &c.	you had been
	tiveraõ, &c.	they had been

Second Preterpluperfect.

It is compounded of the fecond preterimperfect fubjunctive of the verb *ter*, and its own participle *fido* or *eftado*.

Sing.	*eu teria fido or eftado*	I fhould *or* would have been
	terias, &c.	thou fhouldft have been
	teria, &c.	he fhould have been
Plur.	*teriámos, &c.*	we fhould have been
	terieis, &c.	you fhould have been
	teriaõ, &c.	they fhould have been

Firft Future.

Sing.	*quando eu for or eftiver*	when I fhall be
	fores or eftiveres	thou fhalt be
	for or eftiver	he fhall be
Plur.	*formos or eftivermos*	we fhall be
	fordes or eftiverdes	you fhall be
	forem or eftiverem	they fhall be

Second Future.

It is compounded of the future fubjunctive of the verb *ter* and its own participle.

Sing.	*quando eu tiver fido or eftada*	when I fhall have been
	tiveres fido, &c.	thou fhalt have been
	tiver fido, &c.	he fhall have been
Plur.	*tivermos fido, &c*	we fhall have been
	tiverdes fido, &c.	you fhall have been
	tiverem fido, &c.	they fhall have been

Infinitive.
Prefent.

fer or *eftar*   to be.

Preterperfect.

ter fido or *eftada*   to have been.

Parti-

Participles.

Pret.
fido or *eftado*   been.

Future.
futuro, or *que ha de fer,* or *eftar*   future, *or* that is to be.

Gerunds.
fendo or *eftando*   being
tendo fido or *eftado*   having been

Supine.
para fer or *eftar*   to be.

Remarks upon the verb *fer* and *eftar.*

There is a confiderable difference between thefe verbs *fer* and *eftar* both in Portuguefe and Spanifh. In Englifh there is no word to diftinguifh them, fince they are both rendered into Englifh by *to be.* *Ser* fignifies the proper and infeparable effence of a thing, its quality or quantity ; as, *fer homem,* to be a man ; *fer bom,* to be good ; *fer alto,* to be tall ; *fer largo,* to be wide ; *fer branca,* to be white, &c. But *eftar* denotes a place, or any adventitious quality ; as, *eftar em Londres,* to be in London ; *eftar de faude,* to be in health ; *eftar frio,* to be cold ; *eftar quente,* to be warm ; *eftar doente,* to be fick ; *eftar enfadado,* to be angry ; *eftar allegre,* to be merry, &c.

Take notice, that you may ufe *eftar* before the gerunds, but not *fer* ; therefore you may fay, *eftou fallando, lendo,* &c. I am fpeaking, reading, &c. but not *fou fallando,* &c.

The three Conjugations of regular Active Verbs.

A regular verb is fuch as is confined to general rules in its conjugation.

E 4   A verb

A verb active denotes the action or impression of the subject, and governs a noun which is the object of that action or impression; as, *amar a vertude*, to love virtue; *receber cartas*, to receive letters.

The regular Portuguese verbs have three different terminations in the infinitive; to wit, in *ar, er, ir*; as, *amar*, to love; *temer*, to fear; *admittir*, to admit.

An easy Method of learning to conjugate Portuguese Verbs.

I have reduced all the tenses of the Portuguese verbs to eight; four of which are general, and have the same terminations in all the verbs; and the other four may be likewise made general by changing some letters, and all the conjugations reduced to one.

The general tenses are, the Future Indicative, the first and second preterimperfect subjunctive, and the first future subjunctive.

The future indicative is terminated in all the verbs, in
rei, ras, ra; remo, reis, raõ.

The imperfect subjunctive, in
ra or *sse, ras* or *sses, ra* or *sse; ramos* or *ssemos, reis* or *sseis, raõ* or *ssem.*

The second imperfect, in
ria, rias, ria; riamos, rieis, riaõ.

The first future subjunctive, in
es, mos, des, im.

Note, that I have only put the termination of the second person singular of the future subjunctive, because the first and third of the same number are like their respective infinitives of the three conjugations, which however keep both their last consonant

7   and

and vowel before the terminations I have marked for the second person singular, and for the whole plural. As to the future indicative, you have nothing to do but add *ei* to the respective present infinitive of the three conjugations, in order to form the first person singular; and if you add to the same infinitive present *as*, you shall form the second person singular of it, and so of all the rest, by adding to the infinitive present *a, emos, eis, aõ.*

The imperfect subjunctive has two terminations for every person, both in the singular and plural; but if you cut off the last consonant *r* of the infinitive, and then add to it the terminations above-mentioned, you shall form the imperfect subjunctive, according to its two different terminations. Lastly, if you cut off the last consonant of the infinitive, and add to it the terminations above proposed, you shall form the second imperfect subjunctive.

The present indicative of all the three conjugations is formed by changing the last letters of the infinitive, viz. *ar, er, ir,* into *o*; as, *amo, entendo, admitto,* from *amar, entender, admittir.*

The preterimperfect indicative is formed in the first conjugation, by changing the last consonant of the infinitive, viz. *r,* into *va, vas, va, vamos, veis, vaõ*; but in the second conjugation it is formed by changing the termination *er* of the infinitive into *ia, ias, ia, iamos, ieis, iaõ*; and in the third by changing only the last consonant *r* of the infinitive into *a, as, a; amos, eis, aõ.*

The perfect definite in the first conjugation is formed by changing the termination *ar* of the infinitive into *ei, afte, ou, amos, aftes, araõ*; and in the second conjugation it is formed by changing the termination *er* of the infinitive into *i, efte, eo, emos, eftes, eraõ.* In the third conjugation the same tense is is formed by changing the termination *ir* of the infinitive into *i, ifte, io, imos, iftes, iraō.*

The prefent fubjunctive in the firſt conjugation is formed by changing the termination *ar* of the infinitive into *e, es, e, emos, eis, em;* and in the fecond conjugation it is formed by changing the termination *er* of the infinitive into *a, as, a, amos, ais, aō.* In the third conjugation the fame tenſe is formed by changing the termination *ir* of the infinitive into the fame terminations, *a, as, a,* &c.

As to the imperative mood, you may only obſerve, that the fecond perſon ſingular is always the fame as the third perſon ſingular of the prefent indicative, in all the conjugations.

The participles of the preterperfect tenſe in the firſt conjugation are formed by changing the laſt confonant *r* of the infinitive into *do* for the maſculine, and *da* for the feminine; and into *dos, das,* for the plural: but when you come to verbs of the fecond conjugation, you change the termination *r* of the infinitive into *ido, ida,* &c.

In the third conjugation you muſt change the laſt confonant *r* of the infinitive into *do* for the maſculine, *da* for the feminine, &c.

The firſt Conjugation of the Verbs in ar.

The Indicative Mood.

I ſhall put the pronouns perſonal, *eu, tu, elle,* &c. no more.

Prefent.

ame	I love
amas	thou loveſt
ama	he loves
amamos,	we love
amais	ye love
amaō,	they love

Preterimperfect.

amáva	I did love
amávas	thou didſt love
amáva	he did love
amávamos	we did love
amáveis	you did love
amávaõ	they did love

Preterperfect definite.

amei	I loved
amáſte	thou loved'ſt
amou	he loved
amâmos	we loved
amâſtes	you loved
amáraõ	they loved

Preterperfect.

This tenſe is compoſed of the participle *amado* and the preſent indicative of the auxiliary verb *ter*.

tenho amado	I have loved
tens amado	thou haſt loved
tem amado	he has loved
temos amado	we have loved
tendes amado	you have loved
tem amado	they have loved

Preterpluperfect.

This tenſe is compoſed of the participle *amado*, and the imperfect of the auxiliary verb *ter*.

N. B. This tenſe may be conjugated thus, *amara, amaras, amara, amaramos, amareis, amaraõ*; or,

tinha amado	I had loved
tinhas amado	thou hadſt loved
tinha amado	he had loved
tinhamos amada	we had loved
tinheis amado	you had loved
tinhaõ amada	they had loved

Future.

amarei	I ſhall *or* will love
amarás	thou ſhalt love
amará	he ſhall love

amaremos	we shall love
amareis	you shall love
amaraõ	they shall love

Imperative.

ama tu	love thou
ame elle	let him love
amemos nós	let us love
amai vós	love ye
amem elles	let them love

Optative and Subjunctive.

que eu ame	that I may love
ames	thou mayest love
ame	he may love
amemos	we may love
ameis	you may love
amem	they may love

First Preterimperfect.

que eu amára or *amásse*	that I might or could love
amáras or *amásses*	thou mightest love
amára or *amásse*	he might love
amáramos or *amáss mas*	we might love
amáreis or *amásseis*	you might love
amáraõ or *amássem*	they might love

When we find the conjunction *if* before the indicative imperfect, we must use the imperfect of the subjunctive or optative, when we speak by way of wish or desire; as, If I did love, *se eu amasse*, or *amara*, and not *se eu amava*, if I had loved; If I had, *se eu tivera*, or *tivesse*, and not *se eu tinha*; and so in all the verbs.

Second preterimperfect.

amaría	I should love
amarías	thou shouldst love
amaría	he should love
amariamos	we should love
amarieis	you should love
amariaõ	they should love

Preter-

Preterperfect.

It is compofed of the participle *amado* and the prefent fubjunctive of the auxiliary verb *ter*.

que eu tenho amado	that I have loved
tenhas amado	thou haft loved
tenha amado	he has loved
tenhamos amado	we have loved
tenhais amado	you have loved
tenhaõ amado	they have loved.

Preterpluperfect.

It is compofed of the participle *amado* and the firft preterimperfect fubjunctive of the auxiliary verb *ter*.

fe eu tivera or *tiveffe amado*	if I had loved
tiveras or *tiveffes amado*	thou hadft loved
tivera or *tiveffe amado*	he had loved
tiveramos or *tiveffemos amado*	we had loved
tivereis or *tiveffeis amado*	you had loved
tiveraõ or *tiveffem amado*	they had loved

Second Preterpluperfect.

It is compofed of the participle *amado* and the fecond preterimperfect fubjunctive of the auxiliary verb *ter*.

teria amado	I fhould have loved
terias amado	thou fhouldft have loved
teria amado	he fhould have loved
teriamos amádo	we fhould have loved
terieis amado	ye fhould have loved
teriaõ amado	they fhould have loved

Future.

quando eu amar	when I fhall love
amares	thou fhalt love
amar	he fhall love
amarmos	we fhall love
amardes	you fhall love
amarem	they fhall love

Second

Second Future.

It is compofed of the participle *amado*, and the future fubjunctive of the auxiliary verb *tir*.

quando eu tiver amado	when I fhall have loved
tiveres amado	thou fhalt have loved
tiver amado	he fhall have loved
tivermos amado	we fhall have loved
tiverdes amado	you fhall have loved
tiverem amado	they fhall have loved

Infinitive.

Prefent.

amar	to love.

Preterperfect.

ter amado	to have loved.

Participle.

Prefent.

que ama, or amante	that loves.

Pret.

amado, mafc. amada, fem.	loved.

Future.

que ha de amar	that is to love.

Gerunds.

amando	loving
tendo amado	having loved.

Supine.

parà amar	to love.

Note, the verbs terminating in the infinitive in *car* take *qu* in thofe tenfes, where the *c* would otherwife meet with the vowel *e*; and thofe terminating in the infinitive in *gar* take an *u* in thofe tenfes where the *g* would otherwife meet with the fame vowel *e*; that is to fay, in the firft perfon fingular of the preterperfect definite, in the third perfon fingular, singular, in the first and third plural of the imperative, and in the whole present subjunctive, which are the tenses I shall give you by way of example, in the verbs *peccar* and *pagar*.

Peccar, to sin.

Preterperfect definite.
eu pequei, I sinned----instead of *peccei*.

Imperative.
peque elle, let him sin ; *pequemos nos*, let us sin ; *pequem elles*, let them sin---- and not *pecce elles*, &c.

Present subjunctive.
que eu peque, tu peques, that I may sin--- and not *que eu pecce, pecces*, &c.

Pagar, to pay.
Preterperfect definite.
paguei I paid.

Imperative.
pague elle, paguemos nos, paguem elles, let him pay, &c.

Present Subjunctive.
que eu pague, pagues, pague, paguemos, pagueis, paguem, that I may pay, &c.----and not *page, pages*, &c.

The other tenses are conjugated like *amar*.

Regular verbs in *ar*.

Abafar, to choke, *or* to smother
Abalar, to shake
Abanar, to fan
Abastar, to satiate
Abaxar, to bring, *or* let down
Abençoar, to bless
Abocanhar, to carp
Abominar, to abominate
Abotoar, to button
Acabar, to finish
Admoestar, to admonish
Affrontar, to abuse

Agarrar, to lay hold of
Alagar, to overflow
Amaldiçoar, to curse
Annular, to annul, *or* to make void
Apressar, to press *or* hasten
Aquentar, to warm
Argumentar, to argue
Assoprar, to blow
Atar, to tie
Avassalar, to subdue, to conquer
Azedar, to sour.

Of

Of the Verbs Paſſive.

Before we proceed to the ſecond conjugation, it is neceſſary to know that the verbs paſſive, which expreſs the ſuffering or reception of an action, are nothing more than the participles of verbs active, conjugated with the verb *ſer*, to be.

EXAMPLE.

Preſent tenſe.

eu ſou amado	I am loved
tu es amado	thou art loved
elle he amado	he is loved
nos ſomos amados	we are loved
-vos ſois amados	you are loved
elles. ſaõ amados	they are loved

and ſo throughout the other moods and tenſes.

The ſecond conjugation of the verbs in *er*.

Indicative Mood.

Preſent.

vendo	I ſell
vendes	thou ſelleſt
vende	he ſells
vendemos	we ſell
vendeis	you ſell
vendem	they ſell

Preterimperfect.

vendia	I did ſell
vendias	thou didſt ſell
vendia	he did ſell
vendiamos	we did ſell
vendieis	you did ſell
vendiaõ	they did ſell

Preterperfect definite.

vendi	I ſold
vendeſte	thou ſoldeſt
vendeo	he ſold

ven-

vendemos	we fold
vendeftes	you fold
venderaõ	they fold

Preterperfect.

$\left.\begin{array}{l} \textit{tenbo} \\ \textit{tens} \\ \textit{tem} \\ \textit{temos} \\ \textit{tendes} \\ \textit{tem} \end{array}\right\}$ *vendido* $\Big\{$ I have fold, &c.

Preterpluperfect.

$\left.\begin{array}{l} \textit{tinba} \\ \textit{tinbas} \\ \textit{tinba} \\ \textit{tinbamos} \\ \textit{tinbeis} \\ \textit{tinbaõ} \end{array}\right\}$ *véndido* $\Big\{$ I had fold, &c.

This tenfe may be alfo conjugated thus; *vendera, venderas, vendera, venderamos, vendereis, venderaõ.*

Future.

$\left.\begin{array}{l} \textit{venderei} \\ \textit{venderás} \\ \textit{venderá} \\ \textit{venderemos} \\ \textit{vendereis} \\ \textit{venderaõ} \end{array}\right\}$ I fhall *or* will fell, &c.

Imperative Mood.

vénde tu	fell thou
vénda elle	let him fell
vendámos nos	let us fell
vendei vos	fell ye
véndaõ elles	let them fell

Optative and Subjunctive.

que eu vénda
  vendas
  venda $\Big\}$ that I may fell, &c.
  vendamos
  vendáis
  vendaõ

F   Preter-

Preterimperfect.

que eu *venedra* or *vendeſſe*   that I might or could fell,
     venedras or *vendeſſes*   *&c.*
     vendera or *vendeſſe*
     venderamos or *vendeſſemos*
     vendereis or *vendeſſeis*
     venderaõ or *vendeſſem*

Second Preterimperfect.

     venderia   I ſhould fell, *&c.*
     venderias
     venderia
     venderiamos
     venderieis
     venderiaõ

Preterperfect.

que eu *tenha*
     tenhas
     tenha   } *vendido* {   that I have ſold,
     tenhamos   *&c.*
     tenhais
     tenhaõ

Preterpluperfect.

ſe eu *tivéra* or *tivéſſe*
     tivéras or *tivéſſes*
     tivéra or *tivéſſe*
     tivéramos or *tivéſſemos*   } *vendido* {   if I had ſold,
     tivéreis or *tivéſſeis*   &c.
     tivéraõ or *tivéſſem*

Second Preterpluperfect.

eu *teria*
     terias
     teria   } *vendido* {   I ſhould have ſold,
     teriamos   *&c.*
     terieis
     teriaõ

Future.

Future.

quando eu vendér	when I shall sell, &c.
vendéres	
vendér	
vendérmos	
vendérdes	
vendérem	

Second Future.

quando eu tivér
tivéres
tivér } *vendido* { when I shall have sold,
tivérmos &c.
tivérdes
tivérem

Infinitive Mood.

Prefent.

vender	to fell.

Preterperfect.

ter vendido	to have fold.

Participle.

Prefent.

que vende	that fell, that fells.

Preterit.

vendido, mafc. *vendida*, fem. Plur. *vendidos, vendidas*, fold.

Future.

que ha de vender	that is to fell

Gerund.

vendendo	felling
tendo vendido	having fold

Supine.

para vender	to fell.

After the fame manner as the verb *vender* are conjugated all the other regular verbs of the fecond conjugation ending in *er*; as the following:

Acometer,

Accometer, to attack
Beber, to drink
Comer, to eat
Comprehender, to perceive, or apprehend
Cometer, to commit
Conceder, to grant
Correr, to run
Dever, to owe

Esconder, to hide
Emprender, to undertake
Meter, to put in
Offender, to offend
Prometer, to promise
Responder, to answer
Reprehender, to reprove
Temer, to fear
Varrer, to sweep, &c.

The third conjugation of the verbs ending in *ir*.

Indicative Mood.

Present.

admitto	I admit, &c.	admittimos
admittes		admittis
admitte		admittem

Preterimperfect.

admittia	I did admit, &c.	admittiamos
admittias		admittieis
admittia		admit.iaō

Preterperfect definite.

admitti	I admitted	admittimos
admittiste		admittistes
admittio		admittiraō

Preterperfect.

This tense is composed of the participle *admittido*, and the present indicative of the auxiliary verb *ter*.

tenho admittido	I have admitted
tens admittido, &c.	thou hast, &c.

Preterpluperfect.

This tense is composed of the participle *admittido* and the imperfect of the auxiliary verb *ter*.

tinha admittido	I had admitted
tinhas admittido, &c.	thou hadst, &c.

This tense may also be conjugated thus ; *admittira, admittiras, admittira, admittiramos, admittireis, admittiraō*:

Future.

Future.

admittirei	I fhall *or* will admit
admittirás	
admittirá	
admittiremos	
admittireis	
admittiraõ	

Imperative.

admitte tu	admit thou
admitta elle	let him admit
admittamos nós	let us admit
admitti vos.	admit ye
admittaõ elles	let them admit.

Optative and Subjunctive.

Prefent.

que eu admitta	that I may admit, *&c.*
admittas	
admitta	
admittamos	
admittais	
admittaõ	

Firft Preterimperfect.

que eu admittira or *admittiffe*	that I might admit, *&c.*
admittiras or *admittiffes*	
admittira or *admittiffe*	
admittiramos or *admittiffmos*	
admittireis or *admittiffeis*	
admittiraõ or *admittiffem*	

Second Preterimperfect.

admittiria	I fhould *or* would admit, *&c.*
admittirias	
admittiria	
admittiriamos	
admittirieis	
admittiriaõ	

Preterperfect.

This tenfe is compofed of the participle *admittido*
and the prefent fubjunctive of the verb *ter.*

que eu tenha admittido	that I have admitted
tenhas admittido, &c.	thou haft admitted, *&c.*

Preter-

Preterpluperfect.

It is compofed of the firft preterimperfect fubjunctive of the verb *ter* and the participle *admittido*.

fe eu tivera admittido   if I had admitted
    tiveras, &c.   thou hadft admitted, &c.

Second Preterpluperfect.

It is compofed of the fecond preterimperfect fubjunctive of the verb *ter* and the participle *admittido*.

eu teria admittido   I fhould have admitted
    terias, &c.   thou fhouldft, &c.

Firft Future.

fe eu admittir   if I fhall admit, &c.
admittires
admittir
admittirmos
admittirdes
admittirem

Second Future.

It is compofed of the firft Future Subjunctive of
the verb *ter* and the participle *admittido*.

fe eu tiver admittida   if I fhall have admitted
    tiveres, &c.   thou fhalt, &c.

Infinitive Mood.
Prefent.
admittir   to admit.

Preterperfect.
ter admittido   to have admitted.

Participle.
Pret.
admittido, for the mafc. *admittida*, for the fem.   admitted.

Future.
que ha de admittir   that is to admit.

Gerunds.
admittindo   admitting.
tendo admittido   having admitted.

Supines.
para admittir   to admit.

                                        Conjugate

Conjugate after the fame manner the following verbs:

Abrir, to open.
Conduzir, to conduct.
Introduzir, to introduce.
Induzir, to enduce.
Produzir, to produce,
Luzir, to fhine.

Nutrir, to nourifh.
Reduzir, to reduce, to bring to.
Traduzir, to tranflate.
Deduzir, to deduct, &c.

Of the irregular Verbs in ar.

There are in each conjugation fome verbs which do not conform to the common rule, and on that account are called irregulars.

There are but two of the firft conjugation, which in fome of their tenfes depart from the rule of the verb *amar*, viz. *eftár* and *dar*. We have already conjugated the firft, and the fecond is conjugated in the following manner.

Indicative.

Prefent.

dou,	I give	*damos*,	we give
dás,	thou giveft	*dais*,	you give
dá,	he gives	*daõ*,	they give

Preterimperfect.

dava,   I did give, &c. (as in regular verbs of the firft
davas, &c.   conjugation.

Preterperfect definite.

dei,	I gave	*démos*,	we gave
défte,	thou gaveft	*deftes*,	you gave
deu,	he gave	*déraõ*,	they gave

Preterperfect.

This tenfe is compofed of the participle *dado* and the prefent indicative of the auxiliary verb *ter*; as *tenho dado*, I have given, &c.

Preterpluperfect.

This tenfe is compofed of the participle *dado* and the imperfect of the auxiliary verb *ter*; as *eu tinha dado*, &c. I had given, &c.

Future.

Future.

darei, I fhall *or* will give, &c. (as in the verb *amar*.
daras, &c.

Imperative.

		demos nós,	let us give
dá tu,	give thou	*dai vós,*	give you
de elle,	let him give	*dem'elles,*	let them give.

Optative and Subjunctive.

Prefent.

que eu de, that I may give, &c.
        des,
        de,
        demos,
        deis,
        dem.

Preterimperfect.

que eu déra or *défe,* that I might give, &c.
    deras or *deffes*
    dera or *deffe*
    déramos or *deffemos*
    dereis or *deffeis*
    déraõ or *deffem.*

Second Imperfect.

daria, I fhould give, &c.	*dariamos*
darias	*darieis*
daria	*dariaõ.*

The preterperfect, preterpluperfect, and the fecond preterpluperfect are compofed of the participle
dado and the auxiliary verb *ter,* as in the regular
verbs.

Future.

quando eu dér, When I fhall give, &c.
    déres
    der
    dérmos
    dérdes
    dérem.

Second Future.

It is compofed of the participle *dado,* &c. as the
regular verbs.

Infinitive

Infinitive.

Prefent.

dar, to give, *&c.* as in the regular verbs.

Of *the irregular Verbs in* er.

I begin with *fazer, poder,* and *faber,* becaufe they occur ofteneft in difcourfe.

Fazer, to do *or* make.

Indicative.

Prefent.

faço,	I do	*fazemos,*	we do
fazes,	thou doft	*fazeis,*	you do
faz,	he does	*fazem,*	they do.

Imperfect.

fazia,	I did *or* did make, *&c.*	*faziamos*
fazias		*fazieis*
fazia		*faziaō*

Preterperfect definite.

fiz,	I made, *&c.*	*fizemos*
fizefte		*fizeftes*
fez		*fizeraō*

Preterperfect.

tenho feito, I have done, *&c.*
tens feito, &c.

Preterpluperfect.

tinha feito, I had done, *&c.*
tinhas feito, &c.

Future.

farei, I fhall do, *&c.* (according to the regular verb.)
farás, &c.

Imperative.

		façamos nos, let us do
faze tu,	do thou	*fazei vos,* do you
faça elle,	let him do	*façaō elles,* let them do.

Optative

Optative.

Prefent.

que eu faça,   that I may do, &c. (according to the regu-
  faças,   lar verbs.)
  faça, &c.

Preterimperfeĉt.

que eu fizéra or fizéſſe,   that I might do, &c.
  fizéras or fizéſſes
  fizéra or fizéſſe
  fizéramos or fizéſſemos
  fizéreis or fizéſſeis
  fizéraõ or fizéſſem.

Second Imperfeĉt.

faria,   I fhould do, &c.   fariamos
farias,   farieis
faria,   fariaā.

Future.

quando eu fizér,   when I fhall do, &c.
  fizéres
  fizér
  fizérmos
  fizérdes
  fizérem.

Second Future.

quando eu tiver feito,   when I fhall have done
  tiveres feito, &c.

Infinitive.

fazer, to do.

Gerunds.

fazendo, doing or in doing.

Participle.

feito, made or done.

After the fame manner are conjugated *desfazer*,
to undo ; *contrafazer*, to counterfeit ; *refazer*, to
make again.

Poder,

Poder, to be able,

Indicative.

Prefent.

poffo,	I can, *or* am able	*podemos*,	we can
podes,	thou canft	*podeis*,	you can
póde,	he can	*podem*,	they can.

Imperfect.

podia, I could, *or* was able, *&c.*
podias, &c.

Preterperfect definite.

pude,	I could	*pudémos*,	we could
pudefte,	thou couldft	*pudeftes*,	you could
pode,	he could	*puderaõ*,	they could

Preterperfect.

tenho podido, &c. I have been able, *&c.*

Future.

poderei, I fhall be able, *&c.*
poderas, &c.

There is no Imperative.

Optative and Subjunctive.

Prefent.

que eu poffa,	that I may be able
poffas,	thou mayft be able, *&c.*
poffa	
poffamos	
poffais	
poffaõ	

Imperfect.

que eu pudéra or *pudéffe*,	that I might be able
pudéras or *pudéffes*,	thou mightft be able, *&c.*
pudéra or *pudéffe*	
pudéramos or *pudéffemos*	
pudéreis or *pudéffeis*	
puderaõ or *pudéffem*	

Second

Second Imperfect.

poderia,   I fhould be able, *&c.*
poderias, &c.

Future.

quando eu puder,   when I fhall be able, *&c.*
      puderes
      puder
      pudermos
      puderdes
      puderem

Infinitive.

Prefent.
poder, to be able.

Gerunds.
podendo, being able.

Participle.
podido, been able.

Saber, to know.

Indicative.

Prefent.

fei,	I know	*fabemos,*	we know
fabes,	thou knoweft	*fabeis,*	you know
fabe,	he knows	*fabem,*	they know

Imperfect.

fabia,   I did know
fabias,   thou didft know, *&c.*
fabia, &c.

Preterperfect definite.

foubé,	I knew, *&c.*	*foubémos*
foubéfte		*foubéftes*
foubé		*foubéraõ*

Preteperfect.

tenho fabido, I have known, *&c.*

                            Future.

Future.

faberei, I fhall *or* will know, *&c.* (according to the
faberas, &c. regular verbs.)

Imperative.

		faibamos nós,	let us know
fabe tu,	know thou	*fabei vós,*	know you
faiba elle,	let him know	*faibaõ elles,*	let them know.

Optative and Subjunctive.

Prefent.

que eu faiba, I may know
faibas, thou mayft know, *&c.*
faiba
faibamos
faibais
faibaõ

Imperfect.

que eu foubéra or *foubéffe,* that I might know, *&c.*
foubéras or *foubéffes*
foubéra or *foubéffe*
foubéramos or *foubéffemos*
foubéreis or *foubéffeis*
foubéraõ or *foubéffem*

Second Imperfect.

faberîa, I fhould know, *&c.* *faberîamos*
faber ias *faberieis*
faberîa *faberîaõ*

Future.

quando eu foubér, when I fhall know, *&c.*
fouberes
fouber
foubermos
fouberdes
fouberem

Infinitive.
Prefent.
faber, to know.
Gerund.
fabendo, knowing.

Participle

Participle.

fabido (for the maſc.), *fabida* (for the feminine), known.

Of the irregular Verb trazer, *to bring*.

Indicative.

Preſent.

trago,	I bring	*trazemos,*	we bring, &c.
trazes,	thou bringeſt	*trazeis*	
traz,	he brings	*trazem*	

Imperfect.

trazia,   I did bring
trazias, &c. thou didſt bring, &c. (according to the regulars.)

Preterperfect definite.

trouxe,	I brought	*trouxémos*
trouxéſte,	thou broughteſt, &c.	*trouxéſtes*
trouxe,		*trouxêraõ*

Preterperfect.

tenho trazido, I have brought, &c.
tens trazido, &c.

Future.

trarie,	I ſhall *or* will bring, &c.	*traremos*
trarás		*trareis*
trará		*traraõ*

Imperative.

		tragamos nós,	let us bring
traze tu,	bring thou	*trazei vós,*	bring you
traga elle,	let him bring	*tragaõ elles,*	let them bring

Optative and Subjunctive.

Preſent.

que eu traga,	that I may bring, &c.
tragas	
traga	
tragamos	
tragais	
tragaõ	

Imperfect

Imperfect.

que eu trouxéra or *trouxéſſe,*	that I might bring, &c.
trouxéras or *trouxéſſes*	
trouxéra or *trouxéſſe*	
trouxéramos or *trouxéſſemos*	
trouxéreis or *trouxéſſeis*	
trouxéraõ or *trouxéſſem*	

Second Imperfect.

eu traría, I ſhould bring, &c.	*trariamos*
trarîas,	*trarîeis*
trarîa,	*trarîaõ*

Future.

quando eu trouxer,	when I ſhall bring, &c.
trouxeres	
trouxer	
trouxermos	
trouxerdes	
trouxerem	

Infinitive.

Preſent.
trazer, to bring.

Gerund.
trazendo, bringing.

Participle.
trazido, maſc. *trazida,* fem. brought.

The conjugation of the irregular Verb ver, *to ſee.*

Indicative.

Preſent.

vejo,	I ſee	*vemos*
ves,	thou ſeeſt	*vedes*
ve,	he ſees, &c.	*vem*

Imperfect.

via,	I did ſee, &c.
vias,	
via, &c.	

4

Preter-

Preterperfect definite.

vi   I faw, &c.   vimos
vifle   vifles
vio   viraõ

Preterperfect.

tenho vifto   I have feen, &c.
tens vifto, &c.

Future.

verei   I fhall fee, &c.
veras, &c.

Imperative.

ve tu   fee thou
veja elle   let him fee
vejamos nos   let us fee
vede vos   fee you
vejaõ elles   let them fee

Optative.

que eu veja   that I may fee, &c.   vejamos
vejas   vejais
veja   vejaõ

Imperfect.

que eu vira or viffe   that I might fee, &c.
viras or viffes
vira or viffe
víramos or viffemos
víreis or vífleis
viraõ or viffem

Second Imperfect.

eu veria   I fhould fee, &c.   veriamos
verias   verieis
veria   veriaõ

Future.

quando eu vir   when I fhall fee, &c.
vires
vir
virmos
virdes
virem

Infini-

Infinitive.

ver   to fee.

Gerund.

vendo   feeing.

Participle.

vifto, vifta   feen:

In like manner are conjugated the compounds *antever, prever,* and *rever.*

The verb *prover,* when it fignifies *to provide for,* or *to take care of,* is conjugated in the prefent indicative thus:

eu provénho I take care of, &c.	*provímos*
provéns	*provindes*
provém	*provém*

But, when it fignifies *to make provifion,* is conjugated in the fame tenfe thus;

eu provéjo I make provifion, &c.	*provémos*
provés	*proveis*
prové	*provem*

The conjugation of the auxiliary verb *dizer,* to fay.

Indicative.

Prefent.

digo I fay, &c.	*dizemos*
dizes	*dizeis*
diz	*dizem*

Preterimperfeƈt.

dizia,   I did fay, &c.
diziai, &c.

Preterperfeƈt definite.

diffe I faid, &c.	*diffemos*
diffefte	*diffeftas*
diffe	*differaõ*

G   Preter-

Preterperfect.

tenho ditto	I have said, &c.
tens ditto, &c.	

Future.

direi	I shall *or* will say, &c.
diras, &c.	

Imperative.

dize tu	say thou
diga elle	let him say
digamos nós	let us say
dizei vos	say you
digaõ elles	let them say

Optative.

que eu diga	that I may say, &c.
digas, &c.	

Imperfect.

que eu dissera or *dissesse*	that I might say, &c.
disseras or *dissesses*	
dissera or *dissesse*	
disséramos or *dissessemos*	
dissereis or *dissesseis*	
disseraõ or *dissessem*	

Second Imperfect.

diria	I should say, &c.
dirias, &c.	

Future.

quando eu disser	when I shall say, &c.
disseres	
disser, &c.	

Infinitive.

dizer	to say.

Gerund.

dizendo	saying.

Participles.

ditto, ditta	said.

2   Observe,

Obferve, that the compounds *defdizer*, to unfay, and *contradizer*, to contradict, are in all points conjugated like *dizer*.

The Conjugation of the irregular Verb querer, *to be willing.*

Indicative Mood.

Prefent.

quero	I will, *or* am willing
queres	thou art willing
quer	he is willing, *&c.*
queremos	
quereis	
querem	

Imperfect.

queria	I was willing, *&c.*
querias, &c.	

Preterperfect definite.

quiz	I have been willing, *&c.*
quizefte	
quiz	
quizemos	
quizeftes	
quizeraõ	

Future.

quererei	I fhall be willing, *&c.*
quererás, &c.	

Imperative.

queiras tu	be thou willing
queira elle	let him be willing
queiramos nos	let us be willing
queirais vos	be you willing
queiraõ elles	let them be willing.

Optative and Subjunctive.

que eu queira	that I may be willing, *&c.*
queiras, &c.	

Imper-

Imperfect.

que eu quizéra or *quizéſſe*	that I were willing
quizéras or *quizéſſes*	thou wert willing
quizéra or *quizéſſe*	he were willing
quizéramos or *quizéſſemos*	we were willing
quizéreis or *quizéſſeis*	you were willing
quizéraõ or *quizéſſem*	they were willing

Second Imperfect.

eu quereria   I ſhould *or* would be willing, &c.
quererias, &c.

Future.

quando eu quizer   when I ſhall be willing, &c.
quizeres, &c.

Infinitive.

querer   to be willing.

Gerunds.

querendo   being willing.

Participle.

querido   been willing.

Note, that *quer* is ſometimes a conjunction, when repeated in a ſentence, and then it is to be rendered into Engliſh by *whether* and *or*; as, *quer vos o tenhais feito, quer naõ*, whether you have done that or no. But when it is not repeated, and is joined to the participle *ſe*, is ſometimes rendered into Engliſh by *at leaſt*; as, *hum ſe quer*, one at leaſt; and ſometimes by *however*, when joined to the participle *que*; as, *como quer que ſeja*, however it be. In all which caſes, it is not to be confounded with the third perſon ſingular of the indicative of the verb *querer*.

Take notice that the verb *querer* is ſometimes uſed with the particle *ſe* inſtead of the verb *dever*; as, *as couſas naõ ſe querem feitas à preſſa*, things muſt not be done in a hurry.

Of

GRAMMAR. 85

Of the irregular Verb valer, *to be worth.*

I shall put no more tenses of this verb than the present indicative, the imperative, and the present subjunctive, none but these being irregular.

Indicative Mood.

Present.

valho	I am worth, &c.
vales	
vale, or *val*	
valemos	
valeis	
valem	

Imperative.

vale tu	be thou worth
valha elle	let him be worth
valhamos nos	let us be worth
valei vos	be you worth
valhaõ elles	let them be worth.

Subjunctive.

que eu valha	that I may be worth, &c.
valhas	
valha	
valhamos	
valhais	
valhaõ	

Of the irregular Verb perder, *to lose.*

This verb changes the *c* before *o* of the present indicative into *d* in the other persons of the same tense, as well as in the other tenses, if you except the imperative and present subjunctive; in which it is conjugated in the following manner:

Indicative.

Present.

perco	I lose, &c.	*perdemos*
perdes		*perdeis*
perde		*perdem*

G 3

Impera-

Imperative.

d	*perde tu*	lofe thou
	perca elle	let him lofe
	percámos nos	let us lofe
	perdei vos	lofe you
	perçaõ elles	let them lofe.

Subjunctive.

que eu perca	that I may lofe, &c.
percas	
perca, &c.	

The compounds of the verb *ter*, as, *contenho*, I contain; *detenho*, I detain, &c. are conjugated like it.

Some verbs of this conjugation are only irregulars in the participle paffive; as, *efcrito*, from *efcrever*; *abfolto*, from *abfolver*.

Thofe that have the *j* before *o* in the prefent indicative change the *j* into *g* in all tenfes and perfons, in which the *j* would otherwife meet with the vowels *i* or *e*; as, *eleger*, to elect; *eu elejo*, *tu eleges*, &c. I elect, &c.

Imperfect.	Preter-def.
elegia, &c.	*elegi, elegefte,* &c. I elected, &c.

The verbs ending in *eyo* in the prefent indicative, change that termination into *ia* in the imperfect, and into *i* in the preter-definite, and are fo conjugated.

Indicative.

Prefent.

eu leyô	I read, &c.	*lemos*
les		*ledes*
le		*lem*

Imperfect.

eu lia	I did read, &c.
lias, &c.	

Preter-

Preter definite.

eu li	I read, &c.
leste, &c.	

Imperative.

		leamos nos	let us read
le tu	read thou	lede vos	read you
lea elle	let him read	leaō elles	let them read

Subjunctive.

que eu lea	that I may read, &c.
leas	
lea, &c.	

You may observe, that they lose the y through all the other moods and tenses. The verb crer, to believe, ought to be conjugated in the same manner.

Of the irregular Verbs in ir.

Ir, to go.

Indicative Mood.

Present tense.

vou	I go	vamos	we go
vás	thou goest	ides	you go
vay	he goes	vaō	they go

Preterimperfect.

bia	I did go, &c.	biamos
bias		bieis
bia		biaō

Preterperfect definite.

fui	I went	fomos	we went
foste	thou wentest	fostes	you went
foi	he went	foraō	they went

Preterperfect.

tenho		
tens, &c.	} ide {	I have gone, &c.

Preter-

Preterpluperfect.

tinha
tinhas, &c. } *ido* { I had gone, &c.

Future.

irei   I shall *or* will go, &c.
iras, &c.

Imperative.

		vamos nos	let us go
vay tu	go thou	*ide vos*	go you
va elle	let him go	*vaõ elles*	let them go

Optative and Subjunctive.

que eu va   that I may go, &c.
    vas
    va
    vamos
    vades
    vaõ

First Preterimperfect.

que eu fora or *fosse*   that I might go, &c.
  foras or *fosses*
  fora or *fosse*
  foramos or *fossemos*
  foreis or *fosseis*
  foraõ or *fossem*

Second Preterimperfect.

iria   I should go, &c.
irias, &c.

Preterperfect.

It is composed of the participle *ido* and the present subjunctive of the auxiliary verb *ter.*

Preterpluperfect.

It is composed of the participle *ido* and the first preterimperfect subjunctive of the auxiliary verb *ter.*

Second

Second Preterpluperfect.

It is compofed of the participle *ido* and the fecond preterimperfect fubjunctive of the auxiliary verb *fer*.

Future.

quando eu for	when I fhall go, *&c.*
fores	
for	
formos	
fordes	
forem	

Second Future.

quando eu tiver tiveres, &c. } *ido* { when I fhall have gone, *&c.*

Infinitive.

Prefent.
ir   to go

Gerunds.
indo   going.

Part.
ido   gone.

Vir, to come.

Indicative.

Prefent.

venho, I come, *&c.*	*vimos*
vens	*vindes*
vem	*vem*

Imperfect.

vinha I did come, *&c.*	*vinhamos*
vinhas	*vinheis*
vinha	*vinhaõ*

Preter definite.

vim I came, *&c.*	*viémos*
viefte	*viéftes*
veyo	*vieraõ*

Preter-

Preterperfect.

tenho vindo   I have come, &c.
tens vindo, &c.

Future.

virei   I shall come, &c.
viras, &c.

Imperative.

		venhamos nos	let us come
vem tu	come thou	*vinde vos*	come you
venha elle	let him come	*venhaõ elles*	let them come

Optative.

Present.

que eu venha.

Imperfect.

que eu viéra,   or *viéffe.*

Second Imperfect.

viria, virias, &c.

Infinitive.

Present.

vir   to come.

Gerund.

vindo   coming.

Part.

vindo   come.

The compounds of *vir*; as, *convir*, to be convenient; *fobrevir*, to come unlooked-for, are conjugated in the fame manner.

Of the irregular Verbs mentir; *to lie,* fentir, *to feel*; fervir, *to ferve*; ferir, *to wound*.

Thefe verbs change the *i* of the firft perfon fingular of the prefent tenfe, indicative, into *e* in the
other

other perfons of the fame tenfe, as well as in the
other tenfes and moods, except the imperative and
the prefent conjunctive, in which they are conjugated thus ;

Indicative.

Prefent.

eu minto	*tu mentes*	*elle mente,* &c.
eu finto	*tu fentes*	*elle fente,* &c.
eu firvo	*tu firves*	*elle ferve,* &c.

Imperative.

mente tu	*minta elle*	*mintamos nos*	*menti vos*	*mintaõ elles*
fente tu	*finta elle*	*fintamos nos*	*fenti vos*	*fintaõ elles*
firve tu	*firva elle*	*firvamos nos*	*fervi vos*	*firvaõ elles*

Subjunctive.

minta,	*mintas,*	&c.
finta,	*fintas,*	&c.
firva,	*firvas,*	&c.

The compounds, *defmentir, affentir, confentir, dif-
fentir, prefentir,* are conjugated like *mentir* and *fentir*; and alfo the verbs *afferir, referir, conferir, de-
ferir, differir, inferir.*

Of the irregular Verbs affligir, *to afflict*; corrigir, *to
correct*; fingir, *to feign*; ungir, *to anoint*; com-
pungir, frigir, dirigir, tingir, cingir, &c.

Thefe verbs change the g of the infinitive mood
into *j* in thofe tenfes where the g would otherwife
meet with the vowels *o,* as in the firft perfon fingular of the prefent indicative, *afflijo*; or *a,* as in the
third perfon of the imperative in both numbers, in
the firft plural of the fame tenfe, and in the prefent
fubjunctive.

Of the irregular Verb feguir, *to follow.*

This verb changes the *e* of the infinitive mood
into *i* in the firft perfon fingular of the prefent indicative,

cative, *eu figo*, I follow ; in the prefent fubjunctive, *que eu figa*, that I may follow ; and in the imperative, where it is conjugated thus : *fegue tu, figa elle, figamos nos, fegui vos, figaõ elles.*

Take notice that the *u* is loft in thofe tenfes where it would otherwife meet with the vowels *o* and *a*, as you fee in the examples ; and this obfervation alfo takes place in the verbs *diftinguir*, to diftinguifh ; *extinguir*, to extinguifh ; &c.

The compounds are *perfeguir*, to perfecute ; *confeguir*, to obtain ; *profeguir*, to purfue.

Of the irregular Verb ouvir, to hear.

This verb changes the *v* of the infinitive mood into *f* in the firft perfon fingular of the prefent indicative, *eu ouço*, I hear, *tu ouves*, &c. in the prefent fubjunctive, and in the imperative mood, where it is conjugated thus : *ouve tu, ouça elle, ouçamos nos, ouvi vos, ouçaõ elles*, hear thou, &c.

Of the irregular Verb dormir, to fleep.

This verb changes the *o* of the infinitive mood into *u* in the firft perfon fingular of the prefent indicative, thus : *eu durmo, tu dormes, elle dorme*, &c. I fleep, &c. In the prefent fubjunctive, *que eu durma*, &c. that I may fleep ; and in the imperative mood, where it is conjugated thus : *dorme tu, durma elle, durmamos nós, dormi vós, durmaõ elles*, fleep thou, &c.

Of the irregular Verb fugir, to fly away.

This verb is irregular in the prefent indicative, and is thus conjugated : *fujo, foges, foge, fugimos, fugis, fogem*, I run away, &c. It is alfo irregular in the imperative mood, where it is conjugated thus : *foge tu, fuja elle, fujamos nós, fugi vós, fujaõ elles.* Finally, it is irregular in the prefent fubjunctive ; *que eu fuja, fujas*, &c.

It

It keeps the *u* in all other tenses and moods, as also the *g*.

The verb *furgir*, to arrive, or to come to an anchor, has the same irregularity, and makes *furto* in the participle passive.

The verbs *fubir, cubrir, encubrir, defcubrir, acudir, bullir, fumir, confumir, cufpir, conftruir, tuffir,* &c. have the same irregularity in regard to the letter *u*.

Of the irregular Verb pedir, to ask.

This verb is irregular in the first person singular of the present indicative and subjunctive, as well as in the imperative, in which it changes the *d* into *f*.

Indicative.

eu peça, I ask, &c.	*nós pedimos*	
tu pedes	*vós pedis*	
elle pede	*elles pedem*	

Imperative.

		peçamos nós,	let us ask
pede tu,	ask thou	*pedis vós,*	ask you
peça elle,	let him ask	*peçaõ elles,*	let them ask

Subjunctive.

que eu peça,	that I may ask, &c.	*peçamos*
peças		*peçais*
peça		*peçaõ*

In like manner is conjugated the verb *medir*, to measure : *eu meço, tu medes,* &c.

Of the irregular Verb veftir, to dress.

Indicative.

Present.

eu vifto,	I dress, &c.	*veftimos*
veftes		*veftis*
vefte		*veftem*

Imperative.

Imperative.

		viſtamos nos,	let us dreſs
veſte tu,	dreſs thou	*veſti vos,*	dreſs you
viſta elle,	let him dreſs	*viſtaõ elles,*	let them dreſs.

Subjunctive.
Preſent.

que eu viſta	that I may dreſs, *&c.*	*viſtamos*
viſtas		*viſtais*
viſta		*viſtaõ*

In all other tenſes and moods it keeps the letter *e*; and in like manner is conjugated the verb *deſpir.*

Of the irregular Verb ſortir, *to furniſh, or ſtock.*

Feyjo ſays, that the *o* of this verb is to be changed into *u*, in thoſe tenſes where the *t* is followed by *e* or *a*, and that is to be kept, when the *t* is followed by *i*; but in the *Fabula dos Planetas* we read, *ſurtio effeyto*, it took effect; and in *Andrade* 2. *Part. Apologet.* we read, *naõ ſortiraõ effeyto*, where the verb *ſortiraõ* is in the ſame tenſe; viz. in the preterperfect definite; therefore nothing can be determined about the irregularity of this verb.

Of the irregular Verb carpir, *to weep.*

This verb is defective, and is only uſed in thoſe tenſes and perſons where the *p* is followed by *i*; as *carpimos, carpis*, we weep, you weep. Preterimperfect, *carpia, carpias*, &c. I did weep, *&c.*

Of the irregular Verb parir, *to bring forth young as any female doth.*

Indicative Mood.
Preſent.

eu pairo,	I bring forth, *&c.*	*parimos*
pares		*paris*
pare		*parem*

Imperfect.

paria, &c.

Imperative

Imperative Mood.

páre tu bring thou forth, *&c.* *pairamos*
paira ella *pari*
  pairaõ

Subjunctive.

Prefent.

que eu paira, that I may, *&c.* *pairámos*
  páiras *pairáes*
  páira *pairaõ*

Of *the irregular Verb* repetir, *to repeat.*

Indicative.

Prefent.

repito, I repeat, *&c.* *repetimos*
  repétes *repetis*
  repéte *repetem*

Imperfect.

repetia, repetias, &c.

Preterperfect definite.

repeti, repetifti, &c.

Imperative.

repete tu, repeat thou, *&c.* *repitamos, &c.*
repita elle,

Subjunctive.

Prefent.

que eu repita, that I may repeat, *&c.*
  repitas, &c.

Imperfect.

repetira or *repetiffe,* that I might repeat.

Of *the irregular Verbs* fahir, *to go out, and* cahir, *to fall.*

Indicative.

Prefent.

fayo, I go out, *&c.* *fahimos*
  fahes *fahis*
  fahe *fahem*

Preterimperfect.

fahia, fahias, &c.

Preter-

Preterperfect definite.
fabi, fabifte, &c.

Imperative.

fabe tu   *fabamos nós*
faya elle   *fabi vós*
                     fayaõ elles

Subjunctive.
que eu foya, fayas, &c.

This is the common way of writing the irregular tenfes of the verb *fabir* as well as of the verb *cabir,* viz. *eu cayo, tu cabes,* &c. I fall, &c. according to *Feyjo.*

Of the irregular Verb, ordir, *to warp in a loom.*

Feyjo fays that this verb changes the *o* into *u,* in thofe perfons where it would otherwife meet with the fyllables *da, de, do.*

Of the irregular Verb advertir, *to warn.*

Advertir is irregular in the following tenfes, only by changing *vir* into *ver.*

Indicative.
Prefent.

advirto, I warn, &c.   *advertimos*
advértes,   *advertîs*
advérte   *advertem*

Imperative.

                            advirtámos nós
adverte tu, warn thou, &c. *advertî vós*
advirta elle   *advirtaõ elles*

Subjunctive.
Prefent.

que eu advirta, that I may warn, &c.   *advirtámos*
advirtas   *advirtáis*
advirta   *advirtaõ*

The Conjugation of the irregular Verb pôr, *to place.*

Indicative.
Prefent.

ponho,	I put, &c.	pomos
poẽs		pondes
põem		põem

Preterimperfect.

punha,	I did put	púnhamos
punhas		púnheis
punha		punhaõ

Preterperfect definite.

pús,	I put, &c.	pufemos
pufefte		pufeftes
pos		puferaõ

Preterperfect.

It is compofed of the prefent indicative of the auxiliary verb *ter*, and the participle *pofto*.

Preterpluperfect.

It is compofed of the participle *pofto*, and the imperfect of the auxiliary verb *ter*.

Future.

porei,	I fhall *or* will put, &c.	poremos
porás		poreis
porá		poraõ

Imperative.

	ponhamos nós
põem *tu,* put thou, &c.	ponde vós
ponha elle.	ponhaõ elles

Optative and Subjunctive.
Prefent.

que eu ponha,   that I may put, &c.
   ponhas, &c.

Firft Preterimperfect.

que eu pufèra or pufeffe,   that I might put, &c.
   puféras or puféffes, &c.

H   S:cond

Second Preterimperfect.

eu poria,   I fhould put, *&c.*
porias, &c.

Preterperfect.

It is compofed of the participle *pofto,* and the prefent fubjunctive of the auxiliary verb *ter.*

Preterpluperfect.

It is compofed of the participle *pofto,* and the firft preterimperfect fubjunctive of the auxiliary verb *ter.*

Second Preterpluperfect.

It is compofed of the participle *pofto,* and the fecond preterimperfect fubjunctive of the auxiliary verb *ter.*

Future.

quando eu pufer,   when I fhall put, *&c.*
puferes, &c.

Second Future.

It is compofed of the participle *pofto,* and the future fubjunctive of the auxiliary verb *ter.*

Infinitive.

Prefent.

pôr, to put.

Gerund.

pondo, putting.

Participle paffive.

pofto, put.

After the fame manner are conjugated the verbs derived from *por;* as *compor,* to compofe ; *difpor,* to difpofe ; *propor,* to propofe, &c.

Some verbs are only irregular in the participle paffive ; as *aberto,* from *abrir* ; *efcrito,* from *efcrever,* &c.

Of Verbs Neuter.

Verbs neuter are thofe which make a complete fenfe of themfelves, and do not govern any cafe af-

ter

ter them; like the verbs active; as *dormir*, to sleep; *andar*, to go; *tremer*, to tremble; &c. But you must take notice that we meet with some verbs neuter which may govern an accusative; as *dormir hum sono profundo*, to sleep soundly; *eu fui andando meu caminho, e naõ disse huma palavra*, I went my way, and said not a word. We may also say, that the verbs neuter are those which, in their compound tenses, are seldom or never conjugated with the verb *ser*, to be; as, I sleep, I tremble, I speak, &c. We may indeed say, *eu tenho dormido*, I have slept; *eu tenho tremido*, I have trembled; but not, I am slept, &c. I said *seldom*, because sometimes the verbs neuter may be conjugated with the verb *ser*; as, *ser bem fallado*, to have a good name.

It is necessary to be acquainted with the nature of a verb neuter, to avoid mistakes in the participles, as may be seen in the Syntax of Participles.

Of the Reciprocal Verbs, which by some are called Passive Neuter.

The name of Reciprocal Verbs is given to such as return the sense backward, and are conjugated through all their tenses with the pronouns conjunctive *me, te, se,* &c.

E X A M P L E.
Indicative. Present.

eu me arrependo,   I repent, &c.
tu te arrependes
elle se arrepende, &c.

Imperfect.
eu me arrependia, &c.   I did repent, &c.

and so of the rest.

Yet we are to take notice that the pronouns conjunctive *me, te,* &c. may be placed either before or after the verb, in the indicative, and consequently we may say, *eu me lembro,* or *eu lembro-me,* I remember;

member ; *me lembrei*, or *lembrei-me*, I remembered, &c. But in the imperative they ought to be placed after the verb, as in the following

lembra-te tu,	remember thou, &c.	*lembremo-nos nós*
lembre-se elle		*lembrai-vos vós*
		lembrem se elles

In which example you muſt obſerve alſo, that the firſt perſon plural, which in the other verbs is like the firſt perſon plural of the preſent ſubjunctive, has the laſt conſonant, *s*, cut off; and ſo from *lembremos* we cut off the *s* to make *lembremo-nos*; and from *arrependamos* we make *arrependamo-nos*, &c. In regard to the infinitive, we may ſay, *he neceſſario arrepender-ſe dos peccados*, it is neceſſary to repent ſins ; *he neceſſario lembrar-ſe*, it is neceſſary to remember ; and not *ſe arrepender*, or *ſe lembrar*. In like manner we may ſay *lembrando me*, remembering, and not *me lembrando*. Yet you muſt take notice that the preſent infinitive may be preceded by the particle *para*, (which forms the Portugueſe ſupine) and then the pronoun conjunctive may be placed either before or after it; and ſo we may ſay, *para lembrar-ſe*, or *para ſe lembrar*, to remember, or in order to remember.

As for the ſubjunctive mood, you muſt put the pronoun conjunctive before the preſent ; but you muſt carefully obſerve, that the pronouns conjunctive muſt be placed before it when preceded by the particles *ſe*, if, *que*, that ; and ſo you may ſay, *que eu me lembra-ſe, ſe eu me lembra-ſe*, that I might remember, &c. but not *que eu lembraſſe-me*, &c. But when the firſt preterimperfect is not preceded by any particle, then you muſt place the pronoun conjunctive after it ; as, *arrependerame eu diſſo*, I wiſh I was repented of it.

In the ſecond preterimperfect we may place the pronouns conjunctive either before or after it, therefore

fore you may say *arrependeria me fe*, &c. or *eu me arrependeria fe*, &c. I should repent if, &c.

In the future you must always place the pronouns conjunctive before it; and so we may say, *quando eu me lembrar*, when I shall remember; but not *quando eu lembrar-me*.

Note, all the verbs active may become reciprocals.

EXAMPLE.

eu me amo, I love myself
tu te amas, thou lovest thyself
elle fe ama, he loves himself
nos nos amamos, we love ourselves, &c.

The Conjugation of the reciprocal Verb ir-fe, *to go away*

Indicative.

Present.
eu me vou,   I go away
tu te vas, &c. thou goeft away, &c.

Preterimperfect.
eu me hia,   I did go away
tu te hias, &c. thou didft go away, &c.

Preterperfect definite.
eu me fu,   I went away
tu te fofte, &c. thou wenteft away, &c.

Preterperfect.
eu me tenho ido,   I am gone away, *or* I have been gone away
tu te tens ido, &c. thou haft been gone away, &c.

Preterpluperfect.
eu me tinha ido,   I was gone away, *or* I had been gone away
tu te tinhas ido, &c. thou hadft been gone away, &c.

Future.
eu me irei,   I shall *or* will go away
tu te iras, &c. thou shalt go away, &c.

Imperative.
vai-te,   go thou away
va-fe,   let him go away
vamo-nos, let us go away
ide-vos,   go away, get away, *or* get you gone.
vao-fe,   let them go away.

Sub-

Subjunctive.

Present.

que eu me va   that I may go away
que tu te vas, &c.   that thou mayeſt go away, &c.

Firſt Preterimperfect.

eu me fora, or *me foſſe*   I went away
te foras, or *te foſſes,* &c.   thou wenteſt away, &c.

Second Preterimperfect.

eu me iria   I would, &c. go away
tu te irias   thou wouldſt, &c.

Preterperfect.

que eu me tenha ido   that I have gone away, &c.

Preterpluperfect.

que eu me tivera, or *me tiveſſe ido*   that I had gone away,

Second Preterpluperfect.

eu me teria ido   I ſhould have gone away, &c.

Future.

quando eu me for   when I ſhall go away, &c.

Second Future.

quando eu me tiver ido   when I ſhall have gone away, &c.

Infinitive.

Present.

ir-ſe   to go away.

Preterperfect.

ter ſe ido   to have gone away.

Participles,

Present.

que ſe vai   that is going away.

Preterit.

Preterit,

ido   gone away,

Future.

que ha de ir-fe   that is to go away.

Gerunds.

indo-fe   going away.
tendo fe ido   having gone away.

Supine.

para ir-fe   to go, *or* in order to go away.

You muſt obſerve, that in the compound tenſes the pronouns *me, te,* &c. are placed before the auxiliary verb.

2dly, This verb is alſo ſaid of veſſels to ſignify their being leaky; as, *vai-fe a cuba,* the tub leaks. It is alſo uſed before the gerunds; as, *o inverno vai-fe acabando,* the winter is drawing towards an end; *elles vaõ-fe preparando,* they are preparing themſelves: in which examples and in the like the verb is to be rendered into Engliſh by the verb *to be* itſelf, and without addition of the adverb *away*; and ſometimes it is placed before the preſent infinitive; as, *ir-fe deitar,* to go to bed.

Of the reciprocal Verb vir-fe, *to come away.*

This verb is to be conjugated like the verb *vir*; but you muſt place the pronouns conjunctive, *me, te,* &c. according to the obſervations we have made above.

Of the reciprocal Verb avir-fe, *to agree.*

This is a compound verb, which is to be conjugated by putting the particle *a* before the verb *vir* in all its tenſes and moods; but you muſt always

H 4   make

make ufe of the obfervations already made about the pronouns conjunctive; and the fame care muft be had with the reciprocal verb *haver-fe*, to behave; in the conjugation of which, you have nothing to do but to add the pronouns conjunctive to the verb *haver*.

Imperfonal Verbs.

There are three forts of verbs imperfonal, which have only the third perfon fingular.

The firft are properly imperfonals of themfelves; as,

 fuccede, it happens
 bafta, it is enough, *or* it fuffices
 chove, it rains
 troveja, it thunders

The fecond are derived from verbs active, followed by the particle *fe*, which renders them imperfonals; as, *ama-fe*, they love; *diz-fe*, they fay; *nota-fe*, it is noted. They are alfo called paffive imperfonals.

The third, which have a great affinity with reciprocal verbs, are conjugated with the pronouns conjunctive, *me, te, lhe, nos, vos, lhes*; as, *doe-me, doe-te, doe-lhe,* &c.

The imperfonal verbs of themfelves are,

 convem, it is convenient
 fuccede, it happens, *or* it falls out
 eftá me bem, it becomes me
 bafta, it is enough
 ha-fe, it is neceffary
 chovifca, it miffes
 chove, *or* *cahe pedra*, it hails
 gea, it freezes
 neva, it fnows
 fuzila, *or* *relampaguea*, it lightens
 importa, it matters, it concerns
 parece, it feems

and

and the like, which are conjugated with the third
person singular of each tense; as,

Indicative.

Present.
chove   it rains

Imperfect.
chovia   it did rain

Preterperfect definite.
choveo   it rained.

Preterperfect.
tem chovido   it has rained.

Preterpluperfect.
tinha chovido   it had rained.

Future.
chovera   it shall *or* will rain.

Imperative.
chova   let it rain.

Optative and Subjunctive.

Present.
que chova   that it may rain.

Imperfect.
que chovera or *chovesse*   that it might rain.

Second Imperfect.
choveria   it should rain.

Future.
quando chover   when it shall rain.

Second Future.
quando tiver chovido   when it shall have rained.

Infinitive.
chover   to rain.

The

The particle *fe*, which compofes the fecond fort of imperfonal verbs, may be placed either before or after them ; as, *diz-fe*, they fay ; *fabe-fe*, it is known ; *fabia-fe*, it was known ; *logo fe foube*, it was immediately known ; *fe diz*, it is faid, &c. but fometimes they make no ufe of the particle *fe*, and only put the verb in the third perfon plural ; as, *dizem*, inftead of *fe diz*, they fay.

In like manner all the verbs active may become imperfonal.

In regard to thefe verbs, take notice, that when the noun that follows them is in the fingular number, you muft put the verb in the fingular ; if the noun be in the plural, you put the verb in the plural.

E X A M P L E.

Louva-fe o capitaõ, they praife the captain.
Louvaõ-fe os capitães, they praife the captains.
Ve-fe hum homem, they fee a man.
Vem-fe homens, they fee men.

When *lhe* is ufed after the *fe*, then *lhe* is to be rendered into Englifh by *his* or *her* ; as, *louva-fe-lhe o valor*, they praife his *or* her courage.

The third fort of imperfonal verbs are fuch as are conjugated with the pronouns perfonal, *me*, *te*, *lhe*, &c. with the third perfon fingular.

E X A M P L E.

Indicative.
Prefent.

defagrada-me	I am difpleafed, *or* it difpleafes me
defagrada-te	thou art difpleafed
defagrada-lhe	he *or* fhe is difpleafed
defagrada-nos	we are difpleafed
defagrada-vos	you are difpleafed
defagrada-lhes	they are difpleafed

Imperfect.

defagradava-me	I was difpleafed.

Preter-

Preterperfect definite.

desagradou-me   I was displeased

Future.

desagrader-me-ba   I shall be displeased

Optative.

que me desagrade   that I may be displeased

Imperfect.

que me desagradara or *me desagradasse*   that I were displeased

Second Imperfect.

desagradar-me-hia   I should be displeased.

Conjugate after the same manner,

succede-me, it happens to me
doe-me, it grieves, *or* it pains me
parece-me, it seems to me
he-me preciso, it behoves me
agrada-me, it pleases me
lembro-me, I remember

Many of those impersonal verbs have the third person singular and plural; as,

doe me a pérna, my leg pains me
doem me os olhos, I have sore eyes
a vosso vestido parece-me novo, your coat appears new to me
os vossos sapatos me parecem muyto compridos, your shoes seem to me too long

Of the Verb ser, to be.

The verb *ser* is also used as an impersonal, as it appears in the following examples : *he tempo de levantar-se*, it is time to get up; *era tempo de hir*, it was time to go, &c. and particularly when it is conjugated with the adjectives *preciso* or *necessario* ; as, *he preciso* or *necessario fazer isto*, this must be done ; *era preciso* or *necessario escrevar*, it was necessary to write ; *eu iria se fosse preciso*, I would go, if it should be necessary ;

ceffary; *he precifo que eu va,* I muft go; *he precifo que eu leya,* I muft read; *he precifo que elle coma,* he muft eat; *feria precifo que eu foffe,* I fhould go. You fee by the laft examples, that when the verb *fer* and the adjective are before the conjunctive mood, with the particle *que,* the conjunctive is rendered in Englifh by the infinitive; but if the verb *fer* is followed by the relative or particle *que,* it muft then be rendered in Englifh in the following manner; as, *eu he que tenho feito aquillo,* 'tis I who have done that; *tu he que tens, &c.* 'tis thou who haft, &c. *elle he que tem, &c.* 'tis he who, &c. *nos he que temos, &c.* 'tis we who have, &c. *vos he que tendes, &c.* 'tis you who have, &c. *elles he que tem, &c.* 'tis they have, &c. *a ley he que o manda,* 'tis the law that prefcribes it; *ella he que o cre,* 'tis fhe who believes it; *elles he que o fizeraõ?* is it they have done it? *eu he que o fiz,* 'twas I who did it; *entaõ he que tu tomo as minhas medidas,* 'tis then I take my meafures; *entaõ he que eu vi,* 'twas then I faw, *or only,* then I faw. You may obferve that *que* is not relative in the laft examples, and that it is left off in Englifh.

Of the Verb haver, when it is imperfonal.

It is to be fo conjugated.

Indicative.

Prefent.

ha, or *hao ha,* there is, or there is not, *or* there are, *or* there are not.

Imperfect.

havia, there was, *or* there were.

Preterperfect definite.

houve,   there was, *or* there were.

Preter-

3

Preterperfect.

tem havido   there has been, *or* there have been.

Preterpluperfect.

tinha havido   there had been.

Future.

haverá.   there shall be.

Imperative.

haja   let there be.

Optative and Subjunctive.

que haja   that there may be.

Imperfect.

que houvera or houvesse   that there were.

Second Imperfect.

haveria   there would be.

Preterperfect.

que tenha havido   that there had been.

Preterpluperfect.

se tivesse havido   if there had been.

Future.

quando houver   when there will *or* shall be.

Second Future.

quando tiver havido   when there shall have been.

Infinitive.

haver   there to be.

Pret.

ter havido   there to have been.

Gerunds.

havendo   there being
tendo havido   in there having been.

Those who learn Portuguese are greatly at a loss how to render the following expressions; *there is not;*
is

is there? &c. and though there is nothing so easy; however, I have explained them at large in the following conjugation.

Conjugation of the Verb impersonal there is, ha, *when it marks the place, through all its tenses.*

There is of it,	*ha lá disso.*
There is not of it,	*naõ ha lá disso.*
Is there of it ?	*ha lá disso ?*
Is there not of it ?	*naõ ha lá disso ?*
There was of it,	*havia lá disso.*
There was not of it,	*naõ havia lá disso.*
Was there of it ?	*havia lá disso ?*
Was there not of it ?	*naõ havia lá disso ?*
There was of it,	*houve lá disso.*
There was not of it,	*naõ houve lá disso.*
Was there of it ?	*houve lá disso ?*
Was there not of it ?	*naõ houve lá disso ?*
There shall be of it,	*havera lá disso.*
There shall not be of it,	*naõ havera lá disso.*
Shall there be of it ?	*havera lá disso ?*
Shall there not be of it ?	*naõ havera lá disso ?*
That there may be of it,	*que haja lá disso.*
There may not be of it,	*naõ haja lá disso.*
That there were of it,	*que houvera* or *houvesse lá disso.*
There were not of it,	*naõ houvera* or *houvesse lá disso.*
There would be of it,	*haveria lá disso.*
There would not be of it,	*naõ haveria lá disso.*
Would there not be of it ?	*naõ haveria lá disso ?*
If there had been of it,	*se tivesse havido lá disso.*
If there had not been of it,	*se naõ tivesse havido lá disso.*
Had there been of it ?	*teria havido lá disso ?*
Had there not been of it ?	*naõ teria havido lá disso ?*
There would have been of it,	*teria havido lá disso.*
There would not have been of it,	*naõ teria havido lá disso.*
Would there have been of it ?	*teria havido lá disso ?*
Would there not have been of it ?	*naõ teria havido lá disso ?*
When there will be of it,	*quando houver lá disso.*
When there will not be of it,	*quando naõ houver lá disso.*

When

When there will have been of it,	*quando tiver havido lá diſſo.*
When there will not have been of it,	*quando naõ tiver havido lá diſſo.*
Will there have been of it?	*tera havido lá diſſo?*
Will there not have been of it?	*naõ tera havido lá diſſo?*
For there having been too much of it,	*por ter havido lá demaſiadamente diſſo*
In there having been too little of it,	*tendo havido lá muyto pouco diſſo.*

Moſt ways of ſpeaking beginning with *ſome*, and the verb *to be*, are expreſſed in Portugueſe by the imperſonal *ha*; as, ſome friends are falſe, *ha amigos falſos*; ſome Chriſtians are unworthy of that name, *ha Chriſtiaõs que naõ ſaõ dignos de tal nome.*

Obſerve, that *ha* comes before a ſubſtantive even of the plural number.

The imperſonal *ha* is beſides uſed to denote a quantity of time, ſpace, and number; as, *ha dez annos que morreo*, he has been dead theſe ten years; or, he died ten years ago; *ha trinta milhoens d'almas em França*, there are thirty millions of ſouls in France; *de Paris a Londres ha 120 legoas*, Paris is 120 leagues from London.

The queſtion of ſpace is aſked thus, *quanto ha de Paris a Londres?* how far is Paris from London?

Of the imperſonal Verb ha-ſe, *it is neceſſary, or muſt.*

This verb anſwers to the Italian *biſogna*, and to the French *il faut*, and always requires after it the particle *de*, and the infinitive. It denotes the neceſſity of doing ſomething, and is Engliſhed by *muſt*, and ſometimes by the verb *to be*, through all its tenſes, with one of theſe words, *neceſſary, requiſite, needful*: and as it denotes the neceſſity of doing ſomething in general, without ſpecifying who *muſt*, therefore the ſubject coming before *muſt* may be either *I* or *we*, *he* or *ſhe*, or *any body*, according to the ſenſe of the ſpeech; as,

Ha-ſe

Ha-ſe de fazer aquillo, one, *or* we, *or* you, he, ſomebody muſt do that.

Ha-ſe de bir, I, *or* you, *or* we, *or* ſomebody, muſt go.

Sometimes the verb coming after this imperſonal, is Engliſhed by the paſſive voice; as, *ha-ſe de fazer iſta*, this muſt be done.

It is very often joined with *miſter*; as, *ha-ſe de miſter dinheiro para demandas*, one muſt have money to go to law; *ha-ſe de miſter hum bom amigo para fazer fortuna no mundo*, to puſh one's fortune in the world, one muſt have a good friend.

As for the conjugation of this verb, you muſt make uſe of the verb *to be* with *neceſſary*, as I have ſaid already.

E x a m p l e.

Preſent. *ha-ſe*, it is neceſſary. Imperfeſt. *havia-ſe*, it was neceſſary; and ſo through all the tenſes and moods.

You muſt take notice, that ſometimes the infinitive that follows the particle *de* is placed between this imperſonal and its particle *ſe*; as, *ha de achar-ſe*, it will be found: and ſometimes the infinitive precedes the imperſonal, and this follows the particle *ſe*; as, *achar-ſe ha*, it will be found; and in this caſe you muſt not join the particle *de* to it. Obſerve alſo, that the infinitive may be alſo placed between the imperfeſt tenſe of this imperſonal verb and its particle *ſe*; as, *havia de achar-ſe*, it was to be found; but when the infinitive precedes both the imperſonal and its particle *ſe*, then you muſt put the particle *ſe* before the imperſonal, and make uſe of the imperfeſt *hia*, and not *havia*; ſo you may ſay, *achar-ſe hia*, and not *achar-ſe-havia*.

Of

Of the defective Verbs carpir *to weep, and* foer, *to be wont.*

The verb *carpir* is ufed only in thofe tenfes and perfons where the *p* is followed by an *i*; as, *carpimos, carpis,* we weep, you weep.   Preterimp. *carpia, carpias,* &c. I did weep, &c.

The verb *foer* is only ufed in the third perfons of the prefent indicative of the preterimperfect of the fame mood, and in the gerund; as, *elle foe,* he is wont; *elles foem,* they are wont.   Impert. *elle foia,* he was wont; *elles foiaõ,* they were wont.   Gerund. *foendo,* being wont.

✸✸✸✸✸✸✸✸✸✸✸✸✸✸✸✸✸✸✸✸✸✸✸✸✸✸✸✸✸✸✸✸

C H A P. V.

Of the Participles.

THE participle is a tenfe of the infinitive, which ferves to form the preterperfects and preterpluperfects of all the verbs; as, *tenho amado,* I have loved; *tinha amado,* I had loved.

Amado is a participle, and all the verbs in *ar* form the participle in *ado*; as, *amado, cantado,* &c.

Amado is likewife a noun adjective.   Example. *Homem amado, molher amada; livros amados, letras amadas.*

Some participles are frequently abridged; as, *envolto* or *envolvido, corrupto* or *corrompido, enxuto* or *exugado*; and feveral others, which the ufe of authors will point out to you.

The regular verbs ending in *er* or in *ir* form the participle in *ido*; as, *vendido, recebido, luzido, nutrido,* &c.

I   There

There are three forts of participles; namely, active, paffive, and abfolute.

The active participles are compofed of the verb *ter*; as, *tenho amado, tinha amado*, &c.

The paffive participles are preceded by the verb *fer*, to be; as, *fou amado, fendo louvado*, &c.

The abfolute participles are of the fame nature as thofe called *abfolute* in Latin; and you muft obferve, that *having* and *being* are often left out in Portuguefe.

EXAMPLE.

Feito ifto, having done this.
Dito ifto, having faid fo.
Acabada a cea, after he *or* they have fupped.

The auxiliary and participle are not always immediately joined together in compound tenfes; as, *Nos temos, com a graça de Deos, vencido os noffos inimigos*, we have, by the grace of God, overcome our enemies.

CHAP. VI.

Of the Adverbs.

THE adverb is that which gives more or lefs force to the verb.

The adverb has the fame effect with the verb as the adjective with the fubftantive: it explains the accidents and circumftances of the action of the verb.

There are a great many forts; as adverbs of time, place, quantity, &c.

Adverbs of time; as, at prefent, *prefentemente*; now, *agora*; yefterday, *ontem*; to-day, *hoje*; never, *nunca*;

nunca; always, *sempre*; in the mean time, *entre-tanto*.

Adverbs of place; as, where, *onde*; here, *aqui*; from whence, *donde*; there, *ali*; from hence, *da-qui*; above, *em cima*; below, *em baxo*; far, *longe*; near, *perto*.

Adverbs of quantity; as, how much, *quanto*; how many, *quantos* or *quantas*; so much, *tanto*; much, *muyto*; little, *pouco*.

A great many adverbs are formed from adjectives, changing *o* into *amente*; *santo*, *santamente*, holily; *rico*, *ricamente*, richly; *douto*, *doutamente*, learnedly.

From adjectives in *e* or *l* we likewise form adverbs by adding *mente* to them; as,

Constante, *constantemente*, constantly.
Diligente, *diligentemente*, diligently.
Prudente, *prudentemente*, prudently.
Fiel, *fielmente*, faithfully.

In order to assist the memory of those who are learning the Portuguese language, I have here collected a large number of adverbs, which, by frequent repetition, may be easily retained, especially those terminated in *mente*.

A Collection of Adverbs.

Abundantemente, abundantly
Com razaō, *justamente*, justly
Absolutamente, absolutely
A Escacbapernas, or *a cavalleiro*, a-straddle
Agora, or *por hora*, now, at this time
Ia para ja, now, immediately
Com condicaō, upon condition
De parte, aside
De travez, askew, asquint; as, *olhar de travez*, to look askew, or asquint
Actualmente, actually

De proposito, purposely
Adeos, farewel
Admiravelmente,
Maravilhosamente } admirably
As mil maravilhas
Astutamente, cunningly
Atreiçoadamente, treacherously
De maravilha, very seldom
A miudo, often
Assim, so
Taō, so
Apressa, in haste
Facilmente, easily
Ao avesso, or *as avessas*, the wrong side outward

I 2   *De*

De improviſo, or improviſa-
    mente, at unawares
Antigamente, anciently
Quaſi, pretty near, almoſt
Entaõ, then
Deſde crtaõ, ſince that time
Deſde quando? ſince when?
De quando aca? from what
    time? how long?
De quando en quando, now and
    then, ever and anon
Quando bem, or ainda quando,
    albeit, although it ſhould
    be
Quando muito, at the moſt
Quando menos, at leaſt
Cà, here, or hither
Lâ, there
Ali, there, in that place
Ahi, { there, expreſſes the
       place where ſtands
       the perſon ſpoken to;
       as, ahi onde eſtas, there
       where you are.
Acolá there
Traz, or detraz, behind
Para traz, backward
Iſto he, to wit
Em vez, inſtead
Tambem, alſo
Tanto que } as ſoon as
logo que   }
De penſado, wilfully
Acaſo, by chance
Fixamente, ſtedfaſtly
Finalmente, finally
Livremente, freely
Muyto, much
Depreſſa, quickly
Aqui, here
Ate aqui, as far as here, or till
    now, or hitherto
D'aqui em diante, henceſor-
    ward, or hereafter
Bem, well

A'manhãa, to-morrow
A'manhãa pela manhãa, to-
    morrow morning
Diſpois d'a'manhãa, after to-
    morrow
Ultimamente, laſtly
Como, as
Como? how?
Cedo, ſoon
Tarde, late
Premeiro que, before that
Premeiro que tudo, before all,
    or in the firſt place
Fora, abroad, out
Ja, already.
De ſalto, at one jump
De quando em quando, from
    time to time
Antes, before
Deſpois, afterwards
Juntamente, together
Enteiramente, entirely
Ao redor, or em torno, about
De balde, in vain
Loucamente, madly
Muyto, very
Atrevidamente, boldly
Felicemente, happily
Vergonhoſamente, ſhamefully
Nunca, never
Nunca mais, never ſince
Logo, immediately
Ainda, yet; as, ainda naõ
    veio, he is not come yet
Ainda, even; as, ſeria vergon-
    ha ainda o fallar niſſo, it
    were a ſhame even to ſpeak
    of it
Nem ſe quer, even
Vilmente, baſely
Mal, ill
Mais, more
Menos, leſs
Ate, until, or even
Sim, yes

Naõ

Naõ, no, not	*Quando*, when
Onde, where	*Nada*, nothing
De côr, by heart	*Verdadeiramente*, truly
A's vezes, sometimes, from	*Dentro*, within
time to time	*Devagar*, softly

CHAP. VII.

Of the Prepositions.

PRepositions are a part of speech indeclinable, most commonly set before a noun, or pronoun, or verb. Every preposition requires some case after it, as you will see in the following collection:

Genitive.

Antes do dia, before day break
Diante de Deos, before God
Dentro da igreja, within the church
Detraz do palacio, behind the palace
Debaxo da mesa, under the table
Em cima da mesa, upon the table
Alem, besides
Alem dos mares, on that side of the seas
Alem diſſo, besides that, moreover
Alem de que, idem
Aquem, or *daquem dos mares*, on this side of the seas
A o redor, or *em contorno da cidade*, round about the city
Perto de Londres, near London
Acerca daquelle negocio, concerning that affair
Fora da casa, out of the house
Fora de prigo, out of danger
Fora de ſi, out of one's wits
　　This preposition governs alſo a nominative ; as, fora ſeu ir-
　　maõ, *except his brother, or, his brother excepted.*
De fronte da minha casa, over-against my house
De fronte da igreja, facing the church
Deſpois de cea, after supper

Dative.

Quanto áquillo, with respect to that
Pegado á muralha, close to the wall

Defde o bico do pe ate á cabeça, from top to toe

Accufative.

Perante o juiz, before the judge

Entre, between, among, *or* amongft

Entre os homens, among men.

Sobre a mefa, upon the table

Conforme, or *fegundo a ley,* according to the law

Por amor de Deos, for God's fake

Pelo mundo, through the world

Pelos mares, through the feas

Pela rua, through the ftreets

Pelas terras, through the lands

Por grande que feja, let it be never fo great

Contra elles, againft them

Traz o templo, behind the temple

Durante, during; as, *durante o inverno,* during the winter.

We fhall be more particular about prepofitions when we examine their conftruction.

★★★

C H A P. VIII.

Of the Conjunctions.

A Conjunction is a part of fpeech indeclinable, which ferves to join the members and parts of fpeech together, in fhewing the dependency of re-lation and coherency between the words and fen-tences.

Some conjunctions are copulative, which join, and, as it were, couple two terms together; as, *e,* and: *Portuguefes e Inglezes,* Portuguefe and Englifh.

Some are disjunctive, which fhew a refpect of fe-paration or divifion; as, *nem,* nor, neither; *ou,* ei-ther, or. Example: *nem efte nem aquelle,* neither this nor that; *ou efte ou aquelle,* either this or that; *nem mais nem menos,* neither more nor lefs; *quer o faça quer naõ, tudo para mim he o mefmo,* it is all one to me whether he does it or no; *quer feja verdade quer naõ,* whether it be true or no; *nem fe quer hum,* never a one.

The

The adverfative denote reftriction, or contrarie-
ty; as, *mas*, or *porem*, but; *comtudo*, yet, however; *mas antes*, or *pello contrario*, nay.

The conjunctions conditional fuppofe a condition,
and ferve to reftrain and limit what has been juft
faid; as, *fe*, if; *com condiçam que*, *com ifto que*, *dado
cafo que*, provided that, or upon condition that, or
in cafe that, &c.

The conceffive, which fhew the affent we give to
a thing; as, *embora*, or *feja embora*, well and good;
eftá feito, done, agreed.

The caufal fhew the reafon of fomething; as, *porque*, for, or becaufe, or why.

The concluding denote a confequence drawn from
what is before: as, *logo*, or *por confequencia*, therefore, then, or confequently.

The tranfitive, which ferve to pafs from one fentence to another; as, *alem diffo*, moreover, or befides that; *fobre tudo*, or *em fumma*, after all, upon
the whole, in the main; *a propofito*, now I think
on't, or now we are fpeaking of that.

There are others of a different fort; as, *fe quer*,
or *ao menos*, at leaft; *aindaque*, although; *de forte
que*, fo that; *antes quero pedir que furtar*, I'll rather
afk than fteal; *antes morrerei que dizer-volo*, I'll rather die than tell you; *já que*, fince, &c.

To the above mentioned parts of fpeech grammarians have added *Interjections*, which are particles ferv-
ing to denote fome paffion or emotion of the mind:
but there is another fort, which may be called demonftrative; as, *aqui* and *la*; Ex. *efte homem aqui*, this man;
aquella molher la, that woman, &c. and fome others
continuative, becaufe they denote continuation in
the fpeech; as, *com effeito*, in effect; *alem diffo*, befides; *ora vejamos*, now let us fee; *finalmente fomo-
nos embora*, and fo, fir, we went away. To which
we may add thofe invented to imitate the founds of
dumb creatures, and the noife which is occafioned
by the clafhing of bodies againft one another; as,
zaz, *traz*, thwick-thwack, &c.   *In-*

Interjective Particles.

Of Joy.

Ha, ba, ba! Ha, ha, ha!
Ob que gosto! Oh joy!

Of Grief.

Ay! Alas! ah!
Ay de mim! Woe is me! lack!
Meu Deos! My God!

Of Pain.

Ay! Ay!
Ob! Oh!

To encourage.

Animo!
Ora vamos! } Come, come on!

To call.

O, olá! Ho, hey, hip!

Of admiration or surprize.

O, O la, abi! Lack-a-day!
Apre! Heyday!

Of aversion.

Irra!
Nada! } Away, away with! fye!
Fera!

For making people go out of the way, or stand away.

Guardem-se, or *arredem-se!* Have a care, clear the
way, *or* stand away!

For shouting.

Viva! Huzza!

Of silence.

Calaivos! Hush! Peace!

Of cursing and threatening.

Aï, guai! Woe!

For derision.

Ab! Ah! oh! oh! oh!

Of wishing.

Q provera a Deos! Would to God!

Oxalá!

Oxala! or *bab!* O that!
O se! Would!

The interjection O ſeryes for different emotions of the mind, as admiration, grief, wiſh, &c. and ſometimes is uſed ironically, but differently uttered, according to the emotion which it expreſſes.

Some Abbreviations uſed in the Portugueſe Language.

An^to	*Antonio*	Anthony
Seb^am	*Sebaſtiam*	Sebaſtian
B^mo P^e	*Beatiſſimo Padre*	The moſt bleſſed Father
Cap^m	*Capitaõ*	Captain
Comp^a	*Companhia*	Company
Corr^o	*Correo*	Poſt
D.	*Dom*	Don
D^r, D^or	*Doutor*	Doctor
D^s	*Deos*	God
D^o, D^a	*Ditto, ditta*	Said
Exmo, Exma	*Excellentiſſimo, ma*	Moſt excellent
V. E.	*Voſſa excellencia*	Your Excellence
V. S.	*Voſſa ſenhoria*	Your Lordſhip
V. A.	*Voſſa alteſa*	Your Highneſs
V. M. *or* Vm^ce	*Voſſa merce*	You
V. P.	*Voſſa paternidade*	Your Paternity
Vmag^de	*Voſſa mageſtade*	Your Majeſty
S.	*Santo*	Saint
Fran^co	*Franciſco*	Francis
G^de	*Guarde*	Save
J. H. S.	*Jeſus*	Jeſus
M^s a^s	*Muntos annos*	Many Years
M^e	*Meſtre*	Maſter
S^or, S^ra	*Senhor, ora*	Sir, Lady
R^mo	*Reverendiſſimo*	Moſt reverend
P^a	*Para*	For
Q'	*Que*	That
Q^do	*Quando*	When
Q^m	*Quem*	Who
Q^to	*Quanto*	How much
Supp^te	*Supplicante*	Petitioner
Gen^al	*General*	General
Ten^te	*Tenente*	Lieutenant
V. G.	*Verbi gratia*	For Example.

And many others, that muſt be learned by uſe.

A NEW

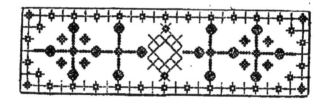

A NEW

PORTUGUESE GRAMMAR.

PART II.

CHAP. I.

Of the Division of Syntax.

SYNTAX is a Greek word, by the Latins called *construction*; and it signifies the right placing and connecting of words in a sentence. It is divided into three sorts; the first, of Order or Arrangement; the second, of Concordance; the third, of Government. The Syntax of Order or Arrangement, is the fit disposition of words in a sentence. The Syntax of Concordance is when the parts of speech agree with one another, as the substantive with the adjective, or the nominative with the verb. The Syntax of Government is when one part of speech governs another.

For

For the sake of those who, perhaps, have not a grammatical knowledge of their own language, I shall lay down some general rules of Portuguese construction.

I. *Of the Order of Words.*

1. The nominative is that to which we attribute the action of the verb, and is generally ranged in the first place; it may be either a noun or pronoun, as *Francisco escreve*, Francis writes; *eu fallo*, I speak.

2. When the action of the verb is attributed to many persons or things, these all belong to the nominative, and are ranged in the first place, together with their conjunction; as *Pedro e Paulo lem*, Peter and Paul read.

3. The adjectives belonging to the nominative substantive, to which the action of the verb is attributed, are put after the substantive and before the verb; as, *os estudantes morigerados e diligentes estudaõ*, the mannerly and diligent scholars do study.

4. If the nominative has an article, this article always takes the first place.

5. Sometimes an infinitive is put for a noun, and stands for a nominative; as, *o dormir faz bem*, sleeping does one good: and sometimes a verb with its case; as, *he acto de humanidade ter compaixaõ dos afflictos*, to have compassion on the afflicted is an act of humanity.

6. The nominative is sometimes understood; as, *amo*, where you understand *eu*; and so of the other persons of the verb.

7. After the nominative you put the verb; and if there is an adverb, it is to be placed immediately after the verb, whose accidents and circumstances it explains; as, *Pedro ama por extremo a gloria*, Peter is extremely fond of glory.

8. The cases governed by the verb are put after it; they may be one, or many, according to the nature of the action; as, *eu amo a Pedro*, I love Peter.

ter. *Faço presente de bum Luro a Paulo*, I make a present of a book to Paul.

9 The prepofition is always put before the cafe it governs; as, *perto de caſa*, near the houfe.

10. The relative is always placed after the antecedent; as, *Pedro o qual eſtuda*, Peter who ftudies.

II. *Of Concordance.*

1. The adjectives agree with their fubftantives in gender, number, and cafe; as, *bomem virtuoſo*, a virtuous man; *bella molher*, a handfome woman; *fumptuoſas palacios*, &c. fumptuous palaces, &c.

2. When two or more fubftantives fingular come together, the adjective belonging to them muft be put in the plural; as, *tanto el rey como a rainba montados a cavallo parecem bem*, both the king and queen look well when they ride.

3. If the fubftantives happen to be one in the fingular and the other in the plural, or to be of different genders, the adjective common to both agrees in number and gender with the laft; as, *elle tinha os olhos e a boca aberta*, or *elle tinha a boca e os olhos abertos*, his eyes and mouth were opened. *As lagoas e rios eſtavaõ congeladas*, the ponds and rivers were frozen.

4. But when there be one or many words between the laft noun and the adjective, that adjective (common to all) agrees with the noun mafculine, though the laft noun be feminine; and if the nouns are in the fingular, then the adjective common fhall be put in the plural number and mafculine gender; as, *a rio e a lagoa eſtavaõ congeladas*, the pond and river were frozen. *O trabalho, a induſtria, e a fortuna unidos*; pains, induftry, and fortune joined together.

5. Every verb perfonal agrees with its nominative, expreffed or underftood, both in number and perfon.

6. The relative *qual* with the article agrees entirely with the antecedent; but without the article, and

and denoting an abfolute quality, it agrees with what follows; as, *aquelle coraçaõ o qual*, &c. that heárt which, *&c. Confiderando quaes feriaõ as condiçoens*, &c. confidering which would be the conditions, *&c.*

⟨ 7. The queftion and anfwer always agree in every thing; as, *a que fenhora pertence vm^{ce}? elle refpondeo, pertenço á rainba*: To what lady do you belong, fir? and he anfwered, I belong to the queen.

III. *Of the Dependence of the Parts of Speech on one another.*

1. The nominative being the bafis of the fentence, the verb depends on it, as the other cafes depend on the verb. The adjective depends on the fub-ftantive that fupports it; and the adverb on the verb whofe accidents it explains.

2. The genitive depends on a fubftantive, ex-preffed or underftood, by which it is governed.

3. The accufative depends either on a verb ac-tive, or a on prepofition.

4. The ablative depends on a prepofition by which it is governed; as, *parto de Roma*, I go from Rome.

5. The dative and vocative have, ftrictly fpeak-ing, no dependence on the other parts: the dative is common, as it were, to all nouns and verbs; the vocative only points out the perfon to whom you fpeak.

I come now to the Conftruction of the feveral parts of fpeech.

CHAP.

CHAP. II.

Of the Syntax of Articles.

BEFORE we come to the fyntax of the articles, remember that *o, a, os, as,* are articles
only when they precede the nouns or pronouns, but
not when joined to the verbs.

Thofe who underſtand Latin will quickly perceive the difference, if they take notice that every
time they render *o, a,* by *illum, illam, illud*; or by
eum, eam, id; and *os, as,* by *illos, illas, illa*; or by
eos, eas, ea; they are relative pronouns.

1. The article is uſed before the names of the ſpe-
cies or things which can be ſpoken of; therefore
nouns of ſubſtances, arts, ſciences, plays, metals,
virtues, and vices, having no article before them in
Engliſh, require the article in Portugueſe; as;

O ouro e a prata naõ podem fazer feliz a o homem,
gold and ſilver cannot make the happineſs of man.

A virtude naõ he compativel com o vicio, virtue cannot agree with vice.

A philofophia he huma ſciencia muito nobre, philoſo-
phy is a very noble ſcience.

Joguemos as cartas, let us play at cards.

2. The article is not placed before a ſubſtantive
which is followed by the adjective of number that
ſtands for a ſurname, or meets with a proper or Chriſ-
tian name; as, *Jofeph Primeiro,* Joſeph the Firſt.

3. When a book or ſome part of it, as chapter,
page, &c. is quoted, the adjective of number may
come either before or after the ſubſtantive; but if
it comes after, the two words are conſtrued without
article; as, *livro primeiro, capitulo fegundo,* &c.
book i.. chapter ii.   If the adjective of number
comes

2

comes before the fubftantive, it takes the article; as, *o primeiro livro*, the firft book.

4. *O* placed before *que* fignifies *what* or *which*; as, *faça o que quifer*, let him do what he likes; *o que eu fiz*, which I did.

5. The article is never made ufe of before proper names of men, women, gods, goddeffes, faints.

6. The article is not ufed in Portuguefe before the pronouns poffeffive relative; as, *de quem he efta cafa? he minha, he tua, &c.* whofe houfe is this? it is mine, it is thine, &c.

7. When a mount's, mountain's, or hill's name, is preceded by the word *monte*, it takes neither article nor prepofition; as, *o Monte Atlante*, Mount Atlas; *os Montes Pireneos*, the Pirenean Mountains; but after the word *ferra*, a ridge of hills, it takes the article; as, *a Serra da Eftrella*, Mount Strella; *Serra do Potofi*, Mount Potofi; however, they fay alfo, *Serra Lioa*.

8. The noun of the meafure, weight, and the number of the things that have been bought, requires the articles; as, *otrigo vende-fe tanto o alqueire*, wheat is fold fo much a peck, three quarts and one pint.

A manteiga vende-fe tanto o arratel, butter coft fo much a pound.

Os ovos vendem-fe tanto a duzia, eggs are fold fo much a dozen.

9. No article is ufed with proper names of perfons and planets, except *a terra*, the earth; *o fol*, the fun; *a lua*, the moon.

10. When proper names are ufed in a determinate fenfe, that is, when they are applied to particular objects, then they take the article; as, *o Deos dos Chriftaõs*, the God of Chriftians; *o Archimedes de Inglaterra*, the Archimedes of England. The proper names of renowned poets and painters keep alfo the article; as, *o Camoens, o Pope, o Taffo, o Ticiano,* &c.

11. The

11. The indefinite article *de* is used before nouns following one of this, *forte, specie, genero*, and any other noun of which they express the *kind, character, quality,* and *nature:* which sort of nouns are usually Englished by an adjective, or even by the substantive itself placed adjectively, and making together, as it were, but a word compound ; as, *Dor de cabeça,* the head-ach ; *huma forte de fruto,* a sort of fruit ; *fallar de tolo,* a foolish speech.

Sometimes the English adjective may be made by an adjective too in Portuguese, as in the last example, *hum fallar tolo,* a foolish speech ; but sometimes too the Portuguese express the English adjective by a substantive of the same signification with *de* before the other noun, though they have an adjective of the same nature as the English adjective ; as, *o diabo de minha molher,* my devilish wife ; and sometimes the adjective is used by them substantively, or the substantive is understood ; as, *o velhaco de meu filho,* my rascally son ; *a velhaca de sua may,* his *or* her rascally mother. Finally, they make also use of the definite article ; as, *o diabo de homem* or *da molher,* the devilish man *or* woman ; *a probre da molher,* the poor woman, &c.

12. Nouns are used without article in the following cases.

1st. At the title of a performance, and in the middle of sentences, where they characterise in a particular manner the person or thing spoken of, in which case the English use especially the particle *a* ; as,

Discurso sobre as obrigações da religiaõ natural, a discourse concerning the obligations of natural religion.

Primeira parte, the first part.

O conde de Clermont, principe do Sangue, morreo, &c. the count of Clermont, a prince of the blood, died, &c.

O S. *An-*

O S. Antonio, não de noventa peças, the St. Anthony, a ninety gun ship.

2dly. In sentences of exclamation; as,

As mais bellas flores saõ as que menos duraõ; qualquer chuva as desmaia, o vento as murcha, o sol as queima, e acaba de secar; sem fallar numa infinidade de insectos que as perseguem e deitaõ a perder: natural e verdadeira image da belleza das senboras! the handsomest flowers last but a very short time; the least rain tarnishes them, the wind withers them, the sun scorches them, and completes the drying of them; without mentioning an infinite number of insects that spoil and hurt them: a natural and true image of the ladies beauty!

3dly. When they meet with a noun of number in an indefinite sense; as, *mil soldados de cavallo contra cem infantes,* a thousand horse against an hundred foot.

Tenho lido dous poetas, I have read two poets, that is, any pair out of all that ever existed.

But before a noun of number, in a definite sense, it would take the article; as,

Tenho lido os dous poetas, I have read both poets; because this plainly indicates a definite pair, of whom some mention has been made already.

Os cem infantes que combateraõ contra os mil de cavallo, que, &c. the hundred foot who fought with the thousand horse, that, &c.

4thly. After the verb *ser,* when it signifies *to become,* and after *ser tomado por,* to be accounted; *passar por,* to pass for; as, *elle será doutor com o tempo,* he will become a doctor in time; *elle passa por marinheiro,* he passes for a sailor.

When the adjective is used substantively, then it must have the neuter Portuguese article *o* before it; as,

O verde offende menos a vista que o vermelho, green hurts the eye less than red.

K   There

There are also some adverbs preceded by the neutral article *o*; as the following, *o melhor que eu puder*, the best I will be able; *o menos que for possivel*, the less it will be possible.

Articles are repeated in Portuguese before as many nouns (requiring the article) as there are in the sentence; as,

O ouro, a prata, a saude, as honras, e os deleites naõ podem fazer feliz a o homem que naõ tem ciencia nem virtude, gold, silver, health, honours, and pleasures, cannot make a man happy without wisdom and virtue.

The article *o* is put before the word *senhor*, sir, or my lord; as,

O senhor duque, my lord duke; *o senhor presidente*, my lord the president; *os senhores*, the gentlemen; *dos senhores*, of the gentlemen.

You must observe the same rule for the feminine article *a*, which is to be prefixed to *senhora*, my lady, *or* madam; as, *a senhora duqueza*, or *condessa de, &c*, my lady duchess, *or* countess of, &c.

The article is never used in Portuguese as it is in English, before *mais* more, or *menos* less, in the following sentences, *quanto mais vivemos, tanto mais aprendemas*, the longer we live, the more we learn; *quanto mais hum hydropico bebe, mais sede tem*, the more an hydropick drinks, the more thirsty he is; *quanto mais hum homem he pobre, quanto menos cuidados tem*, the poorer people are, the less care they have, &c.

Sometimes the English particle *to*, before infinitives, is rendered in Portuguese by the article *o*; as, *he facil o dizer, o ver, &c*. it is easy to say, to see, &c.

In a word, *the natural associators with articles* are those *common appellatives*, which denote the several genera and species of beings, or those words which, though indefinite, are yet capable, through the article, of becoming definite. Therefore *Apollonius*
makes

makes it part of the pronoun's definition, to refuse coalescence with the article; and it would be absurd to say *o eu*, the I ; or *o tu*, the thou ; because nothing can make those pronouns more definite than they are.

N. B. When the adjective *hum, huma*, is used as an article in Portuguese, it respects our primary perception, and denotes individuals as unknown ; but the articles *o*, *a*, respect our secondary perception, and denote individuals as known. To explain by an example : I see an object pass by which I never saw till then ; What do I say ? *Ali vai hum pobre com huma barba comprida*, there goes a beggar with a long beard. The man departs and returns a week after ; What do I say then ? *Ali vai o pobre da barba comprida*, there goes the beggar with the long beard.

CHAP. III.

Of the Syntax of Nouns ; and first, of the Substantives.

WHEN two or more substantives come together without a comma between them, they all govern each the next in the genitive, the first governing the second, the second the third in the same case, and so on ; (that is, the first is always followed by the preposition *de*, or by the article before the next noun) but that genitive can never come in Portuguese before the noun that governs it, as in English :

A philosophia de Newton, Newton's philosophy.
As guardas do principe, the prince's guards.
A porta da casa, the house-gate.

K 2

Eis

Eis aqui a cafa do companbeiro do irmaõ de minba molber, here is my wife's brother's partner's houfe.

When two fubftantives fingular are the nominative of a verb, this muft be put in the plural; as, *meu irmaõ e meu pay eftaõ no campo*, my brother and father are in the country.

If the nominative is a collective name, the verb is always put in the fingular; as, *toda a cidade affiftio*, all the city was prefent.

Of the Syntax of Adjectives.

Of adjectives, fome are put before the noun, and fome after; and others may be put indifferently, either before or after.

The pronouns adjective poffeffive, *meu*, *teu*, *feu*, *&c.* and adjectives of number, come before the fubftantive as in Englifh. Ex. *Meu pay*, my father; *a fua cafa*, their houfe; *duas peçoas*, two people; *o primeiro bomem*, the firft man.

But when the adjective of number ftands for a furname, or meets with a proper or Chriftian name, it comes after the fubftantive, without the article; as, *Joaõ* V. John the fifth.

Thefe following Adjectives come after the Subftantive.

1ft. Verbal adjectives and participles; as, *bum bomem divertido*, a comical *or* merry man; *buma molber eftimada*, a woman efteemed.

2dly. Adjectives of names of nations; as, *bum mathematico Inglez*, an Englifh mathematician; *bum alfaiate Francez*, a French taylor; *mufica Italiana*, Italian mufick.

3dly. Adjectives of colour; as, *bum veftido negro*, a black fuit of cloaths; *bum capote vermelbo*, a red cloak, &c.

4thly.

4thly. Adjectives of figure; as, *huma mesa redonda*, a round table; *bum campo triangular*, a triangular field, &c.

5thly. Adjectives expressing some physical or natural quality; such are, *quente*, hot; *frio*, cold; *humido*, wet; *corcovado*, bunch-backed, &c.

Most other adjectives are differently placed before or after the substantive; as, *santo*, holy; *verdadeiro*, true, &c.

If the substantive has three or more adjectives belonging to it, they must absolutely be put after it with the enclitic *e* before the last, which must likewise be observed, even when there be but two adjectives; for the Portuguese don't say, *huma desagradavel enfadonha obra*, &c. but *huma desagradavel e enfandonha*, &c. a disagreeable, tedious work.

Of adjectives, some always require after them either a noun or a verb, which they govern; as, *digno de louvor*, praise-worthy; *digno de ser amado*, worthy to be loved; *capaz de ensinar*, capable to teach; and these have always the particle *de* after them.

Some will be used absolutely without being ever attended by any noun or verb; as, *prudente*, wise; *incuravel*, incurable, &c.

Others may be construed both with and without a noun, which they govern; as, *ella he huma molher insensivel*, she is a woman without any sensibilty; *ella he insensivel ao amor*, she is insensible and a stranger to the passion of love.

The following adjectives, which require the preposition *de* before the next infinitive, govern the genitive case. Observe, that some of them require in English the preposition *at* or *with* before the next noun.

Digno, worthy: as, *elle he digno de louvor*, he is worthy of praise. This adjective is sometimes followed by *que*; as, *digna que seu nome fosse*, &c. her name deserved to be, &c.

K 3

Indigno,

Indigno, unworthy; as, *indigno da eſtimacaõ que faço delle*, unworthy of the eſteem which I have for him.

Capaz, capable; *incapaz*, incapable; as, *capaz, ou incapaz, de ſervir a propria patria*, capable, *or* incapable to ſerve one's country.

Notado, charged; as, *notado de avareza*, charged with avarice.

Contente, glad; as, *eſtou contente do ſucceſſo que elle teve*, I am glad *or* overjoyed at his ſucceſs.

Cançado, tired; as, *cançado de eſtudar*, tired of ſtudying.

Dezejoſo, greedy; as, *dezejoſo de gloria*, greedy of glory, &c. as likewiſe adjectives ſignifying fulneſs, emptineſs, plenty, want, deſire, knowledge, remembrance, ignorance, or forgetting.

All adjectives ſignifying inclination, advantage and diſadvantage, profit or diſprofit, pleaſure or diſ--pleaſure, due ſubmiſſion, reſiſtance, likeneſs, govern the dative caſe; as, *inſenſivel ás affrontas*, inſenſible of affronts; *ſer inclinado a alguma couſa*, to be inclined to ſomething; *nocivo á ſaude*, hurtful to health.

Theſe adjectives ſignifying dimenſion, as, *alto*, high, tall; *largo*, wide, broad; and *comprido*, long, come after the words of the meaſure of magnitude, both in Engliſh and Portugueſe; but they are preceded by *de* in Portugueſe; as, *des pes de largo*, ten feet broad; *ſeis pes de comprido*, ſix feet long, &c. they alſo turn the adjective of the dimenſion into its ſubſtantive, with the word of the meaſure before; but the word of the dimenſion is always preceded by *de*; as, *ſeis pes de altura*, ſix feet high; *des pes de largura*, ten feet broad.

The adjectives ſignifying experience, knowledge, or ſcience, require *em*, or *no, na, nos, nas*, after them; as, *verſado nos livros*, verſed in books; *experto na medicina*, expert in medicine.

The cardinal nouns require the genitive caſe after them; as, *hum dos dous*, one of the two.

The

The ordinal nouns, as well as the collective and proportional, likewise require the genitive afte them; as, *o primeiro dos reys,* the first of the kings *huma duzia de ovos,* a dozen of eggs, &c.

Of the Syntax of the Comparatives and Superlatives.

The comparative is not made of the positive in Portuguese, as in Latin and English, but by adding. *mais* more, or *menos* less, which govern *que,* signifying *than;* as, *o todo he mayor que a parte,* the whole is greater than the part; *o seu amante he mais bello, mais moço, e mais rico que ella,* her lover is handsomer, younger, and richer than she is; *eu acho-o agora menos bello do que quando o comprei,* I now find it less handsome than when I bought it.

The simple comparatives *mais,* and *menos,* meeting with a noun of number, are attended by *de;* as, *ainda que elle tivesse mais de cem homens,* though he had above an hundred men; *elle tem mais de vinte annos,* he is above twenty.

When the comparison is made by *so as, as much as,* they must all be rendered by *como.*

E X A M P L E.

O meu livro he tão bello como o vosso, my book is as handsome as yours; *hum principe não he tão poderoso como hum rey,* a prince is not so powerful as a king.

They put sometimes *muito* and *pouco* before the simple comparatives *mais* and *menos;* as, *elle he muito mais grande,* he is taller by much; *elle he pouco mais grande,* he is taller by little, &c.

K 4   C H A P.

CHAP. IV.

Of the Syntax of Pronouns.

WE have fufficiently explained the pronouns
in the firft part; and to avoid any further
repetition, I fhall only obferve, that,

1ft. The Englifh make ufe of the verb *to be*, put
imperfonally through all its tenfes in the third perfon, before the pronouns perfonal *I, thou, he, fhe, we,
you, they*; it is I; it is he, &c. In Portuguefe the
verb *to be*, on this occafion, is not imperfonal; and
they exprefs, it is I, by *fou eu*; it is thou, *es tu*;
it is he, *be elle*; it is we, *fomos nos*; it is ye, *fois vos*;
it is fhe, *be ella*; it is they, mafc. *faõ elles*; it is they,
fem. *faõ ellas*; and in like manner through all the
tenfes; as, it was I, *era eu*; it was we, *eramos nos*,
&c.

2dly. The Portuguefe feldom make ufe of the fecond perfon fingular or plural, but when through a
great familiarity among friends, or fpeaking to God,
or a father and mother to their children, or to fer-
vants; thus, you are in the right of it, is expreffed
by *vmᶜᵉ tem razaõ*, inftead of *tendes razaõ; como eftá
vmᶜᵃ?* how do you do? In the plural they fay
vmᶜᵃˢ.

Obferve here, that when an adjective comes after
vmᶜᵉ V. S. V. E. &c. it does not agree in gender
with *vmᶜᵉ V. S.* &c. but with the perfon we fpeak
to or we fpeak of; therefore they fpeak to a lady or
woman thus; *vmᶜᵃ be muito bella*, you are very beautiful; and to a man they fay, *vmᶜᵉ be muito bom*, you
are very good.

3dly, *Nos* is generally ufed by the king, a governor, or a bifhop, in their writings, and then it fignifies in Englifh *we*; as, *nos mandamos*, or *mandamos*,
we command; but *nos* before or after a verb in Portuguefe

tuguefe fignifies *us* in Englifh ; as, *elle nos diffe*, he told us ; *dai-nos tempo*, give us time.

4thly, *Vós* is alfo applied to a fingle perfon, but only fpeaking to inferiors, or between familiar friends, to avoid the word thou, *tu*, which would be too grofs and unmannerly.

5thly. The pronouns conjunctive are joined to verbs, and ftand for the dative and accufative cafes ; as, *deu-me*, he gave me ; *ama-me*, love me ; but the pronouns perfonal are ufed inftead of them when they are preceded by a prepofition, and not immediately followed by a verb ; as, *elle fallou contra mim*, he fpoke againft me.

6thly. When *o, a, os, as*, are joined to the prefent infinitive mood, they change the laft *r* of it into *lo, la, &c.* thus ; *para ama-lo*, to love him ; *para ve-la*, or *ve-las*, to fee her, *or* them, &c. and when they are joined to the preterperfect indicative of the verb *fazer*, and fome others that have that tenfe ending in *iz*, they change the laft *z* of them into *lo, la, &c.* as, *fi-lo*, I did it ; *elle fe-lo*, he did, *or* made it, &c. but when they are joined to the future indicative of any verb with the auxiliary verb *haver*, then they change the terminations *rei, ras*, &c. of the futures into *lo, la, &c.* as, *fa-lo-hei*, I'll do it ; *ama-lo-hei*, I'll love him, &c.

Remarks on the Pronouns.

1ft. *Him*, or *it*, which follow the verb in Englifh, muft be expreffed in Portuguefe, as in the following examples :

When *him* or *it* in Englifh follow the verb in the firft perfon of the fingular number, it muft be expreffed in Portuguefe by *o* before or after the verb. Exam. I call him *or* it, *eu o chamo*, or *eu chamo-o*.

When *him* or *it* in Englifh follow the verb in the fecond perfon of the fingular number, it may be expreffed in Portuguefe either by *o* before the verb, or *lo* after it, making an elifion of the laft confonant of of the verb. Exam. Thou calleſt him *or it*, *tu o chamas*, or *tu chama-lo*.

When *him* or *it* is joined with the third perſon ſingular of a verb, it may be expreſſed by *o* before or after the verb. Ex. He calls him *or it*, *elle o chama*, ou *elle chama-o*.

When *him* or *it* is with a verb in the firſt perſon plural, it may be expreſſed in Portugueſe either by *o* before the verb, or *lo* after it, making an eliſion as in the ſecond caſe. Ex. We call him *or it*, *nos o chamamos*, or *nos chamamo-lo*.

When *him* or *it* is after a verb in the ſecond perſon plural, it is expreſſed in Portugueſe either by *o* before the verb, or *lo* after it, making an eliſion, &c. Ex. You call him *or it*, *vos o chamays*, or *vos chamay-lo*.

When *him* or *it* follows the verb in the third perſon plural, it may be expreſſed in Portugueſe either by *o* before the verb, or *no* after it. Examp. They call him *or it*, *elles o chamaõ*, or *elles chamaõ-no*.

2dly. *Her* or *it* after a verb in Engliſh is expreſſed in Portugueſe by *a*, according to the rules juſt now propoſed.

3dly. *Them* after a verb is expreſſed in Portugueſe by *os* for the maſculine, and by *as* for the feminine, according to the gender and the rules propoſed.

4thly. The words *o*, *a*, *os*, *as*, muſt be always put after the gerunds, but before the infinitives. Examp. Seeing him, we muſt not ſay *o vendo*, but *vendo-o*, becauſe *vendo* is a gerund. To ſee him, inſtead of ſaying *para ver-o*, you muſt ſay, *para o ver*, becauſe *ver* is in the infinitive.

5thly. The words *lo*, *la*, *los*, *las*, muſt be always put after the verbs. Examp. To ſee him, you muſt ſay, *para ve-lo*, or *para o ver*, and not *para lo ver*. The ſame words muſt follow alſo the adverb *eis*; and ſo you muſt ſay, *ei-lo aqui*, here he is; *ei-lo ali*, there he is; *ei-los aqui*, here they are; *ei-la ali*, there
ſhe

she is ; *ei-las ali*, there they are. They follow likewife the perfons of the verbs ; as, *eu fi-lo* ; *tu fizef-
telo* ; *elle fe-lo* ; *nos fizemo-lo*, &c. I made it, &c.

Note, that I have been fpeaking of the words
o, a, os, as, lo, la, los, las, and not of the articles
o, a, os, as ; becaufe when thofe words precede,
and fometimes when they follow the verbs, are not
articles, but pronouns relative. They are articles
only when they precede the nouns or pronouns.

CHAP. V.

Of the Syntax of Verbs.

THE verbs through every tenfe and mood
(except the infinitive) ought to be preceded
by a nominative cafe, either expreffed or underftood, with which they muft agree in number and
perfon. The nominative is expreffed when we fay,
eu amo, tu cantas; underftood when we fay, *canto,
digo*, &c.

The Portuguefe, as well as Englifh, ufe the fecond perfon plural, though they addrefs themfelves
but to a fingle perfon.

EXAMPLE.

Meu amigo, vos naō tendes razaō, my friend, you
are in the wrong.

And if we would fpeak in the third perfon, we
muft fay, *vmce tem razaō*, fir, you are in the right.

The verb active governs the accufative ; as, *amo
a virtude*, I love virtue.

The

The verb paſſive requires an ablative after it; as, *os doutos ſaõ envejados pellos ignorantes*, the learned are envied by the ignorant.

You muſt obſerve, that there is in Portugueſe another way of making the paſſive, by adding the relative *ſe* to the third perſon ſingular or plural; as, *ama-ſe a Deos*, God is loved.

When there are two nominatives ſingular before a verb, in muſt be put in the plural number.

When a noun is collective, the verb requires the ſingular, not the plural; as, *a gente eſtá olhando*, the people are looking.

Syntax of the auxiliary Verbs.

The verb *ter* is made uſe of to conjugate all the compound tenſes of verbs; as, *tenho amado, tinha amado*, I have loved, I had loved.

Ter ſignifies alſo to poſſeſs, to obtain; as, *tenho dinheiro*, I have money; *tem muita capacidade*, he has a great deal of capacity.

Haver, in account-books and trade, expreſſes credit or diſcharge.

Haver is alſo taken imperſonally in Portugueſe, and it ſignifies in Engliſh *there be*; as, *ha muito ouro no Mexico*, there is a great quantity of gold in Mexico.

Haver-ſe, made reciprocal, is the ſame as *to behave, to act*; as, *houve-ſe o governador com tal prudencia, que*, &c. the governor behaved with ſuch wiſdom, that, &c.

We have already obſerved the difference betwixt *ſer* and *eſtar*.

The verb *eſtar* is alſo uſed to conjugate the other verbs, chiefly expreſſing action; as, *eſtou lendo, eſtou eſcrevendo*, I am reading, I am writing.

Eſtar, with the prepoſition *em*, in, or with *no, na, nos, nas*, ſignifies *to be preſent in a place*; as, *eſtou no campo*, I am in the country.

Eſtar,

Eftar, with the prepofition *para*, denotes the inclination of doing what the following verb expreffes, but without a full determination ; as, *eftou para
ir-me de Londres*, I have a mind to go and live in
London.

Eftar, with the prepofition *por*, and the infinitive
of the verb following, means, that the thing expreffed by the verb is not yet done ; as, *ifto eftá por
efcrever*, this is not yet written ; *ifto eftá por alimpar*,
this is not yet cleaned ; *eftar por alguem*, fignifies to
agree with one, or to be of his opinion.

N. B. See in the Third Part the different fignifi-
cations of the verbs *eftar* and *haver*.

When *fer* fignifies the poffeffion of one thing, it
governs the genitive ; as, *a rua he d'el-rey*, the ftreet
belongs to the king ; *efta cafa he de meu pay*, this
houfe belongs to my father.

Em fer is taken for a thing to be whole or en-
tire, without any alteration on mutilation ; as, *as
fazendas eftaõ em fer*, the goods are not fold.

Of the Syntax of Verbs active, paffive, &c.

When two verbs come together, with or without
any nominative cafe, then the latter muft be in the
infinitive mood ; as, *quer vm^{ce} aprender a fallar Inglez?* will you learn to fpeak Englifh ?

All verbs active govern the accufative ; but if
they are followed by a proper name of God, man,
or woman, or any noun expreffing their qualities or
title, then it governs the dative cafe ; as, *conheço a
feu pay*, I know his father. *Acháraõ a Joaõ no cami-*
they found John in the road.

All verbs of gefture, moving, going, refting, or
doing, as alfo all the verbs that have the word that
goes before, and the word that comes after, both
belonging to one thing, require the nominative after
them ; as, *Pedro vai errado*, Peter goes on wrong ;
o pobre

o pobre dorme defcançado, the poor fleep without care. Alfo the verb of the infinitive mood has the fame cafe, when verbs of wifhing and the like come after them; as, *todos dezejaõ fer rioos*, every body wifhes to be rich; *antes quifera fer douto que parecelo*, I had rather be learned than to be accounted fo.

After verbs the Portuguefe exprefs *yes* and *no* by *que fim* and *que naõ*. Example, *treyo que fim*, I believe yes; *creyo que naõ*, I believe not; *digo que fim*, I fay yes; *cuido que naõ*, I think not; *apofto que fim*, I lay yes; *quereis apoftar que naõ?* have you a mind to lay not?

Verbs fignifying *grief, compaffion, want, remembrance, forgetting,* &c. will have the genitive; as, *pefame muito dà morte de feu irmaõ*, I am very forry for the death of your brother; *elle morre de fome*, he perifhes by hunger; *lembre-fe do que me diffe*, remember what you faid to me; *compadeçi-me das fuas difgraças*, I pitied him for his misfortunes; *efquecime de tudo ifto*, all this I forgot.

The reciprocals of jeering, boafting, and diftrufting, govern alfo the genitive; as, *jaEtar-fe, gloriar-fe, picar-fe, envergonhar-fe*, &c.

All the verbs active govern the dative only when the fubftantive reprefents a perfon; as, *eu conheço a vm^ce*, &c, I know you, &c.

The following verbs belong to this rule of the dative:

Jogar, to play; as *jogar ás cartas*, to play at cards; *jogar aos centos*, to play at piquet; *jogar ao xadrez*, to play at chefs, &c.

Obedecer, defobedecer, agradar, comprazer; as, *eu obedeço a Deos e a el rey*, I obey God and the king; *comprazeo em tudo aos foldados*, in all he pleafed the foldiers.

Mandar, when it fignifies to command an army, company, &c. requires the accufative, but when other things, the dative; as *elle mandava a cavallaria*, he commanded the horfe; *o governador mandou*

*dou a todos os moradores que se retiraſſem para ſuas ca-
ſas,* the governor ordered all the inhabitants to re-
tire into their houſes.

Ir, to go; as, *vou a Paris,* I go to Paris.

Aſſiſtir, ajudar, ſocorrer, to help; as, *aſſiſtir ao officio divino,* to aſſiſt at divine ſervice.

Saudar, to ſalute, or greet; as, *elle ſauda a todos,*
he ſalutes every body.

Fallar, to ſpeak; *ſatisfazer,* to ſatisfy; *ſervir,* to.
ſerve; *favorecer,* to favour; *ameaçar,* to threaten.

The verbs of pleaſing, diſpleaſing, granting, de-
nying, pardoning, will have the perſon in the dative caſe.

The imperſonals *acontecer, ſucceder, importar, per-
tencer,* and the like to theſe, will have often two
datives of perſon; as, *a mim me ſuccedeo,* it happen-
ed to me; *a elle lhe convem,* it ſuits him, *or* it is
convenient for him; *a elle naõ lhe importa,* it does not
concern him, &c.

All the active verbs require an accuſative; and
the Latin verbs which govern the accuſative of the.
thing, and the dative of the perſon, govern generally the ſame in Portugueſe; as, *eſcrevei o que diga.
a voſſo irmaõ,* write to your brother what I do ſay.

Verbs of aſking, teaching, arraying, will have an
accuſative of the doer or ſufferer, and ſometimes
verbs neuter will have an accuſative of the thing;
as, *gozar ſaude,* to enjoy health; *peço eſte favor,* I
aſk this favour; *elle toca muito bem flauta,* he plays
very well on the flute; *curar huma doença,* to cure a
ſickneſs.

Verbs paſſive, and the greateſt part of the reciprocals, require the ablative, with *de, do, da, dos,
das, por,* or *pello, pella, pellos, pellas;* as, *fui cha-
mado por el rey,* I was called by the king; *retireime
da cidade,* I retired from the city; *elle foi amado do
povo,* he was loved by the people. But you muſt
except *acoſtar-ſe,* which requires a dative preceded
by *a; encoſtar-ſe,* which ſometimes will have a da-

2   tive,

tive, and sometimes an ablative preceded by *em, no, na, nos,* or *nas*; *meter-se,* which requires an ablative; *sentar-se, introduzir-se,* &c. which must have the ablative with the prepofition *em, no, na, nos, nas.*

The verbs joined with a noun which they govern, muft have the infinitive with *de*; as, *tenho vontade de rir,* I am near laughing.

The price of any thing bought, or fold, or bartered, will have the accufative with *por.*

The verb *por-se,* when it fignifies *to begin,* muft have the infinitive, with the particle *a*; as *por-se a chorar,* to begin to cry.

Verbs of plenty, filling, emptying, loading, unloading, will have the ablative; as, *efta terra abunda de trigo*; this country abounds with corn; *elle efiá carregado de miferias,* he is loaded with calamities.

Verbs denoting cuftom, help, beginning, exhortation, invitation, require the infinitive with the particle *a*; as *ajudar a femear,* to help fowing; *convidou me a cear,* he invited me to fupper.

Verbs that fignify diftance, receiving, or taking away, will have the ablative; as, *a Madeira difta de Marrocos* 320 *milhas,* Madeira lies 320 miles from Morocco.

Note, that the verbs fignifying receiving, or taking away, generally require the ablative of perfon; but they fometimes require an accufative, particularly the verb *receber,* when it fignifies *to welcome,* or *to entertain*; as, *elle recebe todos com muito agrado,* he gives his company a hearty reception, he makes them very welcome.

Verbs denoting obligation, govern the following infinitive with the prepofition *a*; as, *eu o obrigarei a fazer ifto,* I will oblige him to do it.

Verbs of arguing, quarrelling, fighting, &c. will have the ablative with *com*; as, *pelejou mais de huma hora com feu irmaõ,* he quarrelled more than one hour with his brother.

After

GRAMMAR. 145

After the verb fubftantive *fer*, to be, *para* is made ufe of as well as *a* : the firft is employed to denote the ufe or deftination of any thing; as, *efta penna he para efcrever*, this pen is to write with. But the particle *a* is ufed to denote only the action ; as, *elle foy o primeiro a fugir*, he was the firft to run away.

The verbs of motion to a place always govern the dative; as, *vou á comedia*, I go to the play. Though the verb *voltar*, to return, may alfo have an accufative, with the prepofition *para*. But the verbs of motion from a place govern the ablative with *de, do, da, dos, das*; as, *venho do campo*, I come from the country. If the motion is through a place, then the verbs govern the accufative, with *por*; as, *paffarei por Londres*, I will come by the way of London.

Of the Ufe and Conftruction of the Tenfes.

Though we have fpoken at large upon the tenfes in the Firft Part, you muft, however, take notice,

1. That they make ufe of the infinitive and the auxiliary verb *haver*, together with the pronouns *lo, la, los, las*, inftead of the future indicative ; as, *ouvi-lo-hei*, I will hear him ; and then the *r* of the infinitive is changed into *lo, la, los, las*, ; and fometimes they make ufe of the infinitive mood and the auxiliary verb *haver*, with the pronouns conjunctive *me, te, fe*, &c. inftead of the fame future; as, *dar-lhe-hei*, I will give him ; *agaftar-fe-há*, he will be angry.

2. That when we find the particle *if*, which in Portuguefe is expreffed by *fe*, before the imperfect indicative, we muft generally ufe the imperfect fubjunctive in Portuguefe; example, *fe eu tiveffe*, if I had ; *fe eu pudeffe*, if I could. But fometimes they ufe the imperfect indicative ; as, *diffe-lhe que fe queria*, &c. he told him that if he was willing, &c.

L
3. That

3. That the first imperfect subjunctive in Portuguese is also used in a sense that denotes the present, especially in sentences of wishing; as, *quizera que Domingo fizesse bom tempo*, I wish it would be fine weather on Sunday. But if the same tense is preceded by *ainda que*, although, then it must be rendered into English by the second imperfect subjunctive, or by the imperfect indicative ; as, *eu naõ a quizera ainda que tivesse milhoens de seu*, though she was worth several millions I would not have her; *ainda que elle consentisse nisso naõ se podia fazer*, although he would consent to it that could not be done. Lastly, when the first imperfect subjunctive is preceded by *se*, it is sometimes rendered into English by the second imperfect subjunctive ; as *se elle viesse*, if he should come.

The English are apt to put the first imperfect of the subjunctive where the Portuguese make use of the second ; as, I had been in the wrong, *naõ teria tido razaõ*; and though they may say *naõ tivera tido razaõ*, they may not say *naõ tivesse tido razaõ*, to express the English of, *I should have been in the wrong*, or *I had been in the wrong*.

Note, that to express in Portuguese, *though that should be*, we must say *quando isso fosse*, and not *seria*.

The Portuguese use the future tense subjunctive after the conjunction *if*, when they speak of a future action, but the English the present indicative : example, tomorrow if I have time, *amanhãa se tiver tempo*, and not *se tenho*; if he comes we shall see him, *nos o veremos se elle vier*.

A conjunction between two verbs obliges the last to be of the same number, person, and tense as the first : example, the king wills and commands, *el rey quer e ordena*; I see and I know, *eu vejo e conheço*.

Sometimes the present is made use of, instead of the preter definite, in narrations ; as, *no mesmo tempo que hia andando, o encontra o despe, e o ata a huma arvore,*

arvore, as he was going he meets him, he strips him, and ties him to a tree.

When the Portuguese use the infinitive with a third person in the plural, they add *em* to it, and it is generally preceded by *por,* for, and *para,* in order to, that, or to the end that; as, *elles foraõ enforcados por furtarem,* they were hanged for robbing; *para serem enformados,* that, to the end that, they may be informed; *para poderem dizer,* that they may be able to say.

Observe, that when the Portuguese put *por* before the first future subjunctive, they speak of a time past; as, *por fallardes,* because you have spoken. But when they put *para* before it, then they speak of a time to come; as, *para fallarmos,* that, *or* to the end that we may speak, in in order to speak.

Of Moods.

All the tenses of the indicative mood may be employed without any conjunction before them; but they admit also of some. Besides the conjunction *que,* those that may be made use of are *se, como,* and *quando,* with some distinction in respect to *se,* because this conjunction is seldom used before the future tense, and then it is governed by a verb signifying ignorance, doubt, or interrogation; as, *naõ sei se haõ de vir,* I do not know if they shall come; *estou em dúvida se os inimigos passaraõ o rio,* I doubt if the enemies will pass the river; *naõ pergunto se partirá,* I do not ask if he will set out.

The optative or subjunctive in Portuguese has always some sign annexed; as, *oxalá, prouvera a Deos, ò se!* would to God, I pray God, God grant! &c. *que, para que,* &c. that, &c.

The particle *que* is not expressed in the present of this mood; but it is understood in sentences of wishing or praying; as, *Deos o faça bom,* let God amend him.

When

When *que* is between two verbs, the laft is not always put in the fubjunctive, becaufe though fome fay *creyo que venha*, I believe he comes; I think it is better to fay *creyo que vem*; but when there is a negation, the verb following *que* muft be put in the fubjunctive; as, *naõ creyo que venha*, I do not believe he will come; *naõ creyo que venha taõ cedo*, I do not believe he will come fo foon.

When the verbs *crêr*, to believe, *faber*, to know, are ufed interrogatively, and followed by the particle *que*, the next verb is put in the indicative, when the perfon that asked the queftion makes no doubt of the thing which is the object in queftion; as, if knowing that peace is made, I want to know if the people whom I converfe with know it too, I will exprefs myfelf thus, *fabeis vos que eftá feita a paz?* do you know that peace is made? But if I have it only by a report, and doubt of it, and want to be informed of it, I muft ask the queftion thus, *fabeis vos que a paz efteja feita?* and by no means *fabeis vos que eftá feita a paz?*

You muft obferve alfo, that the prefent fubjunctive of *faber* is elegantly ufed when it is attended by a negative and the particle *que* in this phrafe, *naõ que eu faiba*, not that I know of.

All the verbs ufed imperfonally with the particle *que*, require the fubjunctive; as, *he precifo que elle venha*, he muft come; *convem que ifto fe faça*, it is convenient that this be done. You muft only except fuch fentences as exprefs any pofitive affurance, or certainty; as, *he certo que vem*, it is certain that he comes; *fei que eftá em cafa*, I know he is at home.

From thefe obfervations it follows, that all the verbs not expreffing a pofitive affurance, or believing, but only denoting *ignorance, doubt, fear, aftonifhment, admiration, wifhing, praying, pretenfion,* or *defire,* govern all the fubjunctive mood after *que*; as, *as duvido que poffa*, I doubt it is in his power; *temo que morra*, I am afraid he will die; *admiro-me que*

que confinta niffo, I wonder he agrees to it, &c. to all which they add *oxalá*, an Arabic word, fignifying *God grant*, which is ufed in Portuguefe before all the tenfes of the optative or conjunctive, as well as *praza a Deos*, may it pleafe God; or, *prouvera a Deos*, might it pleafe God.

When *que* is relative, and there is a verb in the imperative or in the indicative, with a negative or interrogation before it, it governs likewife the fubjunctive; as, *naõ ha coufa que mais me inquiete*, there is nothing that difturbs me more; *ha coufa no mundo que me poffa dar tanto gofto?* is there any thing in the world that may give me more pleafure? *allegai-lhe tantas razoens que o poffaõ perfuadir*, give him fo many reafons that he may be perfuaded.

The prefent fubjunctive is fometimes rendered into Englifh by the fecond preterimperfect fubjunctive, when it is followed by a verb in the future tenfe; as, *ainda que eu trabalhe nunca hei de canfar*, though I fhould work I never would be tired.

The Portuguefe ufe fpecially the fame prefent fubjunctive for the future; as in thefe fentences, and others like:

Naõ duvido que venha, I do not doubt but he will come.

Duvido que o faça, I doubt that, *or* whether he will do it.

Therefore avoid carefully thofe faults which foreigners are fo apt to make, in confidering rather the tenfe which they want to turn into Portuguefe, than the mood which the genius of the language requires.

The prefent indicative is alfo ufed for the future, as well as in Englifh: example, *jantais hoje em cafa?* do you dine at home to-day?

Of

Of the Particles governing the Optative or Subjunctive.

The conjunction *que*, that, generally requires the subjunctive after it; but *antes que*, *primeiro que*, before that, always require it.

Take notice, that *que* makes all the words to which it is joined become conjunctives; as, *para que*, to the end that; *bem que*, *ainda que*, &c. *Poste que*, although; *até que*, till; *quando*, *como quei que*, which commonly govern the subjunctive. But *com que assim* governs the indicative; as, *com que*, or *com que assim*, *virá amanhaã*, so he will come to-morrow.

In Portuguese you must take care how you express *though* or *although*; if it is by *ainda que*, you may put either the subjunctive or indicative after it: example, *ainda que seja homem honrado*, though he is an honest man; *ainda que elle faz aquillo*, though he does that. But if you render *although* or *though* by *naõ obstante*, then you must use the infinitive: example, though he is an honest man, *naõ obstante ser elle homem honrado*; though he does this, *naõ obstante fazer elle isto*.

The impersonal verbs generally govern the subjunctive with *que*; but with this distinction, when the impersonal is in the present tense or future, of the indicative mood, then it requires the present subjunctive mood; but when the impersonal, or any other verb taken impersonally, is in any of the preterites indicative, then it governs the imperfect, perfect, or pluperfect of the subjunctive, according to the meaning of speech; as *importa muito que el rey veja tudo*, it is of great moment that the king may see all; *foy conveniente que o principe fosse com elle*, it was convenient that the prince should go with him.

The present subjunctive is likewise construed when the particle *por* is separated from *que*, by an adjective; as, *por grande*, *por admiravel*, *por douto que seja*, though he be great, admirable, learned.

An

An imperative often requires the future of the subjunctive; as *succeda o que succeder*, or *seja o que for*, happen what shall happen, at all events.

The imperfect subjunctive is repeated in this phrase, and others like, *succedesse o que succedesse*, let happen what would.

The future of the subjunctive mood follow generally these, *logo que, quando, se, como*, &c. as, *logo que chegar iremos a passear*, as soon as he comes we will go and take a walk; *quando vier estaremos promptos*, when he comes we will be ready.

Observe, that *quando* and *logo que* may also be construed with the indicative mood; as, *quando el rey ve tudo naõ o enganaõ*, when the king sees every thing he is not deceived; *logo que chegou fallei com elle*, as soon as he came he spoke with him.

Of the Infinitive Mood.

In Portuguese there is not a general sign before the infinitive, as in English the particle *to*; but there are several particles used before the infinitive, denoting the same as *to* does in English, and they are governed by the preceding verbs or nouns. These particles are the following: *á para, de, com, em, por, até, despois de*; and the article *o*, when the infinitive serves as a nominative to another verb; as, *o dizer e o fazer saõ duas cousas*, saying and doing are two different things.

A coming between two verbs, notes the second as the object of the first; as, *a tardança das nossas esperanças nos ensina a mortificar os nossos dezejos*, the delay of our hopes teaches us to mortify our desires; *elle começa a discorrer*, he begins to reason.

Para notes the intention or usefulness; as, *a adversidade servé para experimentar a paciencia*, adversity serves to try one's patience. *Para* after an adjective denotes its object; as, *está prompto para obedecer*, he is ready to obey.

L 4

De

De is put between two verbs; if the firſt governs the genitive or ablative; and when the ſubſtantive or adjective governs either of theſe two
caſes, *de* muſt go before the following verbs, or infinitive; as, *venho de ver a meu pay*, I have juſt ſeen
my father; *he tempo de hir-ſe*, it is time to go away;
el-rey foi ſeruido de mandar, the king has been pleaſ-
ed to order.

The infinitive is on ſeveral occaſions governed by
prepoſitions or conjunctions; as, *ſem dizer palavra*,
without ſpeaking a word: where you may obſerve,
it is expreſſed in Engliſh by the participle preſent;
as, *nunca ſe cança de jugar*, he is never weary of play-
ing; *diverte-ſe em caçar*, he delights in hunting;
elle eſtá doente por trabalhar demoſiadamente, by working too much he is ſick; *perde o ſeu tempo em paſſear*,
he loſes his time in walking; *hei-de ir-me, ſem me deſ-
pedir?* ſhall I go away without taking my leave?

The infinitive is alſo uſed paſſively; as, *naõ ha
que dizer, que ver*, &c. there is nothing to be ſaid,
ſeen, &c.

The gerund of any verb active may be conjugated
with the verb *eſtar*, to be, after the ſame manner as
in Engliſh; as, *eſtou eſcrevendo*, I am writing; *elle
eſtava dormindo*, he was aſleep, &c.

CHAP. VI.

Of the Syntax of Participles and Gerunds.

THE participle in the Portugueſe language
generally ends in *do*, or *to*; as, *amado, viſto,
dito*, &c.

The active participles that follow the verb *ter*, to
have, muſt end in *o*; as,

Tenho viſto el rey, I have ſeen the king.

Tenho

Tenbo visto a rainba, I have feen the queen.
Eu tinha amado os livros, I had loved books.
Eu tinha levado as cartas, I had carried the letters.

We meet with authors who fometimes make the participles agree with the thing of which they are fpeaking; as, in *Camoens,* Canto. 1. Stanza xxix.

E porque, como viftes, tem paffados
Na viagem taõ afperos perigos
Tantos climas, e ceos exprimentados, &c.

And Canto 2. Stan. lxxvi.

Saõ offerecimentos verdadeiros,
E palavras finceras, naõ dobradas,
As que o rey manda a os nobres cavaleiros,
Que tanto mar e terras tem paffadas.

If it be a verb neuter, the participle ought always to terminate in *o :* example.

El rey tem jantado, the king has dined ; *a rainba tem, ceado,* the queen has fupped ; *os voffos amigos tem rido,* your friends have laughed ; *minhas irmaãs tem dormido,* my fifters have flept.

When the active participle happens to precede an infinitive, it muft be terminated in *o ;* as, *o juiz lhe tinba feito cortar a cabeça,* the judge had caufed his head to be cut off.

The paffive participles which are joined with the tenfes of the verb *fer,* to be, agree with the fubftantive that precedes the verb *fer ;* as, *o capitaõ foy louvado,* the captain was praifed ; *a virtude be eftimada,* virtue is efteemed ; *os preguiçofos faõ cenfurados,* the lazy are blamed ; *as voffas joyas foraõ vendidas,* your jewels were fold.

The Portuguefe generally fupprefs the gerunds *baving* and *being* before participles ; as, *dito ifto,* having faid fo ; *acabado o fermaõ,* the fermon being ended. This manner of fpeaking is called by grammarians ablatives abfolute.

The participle of the prefent tenfe in Portuguefe has fingular and plural, but one termination ferves for both genders ; as, *bum bomem temente á Deos,* a
man

man fearing God; *huma molher temente a Deos,* a woman fearing God; *homens tementes a Deos,* people fearing God.

There are in Portuguese a great many participles which are used substantively; as, *ignorante, amante, ouvinte, estudante,* &c. an ignorant, a lover, an auditor or hearer, a scholar, *&c.*

It is better to place the nominative after the gerund than before; as, *estando el rey na comedia,* the king being at the play.

****

CHAP. VII.

Of Prepositions.

A Preposition is a part of speech which is put before nouns, and sometimes before verbs, to explain some particular circumstance.

Prepositions may be divided into separable and inseparable. An inseparable preposition is never found but in compound words, and signifies nothing of itself. A separable preposition is generally separated from other words, and signifies something of itself.

The inseparable prepositions are,

Ab and *abs*; as, *abrogar,* to abrogate; *abster-se,* to abstain.

Arce, or *archi*; as, *arcebispo,* an archbishop; *archiduque,* an archduke.

Ad; as, *adventicio,* adventitious.

Am; as, *ambiguo,* ambiguous; *amparo,* protection, shelter.

Circum; as, *circumstancia,* circumstance.

Co; as, *cohabitar,* to live together, to cohabit.

Des, serves to express the contrary of the word it is joined to; as, *d ſacerto,* mistake; *desfazer,* to undo;

do ; *defenganar*, to undeceive ; are the contrary of *acerto*, *fazer*, and *enganar*.

Dis ; as, *difpor*, to difpofe ; *diftinguir*, to diftinguifh ; *diftribuir*, to diftribute.

Ex ; as, *extrahir*, to extract.

In, has commonly a negative or privative fenfe, denoting the contrary of the meaning of the word it precedes ; as, *incapaz*, unable ; *infeliz*, unhappy ; *inaccaõ*, inaction, &c. but fometimes it is affirmative, as in Latin.

Obferve, that *in* before *r* is changed into *ir* ; as, *irregular*, irregular ; *irracional*, irrational : before *l*, into *il* ; as, *illeg.timo*, illegitimate ; before *m*, *in* is changed into *im* ; as, *immaterial*, immaterial.

Ob ; as, *obviar*, to obviate.

Pos ; as, *pofpor*, to poftpofe, or to poftpone.

Pre ; as, *preceder*, to go before ; *predeceffor*, an anceftor.

Pro ; as, *prepôr*, to proppfe ; *prometer*, to promife.

Re, is a borrowed particle from the Latins, which generally denotes iteration, or backward action ; as, *reedficar*, to rebuild ; *repercutir*, to repercute, or ftr ke back.

So ; as, *focorrer*, to help, to fuccour.

Sor ; as, *forrir*, to fmile.

Sos ; as, *fofter*, to fupport.

Soto ; as, *fotopor*, to put or lay under.

Sub, or *fob* ; as, *fubalterno*, fubaltern ; *fubfcrever*, to fubfcribe ; *fobpena*, *fobcolor*, &c.

The Arabic article *al*, which is common to all genders and both numbers, is found in the beginning of almoft all the words that remain in the Portuguefe language from the Arabic, and it is the fureft way to diftinguifh them. But the Portuguefe articles are added to the Arabic nouns, without taking off their article *al*, as *a almofada*, the cufhion ; *o Alcoraõ*, the Coran, &c.

The

The Greek prepofition *anti* enters into the compofition of a great many Portuguefe words, which cannot be fet down here. It is enough to obferve, that it fignifies generally oppofite; as in *Antipodas*, Antipodes; *antipapa*, antipope; and fometimes it fignifies *before*; as in *antiloquio*, a preface, a fpeaking firft; but in this laft fenfe it is derived from the Latin prepofition *ante*.

Of feparable Prepofitions.

It is abfolutely impoffible ever to attain to the knowledge of any language whatever, without thoroughly underftanding the divers relations denoted by the prepofitions, and the feveral cafes of nouns which they govern; both which relations and cafes being arbitrary, vary and differ much in all languages. This only inftance will evince it: the Englifh fay, *to think of a thing*; the French, *to think to a thing*; the Germans and Dutch, *to think on*, or *upon a thing*; the Spaniards and Portuguefe, *to think in a thing*, &c. Now it will avail an Englifhman but little to know that *of* is expreffed in Portuguefe by *de*, if he does not know which relations *em* and *de* denote in that language; fince the Portuguefe fay, to think *in* a thing, and not *of* a thing; therefore we will treat here of each of them, and their conftruction, feparately.

1ft. *A*, or rather *ao*, *as*, *aos*, (at, in, on, &c.) denote the place whither one is going; as,

Eu vou a Londres, I go to London.

Voltar a Portugal, to return, *or* go back to Portugal. .

A, in this fenfe, is a prepofition, but in the next obfervations it is a particle.

2dly. *A* denotes time; as, *chegar a tempo*, to arrive in time; *a todo o tempo*, at all times.

3dly. *A* denotes the way of being, or of doing of people; as alfo their pofture, gefture, or action; as,   *Eftar*

Eſtar a ſua vontade, to be at one's eaſe.

A direita, on the right hand ; *a eſquerda,* on the left hand.

Viver á ſua vontade, to live to one's mind, as one likes.

Andar á pé ou a cavallo, to go on foot, or a-horſeback.

Montar a cavallo, to ride a horſeback.

Correr á redea ſolta, to ride full ſpeed.

Trajar a Franceſa, to dreſs after the French way.

Viver á Ingleza, to live after the Engliſh faſhion.

Andar a grandes paſſos, to walk at a great rate.

Andar a paſſos lentos, to walk very ſlowly.

4thly. *A* denotes the price of things ; as, *a oito xelins,* at eight ſhillings. It denotes alſo the weight ; but as the nouns ſignifying weight are generally uſed in the plural number, hence it is that they add *s* to *a,* when it is placed before nouns of the feminine gender, and *os* when it precedes nouns of the maſculine gender : ſo they ſay, *as onças,* by the ounce ; *aos arrateis,* by the pound, *&c.* *A* denotes alſo the meaſure ; as, *medir a palmos,* to ſpan or meaſure by the hand extended.

When *a* is preceded by *daqui,* and followed by a noun of time, it denotes the ſpace of time after which ſomething is to be done ; as, *el rey partira daqui a tres dias,* the king will ſet out three days hence.

5thly. *A* denotes the tools uſed in working, as likewiſe the games one plays at ; as, *abrir ao buril,* to grave ; wherein you ſee they add *o* to *a* ; *trabalhar á candea,* to do any thing by candle-light ; *á gulba,* with the needle.

Andar á vela, to ſail, or to be under ſail.

Jogar á pela, to play at tennis.

Jogar ás cartas, to play at cards : wherein you ſee they add *s* to *a* when the noun is of the feminine gender, and placed in the plural number.

Jogar

Jogar aos centos, to play at piquet; wherein you see they add *os* to *a* when it precedes nouns signifying games, when they are of the masculine gender, and put in the plural number.

6thly. *A* signifies sometimes *as*. Examp. *Está isto a seu gosto?* is this as you like it? And sometimes it signifies *after*; as, *a seu modo*, after his *or* her way. It signifies also *in*; as, *ao principio*, in the beginning; but then they add *o* to it.

7thly. *A* is also put before the infinitives, preceded by another verb; as, *ensinar a cantar*, to teach to sing. It is also placed between two equal numbers, to denote order; as, *dous a dous*, two by two; *quatro a quatro*, four by four: and sometimes it is preceded by a participle or adjective, and followed by an infinitive mood.

8thly. *A* is a particle of composition, serving to many nouns, verbs, and adverbs, of which it often increases the meaning; as, *adinheirado*, very rich, that has a great deal of money; but it generally expresses in verbs the action of the nouns they are composed of; as, *ajoelhar*, to kneel down, which is formed from *a* and *joelho*, knee; *abrandar*, to appease; *alargar*, to enlarge; from *brando*, soft; *largo*, wide, &c.

9thly. *A*, when it is preceded by the verb *ser*, and followed by the pronouns personal, signifies *in the stead of*; as, *se eu fosse a vos faria aquilo*, if I was you (in your place) I would do that.

10thly. When *á* is placed before *casa*, and the sense implies *going to*, it is Englished by *to*, but the word *casa* is left out; as, *elle foi á casa do governador*, he went to the governor's. You must observe, that *a* in this sense is a preposition.

11th, *A pe* signifies *near*; as, *ponde hum ao pé do outro*, place, put, or set them near one another. Sometimes *mesmo* comes before *ao pe*, to express still more the nearness of a thing, and *mesmo ao pe*

1S

3

is Englished by *hard by, juft by*, &c. as, *a fua cafa eftá
mefmo ao pé da minha*, his houfe is juft by mine.

12th. When the noun *refpeito* is preceded by *a*,
it is ufed in the fame fenfe as *em comparaçaõ*, but requires one of thefe particles, *do, da, dos, das*, after
it, and fignifies *in comparifon of, in regard to, in refpect of*; as, *ifto be nada a refpeito do que poffo dizer*,
this is nothing to other things that I can fay.

13thly. When *a* comes after a verb neuter, it
marks a dative; and after a verb active, an accufative cafe.

A before the word *propofito* is ufed in familiar dif-
courfes; as, *a propofito, efquecime de dizervos o outro
dia*; now I think on't, I forgot to tell you t'other
day.

14th. *Ao revez*, or, *as aveffas*, are alfo ufed as
prepofitions, attended by *de, do, da*, &c. and it fignifies *quite the reverfe*, or *contrary*; as, *elle faz tudo
ao revez*, or *as aveffas do que houvera de fer, ou do que
lhe dizem*, he does every thing quite the reverfe of
right, or contrary to what he is bid.

15thly. *A* before *treco* fignifies *provided that*. It
is alfo ufed before the word *tiro*; as, *a tiro de peça*,
within cannon-fhot.

16thly. *Cara a cara, corpo a corpo*, fignify, face to
face, body to body. *Tomar huma coufa á boa ou á
má parte*, fignifies to take a thing well or ill.

Such are the chief relations denoted by the particle *a*. The others muft be learned in conftruing
and reading good Portuguefe books.

II. *De*, or rather, *do, da, dos, dás*, (of, from,
&c.) denote, firft, the place one comes from; as,
fabir de Londres, to go out of London; *vir de França, das Indias*, &c. to come from France, from the
Indies, &c.

2d. *De* between two nouns denotes the quality of
the perfon expreffed by the firft noun; as, *hum homem de honra*, a man of honour: or the matter which
the thing of the fi.ft noun is made of; as,

Huma

Huma eſtátua de marmore, a ſtatue of marble.

Huma ponte de madeira ou de pedra, a wood or ſtone bridge.

Note, that two nouns ſo joined with *de* are commonly Engliſhed by two nouns likewiſe, but without a prepoſition, or rather by a compound word, whoſe firſt noun (whether ſubſtantive or adjective) expreſſes the matter and quality, manner, form, and uſe of the other; as, a ſtone-bridge, *huma ponte de pedra*; a dancing-maſter, *hum meſtre de dança*.

3d. *De, do, da, dos, das*, are uſed in Portugueſe after the participles of the preterit, with *ſer*; as, *ſer amado, ou bem viſto do povo, dos ſabios, &c.* to be beloved by the people, by the learned, *&c.*

Note, that *do* ſerves for the maſculine, *da* for the feminine, and *de* for both.

4th. *De* ſometimes ſignifies *by*; as, *de noite*, by night; *de dia*, by day.

5th. *De* before *em*, and many nouns of time denotes the regular interval of the time after which ſomething begins again; as, *eu vou velo de dous em dous dias*, I go to ſee him every other day; and before nouns of place and adverbs repeated with *em* or *para* between, *de* denotes the paſſing from one place or condition to another; as, *correr de rua em rua*, to run from ſtreet to ſtreet; *de mal para peor*, worſe and worſe.

6th. *De*, after ſome verbs, ſignifies *after* or *in*; as, *elle portou-ſe d'eſta ſorte*, he behaved *in* or after this manner.

7th. *De* is uſed before an infinitive, and is then governed by ſome previous noun or verb; as, *capaz de enſinar*, capable to teach; *digno de ſer amado*, worthy to be loved, &c. *procurar de fazer*, to endeavour to do; *authoridade de pregar*, the power or authority of preaching, *&c.*

8th. *De* is ſometimes Engliſhed by *on*; as, *por-ſe de joelhos*, to kneel down *on* one's knees.

9. *De*

9. *De* between two nouns denotes the use which a thing is defigned for ; as, *azeite de candeá,* lamp-oil ; *arma de fogo,* a fire-arm ; *moinho de vento,* a wind-mill.

. Note, that this relation is expreffed in Englifh by two nouns, making a compound word ; the firft of which fignifies the manner, form, and ufe, denoted by the Portuguefe prepofition ; as, *cadeira de braços,* an arm-chair, or elbow-chair ; *vela de cera,* a wax-candle, &c.

10. *De* denotes fometimes the quality of things ; as, *meas de tres fios,* ftockings with three threads. Sometimes it denotes alfo the price ; as, *panno de dezoito xelins,* eighteen fhillings cloth.

11. *De* is fometimes Englifhed by *upon* ; as, *viver* ou *fuftentar fe de peixe,* to live upon fifh. Sometimes it is Englifhed by *with* ; as, *morrer de frio,* to ftarve with cold.

12. *De* fometimes fignifies *for* or *out of* ; as, *faltar de alegria,* to leap for joy ; *de modefto,* out of modefty.

13. *De* fignifies fometimes *at* ; as, *zombar de alguem,* to laugh at one.

14. *De* is fometimes left out in Englifh ; as, *gozar de huma coufa,* to enjoy a thing.

15. *De* followed by two nouns of number and the prepofition *até* between them, is Englifhed by *between* ; as, *hum homem de quarenta até cincoenta annos,* a man between forty and fifty.

16. *De,* preceded by the prepofition *diante,* is left out in Englifh ; as, *diante de mim,* before me ; *diante de Deos,* before God.

17. *De,* when it is placed before *cafa,* and the fenfe implies *coming from,* is Englifhed by *from* ; but the word *cafa* fometimes is left out in Englifh, and fometimes not ; as, *venho de cafa* (meaning my houfe) I come from home, from my houfe : but when they fay, *venho de cafa da Senhora C,* we muft

rendeɽ

render it in Englifh thus, *I am returning from Mrs. C's.*

Finally, *de* is ufed before feveral words; as, *de bruços*, lying all along on the ground; *de madrugada*, foon in the morning; *de veras*, in earneft, ferioufly; *de veraõ*, in fummer; *homem de palavra*, a man as good as his word; *de coftas*, backwards, or oh one's back; *andar de pe*, to be fickifh without being bed-rid: and many others which muft be learnt by ufe.

Antes.

III. *Antes*, before, fhews a relation of time, of which it denotes priority; and is always oppofite to *depois*, after; as, *antes da criaçaõ do mundo*, before the creation of the world.

Primeiro is alfo a prepofition; as, *elle chegou primeiro que eu*, he arrived before me.

Diante.

IV. *Diante*, before, fhews a relation of place, and it is always oppofite to *detraz*, behind. It fignifies alfo fometimes *em*, or *na prefença*; as, *ha arvores diante da fua cafa*, there are trees before his houfe; *ponde aquillo diante do fogo*, fet or put that before the fire; *pregar diante del rey*, to preach before the king.

Diante is alfo fometimes an adverb, and may be ufed inftead of *adiante*; as, *ir diante* or *adiante*, to go before: but in the following phrafe you muft fay, *naõ vades tanto adiante*, and not *diante*, don't go fo far; *por diante* is to be Englifhed by *on* in the following phrafe, *ide por diante*, go on.

Depois.

V. *Depois*, after, denotes pofteriority of time, and it is ufed in oppofition to *antes*; as, *depois do deluvio*, after the deluge: *depois do meio dia*, after noon.

Depois alfo is ufed with an infinitive; as, *feito aquillo*, or *tendo feito aquillo*, or *depois de fazer aquillo*,

after

after having done that; and it is also made a conjunction with *que*, governing the indicative; as, *depois que teve feito aquillo*, after he had done that.

Detraz.

VI. *Detraz*, behind, denotes posteriority both of place and order, and it is said in opposition to *diante*; as, *a sua casa está detraz da vossa*, his house is behind your's; *elle vinha detraz de mim*, he walked after me.

Em.

VII. *Em*, or *no*, *na*, *nos*, *nas*, (in, into, within, &c.) denote a relation both of time and place. The many various significations in which these prepositions are used, must be accurately observed, and much regard had to them in the practice.

No and *na* are sometimes rendered into English by *a*; as, *duas vezes no dia*, *na semana*, &c. twice a day, a week, &c.

No, *na*, &c. are always used before nouns denoting the place wherein something is kept; as, *está no gabinete*, it is in the closet; *na papeleira*, in the bureau; *nas gavetas*, in the drawers; *na rua*, in the street, &c. but sometimes they are Englished by *upon*; as, *cahir no chaō*, to fall upon the ground.

Em, *no*, *na*, &c. signifies commonly *in*; as, *em Londres*, in London; *está na graça del rey*, he is in favour with the king; but in some cases it has a very particular meaning; as, *estar em corpo*, which signifies literally *to be in body*; but the true sense of it is *to be without a cloak*; so that the body is more exposed to view without an upper garment. *Estar em pernas*, literally, *to be in legs*, signifies *to be bare-legged*; that is, the legs exposed without stockings. *Estar em camiza* is said of one that has only the shirt on his back.

When this preposition *em* is before an infinitive in Portuguese, then it is an English gerund; as, *consiste em fallar bem*, it consists in speaking well;

M 2   but

but when it is found before a gerund, it signifies *as soon as*; as, *em acabando irei*, as soon as I have done I will go.

Nos nossos tempos is Englished by *new-a-days*.

Em is used in sentences that imply a general sense; as, *Elle está em miseravel estado*, he is in a wretched condition; and not *no miseravel:* but if the sentences imply a particular sense, you must make use of *no, nas*, &c. as, *no miseravel estado em que elle está*, in the wretched condition wherein he is; and not *em miseravel*. You must observe in this last example and the like, that you ought to make use of *em* before *que*, and not of *no, na*, &c. which only are to be placed before *qual*; therefore you must not say, *no miseravel estado no que elle está*; but you may say, *no miseravel estado no qual elle está*.

Note, that *em* construed with pronouns without an article, makes a sort of adverb, rendered into English by a preposition and a noun; thus in this sentence, *nos iremos em coche*, we shall go in a coach, *em coche* is an adverb of manner, which shews how we shall go: but *no coche* denotes something besides; as if a company were considering how they shall ride to a place, somebody would say, *vos ireis na cadeirinha, e nós no coche*, you shall go in the chair and we in the coach; *no coche* would be said in opposition to *na cadeirinha*, and both respectively to some specified chair and coach; or else they should say, *vos ireis em cadeirinha e nos em coche*. But in this other sentence, *eu deixei o meu chapeo no coche*, I left my hat in the coach, it would be improper to say *em coche*, because some particular coach is meant, to wit, that which has drove me here or there, or which has been spoken of.

We say *de verão, no verão*, or *em o verão*; *de inverno, no inverno*, &c. in summer; in winter, &c.

Em is also rendered into English by *at*; as, *em todo o tempo*, at all times.

Em

Em is ufed, and never *no, na,* &c. before proper
names of cities and authors; as, *elle eftá em Londres,* he is in London ; *nós lemos em Ciçero,* we read
in Tully. But they fay *no Porto,* in Oporto.

Em, and *no, na,* &c. are conftrued with names of
kingdoms; as, *em* or *na Inglaterra,* in England :
but *no, na,* is moft commonly conftrued with
names of provinces; as, *no Alentejo, na Beira,* &c.
in Alentejo, in Beira, &c.

Em is fometimes rendered into Englifh by *into ;*
as, *Narçifo foi transformado em flor,* Narciffus was
metamorphofed into a flower : and fometimes by *to;*
as, *de rua em rua,* from ftreet to ftreet.

No, na, are fometimes rendered into Englifh by
againft ; as, *dar coa cabeça na parede,* to dafh one's
head againft the wall.

No, na, &c. are alfo rendered into Englifh by *in,*
and fometimes by *into ;* as, *ter hum menino nos braços,* to hold a child in one's arms ; *entregar alguma
coufa nas maõs de alguem,* to deliver a thing into fome
body's hands.

Em is ufed before the word *travez,* as in this
phrafe, *por-fe de mar em travez com alguem,* to fall
out together.

Em before a noun of time, denotes the fpace of
time that flides away in doing fomething ; as, *el rey
foi a Hanover em tres dias,* the king went to Hanover
in three days; that is, he was no longer than three
days in going.

Em is fometimes ufed after the verb *hir,* to go ;
as, *vai em quatro mefes que eu aqui cheguei,* it is now
going on four months fince I came hither.

Em before *quanto,* and fometimes without it, is
rendered into Englifh by *while* or *whilft* ; as *em
quanto vos fazeis aquillo eu farei ifto,* while you do
that I fhall do this: but if they are followed by a
noun of time with an interrogation, then they muft
be rendered into Englifh by *in how much,* or *many;*
as, *em quanto tempo?* in how much time? You muft

M 3 obferve

obferve, that *em quanto a mim, ati, elle,* &c. are rendered into Englifh by *for what concerns me, thee, him,*
&c.

You muft obferve, that *no* ferves for the mafculine, *na* for the feminine, and *em* for both.

Em fignifies *as* ; as, *em final da fua amizade,* as a
token of his friendfhip ; *em premio,* as a reward.

The prepofitions *em, no, na,* &c. and *dentro,* have
very often the fame fignification, therefore they may
fometimes be ufed one inftead of the other ; as, *eftá na gaveta,* or *dentro da gaveta,* it is in the
drawer ; *eftá na cidade,* or *dentro da cidade,* he is in
town.

Em before the words *favor, utilidade, confidera-
çam, razaõ,* and the like, fignifies *in behalf of, for
the fake of, on account of,* &c. as, *em razaõ das bellas
acçoens que elle tem feito,* in confideration of the great
things he has performed.

Obferve, that they very often make an elifion of
the laft vowels, *o, a,* of the prepofition *no, na,*
when there is a vowel in the beginning of the next
word ; as, *n'agoa* inftead of *na agoa* ; they alfo cut
off the *e* of the prepofition *em,* and change the *m*
into *n,* as you may fee in *Camoens,* Canto 2. Stanza
XXXII. *n'algum porto* inftead of *em algum porto,* wherein you muft obferve that *n'* is to be Englifhed by *to*
or *into.*

Com.

VII. This prepofition fignifies *with,* and it denotes
conjunction, union, mixing, affembling, keeping
company ; as, *cafar huma donzella com hum homem
honrado,* to marry a maid with an honeft man ; *bir
com alguem,* to go with one ; *com a ajuda de Deos,* by
God's help, &c.

Obferve, that moft of the adverbs formed of the
adjectives are turned in Portuguefe by the prepofition *com* and the fubftantive ; as, *atrevidamente,*
boldly, *com atrevimento,* with boldnefs ; *elegante-
                                                    mente,*

mente, elegantly ; *com elegancia*, with elegance; *cortezmente*, politely, *com cortezia*, with politeness, &c.

You must observe, that the last confonant *m* is very often cut off, even before the noun of number *hum*, one ; and so they say *cum*, instead of *com hum*, as you may see in *Camoens*, Cant. 2. Stanza xxxvii.

Note that *with me*, *with thee*, *with himself*, &c. are rendered into Portuguese by *commigo*, *comtigo*, or *comvofco*, *comfigo*, *comnofco*, *comvofco*, *comfigo*.

When *com* is preceded by *para*, it fignifies *towards*, and sometimes *over*, in English ; as, *fejamos piedofos para com os pobres*, let us be merciful towards the poor. *Ter grande poder para com alguem*, to have a great influence over some body's mind.

Com before the word *capa* is used metaphorically, and then it fignifies *under colour*, or *pretext*.

Para.

VIII. *Para* is rendered into English by *for* ; but it fignifies also *to*, when it is found before the infinitive, and denotes the intention, or purpose in doing something ; as, *efte livro he para meu irmaõ*, this book is for my brother; *efta penna he para efcrever*, this pen is to write ; *Deos nos fez para amalo*, God made us for to love him ; *o comer he neceffario para confervar a vida*, eating is neceffary for preferving life.

Para que is rendered into English by *for what* ; as, *para que he ifto?* for what is this? and sometimes by *that*, or *in order that* ; as, *para que venha verme*, that he may come and fee me. But *porque* fignifies *why*, *for what*, *upon what account*, as, *porque naõ vindes?* why don't you come? but when it is not followed by an interrogation, it fignifies *becaufe*.

Para ferves likewife before the verbs, to denote what one is able to do in confequence of his prefent difpofition ; as, *elle he baftantemente forte para àndar a cavallo*, he is ftrong enough to ride ; *elle tem ba-*

M 4
ftante

ftante cabedal para fuftentar-fe, he has means enough to maintain himfelf : *a occafiaõ be muite favoravel para nos naõ fervir-mos della*, the occafion is too favourable to let it flip.

Para expreffes alfo the capacity or incapacity of doing any thing; as, *elle be bomem para ifto*, he is the proper man wanted for this; *be bomem para pouco*, he is good for little; *be bomem para nada*, he is good for nothing.

This prepofition is alfo ufed to denote the end or motive of doing any thing; as, *trabalho para o bem publico*, I work for the public good; *bum hofpital para os pobres*, an hofpital for the poor.

Para is a prepofition of time; as, *ifto me bafta para todo o anno*; this is fufficient to me for all the year; *eftaõ unidos para fempre*, they united for ever; *para dous mefes era muito pouco*, for two months it was too little.

Para is fometimes preceded by the adverb *lá*, and followed by a noun of time, and then it is Englifhed by *againft* or *towards*; as, *lá para o fim da femana*, againft the end of the week, *or* towards the end of the week.

Para is fometimes Englifhed by *confidering*, or *with refpect to*; as, *efte menino eftá muito adiantado para a idade que tem*, or *para o pouco tempo que aprende*, this child is very forward for his age, *or* confidering the little time he has learned; *para Inglez falla demafiadamente*, he talks too much confidering that he is an Englifhman.

Para fignifies fometimes *juft* or *ready to*; as, *elle eftá para partir*, he is juft going away, he is ready to go.

Para is alfo ufed before the word *graças*; as, *elle naõ be para graças*, he takes no jeft; *elle naõ eftá para graças*, he is out of humour, *or* he is in an ill humour.

Para onde? fignifies *whither? to what place?*

Para

Para que? or *para que fim?* fignifies *to what end* or *purpofe? Para cima* fignifies upward.

Para huma e outra parte, fignifies *to both fides, places,* or *parts.*

Para is alfo Englifhed by *towards,* and is faid of places; as, *para o oriente,* towards, *or* to the eaft.

Para onde quer que, fignifies *whether,* or *to what place thou wilt, any whither.*

Para outra parte, fignifies *towards another place.*

Para comigo, towards me.

Para o diante, fignifies, *for the time to come.*

De mim para mim, fignifies *for what concerns me.*

Para is ufed by *Camoens,* Cant. 2. Stanza xxiv. before the prepofition *detraz,* and fignifies *backwards.*

Para between two nouns of number is Englifhed by *or,* and fometimes by *and;* as, *hum homem de quarenta para cincoenta annos,* a man between forty and fifty; *difta quatro para cinco legoas,* it is about four or five leagues diftant.

Por.

IX. *Por, pello, pella, pellos,* or *pellas,* fignify *for;* as, *por amor de vos,* for your fake; *por feis femanas,* for fix weeks; *palavra por palavra,* word for word.

Polo and *pola* inftead of *pelo* and *pela,* are out of ufe.

Por fometimes denotes that the thing is not yet done; as, *efta obra eftá por acabar,* this work is not yet finifhed.

Por, by, for, over, or through; as, *alcancei-o por empenho,* I obtained it by protection; *eu vou por dinheiro,* I am going for money; *paffeo pellos campos,* I walk through the fields; *por todo o reino,* all over the kingdom.

When *por* is before an infinitive, and followed by a negative, in the latter part of the fentence, it is Englifhed by *although,* or *though;* as, *por fer devota,* or *por devota que feja, naõ deixa de*

fer

fer molber, though she is a religious woman, yet she is a woman ; *por fer pobre*, or *por pobre que feja naõ deixa de fer foberba*, though she has no fortune, she is neverthelefs, *or* for all that, proud. Wherein you fee, that the negative with the verb *deixar*, are rendered into Englifh by the verb *to be*, and the particles *neverthelefs*, *yet*, &c. You muft obferve that they fometimes put the words *nem por iſſo* before the verb *deixar*, but the fenfe is the fame, and you may as well fay, *por fer pobre nem por iſſo deixa*, &c.

Por followed by an adjective and the particle *que* with a verb in the fubjunctive mood, is rendered into Englifh by *never ſo* ; as, *por grande que elle feja*, let him be never ſo great ; *por pouco que feja*, never ſo little.

Por before *menos*, fignifies *far lefs than*, or *under* ; as, *vmce naõ o terá por menos de vinte libras*, you shall not have it under twenty pounds.

Por before *quanto*, with an interrogation, fignifies *for how much*, *at what rate ?* But if there is no interrogation, as in the following and the like fentences, then it is to be Englifhed by *for never ſo much* ; as, *naõ o faria por quanto me deſſem*, I would not do it for never ſo much.

Por before *cima* fignifies *upwards*, and before *baxo* is Englifhed by *downwards* ; as, *o remedio obra por cima e por baxo*, the medicine operates, *or* works, upwards and downwards.

Por before *pouco*, *muito*, *bem*, &c. and followed by *que*, makes a fort of conjunction governing the fubjunctive, and is Englifhed by *if*, followed by *ever* or *never ſo little, much, well*, &c. as, *por pouco que erreis*, if you do amifs never ſo little ; *por bem que eu faça*, if I do never ſo well, &c.

Por before *mim* fignifies fometimes *as for*, or *for all* ; as, *por mim eſtou prompto*, as for me, *or*, for my part I am ready ; *por mim podeis dormir ſe quizerdes*, you may sleep for all me.

Por,

Por, pello, pella, &c. denote the efficient cause of a thing, as also the motive and means, or ways of doing; in all which significations they are Englished by *by, through, out of, at,* &c. as,

A Asia foi conquistada por Alexandre, Asia was conquered by Alexander.

Vos fallais nisso so porexveja, it is out of envy only you speak of it.

Elle entrou pella porta, mas sabio pella janella, he got in at the door, but he got out at the window, &c.

Por denotes place, after the verbs *ir* and *passar;* as, *por onde ireis vos?* which way shall you go?

Eu passarei por França, I'll go through France; *por onde passou elle?* which way did he go?

Por construed with nouns without an article, denotes most times *distribution of people, time,* and *place;* and it is Englished by *a,* or *every,* before the noun; as,

Elle deu tanto por cabeça, he gave so much a head.

Tanto por soldado, por anno, por mes, por semana, &c. so much a soldier, a year, a month, a week; *a razão de vinte por cento,* at the rate of twenty per cent.

Elle pede tanto por legoa, he asks so much a league, or every league.

Por, between two nouns without an article, or between two infinitives without a preposition, denotes the choice which one makes between two things, alike in their nature, but different in their circumstances; as,

Casa por casa antes quero esta que aquella, since I must have one of these two houses, I like this better than that; *morrer por morrer melhor he morrer combatendo que fugindo,* when a man must die, it is better to die in fighting than in running away.

Pello meyo is rendered into English by *through;* as, *pello meyo dos campos,* through the fields.

Por meyo is rendered into English by *by;* as, *elle alcançou o seu intento por meyo de astucias,* he has compassed his ends by devices. *Por*

Por turna fignifies *in one's turn.*

Por before the infinitives is ufed inftead of *para* by the beft Portuguefe writers; and *porque* inftead of *para que*; as you may fee particularly in *Camoens,* Canto 2. Stanza VII. and VIII. and in the following example, *por naõ,* or *para naõ repetir o que ja temos dito,* not to repeat what we have already faid.

Por is fometimes Englifhed by *fer, upon the account of, for fake,* &c. as. *elle fará ifto por amor de vos,* he will do this upon your account, *or* for your fake; *deixaraõ-no por morto,* he was left for dead; *eu tenho-o por meu amigo,* I take him to be my friend; *todos os homens de bem faõ,* or *eftaõ por elle,* all honeft people are for him, *or* are on his fide; *por quem me tomais vos?* who do you take me for?

We have already obferved, that *porque* without an interrogation fignifies *becaufe;* but it has the fame fig-nification in the following fentence and the like; *porque elle he mentirofo fegue-fe que tambem eu o feja?* becaufe he is a liar, does it follow therefore that I am one?

Por ifto, or *por efta razaõ* fignifies *therefore.*

O porque fignifies the reafon, the caufe, or the fubject; as, *fabe-fe o porque?* is it known upon what account?

Por modo de dizer fignifies, *as one may fay, if I,* or *we, may fay,* &c.

Por diante fignifies *before;* and *por detraz* fignifies *behind.*

Por ventura fignifies *perhaps.*

Pello paffado, fignifies *formerly, in time paft, heretofore.*

Por nenhum cafo, by no means.

Por mar e por terra, by sea and land.

Hum pòr kum fignifies *one by one.*

Por is fometimes Englifhed by *in;* as, *elles faõ vinte por todos,* they are twenty in all.

When the verb *paffar* is followed by *por* and the word *alto* fignifies *to forget;* as, *paffou lhe aquillo por alto,*

alto, he forgot that; but speaking of goods it signifies *to smuggle*.

Por joined with the verb *ir*, signifies *to fetch*, and
seek after; as, *vai por vinho*, go fetch some wine;
vai pello medico, go see for the physician.

Por is commonly used before the substantives; as,
por exemplo, for example; *por commodidade*, for con-
veniency; *por costume*, for custom sake; and many
others, that may only be learned by use.

You must observe, that *pello* serves for the masculine, *pella* for the feminine, and *por* for both.

Contra,

X. *Contra* (against, contrary to), denotes opposition;
as, *que diz vm^ce contra isto?* what do you say against
this? It signifies also *overagainst*, *opposite to*.

Pro e contra, signifies in English *pro and con*.

Desde.

XI. *Desde*, denotes both time and place, and enu-
meration of things, and is commonly followed in the
sentence by the preposition *até* (*to*); then *desde* denotes the term *from whence*, and *até* that of *hitherto*;
as,

Desde o principio até o fim, from the beginning to
the end.

Elle foi a pê desde Windsor até Londres, he walked
from Windsor to London.

Eu tenho visto todos desde o primeiro até o ultimo, I
have seen them all from first to last; *foraõ todos mortos desde o primeiro até o ultimo*, they were all slain to
a man.

Desde a criaçaõ do mundo, from, or since the creation.

Desde o berço, ou infancia, from the cradle, from a
child.

Desde

Defde ja, even now; as, *defde ja prevejo*, I even now forefee.

Defde agora, from this time forward.

Defde entaõ, from that time ever fince.

Defde que, as foon as, when.

Defde quando? how long fince, *or* ago?

Rio navegavel defde o feu nacimento, a river navigable at its very rife.

Até.

XII. *Até* fignifies *till, even, to*, &c. as you may fee in the following examples.

Até onde? how far?

Até Roma, as far as Rome.

Até quando? till when, *or* how long?

Até que eu viva, as long as I live.

He hum homem de tanta bondade, que até os feus inimigos faõ obrigados a eftimalo, he is fo good a man that even his enemies have a value for him.

Até os mais vis homens tomavaõ a liberdade de, &c. the very worft of men took fuch a liberty as to, &c.

Até que, until, till.

Até as orelhas, up to the ears.

Elle vendeo até a camiza, he has fold the very fhirt off his back.

Até agora or *até aqui*, till now, *or* hitherto.

Até aqui, (fpeaking of a place) to this place, hither, fo far.

Até lá, to that place, fo far.

Até tanto que ifto fe faça, till it be done.

Até entaõ, till then, till that time.

Até is alfo ufed before an infinitive; as, *gritar até enrouquecer*, to bawl one's felf hoarfe.

Rir até arrebentar pellas ilhargas, to fplit one's fides with laughing.

Dar de comer a alguem até arrebentar, to fill *or* cram one with victuals till he burfts.

Até á primeira, till our next meeting, till we meet again.

Por cima.

XIII. *Por cima* (above, over), denotes fuperiority of place ; as,

Morar por cima de alguem, to live or lodge above fomebody,

A balla lhe paffou por cima da cabeça, the ball went over his head.

Por cima de tudo, upon the whole.

Para cima.

XIV. *Para cima* (above) denotes fuperiority of age, and is fometimes put at the end of the fentence ; as,

Elles aliftaraõ todos que tinhaõ de dez annos para cima, they enlifted every body above ten.

A cima.

XV. *A cima* (above) denotes rank, and fome moral fubjects ; as,

A cima delle, above him, *or* fuperior to him.

Eftar a cima de tudo, to be above the world.

Huma molher que eftá a cima de tudo, nem fe lhe dá do que o mundo diz della, a woman who is above the public's cenfure, who don't care what people fay of her.

Em cima.

XVI. *Em cima* (upon) ; as *em cima da mefa,* upon the table.

Em cima de tudo ifto, or only *em cima,* fignifies *and befides all that, over and above all that.*

De cima.

XVII. *De cima,* when it is an adverb, fignifies *from above*; but when a prepofition, it is Englifhed by *from, off,* or *from off;* as,

Tirai

Tirai aquillo de cima da mesa, take that from off the table.

Elle nunca tirou os seus olhos de cima della, he never turned his eyes from her.

Cahir de cima das arvores, to fall off the trees.

Debaxo.

XVIII. The prepofition *debaxo*, (*under, below, or from under*) denotes the time and place; I fay the time of a denomination of a reign, or governtment; as, *debaxo do imperio de Augusto*, under the empire of Augustus.

Debaxo, as a prepofition of place, marks out inferiority of pofition; as,

Tudo o que há debaxo dos ceos, all there is under heaven.

Ter huma almofada debaxo dos joelhos, to have a cushion under the knees.

Estar debaxo da chave, to be under lock and key.

Debaxo is fometimes rendered into Englifh by *upon*; as, *affirmar huma coufa debaxo de juramento*, to fwear to a thing, to declare upon oath.

Abaxo.

XIX. This propofition is rendered into Englifh by *under, inferior*, or *next*; as, *affentou-fe abaxo delles*, he fat inferior, *or* under them; *affentou-fe logo abaxo de mim*, he fat next inferior to me, *or* he was the next man to me; *abaxo del rey elle he o primeiro*, he is the next man to the king.

This prepofition is fometimes put at the end of the next phrafes, *de telhas abaxo*, here below, in this lower world; *de cabeça abaxo*, headlong.

Fora.

XX. *Fora*, (*out, without, except, but,*) denotes exclufion, and exception. It requires generally a genitive before a noun of time, or place; but it governs alfo the nominative; as,   *Fora*

Fora do reyno, out of the kingdom.

Fora da cidade, out of town.

Fora de tempo, out of feafon.

Procurai-o fora de cafa, look for him without doors.

Elles fahiraõ todos, fora dous ou tres, they all went out except, *or* but, two or three.

Elle lhe permete tudo, fora o ir ás affembleas, he indulges her in every thing, but in going to affemblies.

Elle tem todos os poderes, fora o de concluir, he has full powers, except of concluding.

Fora is fometimes preceded by *taõ*, and then it is to be rendered into Englifh by *fo far*; as, *elle eftá taõ fora de focorrer os feus alliados, que fe declara contra elles*, he is fo far trom affifting his allies, that he declares himfelf againft them.

Fora is fometimes rendered into Englifh by *befides*; as, *fora daquelles que*, &c. befides thofe that, &c. and fometimes by *beyond*; as, *fora de medida*, beyond meafure.

Fora de horas fignifies *beyond the hour*, or *very late*.

Pôr alguem fora da porta, or *mandar alguem pella porta fora*, to turn one out of doors.

De fronte, or fronte.

This prepofition governs the genitive, and fignifies *over-againft*. It is followed by *de, do, da*, &c. as,

De fronte da fua cafa eftá hum outeiro, over-againft his houfe is a hill.

Eu eftava de fronte delle, I was over-againft him.

Sem.

Sem fignifies *without*; as,

Sem dinheiro, without money.

Sem duvida, without doubt.

Sem fim, without end.

Sem dar a entender, or *fem fazer conhecer*, as though he did not.

N *Sem*

Sem mais nem menos, without any reason, *or* provocation.

Eſtar ſem amo, to be out of place.

Sem que algum aɛlo precedente poſſa derrogar o preſente, any former act to the contrary of the preſent notwithſtanding.

Sem governs alſo the infinitive, which is rendered into Engliſh with the participle ; as, *fallar ſem ſaber,* to ſpeak without knowing.

It is alſo a conjunction with *que,* governing the ſubjunctive ; as.

Enfada-ſe ſem que lhe digaõ nada, he is angry without any body ſaying any thing to him.

Naõ era eu ja baſtantemente infeliz, ſemque procuraſſeis de acrecentar a minha infelicidade ? was I not miſerable enough before, but you muſt ſtill labour to make me more ſo?

Lembro-me ſem que mo digais, I remember without your telling.

Elle virá ſem que mandem por elle, he will come without ſending for.

Conforme, or *ſegundo.*

XXIII. *Conforme* or *ſegundo* (according to, conformable to), govern the nominative, and never the dative as in Engliſh ; as,

Elle foi tratado conforme o ſeu merecimento, he was treated according to his deſerts.

Conforme o meu parecer, in my judgment, in my opinion.

In common converſation *conforme* is uſed adverbially, and Engliſhed as follows :

Iſſo he conforme, or only *conforme,* it is as it happens ; may be yes, may be not ; that is according.

Conforme a occaſiaõ o pedir, according as there ſhall be need.

Sobre.

XXIV. *Sobre* ſignifies *upon* ; as, *ſobre a meſa,* upon the table ; *ſobre o rio,* upon the river.

Sobre

Sobre tudo, or *sobre todas as cousas*, over all, above all, above all things, above any thing, especially ; as, *sobre tudo tende cuidado na saude*, but howsoever the matter be, mind your health.

Pôr alguem sobre si, or *dar lhe o primeiro lugar*, to place one above himself.

Ir sobre huma cidade, to besiege a town.

Ir sobre alguem, to fall *or* to rush upon one.

Ir sobre seguro, to go upon sure grounds.

Sobre a noite, about *or* towards the evening.

Sobre o verde, somewhat green.

Sobre a minha palavra, upon my word.

Sobre palavra, upon parole.

Mandar carta sobre carta, to send letter upon letter.

Elle recebeo a carta sobre jantar, he had just dined when he received the letter.

Elle dorme sobre jantar, he sleeps presently after dinner.

Sobre isto, or *sobre estas cousas*, is sometimes Englished by *more than that*, or *besides that* ; as,

Elle roubou-o e sobre isto matou-o, he robbed him, and, more than that, he killed him.

Sobre que, is rendered into English by *though* or *although* ; as,

Este negocio sobre que he difficultoso, naõ he impossivel, altho' this is a hard affair, yet it is not impossible.

Sobre is Englished sometimes by *besides* ; as,

Sobre as miserias da guerra, elle teve a disgraça, &c. besides the miseries of the war, he had the misfortune of, *&c,*

Estar sobre si, or *andar sobre si*, signifies to stand upon one's guard.

Eu vos escreverei sobre esta materia, I will write to you about this matter.

Acerca.

XXV. *Acerca* signifies *about* ; as, *acerca disto lhe disse*, about this I told him ; *acerca de lá ir lhe respondi*, about going there I answered him.

Perto

Perto, junto, ao pé, pegado.

XXVI. *Perto* (near by, about) denotes proximity of place and time, and governs the genitive case; as *aquillo está muito perto do lume*, that is too near the fire; *perto das oito horas*, about eight o'clock.

Perto do rio, near the river.

Estamos perto do Natal, we are near Christmas.

Ao pé requires also the genitive case; as,

Assentaivos ao pé de mim, sit down by me, or near me; *ao pé do rio*, near the river, &c.

Note, that *junto* (near or by) and *pegado* (hard by) require the dative case; as,

Junto á cidade, near the town.

Pegado ao palacio, hard by the palace.

Longe.

Longe, far, a great way off, governs the genitive, and the particle *de*, or *do*, *da*, &c. as,

Longe da casa, far from home.

Longe daqui, far from hence.

De longo, or ao longo.

This preposition requires the genitive case; as,

Ao longo da praya, along the shore.

Ao longo da costa, *do prado*, &c. along the coast, the meadow, &c.

Of further Particles.

Ainda, ainda que, postoque or *quando bem, ainda assim* or *com tudo*.

Ainda signifies *yet*; as, *elle ainda naõ veyo*, he is not come yet. It signifies also *even*; as, *seria vergonha ainda o fallar nisso*, it were a shame even to speak of it; *nem ainda por cem libras*, no not for a hundred pounds.

Ainda que signifies *though*, or *although*; as, *ainda que vos sois mais velho do que elle*, though you be older than he; *ainda que assim fosse*, though it were so.

Ainda

Ainda que, is very often followed by *com tudo,*
yet for all that ; as, *ainda que elle naõ tiveſſe neceſſidade
diſſo, com tudo,* &c. though he had no need of it,
yet, *&c.*

Ainda aſſim, or *com tudo,* is ſometimes Engliſhed
by *nevertheleſs,* or *for all that* ; as *ainda aſſim ſempre
elle foi louvavel,* he was praiſe-worthy for all that.

Ja deſde, ja que and *ja por que.*

Ja deſde is rendered into Engliſh by *even from* ; as
ja deſde o principio, even from the beginning.

Ja que ſignifies *ſince* ; as,
Ja que iſſo aſſim be, ſince it is ſo.

The particle *que* ſometimes is not placed immediately after *ja* ; as *ja ha dous annos que morreo,* he
died two years ſince, or ago.

Ja ha muito tempo que ſahiſtes de caſa, it is a long
time ſince you went from home.

Ja por que, is repeated in the ſame ſentence, and
then the firſt is rendered into Engliſh by *firſt, becauſe* ; and the ſecond by *ſecondly, becauſe* ; as *ja por
que era cego, ja por que era coxo,* firſt becauſe he was
blind, and ſecondly becauſe he was lame.

Depois que,

Depois que is rendered into Engliſh by *after* ; as,
Depois que eu tinha entrado, after I was gone in.

Com que.

Com que is only a note either of introduction, or
connexion ; as,
Com que havia hum homem enfermo, &c. now a certain man was ſick ; ſometimes they add to it the
particle *aſſim,* and then it is to be rendered into Engliſh by *and ſo.*

Ou.

Ou ſignifies *or,* or *either* ; as, *eu bom, ou mao,*
either good or bad ; *mais ou menos,* more or leſs ;
ou elle queira ou naõ, whether he will or no.

Quer.

Quer.

Quer, when a particle muſt be repeated, and the firſt is rendered into Engliſh by *either*, or *whether*, and the ſecond by *or*; as, *quer elle queira quer naõ*, whether he will or no; *quer vos o tenhaes feito quer naõ*, whether you have done that or no.

Se quer, or *ao menos.*

Se quer, or *ao menos*, &c. ſignifies *at leaſt, however*; as, *ſe vos naõ quereis ſer por elle naõ ſejais ſe quer contra elle*, If you don't chuſe to be for him, at leaſt don't oppoſe him; *dai lhe ſe quer com que ſuſtentar-ſe*, give him at leaſt a ſubſiſtence; *o noſſo primeiro fim he de livrarnos de todos os males, ao menos dos moyores*, our chief end is to be freed from all, however the greateſt evils.

Nem ſe quer hum, is rendered into Engliſh by *never a one, ſo much*, or *in the following manner*; as, *foraõ todos mortos, e nem ſe quer hum eſcapou*, they were all ſlain to a man.

Quando muito.

Quando muito, (at moſt, at fartheſt, at long run,) is generally uſed before the nouns of time and price; as, *elle eſtará aqui dentro em hum mez quando muito*, he will be here in a month at fartheſt; *dez libras quando muito*, ten pounds at moſt.

Tanto.

Tanto, ſo much, is ſometimes followed by *como*, and then it is rendered into Engliſh by *as well as, as much as*, &c. as,

Amo-te tanto como a mim meſmo, I love thee as well as myſelf.

Elle teme tanto como qualquer de vos, que lhe reſulte algum dano, he is afraid of a harm as much as any of you.

Cuidei

Cuidei que a eftimaffe tanto como a fi mefmo, I thought he made as high account of her as of himfelf.

Elles vem tanto de dia como de noite, they can fee as well by day, as by night.

Eu tive tanto como vos, I had as much as you.

Outro tanto is rendered into Englifh by, *the double, twice as much,* or *as much;* as,

Eu alcancei outro tanto mais por iffo, I had as much more for it; *eu poffo fazer outro tanto,* I can do as much.

Tanto followed by *affim* is a particle merely expletive; as,

Tanto affim que lhe poffo eu fazer? how can I help it; *vaite, tanto affim naõ ha nada para ti,* go away, there is nothing for you.

Tanto affim followed by *que* without an interrogation, is fometimes rendered by *fo that, in fo much that;* as, *tanto affim que elle naõ quer ouvir mais fallar niffo,* fo that he will hear no more of it.

Tanto mais is followed by *que,* and Englifhed by *and the more fo as,* as

Eu eftou prompto para ir com vm^ce hum dia deftes á comedia, fe vm^ce quizer. Tanto mais que fe deve reprefentar huma nova, I am at your fervice to wait on you fome day or other to the play, if you'll give me leave; and the more fo, as a new one is to be acted.

Tanto que, or *logo que,* is rendered into Englifh by *as foon as;* as, *tanto que eu o vi,* as foon as I faw him.

Tanto melhor is rendered into Englifh by *fo much the better.*

Tanto is fometimes preceded by *com,* and followed by *que,* and is Englifhed by *fo, provided that;* as, *com tanto que o façais,* provided that you do it: *com tanto que me naõ faça mal,* fo he do me no hurt.

Tanto quanto is Englifhed by *as much as;* as,

Tanto quanto poffo, as much as I can.

Taõ.

Taõ, fo, is generally followed by *como;* as,

Efte

Eſte naõ he taõ bom como o outro, this is not ſo good as the other ; *eu ſei iſſo taõ bem como vos*, I know it, as well as you.

Taõ is ſometimes followed by *que*, and Engliſhed by *ſo*, *ſuch*, *to that degree* ; as,

Elle he taõ prudente que naõ tem igual, he is ſo wiſe that he has not his match ; *naõ ſou taõ louco que o creya*, I am not ſo ſimple, *or* I am not ſuch a fool as to believe it ; *faz taõ grande vento que*, &c. the wind is ſo high, that, &c. *or* the wind blows to that de-gree, &c.

Como.

Como, is Engliſhed by *as*, *like*, *how*, &c. as you may ſee in the following expreſſions.

Como ? how.

Dizeime como lhe hei de fallar ? tell me how I may ſpeak to him?

Como aſſim ? how ſo ?

Como ! what !

Como quer que, whereas.

Como quer que ſeja, howſoever, in what manner, *or* faſhion ſoever.

Seja como for, be it as it will.

Como iſto aſſim be, ſince it is ſo.

Como, as it were, *or* almoſt.

Como ſe, as if, *or* even as if ; as, *como ſe elles ti-veſſem ja vencido*, as if they had already over-come.

Como tambem, as well as.

Rico como elle he, as rich as he is.

Como ſois meu amigo, quero, &c. as (*or* becauſe) you are my friend, I'll, &c.

Dizeime o como, tell me how.

Eu ſei como fazer para que elle venha, I know the way I ſhall take to make him come.

Como elle lá naõ eſteja, eu irei, provided he is not there I will come.

Aſſim.

Affim.

Affim, fo, thus, is rendered into Englifh as you may fee in the following expreffions.

Pois he affim de veras? de veras que affim he, is it even fo? it is even fo.

Affim feja, or *feja affim,* fo be it, *or* be it fo.

Affim he, it is fo.

Para affim dizer, as it were.

Affim fou eu tolo, que, &c. I am not fo foolifh as to, &c.

Affim Deos me falve, as I hope to be faved.

Tanto affim, fo that.

Affim he que vos, &c. is this your way, &c.

Affim como affim, after all, neverthelefs, *or* for all that; as, *em vaõ dilatais a voffa jornada, affim como affim he precifo que vades,* it is in vain for you to put off your journey, you muft go thither neverthelefs, *or* for all that, you muft go after all.

Affim como, as well as, *or* as foon as.

Bafta affim por agora, thus much for this time.

Affim na paz, como na guerra, both in time of peace and war.

Affim affim, fo fo, indifferent.

Affim queira elle como pode, he can if he will.

Affim is fometimes preceded by *e*; as, *e affim que quer ifto dizer?* how now? what do you mean by this? And fometimes *affim* is followed by *como*; as, *affim como o fol eclipfa os outros planetas, da mefma forte,* &c. as the fun eclipfes the other planets, fo, &c.

Se.

Se, if; as *fe elle vier,* if he comes; *fe me amaffes,* fhould you love him; *fe elle foffe homem de honra,* were he but an honeft man; *fe foubeffem quem eu fou, todos diriaõ,* &c. were it told who I am, every one would fay, &c. *fe he verdade que,* &c. if fo be that, &c.

The

The reciprocal verbs, as well as thofe that are ufed imperfonally, may have two *fe's* joined together; as, *fe fe for*, if he goes away; *fe fe falla niffo*, if they fpeak of it.

Se is fometimes rendered into Englifh by *whether*; and when it is repeated, the fecond is Englifhed by *or*; as,

Quifera faber fe a culpa he noffa, fe voffa, I would know whether it is your fault, or ours.

Aliás.

Aliás, is fometimes rendered into Englifh by *elfe*; as, *entrai porque aliás fecharei a porta*, come in, or elfe I'll fhut the door; *porque aliás feriaõ os voffos filhos immundos*, elfe were your children unclean. And fometimes it is rendered into Englifh by *otherwife*, *in other things*, or *refpects*.

Embora.

Embora is fometimes rendered into Englifh by *profperoufly*, *aufpicioufly*; but fometimes it is a particle merely expletive, and anfwers to the Italian *pure*; as *dizei muito embora o que quizerdes*, fay what you pleafe: the Italian fays, *dite pur quel che vi piacerá*.

Muito embora, feja affim, well, let it be fo.

Embora is fometimes Englifhed by *away*; as, *vaite embora*, go away.

Senaõ.

Senaõ fignifies *if not, did not, were it not that, but that*; as,

Senaõ tiveffe medo de meu pay, but that I fear my father.

Se elle naõ tiveffe vergonha de confeffar, but that he was afhamed to confefs.

Note, that the following expreffions, in which they make ufe of this particle, may be Englifhed by *but*, *for*, and fome other variations.

Senaõ foffe por elle, but for him, *or* had it not been for him, *or* had he not been.

Senaõ foffe por vos, had you not been, *or* had it not been for you, without you, without your help, hindrance, &c.

Senaõ foffe por mim elle morreria de fome, were it not for me, he would ftarve.

Senaõ is fometimes Englifhed by *but ;* as, *nem elles tem outro intento, fenaõ,* &c. nor do they aim at any thing elfe but, &c.

Ninguem diffe affim fenaõ Cicero, nobody faid fo but Cicero.

Senaõ may be alfo expreffed in Portuguefe by *mais que* in the following fentence, and the like.

Elle naõ faz fenaõ jogar, or *elle naõ faz mais que jogar,* he does nothing but play.

Nao, naõ porque.

Naõ, not, or *no,* when followed by *porque,* is Englifhed by *not that, not but that ;* as, *naõ porque lhe faltaffe engenho,* not but that he had wit ; *naõ porque naõ foffe jufto, mas porque,* &c. not but that it was right, but becaufe, &c. *naõ porque a coufa feja impoffivel, mas porque,* &c. not that the thing is impoffible, but becaufe, &c.

Tambem, or outrofi.

Tambem, or *outrofi,* fignifies *alfo, too, likewife ;* as *vos affim o quereis e eu tambem,* you'll have it fo, and I too.

Para que, porque.

See the prepofitions *para* and *por.*

Pois.

This particle is very much ufed by the Portuguefe, and it is rendered into Englifh feveral ways, as you may fee in the following examples.

Pois ide, evinde logo, go then and come back prefently.

Pois naõ fou eu capaz de fazello ? what, am I not capable to do it ?

Pois,

Pois, or *pois entaō que quer dizer ifto?* well, and what of all this?

Pois, or *pois entaō que hei de fazer?* What fhall I do then?

Pois eu digo que elle eftá dentro, why, he is here within, I fay.

Pois porque me vigiais? why then do you watch me?

Elle tem cabeça; pois tambem hum alfinete a tem, he has got a head, and fo has a pin.

Pois before *naō*, and preceded by an interrogation, denotes a ftrong affertion, and is Englifhed by *without doubt*, *yes*, *furely*, *to be fure*, &c. as, *virá elle? pois naō!* will he come? yes to be fure.

Antes, or *mais depreffa*.

Thefe particles are fometimes rendered into Englifh by *rather* or *fooner* ; as, *antes* or *mais depreffa quizera morrer*, I would rather die; *antez quizera viver fó que na voffa companhia*, I would fooner live alone than be in your company. Sometimes *antes* is Englifhed by *before*; as, *Idevos antes que elle venha*, go away before he comes ; *antes que eu morra*, before I die.

Mas antes, *pelo contrario*, *mas pelo contrario*.

Thefe particles are rendered into Englifh by *on the contrary*, *on the other hand*, *nay*; as, *mas antes, mas pelo contrario*, or *pelo contrario ifto he muito differente*, nay it is quite another thing ; *mas antes, pelo contrario*,&c. *elle he avarento*, nay, or on the contrary he is a covetous man.

Para melhor dizer.

This phrafe is rendered into Englifh by *nay*; as *elle tem ja baftante, ou para melhor dizer, mais do neceffario*, he has already enough, nay too much; *Aifto he que nos chamamos direito das gentes, ou para-melhor dizer, da razaō*, this is what we call the law of nations,

nations, which may be called more properly the law of reafon.

Que.

We have already obferved that *que* is a particle which moſt conjunctions are compoſed of; as *ainda que*, although; *de ſorte que*, ſo that, &c.

The particle *que* ſometimes is the ſign of the third perſons of the imperative, as *let* in *Engliſh*; as, *que falle*, let him ſpeak; *que riaõ*, let them laugh.

Que is uſed between two verbs, to determine and ſpecify the ſenſe of the firſt, as *eu vos aſſeguro que aſſim be*, I aſſure you that it is ſo; *duvido que aſſim ſeja*, I doubt whether it is ſo or no.

Que is alſo uſed after *bora* in the beginning of a ſentence, and followed by a verb in the ſubjunctive, to denote by exclamation one's ſurprize, averſion, and reluctance of ſomething; in which caſe there is a verb grammatically underſtood before *que*; as *bora que ſe eſqueceſſe elle de ſi meſmo!* I wonder, or is it poſſible for him to have forgot himſelf!

The exclamation, or admiration, is ſometimes expreſſed without any verb; as, *que goſto; e no meſmo tempo que pena!* how much pleaſure and trouble at once!

Que is ſometimes repeated; as,

Que bellos livros que tendes! what fine books you have got! *que bella que be a virtude!* how beautiful is virtue!

Que is ſometimes followed by *de*; as, *que de loucos ba no mundo!* how many fools there are in the world!

Que is uſed after nouns denoting time, and is ſometimes Engliſhed by *when* or *ſince*, &c. and ſometimes left out; as,

O dia que elle partio, the day when he ſat out.

Quanto tempo ba que eſtais em Londres? how long have you lived at London? how long is it ſince you lived at London?

Ha dez annos que faz a meſma couſa, he has done the ſame thing theſe ten years.

7

Há

Há dez annos que morreo, he died ten years ago.

Que is sometimes rendered into English by *because*, as you may see in Camoens canto 2. Stanza XVI. *que levemente hum animo*, &c. and sometimes by *that*, *to the end that*, *in order to*; as you may see ibid. Stanza XVII. *que como vissem*, *que no rio*, &c.

Que before *se* in the beginning of a sentence, is a redundancy not expressed in English; as *que se vos dizeis que*, &c. if you say that, &c.

Que is used after the conjunction *a penas* (scarce or hardly), and is Englished by *but*; as, *a penas acabou de fallar que logo morreo*, he had hardly done speaking but he expired.

Que sometimes is preceded by *de forte*, *de maneira*, *de jeito*, and then it is Englished by *so that*, *in such a manner*, *insomuch that*; as, *eu o farei de forte que fiqueis contente*, I will do it so that, *or* in that manner that, you shall be contented.

De veras.

De veras signifies *in earnest*; but sometimes it is Englished by *no fure*; as, *de veras! naõ o posso crer*, no fure!

Hora.

Hora, or *ora*, is an interjection that serves to encourage, as we have seen above; but when it is repeated, it is Englished by *sometimes*, *one while*, *another while*; as, *ora está bem ora está mal*, sometimes he is well, sometimes ill; *elle ora está de hum parecer e ora de outro*, he is now of one opinion, and next moment of another. *Por ora* signifies *now*, *for the present*.

C H A P.

CHAP. VIII.

Of the Portuguese Orthography; and first of Capitals and Stops.

I. THE proper names, as well as the surnames, always begin with a capital.

II. The names of nations, kingdoms, and provinces, also begin with a capital; as, *Francez,* French; *Inglez,* English, &c.

III. All names of dignities, degrees, and honours, require a capital; as, *Rey, Bispo,* &c. King, Bishop, &c.

IV. At the beginning of a period, as well as of a verse, the first letter is always a capital.

V. The names of arts and sciences, as well as those of kindred, begin with a capital.

Of Stops.

The use of stops, or points, is to distinguish words and sentences.

The Portuguese have six stops, or pauses, viz.

1. The *ponto final,* the same as our period or full stop (.), and is used at the end of a period, to shew that the sentence is completely finished.

2. The *dous pontos,* which is our colon (:), and is the pause made between two members of a period; that is, when the sense is complete, but the sentence not ended.

3. The *ponto e virgula,* our semicolon (;) and denotes that short pause which is made in the subdivision of the members or parts of a sentence.

4. The *ponto e interrogaçam,* the point of interrogation thus (?)

4. *Ponto e admiraçam,* the point of admiration thus (!)

6. The *virgula,* the same with our comma (,) and is the shortest pause or resting, in speech, being used chiefly to distinguish nouns, verbs, and adverbs, as also the parts of a shorter sentence.

The

The conjunction *e*, the relative *qual*, and the disjunctions *ou* and *nem*, require a comma before them.

The Portuguese make use also of a parenthesis, thus ( ); but they do not make use of the diærefis, called by the printers *crema* (¨); they make use also of the *angulo*, thus ∧, called by the printers *caret*.

The apoftrophe, or, as they call it, *viracento*, likewife takes place in this as in other languages, being defigned only for the more pleafant and eafy pronunciation of words, by cutting off an antecedent vowel; as, *d'armas*, *d'elvas*, and not *darmas*, *delvas*, &c. But this is fomewhat excufable in cafes wherein, by ufage, they feem to be one word; as, *nefta*, *nefte*, *defta*, *defte*, *nalgum*, *daquelle*, *nello*, *nella*, *daqui*, *dali*, *atequi*, *ategora*; and not *em elle*, *de elle*, &c.

Of the Accents.

The accent, which is the very foul of articulated words, is a found of the voice by which we pronounce fome fyllables fhorter, others longer.

I intend to fpeak here only of the accents the Portuguefe ought to make ufe of, according to *Madureira*, in his *Portuguefe Orthography*.

The Portuguefe indeed are acquainted with three accents, but they ought to make ufe of two only, namely, the acute, which defcends from the right to the left (´), and the circumflex, thus (ˆ).

1. The acute ferves to prolong the pronunciation, and is put, according to *Madureira*, on the third perfon fingular of the future tenfe; as, *amará*, *lerá*, &c.

2. On the penultima of the preterpluperfect tenfe of the indicative mood; as, *amára*, *enfinára*, &c.

3. The acute accent ought to be put alfo on the penultima of the third perfons of the prefent tenfe of the verbs *renunciar*, *pronunciar*, *duvidar*, &c. thus *renuncía*, *pronuncía*, *duvída*, &c. that they may be

be diftinguifhed from the nouns *renúncia, pronúncia, dúvida,* &c. The fame accent is alfo put on *eftá, nó,* to diftinguifh them from *efta,* this, and *no,* in the.

The vowel *o* has two founds, according to the two accents that may be put on it; one open, when it is markt with the acute accent, and it is pronounced like *o* in *fcre*; the other clofe, when it is markt with the circumflex accent, and then it is pronounced like *u* in *ftumble.*

There are many nouns, both fubftantive and adjective, which are accented in the fingular with the circumflex, and in the plural with the acute; and the adjectives that have two terminations, particularly thofe ending in *ofo, ofa,* muft be accented (in the fingular) with the circumflex in the mafculine, and with the acute in the feminine; as,

Fôgo, fire; plural, *fógos.*
Fôrno, oven; plural, *fórnos.*
ôlho, eye; plural, *ólhos.*
ôvo, egg; plural, *óvos.*
ôffo, bone; plural, *óffos.*
Pôço, well; plural, *póços.*
Pôrco, hog; plural, *pórcos.*
Rôgo, prayer; plural *rógos.* And fo *fôjo, tôrno, formôfo, fequiôfo, fuppôfto, pôvo, tôrto, tórta, copiôfo, copiófa,* &c.

The following keep the circumflex accent in both numbers: *bôlo, bôlos; bôjo, bôjos; bôto, bôtos; côco, côcos; chôro, chôros; côto, côtos; fôrro, fôrros; gôrdo, gôrdos; gôfto, gôftos; gôzo, gôzos; lôbo, lôbos; môço, môços; nôjo, nôjos; pôtro, pôtros; tôlo, tôlos; ferrôlho, ferrôlhos; rapôfo, rapôfos; arrôz, arrôzes; algôz, algôzes,* &c.

On the contrary, the following keep the acute accent in both numbers: *cópo, cópos; módo, módos; nóffo, nóffos; vóffo, vóffos,* &c.

When the accent circumflex is put on the *ê,* then the *e* is pronounced like the French mafculine *e*; but when *e* is accented with the acute accent, then

O the

the _e_ is to be pronounced like the _e_ open in French, and it is exceeding sonorous and long. See the pronunciation of the vowel _e_.

The nouns ending in _az, iz, oz, uz_, must have the acute accent on the vowel before the _z_; as, _rapáz_, a boy; _nóz_, a walnut; _alcaçúz_, liquorish: but you must except _arróz_, rice; _algóz_, a hang-man.

Nouns ending in _ez_ generally have the circumflex accent; as, _méz_, a month; _marquêz_, a marquis; &c. except the surnames; as, _Alvarez, Antunez, Lopez, Henriquez, Gonçalvez, Rodriguez, Perez, Nunez, Tellez_, &c.

Some Observations upon the Portuguese Orthography.

Both the Portuguese orthographers and best authors vary so much in their rules and ways of writing, that it is a hard matter, and quite out of any grammarian's way, to clear up this part of the Portuguese grammar; since it requires no less authority than that of the Royal Portuguese Academy. However, not to omit such a material part of the Grammar, I shall present the learners with the following observations.

I. When the Latin words which the Portuguese are derived from, begin with a _b_, the Portuguese likewise must begin with it; therefore you must write and pronounce the _b_ in the following words, _bom, bondade, bem, bento_, &c. because they are derived from _bonus, bonitas, &c._ But you must except _bainha, bexiga, bairro_, which begin with a _b_, though they are derived from _vagina, vesica, vicus_.

II. Likewise if the Latin words begin with a _v_, the Portuguese words derived from them must also begin with it; as, _vida, viver, varrer, ver, vinho_, &c. from _vita, vivere, verrere, videre, vinum_, &c.

Though _b_ ought to be pronounced only by closing the lips, and _v_ by touching the superior teeth with the inferior lips; yet, by a certain affinity be-

7   tween

tween thefe two letters, in fpeaking there is a great confufion in the pronunciation of them in the province of *Entre Douro e Minho*: and this confufion has not been peculiar to the Portuguefe language, becaufe *Nebrixa* fays, in his *Caftilian Orthography*, that in his time fome Spaniards could hardly make any diftinction between thefe two letters.

III. The *p* found in fome words originally Latin, is changed in Portuguefe into a *b*; as, *cabrá*, *cabêllo*, *cabeça*, &c. from *capra*, *capillús*, *cáput*, &c.

IV. The Portuguefe generally make ufe of the *y* in the following words: *ay*, *rey*, *frey*, *ley*, *may*, *pay*, *mayo*, *meyo*, and fome others.

Bluteau fays, that we muft make ufe of the *y* in words having a Greek origin; as, *fyllaba*, *Chryfopeia*, *pyrámide*, *polygono*, *hydrographia*, *hydrípico*, *phyfica*, *hyperbole*, *hypocrita*, *Apocrypho*, &c.

V. The *ph* are ufed by the Portuguefe in fome words taken from the Greek; as, *philofophia*, *philologia*, *philadelphia*, *epitaphio*, &c.

VI. The *r* in Portuguefe has two pronunciations, one foft, expreffed by a fingle *r*, as in *arádo*, a plough; and after the confonants *b*, *c*, *d*, *f*, *g*, *p*, *t*; and another hard, in which two *rr* are ufed; as in *barró*, *carro*, &c. But you muft obferve,

1. That in the beginning of a word two *rr* muft never be ufed, becaufe then the *r* is always pronounced hard in Portuguefe; as in the words *remo*, *rico*, *roda*, &c.

2. When the confonants *l*, *n*, *s*, are before the *r*, either in a fingle word, or a compound, this letter muft never be doubled, becaufe then its found is always ftrong; as in *abalroar*, *enriquecer*, *honra*, *defregrado*, *Henrique*, *Ifraelita*, &c.

3. The *r* after a *b* is alfo pronounced hard in compounds with the prepofitions *ab*, *ob*, *fub*, and yet is not doubled; as in *abrogar*, *obrepçaõ*, *fubrepçaõ*.

VII. The *s* is never doubled in the beginning of words, nor after the confonants; therefore you

muft

muſt write *ſarar, ſaber, falſamente, falſo, manſo,* &c.

The *ſ* is pronounced like *z* between two vowels, in words derived from the Latin, as well as in thoſe that end in *ôſa* and *ôſo*; as, *muſa, caſo, riſo, amorôſo, cuida-dóſa, coſa,* &c. You muſt alſo obſerve, that *coſer* ſignifies *to ſew,* but *cozer* ſignifies *to boil* or *bake.*

VIII. *Th* are generally uſed in words derived from the Greek; as, *amphitheatro, atheiſta, theologo, lethargo, methodo,* &c.

Th is alſo uſed in the Portugueſe prepoſition *athé*; though ſome write it thus, *até.*

IX. When *pt* is found in Latin words, it muſt be kept in the Portugueſe derived from them; as, *apto, inepto, optimo,* &c. from *aptus, ineptus, optimus,* &c. You muſt make the ſame obſervation about *ct.*

X. *Ch* is ſounded like *k* in words derived from the Greek; as, *archanjo, archiduque, Chryſoſtomo, chryſol, chriſologo, Chriſtovaõ, monarchia,* &c. Theſe words muſt be written with *ch,* in order to preſerve to the eye the etymology of words.

Note, that *ch* in words that are not derived from the Greek, is pronounced like *ch* in the Engliſh words *church, chin, much,* &c. but as ſome confound the *ch* with the *x,* and begin with *x* thoſe words that ſhould begin with *ch,* I thought it neceſſary to make a collection of them.

Words beginning with ch.

Chá	Chamar
Chãa	Chamarîz
Cháça	Chambaõ
Chacîna	Chamejar
Cháço	Chamîça
Chácota	Chamîné
Chafarîz	Chamuſcar
Chága	Chança
Chalûpa.	Chancéla
Cháma.	Chancelaria
Chamalóte	Chancelér

Chanconête

Chançonêta
Chanquêta
Chantágem
Chantrado
Chantre
Chaō
Chápa
Chapádo
Chapeádo
Chapelêta
Chapéo
Chapîm
Chapinhar
Chapûz
Charaméla
Charameleiro
Chárco
Charnéca
Charneira
Charóla
Chárpa
Chárro
Charrûa
Cháſco
Chaſôna
Chatîm
Cháto
Chavaō
Chavaſcál
Cháve
Chávêlha
Chavêta
Chavinha.

C H E.

Chêa, or Cheya
Chéfe
Chegar
Cheirar, and its derivatives
Cherîvia
Chérne.

C H I.

Chiar
Chibarro
Chibo
Chîcharos

Chichárro
Chichélos
Chicória
Chicóte
Chífra
Chífrar
Chifre
Chilindraō
Chilrar
Chimbéo
Chincar
Chincheiro
Chinchôrro
Chinéla
Chiqueiro
Chiſpa
Chiſpar
Chiſte
Chîta.

C H O.

Chóça
Chóca
Chocalhar
Chocálho
Chocar
Chocarrear
Chocarrîce
Chôco, and Chócos
Chocoláte
Chôfrado
Chófre
Chóldabolda
Chóque
Chorar
Chorrilho
Chórro
Chover
Choupa
Choupana
Choupo, or Chôpo
Chouriço
Choutar.

C H U.

Chûça
Chupamel
Chupar

O 3

Chuchurriar

Chuchurriar
Cbùço
Chùfa
Chumáço
Chumbar
Chûmbo
Churriaõ

Churûme
Chufma
Chúva
Chuveiro.

C H Y.

Chypre.

The following words begin with *ce* and not *ſe*.

Cêa
Ceado
Ceár

C E B.

Cebôla
Cebolal
Cebolinho.

C E D.

Cedavim
Cedéla
Cedenho
Ceder
Cedilho
Cêdo
Cédro
Cédula.

C E G.

Cega
Cegar
Cégo
Cegonha
Cegûde
Cegueira.

C E I.

Ceifa
Ceifaõ
Ceiraõ
Ceirinha
Ceivar.

C E L.

Celáda
Celebraçaõ
Celebrar
Célebre
Celéſte

Celeſtial
Celeſtrina
Celeuſma
Celga
Celha
Celho
Celibado
Celibáto
Celícola
Celidonia
Cella
Celleiro
Celleireiro
Celtas.

C E M.

Cem
Cemiterio.

C E N.

Cenâculo
Ceno
Cenóbio
Cenobitico
Cenotáphia
Cenoura
Cenrada
Cenreira
Cenſo
Cenſôr
Cenſura
Cenſurádo
Cenſurar
Centauro
Centêna
Centeal
Centeſimo

Centeyo

Centeyo
Cento
Céntóculo
Centopea
Central
Centro
Centuplo
Centuria
Centuriaõ
Céo.

C E P.

Cepa
Cepilho
Cepo
Ceptro.

C E R.

Cera
Ceraferario
Cerbero
Cerca
Cercado
Cercar
Cercador
Cercadura
Cérce
Cerceádo
Cercear
Cercillo
Cerco
Cerdoſo
Cérebro
Cereijas
Cereijal
Ceremonia
Ceremonial
Cerieiro
Cérne
Cernelha
Cerol
Ceroulas
Cerqueiro
Cerraçaõ

Cerrar
Cerralheiro
Cerrálho
Cerrarſe
Cerro
Cérta
Certo
Certãa
Certeza
Certidaõ
Certificar
Cerva
Cerval
Cervêja
Cervilhas
Cerviz
Cerúda
Ceruleo
Cervo
Cerzir.

C E S.

Ceſar
Ceſarea
Ceſma
Ceſmaría
Ceſmeiro
Ceſſaõ
Ceſſacaõ
Ceſſar
Ceſta
Ceſtinha
Ceſtinho
Ceſteiro
Ceſto
Ceſura.

C E V.

Ceva
Cevada
Cevadal
Cevadeira
Cevadóuro
Cevar.

Cezaõ

C E Z.

Cezaõ   Cezimbra.

N. B. *Cerrar* fignifies *to fhut*, or *fhut up*; but *ferrar* fignifies *to faw*, to cut timber or other matter with a faw.

The following words muft have *ci*, and not *fi*, in their beginning.

C I A.

Ciarfe
Ciática.

C I B.

Ciba
Cibalho
Ciborio.

C I C.

Cicatriz
Cicero
Ciciofo.

C I D.

Cidadaõ
Cidadaõs
Cidade
Cidadôa
Cidra
Cidrada
Cidraõ
Cidreira.

C I E.

Ciencia.

C I F.

Cifar
Cifra
Cifrar.

C I G.

Cigâna
Cigano
Cigarra
Cigúde
Cigurelha.

C I L.

Cilada

Cilhas
Cilhar
Cilîcia
Cilîcio
Cilladas.

C I M.

Cima
Cimalha
Cimbalo
Cimeyra)
Cimento
Cimitarra
Cimo.

C I N.

Cinca
Cincar
Cincho
Cinco
Cincoenta
Cingidouro
Cingir
Cingulo
Cinnamômo
Cinta
Cintillar
Cintura
Cinza
Cinzento
Cinzeiro.

C I O.

Cîo
Ciôfo
Ciófa.

C I P.

C I P.

Cipó
Ciprefte
Cipriano.

C I R.

Ciranda
Cirandagem
Cirandar
Circo
Circulaçaō
Circular
Circulo
Circuito
Circumcidar
Circumcifaō
Circumferencia
Circumfpecto
Circumfpecçaō
Circumftancia
Circumftantes
Cîrio
Cirurgîa
Cirurgiaō
Cirzir.

C I S.

Cifcar
Cifco
Cifma
Cifmatico
Cifne
Ciftercienfe
Cifterna
Citaç.ō
Citádo
Citar
Citerior
Cithara
Citharédo
Citrino
Cîvel
Civíl
Civilidade.

C I U.

Ciûme
Ciumes.

C I Z.

Cizânia
Ciziraō.

XI. No Portuguefe word begins with *ço*; but according to *Madureira*, there are fome that begin with *ça* and *çu*; as, *çapato, çapateiro, çargaço, çuja, çugidade, çumo, çurra, çurrar*, and fome others.

The *ç* is ufed after *p* in thofe Portuguefe words that have in their Latin root *pt*; as, *defcripçaō, accepçaō*, &c. from *defcriptio, acceptio*, &c.

Of Double Letters.

It is to be generally obferved, that the confonants are doubled in thofe Portuguefe words, whofe Latin roots have likewife the fame double confonants; as, *accelerar, accento, occidente*, &c. from *accelero, accentus, occidens*, &c. *affligir, affluencia, affirmaçaō*, &c. from *affligo, affluentia, affirmatio*, &c. as you will fee in the following collections.

i

B is

B.

B is to be doubled in *abbade, abbacial, abbadia, abbadeſſa, abbreviatura, abbreviar,* and ſome others.

C.

C is to be doubled in the following words, and ſome of their derivatives.

A.

Abſtracçaõ
Acçaõ
Accento
Acçentuar
Accepçaõ
Acceita
Acceitaçaõ
Acceitador
Acceitar
Acceſſaõ
Acceſſivel
Accéſſo
Acceſſório
Accidental
Accidente
Accelerada
Accelerado
Accelerar
Acclamaçaõ
Acclamar
Accommodaçaõ
Accommodado
Accommodar
Accumulaçaõ
Accumulado
Accumular
Accuſaçaõ
Accuſádo
Accuſadôr
Accuſar
Accuſativo
Adſtricçaõ
Afflicçaõ
Attracçaõ.

B.

Baccho
Bocca
Boccaça
Boccadinho
Boccado
Boccal.

C.

Circumſpecçaõ
Coacçaõ
Cocçaõ
Collecçaõ
Conſtricçaõ
Conſtrucçaõ
Contracçaõ
Correcçaõ.

D.

Decocçaõ
Deducçaõ
Desjecçaõ
Deſóccupaçaõ
Deſoccupado
Deſoccupar
Detracçaõ
Dicçaõ
Diccionario
Direcçaõ
Diſtráeçaõ.

E.

Eccentrico
Ecclefiaſtico
Erécçaõ
Evicçaõ
Exacçaõ
Extracçaõ.

Fácçaõ

F.

Fácçaō
Ficçaō
Fracçaō.

I.

Impeccabilidade
Impeccavel
Inacceſſivel
Indicçaō
Inducçaō
Infécçaō
Infracçaō
Inſpecçaō
Inſtrucçaō
Intellécçaō
Interjécçaō
Interſecçaō
Introducçaō.

M.

Manuducçaō.

O.

Objecçaō
Obſtrucçaō
Occaſiaō
Occaſionar
Occáſo
Occidental
Occidente
Occiduo
Occiſaō
Occorrer
Occultamente
Occultado
Occultar
Occulto
Occupaçaō
Occupado
Occupar
Occurrencia
Occurrente.

P.

Peccado
Peccadôr

Peccadôra
Peccante
Peccar
Predlecçaō
Preoccupar
Producçaō
Projecçaō
Protécçaō
Putrefácçaō.

R.

Rarefacçaō
Reconducçaō
Refecçaō.
Refracçaō
Reſeccaçaō
Reſtricçaō.

S.

Satisfacçaō
Seccar
Secco
Secçaō
Seccura
Sôcco
Soccôrrer
Soccorro
Subtracçaō
Succeder
Succeſſaō
Succéſſo
Succeſſivo
Succeſſivel
Succeſſôr
Succintamente
Succinto
Sûcco
Succoſo
Sûccubo.

T.

Tranſácçaō
Traducçaō.

V.

Vacca
Vaccáda
Vaccum.

D.

D.

This letter is doubled in the following words :
addiçaõ, addicionado, addicionar, additamento, additar.

F.

F is to be doubled in

Affabilidade
Affavel
Affadigado
Affadigar
Affagádo
Affagar
Affágos
Affamádo
Affamarfe
Affaftâdo
Affaftar
Affazendádo
Affazerfe.

A F F E.

Affeádo
Affear
Affeamento
Affectadamente
Affectádo
Affectar
Affécto
Affectuofo
Affeiçaõ
Affeiçoado
Affeiçoar
Affeite
Affeitar
Affeminado
Affeminarfe
Afferradamente
Afferrado
Afferrar
Afferretoado
Afferretoar
Afferrolhado

Afferrolhar
Afferventado
Afferventar
Affervorado
Affervorar.

A F F I.

Affiado
Affiar
Affidalgádo
Affidalgarfe
Affigurado
Affigurar
Affilháda
Affilhado
Affiladôr
Affilar
Affinado
Affinar
Affincado
Affincar
Affirmadamente
Affirmadôr
Affirmar
Affiftularfe
Affixar.

A F F L.

Afflamarfe
Afflicçaõ
Afflicto
Affligir
Affluencia.

A F F O.

Affocinhar
Affogado

Affogádor

Affogadôr
Affogar
Affogamento
Affogueado
Affoguear
Afforàdo
Afforador
Afforár
Afforamento
Afformentar
Afformoſeádo
Afformoſear
Affoutado
Affoutar
Affouteza
Affouto

A F F R.

Affracar
Afframengado
Affreguefado
Affreguefarfe
Affronta
Affrontado
Affrontamento
Affrontar
Affrontofamente
Affrontofo
Affroxadamente
Affroxado
Affroxar.

A F F U.

Affugentado
Affugentar
Affumado
Affumar
Affundado

Affundarſe
Affundirſe
Affuzillar.

D I.

Diffamado
Diffamar
Differença
Differençar
Differenças
Differente
Differentemente
Difficil
Difficuldade
Difficultar
Difficultoſamente
Difficultoſo
Diffuſaõ
Diffuſamende
Diffuſo.

E.

Effectivamente
Effectivo
Effeito
Effeituar
Efficazmente
Efficacia
Efficaz
Efficiente
Effigie.

O.

Offender
Offerecer
Offuſcar

S

Suffocar
Suffragio, *and ſome others.*

G.

This letter is to be doubled in

Aggravante
Aggravar
Aggravado
Aggrávo
Aggreſſôr
Exaggeraçaõ

Exaggerador
Exaggerado
Exaggerar
Suggerir
Suggeſtaõ
Suggerido.

L.

L is to be doubled in

A B.
Aballado
Aballador
Aballar
Aballo
Aballifado
Aballifadôr
Aballifar

A C.
Acafellador
Acafelladura
Acafellar
Acallentado
Acallentar
Acapellado.

A F.
Affillado
Affillador
Affillar.

A L.
Allegaçaõ
Allegado
Allegar
Allegoria
Allegórico
Allegorifar
Alleluia
Alliviar
Allucinaçaõ
Allucinar
Alludir
Allumiar
Allufaõ.

A M.
Amantellado
Amarello
Amarellecerfe
Amarellidaõ
Amollado
Amollar
Amollecer
Amollecido
Amollentar
Ampólla.

A N
Annullaçaõ
Annullar.

A P.
Appellaçaõ
Appellante
Appellar.
Appellidar
Appellido.

A Q.
Aquélla
Aquélle
Aquelloutro
Aquillo.

A R.
Armellas
Arrepellado
Arrepellaõ
Arrepellar.

A T.
Atropellado
Atropellar.

A V.
Avillanado.

B A.
Bacellada
Bacêllo
Barbélla
Barrélla.

B E.
Bella
Béllamente
Bello
Belleza.
Belleguim
Béllico
Bellicôfo.
Belligero
Belluîno.

B U:

B U.

Bulla
Bullário.

C A.

Calliope
Camillo
Cavillaçaõ
Cavillofamente
Caballina
Cadélla
Cadellinha
Callo
Camartello
Cambadella
Cancella
Capella
Capellaõ
Capelláda
Capellania
Capello
Capillar
Caftella
Caftello
Cafullo
Cafulla
Cavalla
Cavallaria
Cavalleiro
Cavállo.

C E.

Cebólla
Cebollál
Cebollinho
Chancellér
Chancellaria
Célla
Celleiro.

C L.

Clavellina

C O.

Codicillo
Colla
Collado
Collar
Colleira
Collaçaõ

Collateral
Collecçaõ
Collecta
Collectivo
Collectôr
Colléga
Collegiada
Collegial
Collégio
Colligar
Colligir
Collyrio
Collo
Collocaçaõ
Collocar
Colloquio.

C O M.

Compellir
Compoftélla
Conftellaçaõ
Corrollario
Covello
Courella.

D E.

Della
Dellas
Delle
Delles
Degollado
Degollaçaõ
Degollar
Degolladouro.

D I.

Diftillaçaõ
Diftillador
Diftillar.

D O.

Donzélla.

D U.

Duéllo.

E B.

Ebulliçâo.

E L L.

Ella

Ellas

Ellas
Elle
Elles
Elléboro
Ellipse
Elliptico.

E M.

Emolliente
Emollir.

E N.

Enallage
Encapellado
Encapellar
Encaftellado
Encaftellar
Encelleirar.

E Q.

Equipollencia
Equipollente.

E S.

Efcabellado.
Efcabello
Efcudélla
Efcudellaõ
Eftillaçaõ
Eftilládo
Eftillar
Eftillicidio
Eftrella
Eftrellado.

E X.

Excellencia
Excellente
Expellir.

F A.

Falla
Fallacha
Fallacia
Fallador
Fallar
Fallecer
Fallecido
Fallencia
Fallido

F E.

Ferdizello

F L.

Flagellante
Flagéllo

F O.

Folle
Follículo
Fontello

G A.

Gabella
Gallado
Galladura
Gallar
Gallego
Gállia
Gallicado
Gallicar
Gallico
Gallinha
Gallinhaço
Gallinheira
Gallinheiro
Gallinhólla
Galliópoli
Galliota
Galliza
Gállo
Gamella
Gazella.

G O.

Golla.

H E.

Hellefponto
Hendecafyllabo
Hollanda
Hypállage.

J A.

Janella
Janelleira
Janellinha
Jarméllo

I.

Illaçaõ
Illaquear
Illativo
Illegitimo

Illiciador

Illéfo
Illiçar
Illiciador
Illicitamente
Illicito
Illocavel
Illudido
Illudir
Illuminação
Illuminado
Illuminar
Illuminativo
Illufaõ
Illufo
Illuftração
Illuftrar
Illuftre
Illuftriſſimo
Illyrio
Imbella
Impellir
Incapillato
Infallivel
Inintelligivel
Intervallo.

L.

Libello
Lordello
Loufella.

M.

Marcella
Marcellina
Marcello
Martellada
Martellar
Martello
Martellinho
Malfallante
Mallogrado
Mamillar
Medulla
Mellifluo
Mello
Metallico
Millenário
Millefimo

Mirandella
Mifcellania
Molle
Molleira
Molleza
Mollice
Mollidaõ
Mollificânte
Mollificar
Mollinar
Monofyllabo.

N.

Nella
Nellas
Nelle
Nelles
Nigélla
Novélla
Novelleiro
Nulla
Nullidade
Nullo
Nuzellos.

O.

Odivellas
Ollaria
Olleiro
Ouguella.

P.

Palla
Palládio
Pallante
Pallas
Palliado
Palliar
Pallidez
Pallido
Pallio
Paradella
Parallaxe
Parallelo
Parallelogramo
Pelle
Pellefinha
Pellica

P   Pellicula

Pellicula
Panella
Pimpinella
Phillis
Pollegada
Pollegar
Pollez
Polluçaõ
Polluto
Polyfyllabo
Portacóllo
Portélla
Poftilla
Poufafolles
Prunélle.
Pulmella
Pupilla
Pupillo
Pufillanimidade
Pufillanime.

Q
Quartella.

R.
Rabadélla
Rebellado
Rebellaõ
Rebellarfe
Rebelliaõ
Rélla
Rodofólle
Rodopello
Rofélla
Ruélla

S E.
Sella
Sellado
Sellador
Sellagaõ
Sellar
Selleiro
Sello
Sentinella
Sibylla
Sigillo
Sigillado

Sobrepelliz
Sugillaçaõ
Syllaba
Syllabático
Syllábico
Syllogifar
Syllogifmo.

T.
Tabélla
Tabelliaõ
Tabelliôa
Titillaçaõ
Titillar
Tólla
Tollice
Tollo
Torcicóllo
Tranquillidade
Tranquillo
Trella
Trifyllabo
Tunicella
Tullio.

V.
Vacillaçaõ
Vacillante
Vacillar
Valla
Vallado
Vallar
Valle
Vaffallagem
Vaffallo.

V E.
Velleidade
Vellicaçam
Vellicar
Vello
Vellofo
Vellûdo
Verdefélla.

V I.
Villa
Villanía

Villa-

Villaāmente   Vitella
Villaõ   Vitellino.
Villaā

N.B. *Annullar* fignifies to *annul*; but *annular* is an adjective, and fignifies *annular*, or in the form of a ring. *L* is doubled by fome in the words *pelo*, *pela* (for) thus *pello*, *pella*.

M.

M is to be doubled in

Accommodar
Commemoraçaõ
Commenda
Commenfurar
Commentar
Commerciar
Commetter
Comminaçaõ
Commiferaçaõ
Commiffaõ
Commiffario
Commoçaõ
Commodo
Commover
Commum
Commungar
Communicar
Communidade
Commutar
Confummar.
Defaccommodat
Defcommodo
Dilemma.
Emmadeirar
Emmadeixar
Emmagrecer
Emmanquecer
Emmaffar
Emmudecer
Engommar
Epigramma.
Flamma
Flammante

Flâmmula.
Gemma
Gomma
Grammatica.
Immaculada
Immanente
Immarceffivel
Immaterial
Immaturo
Immediatamente
Immemoravel
Immenfo
Immenfuravel
Immobilidade
Immoderadamente
Immodefto
Immodico
Immolar
Immortalifar
Immortificado
Immóvel
Immudavel
Immundo
Immunidade
Immutavel
Incómmodo
Incommunicavel
Incommutavel
Inflammar.
Mamma
Mammar.
Recommendar.
Sómma

      Sommar

Sommar Summidade
Summa Symmetria, *and some others.*
Summario

N. B. *M*, and not *n*, is always to be made ufe of before *b, m, p.*

N.

N is likewife doubled in feveral verbs compounded with *an, en, in, con*; as, *annelar, annexa, annaõs annata, annel, Anna, anno, annular, connexaõ, connexo, depennar, empennar, ennaftrar, ennegrecer, innato, innavegavel, innocencia, manná, Marianna, panno, penna* when it fignifies a pen, *tyranno,* and fome others.

P.

This letter is to be doubled in words beginning with *p* compounded with the Latin prepofitions *ad, ob, fub*; as, *apparato, apparecer, oppôr, opprimir, fuppor, Philippe, poppa,* &c.

N. B. *Pappa* fignifies *pap,* or a fort of fpoon-meat for children; but *papa* fignifies *the pope.*

R.

The *r* is doubled in fuch words as are ftrongly pronounced in the middle; as, *guerra, arrancar, arredar, arrimar, arruinar, carregar, carro,* &c.

S.

The *s* is to be doubled in the Portuguefe fuperlatives, becaufe it is doubled in the Latin roots; it is alfo doubled in the following words:

Abbadêffa	Acceffo
Baronêffa	Aggreffor
Condêffa	Apreffar
Priorèffa	Amaffar
Affar	Arremeffar
Affanhar	Affaltar
Affegurar	Affeyo
Affignar	Affeffor
Affolar	Affim

Affiftir

Affiftir	Noffa
Affombrar	Effa
Affoprar	Effe
Affobiar	Iffo
Affuftar	Offo
Atraveffar	Paffear
Neceffitar	Paffar
Niffo	Remeffa
Noffd	Ingreffo, *and many others.*

T.

T is doubled in the following words and their derivatives:

Attemperar	Commétter
Attençaõ	Demittir
Attender	Enfittar
Attentar	Fitta
Attenuaçaõ	Intrometter
Attenuar	Omittir
Attónito	Permittir
Attracçaõ	Promotter
Attractivo	Remetter
Attrahir	Remittir
Attribuir	Sétta
Attribûto	Settenta
Attriçaõ	Settecentos
Attrito	Tranfmittir.

Of the Quantity of Syllables, and their Sound.

Of Words that make their penultima in a.

N. B. You muft remember what we have faid above about the accents.

All words ending in *abo, aba, aco, aca, acho, acha, aço, aça, ado, ada, afo, afa, ago, aga, agem, agre, albo, alba, alo, ala*, have the penultimas long; as, *diába, mangába, macáco, macáca, caváca, mingácho, garnácha, madráço, linháça, amádo, punháda,* (except *relámpago, antropófago, lévado,* and *cágado,* which are fhort in the penultima), *abáfo, abáfa, faramágo, adíga,* (except *eftámago* or *eftômago, ámago, amáraco,*

amáraco, which are short), *trabálho, toálha, badálo*, (except *anomalo, búfalo, escândalo*, which are short), *tanchágem, vinágre.*

Words ending in *amo, ama, anho, anha, ano, ana*, have their penultima long; as, *escámo, couráma, caſtánho, aránha, engáno, peſtána*; except *pámpano, tympano, bîgamo.*

Words ending in *apo, apa, aque, aro, ara*, have their penultima long; as, *guardanapo, ſolapa, baſbaque, empáro, feára*; except *cântaro, púcaro, lápa-ro, búfaro, lúparo, pífaro, pícaro, cámera, támara, páſſaro, Lázaro, barbaro, cócaras*, &c.

Words ending in *arro, arra, ato, ata, avo, ava, axo, axas*, make the penultima long; as, *bizárro, bizárra, biſcáto, pataráta, eſcravo, eſcrava*, (except *concava* and *biſavô*), *cartaxo, tarraxa.*

Of Words that make their Penultima in e.

All words ending in *ebo, eba, edo, eda, eſa*, have their penultima long; as, *mancébo, mancéba, azédo, azéda, ſanefa.*

Words ending in *efe* are long; as, *magaréfe* : as well as thoſe ending in *eco, eca, eço, eça*; as, *bonéco, bonéca, cabéço, cabéça.*

Words ending in *ego, ega*, are long; as, *morcé-go, ſocégo, relégo, entréga, alléga*; except *cónego, tráſego, córrego, ſôfrego, pêcego, fólego, bátega, cócegas.*

Words ending in *ejo, eja, elo, ela*, are long; as, *caranguéjo, bocéjo, igréja, Alentéjo, emvéja, martélo, queréla.*

Words ending in *emo, ema, eno, ena*, are long; as, *suprêmo, poſtêma, acêno, açucéna*; except *apózema.*

N. B. The penultima is short in the word *íngreme.*

Words ending in *epo, epa, epe, eque, ero, era*, are long; as, *decêpo, carépa, julépe, moleque, ſevéro, ſevera, tempéro* (when a noun), and *tempéro* (when a verb) : except *áspero, próspero.*

Words ending in *eſo, eſa, ezo, eza, eto, eta, ete, evo, eva, eve*, are long; as, *acéſo, acéſa, deſprézo,*

gran-

grandéza, and *despréſo* (when a verb), *entremêto, galhêta, ramalhête, bofête, atrêvo, atrêva, atrêve.*

Of words that make their penultima in i.

Words ending in *ibo, iba, ibe, icho, icha, iche, ico, ica, iço, iça, ice, ido, ida, iſo, iſa, iſe,* have the penultima long; as, *eſtribo, arriba, arríbe, eſguicho, eſguicha, azeviche, panico,* (a fort of ſtuff) *botiça;* except *mecânico, ecuménico, critico, politico, pânico* (panick), and ſome others borrowed from the Greek and Latin. In *iço, iça,* &c. as, *roliço, preguiça, velhice, marido, medida;* except *húmido, pálido, hórrido,* and ſome others derived from the Latin. In *iſo, iſa,* &c. as, *borriſo, alcatíſa, patiſe.*

Words ending in *igo* and *iga* are long; as, *amigo, amiga;* except *pródigo, prodiga.*

Words ending in *ijo* and *ija,* are long; as, *afflijo, artemija.*

Words ending in *ilho, ilha,* are long; as, *atilho, beatilha.* Others ending in *ilo, ila;* as, *gorgomilo, perfila, desfila.*

Words ending in *imo, ima,* have the penultima long; as, *opimo, cadimo, eſgrima, laſtima* (when a verb); except *láſtima* (when a noun), *Jeronimo, péſſimo,* and all the ſuperlatives, *anónimo,* and ſome others.

Words ending in *inho, inha, ino, ina, ipo, ipa, ipe,* have the penultima long; as, *conſtipo, conſtipa, Eurípo, acipípe.* Others in *iquo, iqua, ique, iro, ira, ire;* as, *iniquo, iniqua, lambique, retiro, mentira, ſuſpire.*

Words ending in *iſo, iſa, izo, iza, ito, ita, ivo, iva, ixo, ixa,* are long in the penultima; as, *aviſo, camiſa, juizo, ajuiza, altivo, altiva, prolixo, prolixa, apito, cabrito;* except *púlpito, vómito, decrépito, eſpírito, débito,* and ſome others.

Rules for ſuch Words as make their Penultima in o.

Words ending in *oho, oba, obe, obra, obro, obre,* have their penultima long; as, *lého, lôba, arrôba,*

P 4   *arrôbe,*

arrôbe, glóba, alcôva, óbra, óbra, côbre, côbra, dô-bro.

Words ending in *ocho, ocha, oco, oca, oço, oça, odo, oda, ode, oſo, oſa, oſe,* have the penultima long; as, *agarrócho, garrócha, carócha, biôco* (except *alíiloco), maſſaróca, minhóca, almôço, môça* (a girl), *móça* or *moſſa* (a notch), *almóço* (when a verb), *carróça, lôdo, bôda, bóde, póde* (the third perſon ſingular of the preſent indicative of the verb *poder*), *pôde* (the third perſon ſingular of the preterperfect definite of the ſame verb), *galhófa, bófe.*

Words ending in *ofro, ofra, ofre,* are long; as, *alcaxofra, cofre, enxôfre.*

Words ending in *ogo, oga, ogue,* are long; as, *affógo, affóga, affógue, deſafógo* when a verb, and *deſafôgo* when a noun.

Words ending in *ojo, oja,* have the penultima long; as, *deſpójo* when a verb, *nôjo, deſpôjo* when a noun.

Words ending in *olo, ola, ole,* are long; as, *vióla, galinbóla, bóla, engóle, miólo, bóla, rebôlo, tôlo, sebôla;* except *pêrola, frivolo, benévolo, malévolo.*

Words ending in *omo, oma, ome,* have the penultima long; as, *mordômo, redôma, fóme;* except *Thomé.*

Words ending in *onho, onha, ono, ona,* have the penultima long; as, *biſônho, riſônha, dôno, atafôna, dóna;* except *altíſono* and *uníſono.*

Words ending in *opla, opo, opa, ope, opro, opra, opre, oque,* have the penultima long; as, *manópla, tópo. topa, galópe, aſſópro* when a verb, *aſſópra, aſſópre, aſſôpro* when a noun, *botóque.*

Words ending in *oro, ora, ore,* are long in the penultima; as, *penbóro, penbóra, penbóre, chóro* when a noun; *chóro,* when a verb; except *bácoro, rêmora, pólvora, árvore.*

Words ending in *orro, orra,* are long; as, *foccôrro, môrro, cachôrra;* and ſome others ending in *oſo, oſe, oſa, ozo, oza;* as, *primoróſo, primoróſa, induſtriôſo, induſtrióſa, ciôzo, cióza, deſcóſe.*

Words ending in *oto, ota, ote*, have their penultima long; as, *gôto, gôta, béta, devóto, fróta, capéte, garrote.*

Words ending in *ovo, ova, ove*, are long in the penultima; as, *óvo, corcôva, apróve.*

Words ending in *oxo, oxa*, are long in the penultima; as, *rôxo, rôxa, pintarrôxo.*

Rules for such Words as make their Penultima in u.

Words ending in *ubo, uba, ubro, ubra, ucho, ucha, uco, uca, uço, uça*, make the penultima long; as, *adúbo, adúba*; except *súccubo, íncubo*, and some others; *incúbro, incúbra, macbúcho, embúcha, cadúco, cadúca, rebuço, embuça.*

Words ending in *udo, uda, ude, ufo, ufa, ufe, ugo, uga, ujo, uja*, have the penultima long, as, *felpúdo, felpúda, almúde, pantúfo, adúfa, adúfe, sanguesúga, caramújo, azambúja.*

Words ending in *ulbo, ulha, ulbe, ulo, ula, ule, umo, uma, ume, unho, unha, unhe*; as, *bagúlbo, borbúlha, entulbe, engúlo, engúla, bulebúle*; except *vocábulo, vestíbulo, ángulo, régulo, opúsculo, trémulo, patíbulo, thuríbulo*, and some others; *consúmo, consúma, cardúme, testemúnho, testemúnha, empunhe.*

Words ending in *uno, una, une, upo, upa, upe, uque, uro, ura, ure*, are long in the penultima; as, *defúno, fortúna, desúne, apúpo, apúpa, apúpe, estúque, madúro, madura, apúre.*

Words ending in *ufo, ufa, ufe, uzo, uza, uze, uto, uta, ute, uxo, uxa, uxe*, have the penultima long; as, *parafúfo, parafúfa, parafufe, redúzo, reduza, redúze, condúto, labuta, enxúta, labúte*; except *cômputo* when a noun; *repúxo, empúxa, empúxe*; and some others ending in *uvo, uva, uve*; as, *viúvo, viúva, enviúve.*

N. B. When the penultima is immediately followed by another vowel, you must make the following observations.

A before

A before *e* muſt be accentuated with the acute accent, and pronounced accordingly ; as, *ſãe, cãe* : but before *i* has no accent.

A before *o* muſt be pronounced and accentuated thus, *bacalbáo* ; but when the relative *o* is added to the third perſon ſingular of the preſent indicative, then *a* has no accent ; as, *âma·o*.

E before *a* is accentuated thus, *balêa* ; and ſometimes with the acute, as *aſſemblêa, idéa*, and ſome others ; and ſometimes has no accent at all, as in *gávea, fêmea*, and ſome others.

E before *o* is exceeding ſonorous and long, as in *cbapéo, coruçbéo* ; except *páteo, férreo, plúmbeo, au-reo, argênteo*.

I before *a, e, o*, is long ; as, *dizía, fazía, almo-tolía* ; except ſuch as are borrowed from the Latin ; as, *néſcia, comédia, feria, ciéncia, prudência*, and *ſá-bia* when an adjective, &c. *I* before *o* and *e*, is long ; as, *deſvíe, deſvío* ; except *vício* and ſome others.

O before *a* is accentuated thus, *coróa, tôa, móa, eſmôa*.

O before *e* is long in the words *dóe, móe, róe*, and in the verb *ſóe* when it ſignifies *to be wont* ; but when it ſignifies *to ſound*, it is to be accentuated thus, *ſôe*.

U before *a* is long ; as *rúa, cbarrúa* ; except *mel-liflua, înſua*.

U before *e* and *o* is long ; as, *conclúo, recúo, con-clúe, recúe* ; except *mellifluo*, and ſome others derived from the Latin.

CHAP.

CHAP. IX.

Etymology of the Portuguese Tongue from the Latin.

THE Portuguese retains so great an affinity to the Latin, that several words of the last are preserved in the first, by only allowing a small alteration; as it may be easily seen in the following observations.

I. The *o* of the Latin words is preserved in some Portuguese ones; nay, some Latin words are entirely preserved in the Portuguese; as, *hosped:, corda, porta,* &c.

II. The *u* is changed into *o*; as, *forca, goloso, estopa, mosca, amamos,* &c. from *furca, gulosus, stupa, musca, amamus,* &c.

III. The diphthong *au* is frequently changed into *ou*; as, *louvavel, ouro, couve, mouro,* &c. from *laudabilis, aurum, caulis, maurus,* &c.

IV. The *e* is preserved in several Portuguese words; as, *certo, servo, erva, terra, ferro,* &c. from *certus, servus, herba, terra, ferrum,* &c.

V. The *e* takes the place of *i*; as, *enfermo, seco,* &c. from *infirmus, ficus,* &c. and the *i* is sometimes preserved, as in *indigno, benigno,* &c. from *indignus, benignus,* &c.

VI. The *b* is also changed into *v*; as, *arvore, duvidar, dever, estava, amava,* &c. from *arbor, dubitare, debere, stabat, amabat,* &c.

VII. The *c* is changed very often into *g*; as, *digo, agudo, amigo, migalha,* &c. from *dico, acutus, amicus, mica,* &c.

VIII. *Cl* is changed into *ch*; as, *chamar, chave,* from *clamare, clavis,* &c.

IX. When the *c* in Latin is followed by *t*, this letter is changed into *ç*; as, *acção, dicção, liçõ,* &c. from *acto, dictio, lectio,* &c. and sometimes the

the *c* before *t* is changed into *i* ; as, *feito*, *'leito*, *noite*, *leite*, *peito*, &c. from *factus*, *lectum*, *nocte*, *lacte*, *pectus*, &c. Finally, both the *c* and *t* are preserved in a great number of words ; as, *acto*, *afflicto*, *distincto*, &c. from *actus*, *afflictus*, *distinctus*, &c.

X. The *d* is several times lost ; as, *roer*, *excluir*, *raio*, &c. from *rodere*, *excludere*, *radius*, &c.

XI. The *f* is frequently preserved; as in *filho*, *fazer*, *fervor*, *formoso*, &c. from *filius*, *facere*, *fervor*, *formosus*, &c.

XII. The *g* is changed into *i* ; as, *reino*, from *regnum*. Sometimes it is quite lost, as in *dedo*, *frio*, *setta*, *final*, *bainha*, &c. from *digitus*, *frigus*, *sagitta*, *signum*, *vagina*, &c.

XIII. The *h* is placed instead of the *l* ; as, *alho*, from *allium*. Sometimes it is added ; as, *artilho*, *alheo*, *folha*, *conselho*, &c. from *articulus*, *alienus*, *folium*, *consilium*, &c.

XIV. The *n* is sometimes added, and sometimes taken off ; as, *mancha*, *ilha*, *Salitre*, *espôso*, from *macula*, *insula*, *sal nitrum*, *sponsus*, &c.

XV. The *mn* is preserved by many Portuguese writers in the words *alumno*, *calumnia*, *columna*, *damno*, *solemne*, *somno*, from *alumnus*, *calumnia*, *columna*, *damnum*, &c.

XVI. The double *nn* of the Latin is preserved in several words ; as in *anno*, *innocencia*, *innocuo*, *innavegavel*, *innovar*, *connexo*, &c. from *annus*, *innocentia*, *innocuus*, *innavigabilis*, *innovare*, *connexus*, &c.

XVII. The *gn* and *gm* are preserved in several Portuguese words ; as in *augmento*, *fragmento*, *enigma*, *benigno*, *digno*, *indigno*, *ignominia*, &c. from *augmentum*, *fragmentum*, *ænigma*, *benignus*, *dignus*, &c.

XVIII. The *e* and the *i* after *n* are sometimes changed into *h* ; as in *aranha*, *vinha*, *Hespanha*, *castanha*, &c. from *aranea*, *vinea*, *Hispania*, *castanea*, &c.

XIX. The *p* is changed into *b* ; as in *cabra*, *cabello*, *cabeça*, &c. from *capra*, *capillus*, *caput*, &c.

Some-

Sometimes *pl* is changed into *ch*; as, *chaga, chóro, chuva,* &c. from *plaga, ploro, pluvia,* &c.

XX. The *q* is changed into *g*; as, *igual, alguem, antigo, agoa, aguia,* &c. from *equus, aliquis, antiquus, aqua, aquila,* &c.

XXI. The *t* is likewise changed into *d*; as, *cadea, fado, lado, nadar, piedade,* &c. from *catena, fatum, latus, natare, pietas,* &c. The *ti* of the Latin is sometimes changed into *ça,* and sometimes into *ci*; as in *graça, clemencia, paciencia,* &c. from *gratia, clementia, patientia,* &c.

N. B. All these alterations are not general in all the words, but are used in several; and on some occasions the Latin word is preserved without any mutilation or variation. And as it would be endless to pretend to shew all the affinity between the Portuguese and the Latin, I shall only observe, that they sometimes add, and sometimes take off letters from the Latin roots.; as in *facil, debil, final, material, estrepito, estomago, expectadór, especular,* &c. from *facilis, debilis, finalis, strepitus, spectator,* &c.

END of the SECOND PART.

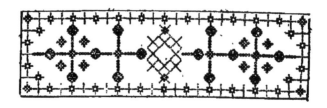

A NEW
PORTUGUESE
GRAMMAR.

The different Significations of andar, *to go.*

ANDAR a pé	TO go on foot.
Andar a cavallo	To ride on horſeback.
Andar pella poſta	To ride *or* go poſt.
Andar em coche,	To ride in a coach.
Andar a vela,	To ſail.
Andar pella bolina,	To ſail with a ſide wind.
Andar para diante.	To go forward.
Andar para traz,	To go backward.
Andar a trás de alguem,	To go behind, *or* after one, *alſo* to follow, to preſs, to ſolicit a perſon.

Andar

Andar ás apalpadellas,	To grope along, to grope *or* feel one's way.
Andar com o tempo,	To go according to the times.
Andar pejáda,	To be with child, *or* big with child.
Andar fahida,	(*speaking of a bitch*) To be proud.
Andar perdido,	To go aftray.
Andar de pé,	To be fickifh, *but not bed-rid.*
Andar com honra,	To act like an honeft man.
Anda,	Go.
Anda para diante,	Go on.
Andar de efguélha,	To go fideling.
Andar de mal para peor,	Out of the frying-pan into .the fire.
Andar de reixa com alguem,	To bear one a grudge, to have a fpleen againft him, to owe him a fpite.
Com o andar do tempo,	At long run.
Andar de galope,	To gallop.
Andar em corpo,	To be in cuerpo, *or* to be without the upper coat or cloak, fo as to difcover the true fhape of the cuerpo or body.
Anda o mundo as aveffas,	The world is come about.
Andar efpalhados,	To lie about.
Andar trabalhando nalguma o-bra,	To be about fome piece of work.
Andar de gatinhas,	To go crawling.
Andar de cócoras,	To go on one's breech.
Andar dizendo,	To publifh *or* report.

The different Significations of dar and dar-fe.

Dar,	To give, to ftrike.
Dar a entender,	To make one believe.
Dar fé,	To credit, to believe, *alfo* to perceive, to defcry, to take notice, to fmell out.
Dar or *vender fiada.*	To fell upon credit.
Dar á luz.	To publifh.
Dar fenhoria,	To call one a gentleman.
Dar tu, or *fallar a alguem por tu,*	To thee, and thou one.

Dar

Dar-ſe a partido, or *lançar-ſe ao partido de alguem*,	To ſide with one, to be for him.
Dar palavra,	To promiſe.
Dar huma ſalva,	To give a volley of ſhot, or to make a diſcharge of guns in honour of ſome perſons of quality.
Dar fiador,	To bail.
Dar principio, or *fim*,	To begin, or end.
Dar conta,	To give an account.
Dar-ſe ao eſtudo,	To apply one's ſelf to ſtudy.
Dar em que fallar,	To make one ſpeak, to give an occaſion to be talked of.
Dar entrada,	To give acceſs to.
Dar cauſa,	To give cauſe.
Dar em que entender,	To vex one ſadly, to trouble one.
Dar de beber,	To give drink.
Dar couces,	To kick.
Dar hum coſcorraõ,	To give a box on the ear.
Dar pancadas,	To beat with a cudgel.
Dar murros,	To cuff.
Dar marradas,	To butt, as rams do.
Dar o faro a alguem de alguma couſa,	To ſmell out a matter.
Dar huma eſtocada,	To give a thruſt.
Dar os bons dias,	To bid one good-morrow.
Dar a guardar,	To give in keeping.
Dar á coſta,	To run a-ground.
Dar com alguem,	To meet with one by chance, to light upon a perſon.
Dar em alguem,	To ſtrike one, alſo to accuſe one.
Dar cartas,	To deal or give the cards.
Dar ſobre o inimigo,	To fall upon the enemy.
Dar os parabens,	To congratulate.
Dar os parabens a alguem da ſua chegada,	To bid one welcome.
Dar a maõ ajudando.	To give a helping hand.
Dar a eſcolher,	To let one take his choice.
Dar enfado a alguem,	To moleſt one.
Dar no alvo,	To hit the mark.
Dar as coſtas,	To run away, to betake one's ſelf to flight.
Dar parte de hum negocio,	To impart a buſineſs.

Dar

Dar pello amor de Deos,	To give for God's fake.
Dar huma furra,	To beat one foundly.
Dar huma volta em redondo,	To walk a turn.
Dar huma vifta de olhos,	To caft an eye on.
Dar alcance ao que fe dezeja,	To obtain, or compafs one's wifh.
Dar fufpiros,	To figh.
Dar ouvidos,	To give hearing.
Dar em rofto,	To upbraid, to caft in the teeth
Da cá,	Give hither.
Deu-me huma dor,	I was taken with a pain.
Dar que fazer a alguem, or occupar alguem,	To employ one, to fet him at work, to fet him upon fome bufinefs.
Dar horas,	To ftrike.
O relogio dá horas,	The clock ftrikes.
Dar a alma a Deos,	To give up the ghoft, to die.
Dar comfigo em alguma parte,	To caft one's felf into a place, or to go to a place.
Dar leite,	To fuckle.
Dar garrote,	To ftrangle.
Dar vozes.	To cry out, to bawl.
Dar o fol nos olhos,	Is for the fun to fhine in one's eyes.
Dar razbens,	To debate, or contend.
Dar comfigo no chaõ,	To fall upon the ground.
Dar fruto,	To bear fruit.
Dar as maõs,	To fhake hands.
Dar com a porta na cara de alguem,	To fhut the door upon one.
Dar com a porta nos olhos a alguma coufa, (metaph.)	To flight, to defpife a thing.
Dar preffa,	To prefs or haften.
Dar tregoas, (metaph.)	To refpite, to give fome refpite
Efta traveffa vai dar á rua larga,	This lane ftrikes, or goes into the broad ftreet.
Dei no penfamento de, &c.	It came into my head to, &c.
Quem me déra eftar em cafa!	How fain wou'd I be at home!
Naõ fabe aonde ha de dar com a cabeça,	He does not know which way to turn himfelf.
Ifto vos ha de dar na cabeça,	The mifchief will light upon your own head.
Dar com a cabeça pellas paredes,	To beat one's head againft the wall.

Q   Dar

Dar em todos, or dizer mal de todos,	To have a satirical virulent tongue, to spare no body.
Dar boa conta de si,	To give a good account of himself, to behave cleverly.
Dar á conta,	To pay on account.
Eu darei conta disso,	I'll be answerable for it.
Elle deu em ir áquelle lugar,	He began to use that place.
Dar em droga,	To grow a very drug.
Dar em ridicularias,	To grow, or become ridiculous.
Dár huma figa a alguem,	To flirt at one, to fig, to give the fico.
Dar-se por culpado,	To acknowledge one's self guilty.
De nenhuma forte vos deis por entendido, or achado,	Take no notice of any thing.
Dar-se por aggravado,	To make a shew of anger.
Dar-se por satisfeito,	To rest satisfied.
Dar-se por vencido,	To submit, to surrender one's self a prisoner, or to yield a point.
Dar-se por desentendido,	To feign one's self ignorant, to take no notice of any thing, to make as if one saw nor knew not.
Quando se der a occasiaõ,	When occasion shall require it
Dar-se pressa,	To be in haste, to make haste
Elle deu-se a toda a forte de vicios,	He gave himself over to all manner of vices.
Naõ se me dá disso,	I matter it not.
Que se vos dá a vos disso?	What have you to do with it?
Pouco se me dá,	I care but little.
Naõ se lhe dá de morrer,	He matters not his dying.
Ellas daõ-se muyto bem,	They agree mighty well together.
Esta carne naõ se dá bem comigo,	This meat does not agree with me.

Of the different Significations of the Verb estar.

We use the verb *estar* to mark an action of repose, by putting the verb that follows in the gerund; as, *elle está escrevendo,* he is writing.

Estar has several other significations; as,

Estar

Estar em pé,	To stand upright.
Estar bem, ou mal,	To be well, or ill.
Estar assentado,	To be sitting.
Estar para sahir para fòra,	To be just going out.
Estar com o sentido em França, or *estar com o sentido em outra parte,*	To have one's wits a woolgathering.
Está muyto bem,	It is well, it is very well.
Está para chover,	It is a going to rain.
Estar para cahir,	To be ready to fall.
Estar para morrer,	To be like to die.
Estar em duvida,	To be in doubt.
Estaremos a ver,	We will expect the issue.
Estar com huma maõ sobre a outra.	To stand idle.
Estar em casa,	To stay at home.
Isto vos está bem,	This becomes you very well.
Aquilo naõ me está bem,	That does not become me well.
Estar dormindo,	To lie sleeping.
Estar fazendo,	To be a doing.
Estar de nojo,	To be in mourning.
Estar álerta,	To look heedfully about.
Estar de sentinella,	To stand centry.
Estar alegre,	To be merry.
Elle está como quer,	He lives in clover.
Estar em perigo,	To be in danger.
Estar encostado,	To lean upon.
Estar esperando,	To expect.
Estar muyto tempo,	To stay a good while.
Estar calado,	To be hushed.
Estar ou viver com outros,	To dwell with others.
Estar de cima,	To lie over.
Estar debaxo,	To lie under.
Estar bem aviado,	To be in an ill taking.
Estar a espera,	To lie in wait.
Estar enamorado,	To be in love.
Estar na cama,	To be a-bed.
Estar de cama,	To be bed-rid.
Estar no campo,	To live in the country.
Estar com saude, or *de saude,*	To be in health.
Estar quieto,	To stand still, or to be quiet.
Estar neutral,	To stand neuter.
Estarei por tudo o que vos parecer mais conveniente,	I shall stand to whatsoever you shall think fitting.

A difficuldade está em, &c.	The difficulty consists in, &c.
Estar por alguem,	To stand for one, to be of his side.
Estar por, or em lugar de, &c.	To stand for, or signify.
Elle estava na altura do Cabo da Boa Esperança,	He stood off the Cape of Good Hope.
Eu naõ quero estar as razoens comvosco,	I won't stand, or dispute, with you.
Está quanto quizeres,	Stay as long as you please.
Aonde estais de casa?	Where do you live?
Estarei pello que disser a pessoa que for de vosso mayor agrado,	I'll refer it to whom you please.
Naõ podemos estar por isso,	We can't stand to that.
Naõ quero estar pella vossa sentença,	I won't take your judgment.
Como está vmce?	How do you do, sir?

Estar, joined with the infinitive of a verb and the particle *para*, signifies to be ready, or about doing a thing, which has always reference to the signification of the verb; as,

Estou para ir,	I am going, I am ready to go.
Estou para comprar hum cavallo,	I am about buying a horse.
Estou para casarme,	I am going to be married.
Esta casa esta para cahir,	This house is ready to fall.
Estou para dizer,	I dare say.
Naõ está no meu poder,	It is not in my power.
Estar com a boca aberta (metaph.)	To stare, to look, to hearken attentively.
Estar de regimento,	To keep to a diet.
Estar fiado em alguem,	To trust to, to rely or depend upon one.
Estar no fundo,	To lie at the bottom.
Estar de fronte,	To lie over-against.
Estar em competencia,	To stand in competition.
Estar ao lume,	To stand by the fire.
Estar de longe,	To stand at a distance.
Estar ao ar,	To stand in the air.
Estar alto,	To stand high, or in a high place.
Estar á maõ direita de alguem,	To be at one's right hand, to have the first place.

Elle

Elle esteve em perigo de afogar-se,	He was like to be drowned.
Naõ estar no caso de, &c.	To not be able, or in the case of, &c.
Estar á ordem de alguem,	To be at one's disposal.
Isso naõ está nos termos,	That is not right, it won't do.
Naõ estou no caso,	I don't understand the case.
Estar ás razoens,	To contend, to strive, or quarrel.
Estar bem com alguem,	To be in favour with one, to live in friendship with him.
Estar bem,	To be well, to be at one's ease.
Bem aviado estaria eu, se, &c.	It wou'd be very bad for me, indeed, if, &c.
Estar em conceito de bomem honrado,	To be looked upon as an honest man.
Estar na fé,	To believe, to think, or suppose.
Estar de posse,	To possess, to have the possession of a thing.
Deixai estar isso,	Let that alone.
Estar em si,	To be in one's right wits.
Estar fora de si,	To be out of one's wits.
Deixaivos estar (a sort of threatening)	I'll be revenged on you, you shall pay for it.

We have already observed the difference between *ser*, and *estar*. See page 55.

Of the different Significations of fazer *and* fazer-se.

Fazer signifies *to do, to make, to create*; also *to form of materials*; also *to feign, to seem, to make as if.*

Elle fez que naõ o via,	He made as if he did not see it
Fazer huma saude,	To drink or to toast a health.
Elle lhe fez cortar a cabeça,	He caused his head to be cut off.
Fazer pé atraz (metaph.)	To fall or draw back, to give ground; also yield, to submit.
Que tendes vos que fazer com isto?	What have you to do with it? or what is that to you?

Q 3   *Fazer*

Fazer brio de alguma cousa,	To make a pride of a thing, to take glory in it.
Fazer fim ao dexejo,	To satisfy one's defire, or longing.
Fazer por alguma cousa,	To take pains, to endeavour, to labour to a certain purpofe, to work for a certain end.
Faço por iffo,	I endeavour after it.
Fazer ao negocio, or *ao cafa,*	To come to the purpofe.
Fazer efmolas,	To give alms.
Fazer gafto,	To fpend.
Fazer gofto,	To like, to be pleafed with.
Fazer o gofto, or *a vontade a alguem,*	To pleafe one, to comply with one's defire.
Fazer parallelo,	To parallel, to compare.
Fazer de comer,	To drefs the meat.
Fazer jumo,	To fmoak.
Fazer auzente a alguem,	To believe one abfent.
Faz frio,	It is cold.
Fazer gente,	To raife men, foldiers.
Fazer em pedaços,	To pull into pieces.
Fazer zombaria de alguem,	To mock, or to laugh at a perfon.
Naõ façais cafo diffo,	Do not mind that.
Fazer agoada,	To take in frefh water.
Ifto me faz vir a agoa á boca,	This makes my teeth, or mouth, water.
Fazer alto,	To halt in a march.
Fazer cofa (in playing at draughts)	To put two men in the fame fquare.
Fazer a cea,	To get fupper ready.
Fazer caras,	To make mouths.
Fazer enredos,	To form a fecret defign againft another.
Fazer carrancas,	To powt.
Fazer cafo,	To make account of, or efteem.
Fazer de tripas coraçaõ,	To make one's utmoft efforts.
Fazer muito cafo de alguma cousa,	To make great account of a thing, to make much of it.
Naõ faço cafo delle,	I don't mind him.
Fazer fefta,	To endear, to fondle.
Fazer huma fefta,	To give an entertainment, to feaft.

Fazer

Fazer as vezes de alguem,	To make any bufinefs for another.
Fazer trapaças,	To chicane, to cavil, to ufe tricks, or quirks.
Fazer lugar,	To make room.
Fazer mercé,	To grant a favour.
Fazer ouvidos de mercador,	To make as if one were deaf.
Fazer fuas neceffidades,	To eafe one's felf, to go to ftool.
Ter que fazer,	To be bufy.
Fazer exercicio,	To ufe exercife.
Fazer exercicio (a military word),	To exercife.
Os foldados eftaõ fazendo exercicio,	The foldiers exercife.
Que fazeis aqui?	What make you here?
Fazer hum veftido,	To make a fuit of cloaths.
Fazer huma ley, hum difcurfo,	To make a law, a fpeech.
Fazer guerra,	To make war.
Fazer faber alguma coufa a alguem,	To make one acquainted with a thing.
Fazer enraivecer alguem,	To make one mad.
Fazer huma conta,	To caft up an account.
Fazer conta,	To intend, or to propofe.
Elle fazia huma conta, e fahio-lhe outra,	He was much difappointed.
Fazer contas com alguem,	To fettle the accounts with one.
Iffo naõ me faz nada,	It makes nothing to me, that does not concern me.
Fazer paufa,	To make a ftand.
Fazer de alguem tolo,	To make a fool of one.
Fazer dinheiro de alguma coufa,	To make money of a thing, to fell it.
Tornar a fazer,	To make a gain.
Fazer a razaõ,	To pledge one.
Ter que fazer com alguem,	To deal with one, *or* to have to do with one.
Fazer a alguem hum gilváz na cara,	To mark one in the face.
Fazer honra,	To honour.
Fazer fé,	To make known, to teftify, to witnefs.
Fazer forte,	To fortify, *or* ftrengthen.

Fazer

Fazer menção,	To mention.
Fazer mal,	To hurt.
Fazer de alguem o que huma pessoa quer,	To dispose of one.
Fazer huma aposta,	To lay a wager.
Faz vento,	The wind blows.
Faz hoje outo dias,	This day se'nnight, *or* a week ago.
Fazer vida com alguem,	To cohabit, *or* dwell together.
Fazer a sua vontade,	To do as one pleases.
Fazer o possivel,	To do one's best, *or* endeavour, to do one's utmost,
Naõ fareis nada com isso,	You will do no good in it.
Naõ façais mais assim,	Do so no more.
Se tornardes a fazer assim,	If ever you do so again.
Dezejo que faça a sua fortuna,	I wish he may do well.
Custou-me muito a fazello vir,	I had much to do to get him to come.
Fazer a outrem o que quizeramos que outrem nos fizesse a nós,	To do by others as we would be done by.
Naõ tenho que fazer com isso,	I have nothing to do with it.
Fazer o que alguem manda,	To do as one is bid.
Ter que fazer cum huma molher carnalmente,	To have carnally to do with a woman.
Fazei de mim o que vos parecer,	Do with me as you shall think fit.
Fazer hum grande estrondo,	To keep a heavy do.
Elle foi o que fez tudo naquelle negocio,	He was the do-all in that business.
Que fareis hoje?	What will you do to-day? *or* how do you employ yourself to-day?
Fazer hum filho a huma molher,	To get a woman with child.
Fazer o seu curso,	To finish its course, as a star does.
Fazer huma boa casa,	To raise, to set up one's family,
Fazer a barba,	To shave.
Fazer a cama,	To make the bed.
Naõ sei que lhe fazer,	I can't help it.
Fazer grande negocio,	To drive a great trade.
Fazer o seu officio,	To exercise, or discharge.
Fazer profissaõ,	To profess.

Todos

Todos o faziaõ morto,	They gave out that he was dead.
Fazer vir,	To call, or send for.
Fazer entrar, ou fabir alguem,	To call in, *or* out, to bid one come in, *or* out.
Ifto naõ faz nada,	It is no matter.
Naõ fei que fazer diffo,	I have no need of it.
Ja naõ tenho que fazer com elle,	I have done with him.
Fazer hum livro,	To write a book.
Fazer amizade com alguem,	To make friendfhip, to get into friendfhip with one.
Fazer exemplo em alguem, or *caftigallo para dar exemplo,*	To make one a public example.
Fazer huma coufa muito ao def-entendido,	To do a thing very covertly, fo that people can't apprehend that it is done on fet purpofe, and with a defign.
Fazer das fuas,	To play the fool, to dodge, to play tricks.
Elle fempre eftá fazendo das fuas,	He is always playing his foolifh tricks.
Fazer fôfcas,	To bully, to provoke, to excite by words, or actions of comtempt; *alfo* to elude, or deceive by falfe fhow.
Fazer de peffoa,	To behave courageoufly.
Fazer jurar alguem,	To tender the oaths to one, to put one to his oaths.
Fazer faltar, or *voar pellos ares,*	To blow up.
Fazer boa vezinhança,	To keep fair with one's neighbours.
Fazer lenha,	To fell wood.
Fazer a ronda,	To walk the rounds.
Fazer dividas,	To run into debt, to contract debts.
Faz luár,	The moon fhines.
Fazer violencia,	To offer violence.
Fazer-fe ao trabalho,	To inure one's felf to hard-fhips.
Fazer-fe tolo,	To play the ninny.
Fazer-fe velho,	To grow old, *or* to grow in years.
Fazer-fè feo,	To grow ugly.
Fazer-fe foberbo,	To grow proud.

Faz-

Fax-ſe tarde,   It grows late.

Fazer-ſe ſignifies alſo *to feign, to pretend, to ſeem, to make as if.*

Fax-ſe mouco,   He won't hear.

The different Significations of ter *and* ter-ſe.

Ter que fazer,	To be buſy.
Ter odio,	To hate.
Ter por coſtume,	To be wont.
Ter alguem por ignorante,	To believe one ignorant.
Ter cuidado de,	To be careful of.
Ter cuidados,	To be full of care, or thoughtful.
Ter faſtio,	To loath, to ſee food with diſlike.
Ter animo,	To have courage.
Ter boa fama,	To be well ſpoken of.
Ter cara d'aço,	To have a brâſen face.
Ter neceſſidade,	To be in want.
Ter preſſa,	To be in haſte.
Ter muitos fumos,	To be very proud.
Ter grande preſumpçaõ,	To preſume much on one's ſelf.
Ter razaã,	To be in the right.
Naõ tér razaõ	To be in the wrong.
Ter alguma couſa debaxo da lingua,	To have a thing at one's tongue's end.

Ter alguma couſa na ponta da lingua, we ſay, to have a thing at one's fingers ends, to have it perfect. They alſo ſay, *ſaber alguma couſa nas pontas dos dedos,* which exactly anſwers to our Engliſh phraſe.

Ter feiçoens feiticeiras,	To have a taking look.
Ter má fama,	To be ill ſpoken of.
Ter ciumes,	To be jealous of.
Ter meyos,	To be able, or have means.
Ter no penſamento,	To bear in mind.
Ter obrigaçaõ,	To be obliged.
Ter medo,	To be fearful.
Ter razaõ, e mais que razaõ,	To have reaſon to ſpare.

Que

Que tendes vos com iffo?	What is that to you?
Ter carruage, e criados,	To keep a coach and fervants.
Ter a alguem fufpenfo,	To hold one in fufpence.
Homem que tem boa feiçaõ,	A man of good addrefs, a polite man.
Ter mefa franca,	To keep open table, to keep a table where a man may come without bidding.
Ter frio,	To be cold.
Ter as coftas quentes em alguem.	To be backed, *or* fupported by one.
Ter por bem.	To approve of, *or* confent.
Tenho o por doudo,	I take him to be mad.
Ter maõ na fua refoluçaõ,	To be ftill in one mind.
Ter com que,	To have wherewith.
Naõ tendes de que vos queixar,	You have no reafon of complaint.
Naõ tendes que, &c.	It is ufelefs, *or* it will be to no purpofe for you to, *&c.*
Ifto naõ tem nada que fazer, com o que eu digo,	That is nothing to the purpofe.
Ter entre maõs,	To have in hand, *or* in one's poffeffion.
Tenho iffo por certo,	I hold that for a certainty.
Ir ter com alguem,	To addrefs one's felf to one.
Venho ter com vmce para faber como paffa a fenhora, fullana,	I addrefs *or* apply myfelf to you to know how mifs fuch a one does.
Ir ter a algum lugar,	To go to a place.
Efta rua vai ter ao mercado,	This ftreet ftrikes *or* goes into the market.
Ter alguem por fi,	To be fupported, *or* protected by one.
Temos por nós a authoridade dos mais prudentes,	We have the wifeft men of our fide, *or* of our opinion.
Ter para fi,	To think, *or* imagine, to reckon.
Ter em muita,	To fet much by.
Ter em pouço,	To value but little.
Ser tido em boa conta,	To be efteemed, regarded, *or* valued, to be in great efteem.
Ter maõ,	To hold *or* keep in, to reftrain.
Ter maõ nalguma coufa,	To bear up, to fupport, to prop, to keep up, to hold up.

A to-

Atomos que tem maõ huns nos outros,	Atoms that ftick together.
Tenha maõ, or *tem maõ,*	Hold, ftop.
Ter,	To contain.
Ter-fe em pé,	To ftand, to ftand up.
Ter-fe bem a cavallo,	To fit faft, *or* well on horfe-back.
Ter-fe em cafa,	To keep at home.
Ter-fe com alguem,	To hold out, to refift, to ftand againft one, to cope with one, to oppofe, *or* refift him.
Naõ me poffo ter com rizo.	I can't forbear laughing.
Naõ fe pode ter, que naõ falle,	He can't forbear fpeaking.

The different Significations of querer.

Querer fignifies *to will, to be willing,* and *to believe;* as,

Querem alguns,	Some believe.
Querer bem,	To love.
Querer mal,	To hate.
Antes querer,	To have rather.
Queira Deos,	God grant it, God fend it may be fo.
Mas quero que affim feja,	I grant it, fuppofe it were fo.
Que quer dizer aquelle homem ?	What does that man mean?
Que quer dizer ifto ?	What means this? what's the meaning of that?
Ifto quer dizer que, &c.	The meaning is that, &c.
Eu quero abfolutamente que, &c.	I pofitively refolve that, &c.
Eu affim o quero,	I'll have it fo.
Elle quer que vós obedeçais,	He will have you obey.
Naõ quero,	I will not, I won't.
Elle o fará quando quizer,	He will do it when he pleafes, *or* when he has a mind to it.
Elle quer partir amanhãa,	He intends, *or* has a mind, to fet out to-morrow.
O mal que lhe eu quero me venha a mim,	I wifh him no more harm than I do myfelf.

Haver, to have.

Tu has de bir,	You muft go.
Elle ha de vir hoje,	He is to come to-day.

If

Se eu houver de hir,	If I shall be obliged to go.
Aindaque isso me houvesse de custar a vida,	Though I were to lose my life for't.
Elle está todo nú, e ha de ter muyto frio,	He is all naked, he must needs be very cold.
Haveis vós de estar em casa,	Shall you be at home?
Eu hei de acharme lá,	I must be there.
Elle há de ser enforcado,	He is to be hanged.
Eu hei de receber dinheiro,	I am to receive money.
Vós he que haveis de jugar,	You are to play.
Aquillo he que vos havieis de fazer,	You should do that.
Haver por bem,	To take in good part.
Haver por mal,	To take in ill part.
Que ha de ser,	That is to be hereafter.
Aquillo nunca ha de ser,	That will never be.
Eu hei de ser a causa da sua morte, ou ruina,	I shall be the death, or ruin of him.
Para haver de fallar, ouvir, &c.	In order to speak, hear, &c.
Que ha de ser de mim?	What is to become of me?
Haver filhos,	To beget, to become the father of children.
Haver filhos de huma molher,	To beget on, or upon a woman.
Livros do deve, e ha de haver,	Books of debtor and creditor.
Haver mister,	To want.
Há mister apressar-se,	It is necessary to haste, or to make haste.

Haver, when impersonal, is rendered into English by the verb *to be*, preceded by *there*; as,

Há,	There is, or there are.
Ha homens taó malvados,	There are men so wicked.
Havia huma molher,	There was a woman.
Há alguns bons e outros máos,	There are some good, and some bad.
Há muytas casas,	There are several houses.
Há alguma cousa de novo?	Is there any news?
Há mais de huma hora,	It is above an hour since.
Há muyto tempo,	Long since.
Há perto de huma hora que, elle sahio,	It is almost an hour since he went out.
Há hum anno,	A year ago.

Há outo dias,	Eight days ago.
Há perto de 20 legoas daqui lá,	It is near upon 20 leagues thither.
Naõ há,	There is not.
Elle cuida que naõ há mais que purgar,	He believes that purging is all in all, *or* that purging is the only remedy in such a case.
Haver-se, v. r.	To carry, to behave one's self.
Elle sabe como se ha de haver, or elle sabe como ha de haver-se,	He knows how to behave himself.
Elle houve-se de maneira que, &c.	He behaved himself in such a manner, that, *&c.*

N. B. When this verb is used impersonally, it is always followed by the particle *de*; as,

Ha se de mister dinheiro,	Money is wanted.
Ha-se de fazer, ou dizer isto,	This must be done or said.
Ha-se de fazer o que elle quizer,	People must do what he pleases.

Hir, a neuter and irregular verb, *to go, to walk, to march*; also, *to grow, to reach any estate gradually, to be going.*

Hir por már e por terra,	To travel by sea and land.
Come vaõ os vossos negocios ?	How go your concerns?
Tudo vai bem,	All is well, all goes well.
As suas coufas vaõ muyto mal,	Things go very ill (or very hard) with him.
Hir á maõ,	To hinder, to obstruct, to prevent, to obviate.
His passando,	To grow out of fashion or use.
Hir andando,	To go on *or* forward, to keep *or* hold on his way; *also* to proceed, to continue on, to prosecute.
Hir andando, or *passando,*	To shift, to pass life not quite well, to live though with difficulty.
Que vai de novo ?	Is there any thing new?
Que vai nisto? or *onde vai isto a dar comsigo ?*	What of all this ?

Hir

Hir debaxo,	To come by the worſt.
Hir para,	To approach, to go near.
Quanto mais vamos para a pri-mavera, mais compridos ſaõ os dias,	The nearer the ſpring, the longer the days.
Hir de mal para peor,	To grow worſe and worſe.
Hir diante,	To go before.
Hir por diante,	To go on, or forward.
Hir ao encontro,	To go to meet.
Hir ao fundo,	To ſink, *or* fall to the bottom.
Hir e vir,	To go to and fro, to go and come.
Naõ faço mais do que hir e voltar,	I will not ſtay, I ſhall be back preſently.
Iſſo ja lá vai,	'Tis a thing paſt and done.
Eilo la vai,	There he goes.
Eilo vai,	So ſo, pretty well.
Que vos parece daquella molher? eilo vai, ella naõ he fea,	How do you like that woman? She is ſo ſo, ſhe may paſs.
Eilo vai, folgo que aſſim ſeja,	Well, well, I am glad on't.
Como as couſas agora vaõ,	As things go now, as the world goes.
Por que parte ides,	Which way d'ye go?
Deos vá comvoſco,	The Lord of heaven go with you.
Hir á roda do mundo,	To go about the world.
Hir com alguem,	To go along with one.
Eſta traveſſa vai ter á rua larga,	This lane goes into the broad ſtreet.
Eu o irei ver de caminho,	I will call upon him as I go along.
Hir continuando o ſeu caminho,	To go along.
Hir fóra do ſeu caminho,	To go out of one's way.
Hir hum de huma banda, e outro da outra,	To go aſunder.
Hir para tráx,	To go backward.
Hir detráx,	To go behind.
Hir atráx de alguem,	To purſue, to go after one.
Hir em akance de alguem,	To go after one, in order to overtake him.
Hir buſcar,	To go for, *or* fetch.
Hir para dentro,	To go in.
Hir para fóra,	To go out.

Hir peregrinando,	To go a pilgrimage.
Hir fazer huma embaxada,	To go on an embaffy.
Hir ver, zantar, &c.	To go to fee, to fing, &c.
Vamos,	Come, come on.
Hir fazer bum negocio,	To go upon a bufinefs.
Hir com a maré,	To go with the tide.
Hir par a par com alguem,	To go cheek by jole with one.
Vai para quatro mefes que eu aqui cheguei,	It is now going on' four months finee I came hither.
Ide em paz,	Depart in peace.
O tempo vai abrandando,	The weather grows mild.
Hir (at cards),	To go, to lay, to ftake, to fet.
Hir-fe, v. r.	To go, to go away, to go one's way, to depart, *alfo* to run *or* leak.
Hir-fe a olha, ou *a panella,*	Is for the pot to boll over.
Hir-fe o enfermo,	Is for a fick man to die.
A quaréfma vai fe acabando,	Lent draws to an end.
Hir-fe,	To flip, or pafs away (as time).
Nada fe vai mais depreffa que o tempo,	Nothing goes fafter than time.
Aquelles montes vaõ fe eftendendo,	Thofe mountains extend, *or* ftretch themfelves.
Hir-fe embora,	To go away, alfo to be over.
Efperai até que a calma fe va embora,	Stay till the heat be over.
Vai-te embora ; que naõ fabes engodar a gente,	Away, or go, you know not how to wheedle people.
Hir-fe de huma carta (at cards)	To throw away a card.
Vai-fe fazendo tarde,	It grows late.
Vai-fe chegando a noite,	The night draws on.
Vai fe chegando o tempo da fega,	It grows near harveft.
Vai-fe acabando o meu confulado,	My confulfhip is almoft at an end.
Hir-fe efcapulindo,	To fneak away.
Hir-fe á maõ,	To refrain, to forbear, to abftain.

Hir-fe imperfonal; as, *vai-fe,* they go ; *foi-fe,* they are gone ; *bir-fe ha,* they fhall go.

To pray.

Senhor, como amigo, façame o favor,	Dear fir, do me the favour
Eu vos peço, or *peçovos,*	I pray you.
Peçolhe em cortesia,	I befeech you.
Peçolho encarecidamente,	I intreat, *or* conjure, you to do it.
Peçolhe por favor que, &c.	I beg of you that, *&c.*
Façame a fineza,	Do me the kindnefs.
Peçolhe perdaõ,	I beg your pardon.

Expreffions of Kindnefs.

Minha vida,	My life.
Minha alma,	My dear foul.
Meu amor	My love.
Meu querido, minha querida,	My little darling.
Meu coraçaõ,	My dear love, my love.
Filho do meu coraçaõ,	My dear child.
Filha da minha alma,	My little honey.

To fhew Civility.

Agradeço a vmce,	I thank you.
Dou a vmce os agradecimentos,	I give you thanks.
Beijo as maõs de vmce,	I kifs your hand.
Falo-hei com todo o gofto,	I will do it chearfully.
Com todo o meu coraçaõ,	With all my heart.
De muito boa vontade,	Heartily, willingly.
Veja vmce fe o poffo fervir nalguma coufa,	See if it is in my power to ferve you.
Difponha vmce como lhe parecer defte feu criado,	Do what you pleafe with your fervant.
Eftou efperando pellas ordens de vmce	I wait for your commands.
Ja que vmce affim ordena,	Since you will have it fo.
As ordens de vmce	At your fervice.
Fico muito obrigado a vmce	I am very much obliged to you.
Quer vmce que eu faça alguma coufa,	Have you any thing to command me?
Sem ceremonia,	Without ceremony.
Naõ tem vmce mais que fallar,	You need but to fpeak.
Façame a honra de me por aos pés da fnra	Prefent my refpects, *or* duty, to my lady.

R   Naõ

Naõ sei como agradecer a vmce tantos favores,	I know not how to make a proper return for so many favours.
Naõ sou de comprimentos,	I am not for ceremonies.
Deixemos estes comprimentos,	Away with these ceremonies, or compliments.
Isso he o melhor,	That is the best way.

To give Tokens of Affirmation, Consent, Belief, and Refusal.

He verdade,	It is true.
He isso verdade?	Is it true?
He muito verdade,	It is but too true.
Para diservos a verdade,	To tell you the truth.
Com effeito he assim,	Really it is so.
Quem duvida disso?	Who doubts it?
Naõ ha duvida nisso,	There is no doubt of it.
Pareceme que sim, que naõ,	I think so, not.
Aposto que sim,	I lay it is.
Aposto que naõ,	I lay it is not.
Creame vmce	Do believe me?
Está vmce zombando?	Don't you jest?
Falla vmce de veras?	Are you in earnest?
Fallo de veras,	I am in earnest.
Pois, esta feito,	Well, let it be so.
Pouco a pouco,	Softly, fair and softly.
Isso naõ he verdade,	It is not true.
Nao ha tal cousa,	There is no such thing.
He mentira,	It is a lie.
Estáva zombando,	I did but jest.
Seja muito embora,	Let it be so.
Naõ quero,	I won't, I will not,

To consult.

Que se ha de fazer?	What is to be done?
Que faremos?	What shall we do?
Que lhe parece a vmce que eu faça?	What do you advise me to do?
Que remedio tem isso?	What remedy is there for it?
Façamos assim,	Let us do so, & so.
Façamos huma cousa,	Let us do one thing.
Sera melhor que,	It will be better that.
Seria melhor que,	It would be better that.

Esperai

Esperai hum pouco,	Stay a little.
Deixaime com iffo,	Let me alone.
Antes quizera.	I had rather.
Se iffo foffe comigo,	Were I in your place
Tudo he o mefmo,	It is all one.

Of Eating and Drinking.

Tenho fome,	I am hungry.
M rro de fome,	I am almoft ftarved.
Coma vmce alguma coufa,	Eat fomething.
Que quer vmce comer ?	What will you eat?
Quer vmce comer mais ?	Will you eat any more?
Tenho fede,	I am dry, *or* thirfty.
Ja matei a fome,	I have no more ftomach.
Tenho muita fede,	I am very dry.
Morro de fede,	I am almoft dead with thirft.
Deme de beber,	Give me fome drink.
Viva vmce muitos annos,	I thank you.
Eu beberia hum copo de vinho,	I could drink a glafs of wine.
Pois beba vmce	Drink then.
Tenho bebido baftante,	I have drank enough.
Naõ poffo beber mais,	I can drink no more.
Ja matei a fede,	I am no more thirfty, *or* my thirft is quenched.

Of Going, Coming, Stirring, &c.

Donde vem vmce ?	From whence do you come?
Para onde vai vmce ?	Where do you go?
Venho de ; vou parà, ot a,	I come from ; I am going to.
Quer vmce fubir, ou defcer ?	Will you come up, *or* come down?
Entre vmce , fabia vmce ,	Come in, go out
Nao fe bula daqui,	Do not ftir from hence.
Chegue-fe para mim,	Come near to me.
Va-fe vmce	Go your way, be gone.
Vem ca,	Come hither.
Efpere por mim,	Stay for me.
Naõ va taõ depreffa,	Do not go fo faft.
Tire-fe de diante de mim,	Get you out of my
Naõ me toque,	Do not touch me.
Deixe eftar iffo,	Let that alone.
Eftou bem aqui,	I am well here.
Abra vmce a porta,	Open the door.

Feche

Feche a porta,	Shut the door.
Abra, ou feche, a janella,	Open the window, *or* shut the window.
Venha vm.ce por aqui,	Come this way.
Passe por lá,	Pass that way.
Que procura vm.ce ?	What do you look for?
Que perdeo vm.ce ?	What have you lost?

To wish well to a Person.

O Ceo vos guarde,	Heavens preserve you.
Deos vos dê boa fortuna,	God send you good luck.
Dezejo-vos todo o bem,	I wish you every thing that is good.
Deos vos ajude,	God assist you.
Deos vos perdoe,	God forgive you.
Ide com Deos,	God be with you.
Até vernos,	Till I see you again.
Bom proveito faça a vm.ce	Much good may do you.

To wish ill.

O diabo te leve,	The devil take thee.
Maldito sejas tu,	A curse on thee.
Vai para os quintos infernos,	Away, go to hell.
Vaite enforcar,	Go and be hanged.
Enforcado sejas tu,	Would thou wert hanged.

To swear.

Assim Deos me salve,	As God shall help me, shall save me.
Arrebentado seja eu,	May I burst.
Em conciencia,	In my conscience.

To threaten and insult.

Olha que te hei de dar,	Take care, I will beat thee.
Deixa te estar, or cala te que mo has de pagar,	Thou wilt pay it me.
Juro que te farei arrepender disso,	I swear thou shalt repent of it.
Se me enfadáres,	If you put me into a passion.
Coitado de ti,	Woe be to thee.
Poucas razoens, or cala essa boca,	Hold your tougue, don't speak to me.
Isto basta.	It is enough, it is sufficient.

To

To mock, to blame, and to call.

Que belo focinho!	O the fine fnout!
Que cara de mono!	What an ape's face!
Cornudo,	A cuckold.
Trapaceiro,	A chicaner.
Embufteiro,	A cheat, an impoftor.
Mexeriqueiro,	A tale bearer, a tell-tale.
Que belo fogeito!	O the dull thing!
Velhaco,	A knave.
Maroto,	A rogue, a rafcal.
Má cafta,	Curfed race.
Tonto,	Giddy-brains, blunderbufs.
Afneiraõ,	A great beaft, a thick-fkull.

To admire.

O Deos!	O God!
He poffivel!	Is it poffible!
Quem teria imaginado, crido, dito!	Who would have thought, believed, faid.
Que animal!	What a beaft it is!
Que maravilha! or o que milogre!	O ftrange!
Naõ me maravilho!	I don't wonder!
Como pode fer ifto! or Como he poffivel!	How can that be!
Eis aqui como faõ as coufas defte mundo!	So goes the world!

To fhew Joy and Difpleafure.

Que gofto!	What pleafure!
Que gloria!	What glory!
Que alegria!	What joy;
O que contentamento he o meu!	How pleafed I am!
Que felicidade!	What happinefs!
Sinto iffo.	I am forry for it.
Sinto iffo na alma,	That touches my very foul.
Sinto iffo na coraçaõ,	It pierces me to the heart.
O que difgracia he a minha!	O how unhappy am I!

To reproach.

Affrontar-me defta forte !	To affront me thus !
Affim he que fe trata ?	Do you deal thus?
Olha maroto !	You rogue !
Que bella cortefia !	O what fine manners !
Naõ deveria tratar comigo de-	Thou oughteft not to treat me
fta forte,	thus.
Parece-te bem ?	Doft thou think that is well?
Aprende, pedaço d'afno,	Learn, beaft as thou art.
Olha como me trata efte animal,	See the brute, how he ufes me.
Olhai que velhaço he efte,	Do but behold that rafcal.
Que diabo tem elle feito ?	What the devil has he done?
Pois, ainda teimais ?	What, are you obftinate ftill?

To call.

Ouve,	Heark.
Onde eftás?	Where art thou ?
Huma palavra,	A word.
Duas palavras fomente,	I'll fpeak but two words to
	you.

To fhew Uneafinefs, Trouble, and Sorrow.

Sinto, or *pefame,*	I am forry.
Deixame,	Let me be quiet.
Peço-te que me deixes,	Prithee get thee gone.
Naõ me quebres a cabeça,	Do not break my head.
Ora vamos, deixame.	Away, away.
Deixame vai com Deos,	Go, go, God be with you.
Vaite daqui, or *vaite embora,*	Get thee gone from hence.
Vai tratar da tua vida,	Go mind your own bufinefs.
Vaite na ma bora, or *vaite co*	Go to the devil.
diabo,	
Naõ me faças a cabeça tonta,	Do not make me giddy.
Ja me tens dito iffo hum cento	You have told it me a hun-
de vezes,	dred times already.

To afk.

Que novas ha ?	What news ?
Que he ifto ? que ha ?	What is this, what is the
	matter ?

Onde

Onde ides?	Where are you a-going?
Donde vindes?	Whence come you?
Que quer dizer?	What means?
De que serve?	To what purpose?
Que vos parece?	What do you think?
Quem teve tal atrevimento?	Who is that has been so bold?
Que dizem? que se diz?	What do they say?
Como diz vmce?	How do you say?
Por que naõ me responde?	What don't you answer for?

To forbid.

Deixai estar isso,	Let that alone.
Naõ toqueis,	Do not touch.
Naõ digais nada,	Say not a word.
Guardaivos,	Have a care.

Of speaking, saying, doing, &c.

Falle vmce alto,	Speak loud.
Falle vmce manso,	Speak low.
Com quem falla vmce?	Who do you speak to?
Falla vmce comigo?	Do you speak to me?
Falle-lhe,	Speak to him, *or* to her.
Falla vmce Portuguez?	Do you speak Portuguese?
Que diz vmce?	What do you say?
Naõ digo nada,	I say nothing.
Ella naõ quer calar-se,	She will not hold her tongue.
Ouvi dizer que ——	I was told that ——
Assim mo disseraõ,	I was told so.
Assim dizem,	They say so.
Assim dizem todos,	Every one says so.
Quem lho disse a vmce?	Who told it you?
Dissemo o Sr A.	Mr. A. told it me.
Pois elle he que lho disse?	Did he tell you so?
Pois ella he que o disse?	Did she tell it?
Quando o ouvio vm. dizer?	When did you hear it?
Disseraõ-mo hoje,	I heard it to-day.
Naõ posso cre-lo,	I can't believe it.
Que diz elle?	What does he say?
Que vos disse elle?	What did he say to you?
Elle naõ me disse nada,	He said nothing to me.
Naõ lho diga vm.	Do not tell him that.
Eu lho direi,	I'll tell him, *or* her of it.
Naõ diga nada,	Say not a word.
Disse vm. aquillo?	Did you say that?

Naõ o diſſe,	I did not ſay it.
Naõ diſſe vm. aſſim ?	Did you not ſay ſo ?
Que eſta vm. fazendo?	What are you doing ?
Que tem vm. feito?	What have you done ?
Naõ faço nada,	I do nothing.
Naõ tenho feito nada,	I have done nothing.
Tem vm. acabado?	Have you done ?
Que eſtá elle fazendo ?	What is he doing?
Que faz ella ?	What does ſhe do ?
Que quer, or *que ordena vm ?*	What is your pleaſure ?
Que lhe falta ?	What do you want ?

Of underſtanding or apprehending.

Entende-o, or *percebeo vm. bem ?*	Do you underſtand him well ?
Percebe vm. o que elle diſſe ?	Did you underſtand what he ſaid ?
Percebe vm, o que elle diz ?	Did you underſtand what he ſays ?
Entendeme, or *percebeme vm. ?*	Do you underſtand me ?
Entendo a vm. muito bem,	I underſtand you very well.
Naõ entendo a vm.	I do not underſtand you.
Sabe vm, a lingua Portugueza?	Do you underſtand Portugueſe ?
Naõ a ſey,	I do not underſtand it.
Tem-me vm. percebido?	Did you underſtand me ?
Agora o percebo,	Now I underſtand you.
Naõ ſe percebe o que elle diz,	One cannot underſtand what he utters.
Parece gago,	He ſpeaks like a ſtammerer.

Of knowing, or having Knowledge of.

Sabe vm. iſſo ?	Do you know that ?
Naõ o ſei,	I do not know it.
Naõ ſei nada diſſo,	I knew nothing of it.
Ella bem o ſabia,	She knew well of it.
Por ventura naõ ſabia elle iſſo ?	Did he not know of it.
Demos que eu o ſoubêſſe,	Suppoſe I knew it.
Elle naõ ſaberá nada diſſo,	He ſhall know nothing of it.
Elle nunca ſoube nada diſto,	He never knew any thing about this.
Eu ſoubeo primeiro, or *antes que vm. o ſoubeſſe,*	I knew it before you.

He,

He iſto aſſim ou naõ?	Is it ſo, or not?
Naõ que eu ſaiba,	Not that I know of,

Of knowing or being acquainted with, forgetting, and remembering.

Conhece-o vm.?	Do you know him?
Conhece-a vm.?	Do you know her?
Combece-os vm.?	Do you know them?
Conheço-o muito bem,	I know him very well.
Naõ os conheço,	I do not know them.
Nós naõ nos conhecemos,	We do not know one another,
Conheço-o de viſta,	I know him by ſight.
Conheço-a de nome,	I have heard of her.
Elle conheceo-me muito bem,	He knew me very well.
Conhece-me vm.?	Do you know me?
Tenho-me eſquecido do ſeu nome,	I have forgot your name.
Tem-ſe vm. eſquecido de mim?	Did you forget me?
Conhece-vos ella?	Does ſhe know you?
Conhece o Sr. a vm.?	Does the gentleman know you?
Parece que naõ me conhece,	It appears he does not know me.
O Sr. bem me conhece,	The gentleman knows me well.
Elle ja me naõ conhece,	He knows me no more.
Tenho a honra de ſer ſu conhe-cido,	I have the honour to be known to him.
Lembra-ſe vm. diſſo?	Do you remember that?
Naõ me lembro diſſo,	I do not remember it.
Lembro me muito bem diſſo,	I do remember it very well.

Of Age, Life, Death, &c.

Que idade tem vm.?	How old are you?
Que idade tem ſeu irmaõ?	How old is your brother?
Tenho vente e cinco annos,	I am five and twenty. .
Tem vinte e dous annos,	He is twenty-two years old.
Vm. tem mais annos do que eu,	You are older than I.
Que idade terá vm.?	How old may you be?
He vm. caſado?	Are you married?
Quin as vezes tem vm. caſado?	How often have you been married?
Quantas molheres tem vm. ti-do?	How many wives have you had?

Tem

Tem vm. ainda pay, e máy?	Have you father and mother ftill alive?
Meu pay morreo,	My father is dead.
Minha may morreo,	My mother is dead.
Ha dous annos que meu pay morreo,	My father has been dead thefe two years.
Minha may cafou outra vez,	My mother is married again.
Quantos filhos tem vm.?	How many children have you?
Tenho quatro,	I have four.
Filhos; ou filhas?	Sons, or daughters?
Tenho hum filho, e tres filhas?	I have one fon and three daughters.
Quantos irmaõs tem vm.?	How many brothers have you?
Naõ tenho nenhum vivo,	I have none alive.
Todos morreraõ,	They are all dead.
Todos havemos de morrer,	We muft all die.

Of the Word hora, as a Noun as well as an Interjection.

Hora,	An hour, *alfo* a particular time.
Eu eftarei lá dentro de huma hora,	I will be there within an hour.
Que horas faõ?	What's o'clock?
Saõ fete horas,	It is feven o'clock.
A que horas eftareis vós lá?	At what hour *or* time will you be there?
As horas que for precifo,	In due *or* good time, at the time appointed.
Horas defoccupadas,	Leifure hours.
A ultima hora, ou a hora da morte,	The laft hour, *or* the dying hour.
Cada hora,	Every hour.
De hora em hora,	Hourly, every hour.
Meya hora,	Half an hour.
Hum quarto de hora,	A quarter of an hour.
Huma hora e meya,	An hour and a half.
Perto das nove horas,	About the ninth hour.
Há huma hora,	An hour ago *or* an hour fince.
Fóra de horas,	Beyond the hour, *or* very late.
A horas,	In time.
Recolher-fe a boas horas,	To keep good hours.
Recolher-fe fora de horas,	To keep bad hours.
Horas de jantar ou de cear,	Dinner or fupper-time.

Perto das horas de jantar,	About dinner-time.
Ainda eſtais na cama a eſtas horas?	Are you a-bed at this time of the day?
O relogio dá horas,	The clock ſtrikes.
Ja deraõ onze horas,	It ſtruck eleven o'clock.
Relogio de hora,	Hour-glaſs.
Muyto a boas horas,	Early, betimes.
A boas horas,	In good time, in time, at the time appointed, in the very nick of time.
Na má hora,	In an ill hour, unluckily, unfortunately.
Vai-te na má hora,	Go to the devil, go and be hanged.
Toda a hora que,	Whenſoever, at what time ſoever.
Toda a hora que quizerdes,	At what time you will.
Hora,	Time *or* hour of child-birth.
Molher que anda para cada hora,	A woman near her time.
Horas de fazer oraçaõ,	Prayer-time.
Horas de hir á igrega,	Church-time.
Horas de hir para a cama,	Bed-time.
Horas de comer,	Times of eating.
Ja naõ ſaõ horas,	The time is paſt, it is too late.
Chegar a hora,	Is for a perſon to die.
Eſtar eſperando pella ſua hora,	To wait for God's time.
Naõ ver a hora,	To long, to deſire earneſtly, to wiſh with eagerneſs continued, with *em,* or *de* before the thing deſired.
Saõ horas de, &c.	Is is time to, &c.
Horas canonicas,	The ſet time for the clergy to ſay their office; alſo thoſe parts of the office itſelf, called *Prime, Tierce, Sixth, None,* &c
Horas,	Any little prayer-book but particularly that in which is the office of the *Bleſſed Virgin.*
As quarenta horas,	So they call the ſpace of three days, in which the conſecrated Hoſt is expoſed and laid to public view.
Conta das horas,	Horography, an account of the hours.
Arte de dividir o tempo em horas,	Horometry.

Hora

Hora *as an Adverb and Interjection.*

Hora deixa-o bir, — Pray let him go.

Hora deixate deſtas parvoices, — Away with theſe fopperies.

Hora, deixeme-nos deſtes comprimentos, — Away with theſe compliments.

Hora vamos, deſpaxate, — Come, come, make haſte.

Hora vamos, naõ ha perigo, — Away, there is no danger.

Hora vamos, tira daqui iſto, — Away with this.

Hora vamos, tem vergonba, — Away for ſhame.

Hora, eu naõ poſſo ſofrer aquillo, — I cannot away with it.

Hora hum, hora outro, — Sometimes one, ſometimes another.

Elles hora eſtaõ ſobre hum pé, hora ſobre outro, — They ſtand now on one foot and then on another.

Hora, que quer dizer iſſo? — How now?

Tudo o que he bom, deve ſer amado ; hora, Deos he infinitamente bom, logo, &c. — All that is good is to be loved, now God is infinitely good, therefore, &c.

Hora, havia hum enfermo, — Now there was a ſick man.

Por hora, — At preſent, for the preſent, now, at this time.

A VO-

A

VOCABULARY.

OF

WORDS most used in DISCOURSE.

Do Ceo e dos Elementos.	Of the Heaven and the Elements.
DEOS,	GOD.
Jesus Christo,	Jesus Christ.
O Espirito Santo,	The Holy Ghost.
A Trindade,	The Trinity.
A Virgem,	The Virgin.
Os anjos.	The angels.
Os archanjos,	The arch-angels.
Os santos,	The saints.
Os bemaventurados,	The blessed.
O ceo,	Heaven.
O paraiso,	Paradise.
Inferno,	Hell.
Purgatorio,	Purgatory.
Os diabos,	The devils.
O fogo,	The fire.
O ar,	The air.
A terra,	The earth.
O mar,	The sea.
O sol,	The sun.
A lua,	The moon.
As estrellas,	The stars.
Os raios,	The rays.

As nuvens,	The clouds.
O vénto,	The wind.
A chuva,	The rain.
O trovaõ,	Thunder.
O relampago,	The lightning.
Saráiva,	Hail.
O rayo,	The thunderbolt.
A neve,	The snow.
A geáda,	The frost.
O caramélo,	The ice.
O orvalho,	The dew.
Névoa,	A fog, or mist.
Nevoeiro,	A thick fog.
O terremoto,	The earthquake.
O diluvio,	The deluge or flood.
O calor,	The heat.
O frio,	The cold.

Do Tempo.

Of the Time.

O dia,	The day:
A noite,	The night.
Meye dia,	Noon.
Meya noite,	Midnight.
A manhãa,	The morning.
Despois de meyo dia,	The afternoon.
Huma hora,	An hour.
Hum quarto de hora,	A quarter of an hour.
Huma meya hora,	Half an hour.
Tres quartos de hora,	Three quarters of an hour.
Hoje,	To-day.
Ontem,	Yesterday.
Amanhãa,	To-morrow.
Antes d'ontem,	The day before yesterday.
Depois de amanhãa,	After to-morrow.
Depois de jantar,	After dinner.
Depois de cea,	After supper.
Huma semana,	A week.
Hum mês,	A month.
Hum anno,	A year.
Dia santo,	A holy-day.
Dia de trabalho,	A working-day.
O nacer do sol,	The sun-rising.
O por do sol,	The sun-set.

Tempo da fega, or *da eeifa,*	The harveft.
Tempo da vindima,	The vintage.

Das Eftaçoens do tempo.	Of the Seafons.
A primavera,	The fpring.
O veraõ,	The fummer.
O outono,	Autumn.
O inverno,	Winter.

Os Dias da Semana,	The Days of the Week.
Domingo,	Sunday.
Segunda feira,	Monday.
Terça feira,	Tuefday.
Quarta feira,	Wednefday.
Quinta feira,	Thurfday.
Sefta feira,	Friday.
Sabado,	Saturday.

Dos Mefes,	Of the Months.
Janeiro,	January.
Fevereiro,	February.
Março,	March.
Abril,	April.
Mayo,	May.
Junho,	June.
Julho,	July.
Agofto,	Auguft.
Setembro,	September.
Outubro,	October.
Novembro,	November.
Dezembro,	December.

Dias Santos,	Holy-days of the Year.
Dia de Anno bom,	New Year's Day.
Dia de Reys, a Epiphania,	Twelfth Day.
A Candelaria,	Candlemas Day.

A Pu-

A Purificaçaõ,	The Purification.
O Entrudo,	The Carnival, *or* Shrovetide.
Quarta feira de Cinzas,	Aſh Wedneſday.
A Quareſma,	The Lent.
Annunciaçaõ,	Lady Day in March.
As Quatro Temporas,	The Ember Weeks.
A Semana ſanta,	The Holy Week.
Domingo de Ramos,	Palm Sunday,
Quarta feira de Trevoas,	Wedneſday before Eaſter.
Quinta feira de Endoenças,	Maundy Thurſday, the laſt Thurſday in Lent
Seſta feira da Paixaõ,	Good Friday.
Paſcoa da Reſurreyçaõ,	Eaſter Day.
Aſſumpçaõ de N. Sᵃ	Lady Day in harveſt.
As Rogaçoens, or *Ladainhas,*	Rogation Week.
Aſcenſaõ,	The Aſcenſion.
Pentecoſte,	The Pentecoſt, *or* Witſuntide.
Dia do Corpo de Deos,	Corpus Chriſti Day.
Dia de S. Joaõ	Midſummer Day.
Dia de S. Pedro,	Lammas Day.
Dia de todos os Santos,	All Saints Day.
Dia dos Finados,	All Souls.
Dia de S. Martinho,	Martinmas.
Dia de Natal,	Chriſtmaſs Day.
Vigilia, or *veſpera,*	The eve.

Da Igreja e Dignidades Ecclesiaſticas,	*Of the Church, and Eccleſiaſtical Dignities.*
A nave,	The iſle of the church.
Zimbório,	The dome.
Pináculo,	Pinnacle.
Coro,	The choir.
Capella,	The chapel.
Eſtante,	A reading deſk, *or* choriſter's deſk.
Sancriſtia,	The veſtry.
Campanário, ou *torre dos ſinos,*	The belfry.
Sino,	The bell,
Badálo,	The clapper of the bell.
Pia,	The font.
Hyſope,	A ſprinkler.
Confeſſionário,	A confeſſion ſeat.

Tribuna,

Tribuna,	A tribune, *or* gallery.
Cemitério,	A church-yard, a burying place.
Carneiro,	A charnel.
Altar,	An altar.
Frontal,	An antipendium.
Pallio,	A canopy.
Toalba do altar,	The altar-cloth.
Miffal,	A miffal, a mafs book.
Sotâna,	A caffock.
Sobrepelliz,	A furplice.
Roquete,	A fhort furplice, a bifhop's furplice.
O papa,	The pope.
Hum cardeal,	A cardinal.
Hum patriarca,	A patriarch.
Hum arcebifpo,	An archbifhop
Hum bifpo,	A bifhop.
Hum legado,	A legate.
Vice-legado,	A vice-legate.
Hum nuncio,	A nuncio.
Hum prelado,	A prelate.
Hum commendador,	A commander.
Hum abbade,	An abbot.
Huma abbadeffa,	An abbefs.
Hum prior,	A prior.
Hum reitor,	A rector.
Beneficiado,	Beneficed clergyman, *or* incumbent.
Frade, or *religiofo,*	A friar.
Coroa,	A fhaven crown.
Hum guardiaõ,	A guardian.
Hum definidor,	A definitor.
Hum provincial,	A provincial.
Hum geral,	A general.
Hum vigario,	A vicar.
Hum vigario geral,	A vicar-general,
Hum deaõ.	A dean.
Hum arcediágo,	Archdeacon.
Diácono,	Deacon.
Subdiácono,	A fub-deacon.
Hum cónego,	A canon.
Arcipréfte,	Arch-prieft.
Hum clérigo,	A prieft.
Capellaõ,	A chaplain.

S *Hum*

Hum esmolér,	An almoner.
Hum párroco,	A curate.
Beneficio simples,	Sinecure.
Freira,	A Nun.
Hum pregador,	A preacher, or lecturer.
Sacristaõ or sancristaõ,	A sexton, a vestry keeper.
Menino do coro,	A singing boy.

Nomes das cousas que geralmente se comem.

Names of things most usually eaten.

Paõ,	Bread.
Agoa,	Water.
Vinho,	Wine.
Carne,	Meat, or flesh.
Peixe,	Fish.
Carne cozida,	Boiled meat.
Carne açada,	Roast meat.
Hum bocado de paõ,	A mouthful of bread.
Hum pastel,	A pie.
Huma sopa,	Soup.
Hum caldo,	Broth.
Huma saláda,	A sallad.
Hum môlho,	Any kind of sauce to dip in, provoking appetite.
Fruta,	Fruit.
Queijo,	Cheese.
Manteiga,	Butter.

Do Serviço de huma Mesa.

Of the Covering of the Table.

A mesa,	The table.
Huma cadeira,	A chair.
A toalha da mesa,	The table cloth.
Toalha de maõs,	A towel.
Hum guardanápo,	A napkin.
Huma faca,	A knife.
Hum garfo,	A fork.
Huma colhér,	A spoon.
Hum prato,	A plate
Hum saleiro,	A saltseller.
Galheta do vinagre,	A vinegar-bottle, a cruit.
Galheta do azeite,	A cruit, or vial for oil.

Talher,

Talber,	A cruit-stand.
Talber do açucar,	Sugar-box.
Bayxella, ou *serviço de prata,*	A set of silver plate.
Huma cuberta,	A courſe.
Prato, guardanapo, fata, garfo, colher (tudo junto);	A cover.
O gomil,	The ewer.
Huma bacia,	A baſin.
Hum copo,	A glaſs.
Huma garrafa,	A bottle.
Huma taça,	A cup.
Castiçal,	A candleſtick.
Vela,	A candle.
Teſouras de eſpevitar,	Snuffers.
Huma ſalva,	A ſalver.
Tigela, or *eſcudella,*	A porringer.
Cesto para por o paõ,	A bread-baſket.
Donzella,	A dumb-waiter.
Faqueiro,	A caſe for knives.
Louça de Barro,	Earthen ware.
Louça de eſtanho,	Pewter.

Do Comer, e Beber,	*Of Eating and Drinking.*
Vaca,	Beef.
Carneiro,	Mutton.
Vitella,	Veal.
Cordeiro,	Lamb.
Gallinha,	Hen.
Gallo,	Cock.
Perú,	A turkey.
Almôndegas,	Puddings.
O jantar,	The dinner.
Almoço,	Breakfaſt.
Cea,	Supper.
Merenda,	Luncheon, *or* the afternoon's luncheon.
Conſoada,	A light ſupper, as upon a faſt day.
Banquete,	An entertainment.
Fome,	Hunger.
Sede,	Thirſt.
Faſtio,	A loathing of meat.
Paõ,	Bread.

Paõ

Paõ fresco, or paõ molle,	New bread.
Paõ quente,	A hot loaf.
Paõ de toda farinha,	Wheaten bread.
Paõ branca, or paõ alvo,	White bread.
Arroz,	Rice.
Paõ de rala,	Brown bread.
Paõ de cevada,	Barley bread.
Paõ de centeo,	Rye bread.
Paõ de avea,	Oaten bread.
Paõ de milho miudo,	Millet bread.
Paõ de milho grande, ou de maiz,	Indian corn bread.
Paõ levedo,	Leavened bread.
Paõ asmo,	Unleavened bread.
Bifcouto,	Bifcuit.
Migalba de paõ,	A crumb of bread.
Fatia de paõ,	A flice of bread.
Côdea de paõ,	A cruft of bread.
Maffa,	Dough.
Torta,	A tart.
Rôfca,	Bread made like a roll.
Eftofado,	Stewed meat.
Fiambre,	Cold meat.
Carne affada fobre grelhos,	Broiled meat.
Carne frita,	Fried meat.
Picado, or carne picada,	A hafh.
Javali, or porco montez,	A wild boar.
Prefunto,	Ham, gammon of bacon.
Pôrco,	Pork.
Cabrito,	Kid,
Toucinho,	Bacon.
Hum lombo,	A loin.
Maõs de carneiro,	Sheeps trotters.
Freffura, or forçura,	A Pluck.
Cachôla de porco,	A hog's haflet.
Linguiça, or lingoiça,	A faufage.
Chouriço de fangue de porco,	Black-pudding.
Payo,	A thick and fhort faufage.
Fricaffé,	A fricaffee.
Figado,	Liver.
Leite,	Milk.
Nata,	Cream.
Soro,	Whey.
Requeijaõ,	A kind of new cheefe.
Coalhada,	Curdled milk, milk turned to curds.

Ovo,

Ovo,	An egg.
Gemma do ovo,	The yolk of an egg.
Clara do ovo,	The white of an egg.
Ovo fresco,	A new-laid egg.
Ovo molle,	A soft egg.
Ovo duro,	A hard egg.
Ovo assado,	A roasted egg.
Ovo gallado,	An egg with a chicken in it.
Ovos reaes,	Sweet eggs spun out like hairs.
Ovos escalfados,	Poached eggs.
Ovos fritos,	Fried eggs.
Ovos mexidos, e fritos,	An amlet.
Bolinholo,	A fritter.
Ovas de peixe,	The roes of fish.
Doces,	Sweetmeats.
Confeitos,	Comfits.
Marmelada,	Marmalade.

O que se Assa, *What is Roasted.*

Hum capaõ,	A capon.
Huma franga,	A pullet.
Hum frango,	A chicken.
Pombos,	Pigeons.
Pombo trocáz,	A wood-culver or, wood-pigeon.
Gallinhola,	A woodcock.
Huma especie de gallinhola pequena á qual os Castelhanos chamaõ gallineta cega,	A snipe.
Perdiz,	A partridge.
Tordo,	A thrush.
Faisaõ,	A pheasant.
Faisaõsinho,	A pheasant-powt.
Hum leitaõ,	A roasting-pig.
Veado,	A stag.
Hum Coelho,	A rabbit.
Láparo,	A young coney.
Lebre,	A hare.
Adem,	A duck.
Ganso, or o macho da adem,	A drake.
Pata,	Goose.
Pato,	Gander, the male of the goose.

Calhandra,

Calhandra,	A sky-lark.
Codorniz,	A quail.

De outros Pássaros,	Of other Birds.
Aguia,	An eagle.
Aguia nova,	An eaglet.
Abutre,	A vulture.
Abestrús,	An ostrich.
Esmerilhaõ,	A merlin.
Gaviaõ,	A sparrow-hawk.
Mocho,	A tassel, the tassel of a sparrow-hawk.
Falçaõ,	A falcon.
Falcaõ que ainda naõ voa,	A jass-hawk.
Gerifalte,	A ger-falcon.
Sacre,	A saker, a saker-hawk.
Garça,	A heron.
Melharuco,	Tomtit.
Garçota,	A little heron.
Milhano, or milhafre,	A kite.
Corvo,	A crow, or raven.
Gralha,	A rook.
Gralho,	A jack-daw, a chough, a jay.
Alveloa, pespita, or rabeta,	A wag-tail.
Canario,	A canary-bird.
Pintasilgo,	A goldfinch.
Mérlo,	A blackbird.
Tentilhaõ,	A chaffinch.
Rouxinol,	A nightingale.
Verdelhaõ,	A green-bird.
Papagayo,	A parrot.
Pega,	A magpye.
Estorninho, or zorzal,	A starling.
Francêlho,	A hobby, a musket.
Mocho,	Owl.
Coruja,	A screech owl.
Morcego,	A bat.
Ave nocturna, como melro, que mama as cabras,	A goat-milker.
O francolim,	A godwit, a moor-cock.
Bufo,	A night-crow, or raven.
Cerceta,	A teal.
Corvo marinho,	A cormorant.

Gaivota,

Gaivóta,	A moor-hen, *or* gull.
Gaivaõ,	A martlet, *or* martin, a kind of swallow.
Andorinha,	A swallow,
Mergulhaõ,	A diver, *or* didapper.
Marreca,	A wild duck.
Picanço,	A wren, a little bird.
Taralhaõ,	A kind of ortolan.
Pavaõ,	A peacock.
Pavôa,	A peahen.
Arára,	A macaw.
Pardál,	A sparrow.
Rôla,	A turtledove.
Alcyon,	A king's fisher.
Cegónha,	A stork.
Cuco,	A cuckow.
Cisne,	A swan.
Pintarroxo,	A red robbin.
Grou,	A crane.
Pavoncino,	A lapwing.
Pelicano,	A pelican.
Tarambóla,	A plover.
Pisco,	A bullfinch, *or* red-tail.

Para os Dias de Peixe, ou de Jejum,	*For Fish Days, or Fast Days.*
Sopa de peixe, ervas, &c.	Soop meagre, *or* lenten pottage.
Peixe,	Fish.
Peixe do mar,	Sea fish.
Peixe do rio, ou *da agoa doce,*	Fresh-water fish.
Sável,	A shad.
Anchôva,	An anchovy.
Anguia, or *Enguia,*	An eel.
Barbo,	A barbel.
Lúcio,	A pike, *or* jack.
Carpe,	A carp.
Siba,	A cuttle.
Lúla,	A calamary.
Cábra,	The miller's thumb.
Goráz,	A rochet, *or* roach.
Congro,	A conger.
Dourada,	Dorado, St. Peter's fish, *or* the gilt head.

Lin-

Linguado,	A sole.
Lagosta,	A lobster.
Bordalo,	A sturgeon; some call it shad-fish.
Mugem,	A mullet.
Rodavalho,	A byrt, or turbot.
Sarda,	A sort of little mackerel.
Cavalla,	A mackerel.
Sardinha,	A pilchard.
Bacalhâs,	Dry cod.
Arenque,	A herring.
Voador,	A flying-fish.
Arenque de fuma,	A red herring.
Arenque com ôvas,	A hard-rowed herring.
Pescada,	A kind of cod-fish.
Cadoz,	A gudgeon.
Ostra,	An oyster.
Lamprea,	A lamprey.
Lamprea, pequena,	A lampern.
Porco marinho,	A porpoise.
Polvo,	Pourcontrell, or many-feet.
Perca,	Perch.
Tinca,	A tench.
Truta,	A trout.
Atûm,	A tunny-fish.
Salmaô,	A salmon.
Camaraô,	A shrimp.
Caranguejo,	A crab.
Ameijoa,	A cockle.
Ervilhas,	Pease.
Favas,	Beans.
Espinafres,	Spinage.
Alcachofras,	Artichoaks.
Espargos,	Asparagus.
Couve,	Cabbage, colewort.
Repolho,	Cabbage.
Nabos,	Turnips.
Grelos de couve,	Sprouts.
Couve crespa,	Curled colewort.
Coliflor, or couliflor,	Cauliflower.
Beldroegas,	Purslane.
Cenouras,	Carrots.
Celgas, or acelgas,	Beets.
Tomates,	Apples of love.

Para

Para temperar o Comer,	To season Meat with.
Sal,	Salt.
Pimenta,	Pepper.
Pimentaõ,	Guiney-pepper.
Azeite,	Oil.
Vinagre,	Vinegar.
Mostarda,	Mustard.
Cravos,	Cloves.
Canela,	Cinnamon.
Loureiro,	Laurel.
Alcaparras.	Capers.
Cogumelos,	Mushrooms.
Tuhara da terra,	Truffles.
Cebôlas,	Onions.
Ouregaõ,	Organy.
Funcho,	Fennel.
Cebolinhas,	Young onions.
Alho,	Garlick.
Laranjas,	Oranges.
Limoens,	Lemons.
Pinhoens,	The kernels of a pine-apple.
Perrexil, .	Wild-parsley.
Salsa,	Garden-parsley.
Ortelaã,	Mint.
Aipo hortense,	Cellery.
Alho porro,	Leek.
Coentro,	Coriander.
Açafram,	Saffron.
Cominhos,	Cummins.

Para Salada,	For a Sallad.
Almeiraõ,	Wild succory.
Almeiraõ hortense, or endivia,	Endive.
Alface,	Lettuce.
Chicória, .	Succory.
Agriões,	Water-cresses.
Mastruços, or masturços,	Cresses.
Cerefólia,	Chervil.
Rabaõ,	Raddish root.

Pará

Para Sobremefa.	For the Deſſert.
Maçaãs,	Apples.
Peras	Pears.
Pera bergamota	A bergamot pear.
Pécegos,	Peaches.
Camoeza,	A pippin.
Albricoque, fruta nova, or da- maſco,	Apricot.
Cerejas,	Cherries.
Cerejas de ſaco,	Hard cherries.
Ginjas,	Sour cherries.
Ginja garrafãl,	A very large ſort of cherry, the fruit of the dwarf cherry-tree.
Laranja da China,	China-orange.
Uvas,	Grapes.
Paſſas de uva,	Raiſins.
Uva eſpim,	Gooſeberries.
Figos,	Figs.
Figos lampos,	The firſt figs that come in May.
Ameixas,	Plumbs.
Paſſas de ameixas,	Prunes.
Amoras de çarça, or de ſylva,	Blackberries.
Amoras que nacem de huma ſorte de ſylva tenra,	Raſpberries.
Amoras que nacem da amoreira,	Mulberries.
Marmelos,	Quinces.
Romaãs,	Pomegranates.
Lima,	A lime.
Azeitonas,	Olives.
Amendoas,	Almonds.
Neſperas,	Medlars.
Melaã,	A melon.
Melancia, or balancia,	Water-melon.
Caſtanhas,	Cheſnuts.
Nozes	Walnuts.
Avelans,	Hazel nuts.
Morangos,	Strawberries.
Medranho,	A ſort of fruit they have in Portugal like a ſtrawberry eating whereof, they ſay, makes people drunk.
	Tâmara.

Tâmara,	A date.
Fiftico,	Piftacho, *or* piftache nut.
Alfarrôba,	A carob.
Bolota,	A fweet acorn.
Sorva,	Service.
Açofeifa, or maçaã de náfega,	A jujub.
Doces,	Sweet meats.

Das Arvores e Arbuftos. Of Trees and Shrubs.

Damafqueiro,	An apricot-tree.
Amendoeira,	An almon tree.
Cerejeira,	A cherry-tree.
Caftanheiro,	A chefnut tree.
Cidreira,	A citron-tree.
Sorveira,	A fervice tree.
Palmeyra,	A palm-tree.
Figueira,	A fig-tree.
Marmeleiro,	A quince-tree.
Maceira,	An apple-tree.
Maceira da náfega,	A jujub-tree.
Romeira,	A pomegranate-tree.
Limoeiro,	A lemon-tree.
Amoreira,	A mulberry-tree.
Oliveira,	An olive-tree.
Nefpereira,	A medlar-tree.
Laranjeira,	An orange-tree.
Murta,	Myrtle.
Nogueira,	A walnut-tree.
Zambujeiro,	A wild olive-tree.
Era,	Ivy.
Pecegueiro,	A peach-tree.
Rofeira,	A rofe bufh.
Ameixieira,	A plumb-tree.
Pereira,	A pear-tree.
Rofmaninho,	Rofemary.
Pinheiro,	A pine-tree.
Giefta,	Broom.

Dos Reptiles, e Animaes amphibios. Of Reptiles and amphibious Creatures,

Minhóca,	An earth-worm.
Serpente,	A ferpent.

Serpente com azas,	A flying serpent.
Aspide,	An asp.
Cobra,	A snake.
Cobra de cascavel,	A rattle-snake.
Vibora,	A viper.
Lagarto,	A lizard.
Osga,	An evet, eft or, newt.
Alacrao,	A scorpion.
Crocodilo,	A crocodile.
Jacaré, or crocodilo da America,	An alligator.
Castor,	A beaver.
Cágado,	A land-tortoise.
Lontra,	An otter.

Dos Insectos.   Of the Insects.

Aranha,	A spider.
Formiga,	A pismire, or ant.
Caracól,	A snail.
Raã,	A frog.
Sapo,	A toad.
Ouçaõ,	Hand-worm.
Escaravélho,	A beetle.
Caruncho,	Wood-worm.
Piolho, or lagarta da hortaliça,	Caterpillar.
Cigarra,	Grashopper.
Borboleta,	A butterfly.
Grillo,	A cricket.
Piôlho,	A louse.
Piolho ladro,	Crab-louse.
Lêndea,	A nit.
Pulga,	A flea.
Mosca,	A fly.
Persovejo,	A bug.
Carrapato,	A tick.
Gafanhoto,	A locust.
Polilha, or traça,	Moth.
Vespa, or abêspora,	A wasp.
Abelha,	A bee.
Zango, or Zangaõ,	A drone.
Tavaõ,	An ox-fly, a guard-bee.
Boy de Deos,	A lady-bird.
Mosquito,	A gnat.

Graos

Graos de Parentesco.	Degrees of Kindred.
Pay,	Father.
May,	Mother.
Avô,	Grandfather.
Avó,	Grandmother.
Bisavô,	Great grandfather.
Bisavó,	Great grandmother.
Filho,	Son.
Filha,	Daughter.
Irmaõ,	Brother.
Irmaã,	Sister.
Primogenito,	The eldeſt ſon.
O filho maîs moço,	The youngeſt ſon.
Tio,	Uncle.
Tia,	Aunt.
Sobrinho,	Nephew.
Sobrinha,	Niece.
Primo,	Couſin.
Prima,	A ſhe couſin.
Primo com irmaõ	The (he) firſt couſin.
Prima com irmaã,	The (ſhe) firſt couſin.
Cunhádo,	Brother-in-law.
Cunháda,	Sister-in-law.
Meyo irmaõ,	Half brother.
Sôgro,	Father-in-law.
Sôgra,	Mother-in-law.
Padráſto,	A ſtep-father.
Madráſta,	A ſtep-mother.
Enteádo,	A ſtep-ſon.
Enteáda,	A ſtep-daughter.
Genro,	A ſon-in-law.
Nôra,	A daughter-in-law.
Néta	A grand-daughter.
Néto,	A grand-ſon.
Bifnéto,	A great grand-ſon.
Bifneta,	A great grand-daughter.
Conſorte, maſc. and fem.	A conſort.
Marido,	Husband.
Mother,	Wife.
Irmaõ gémeo,	A twin-brother.
Coiaço, or irmaõ de leite,	A foster-brother.
Baſtardo,	A baſtard.
Compádre,	A he-goſſip.

Comádre

Comádre,	A she-gossip.
Afilhádo,	A god-son.
Afilháda,	A god-daughter.
Padrinho,	A god-father.
Madrinha,	A god-mother.
O parente,	A he relation.
A parente,	A she relation.
Parente por affinidade, or *consanguinidade*,	A kin, a relation either of affinity, or consanguinity.

Dos differentes Generos de Eftado de hum Homem, ou de huma Molher, e das fuas qualidades,	*Of the Conditions of Man and Woman, as well as of their qualities.*

O Homem,	A man.
A molher,	A woman.
Hum homem de idade,	An aged man.
Huma molher de idade,	An aged woman.
Hum velho,	An old man.
Huma velha,	An old woman.
Hum moço, ou mancebo,	A young man.
Huma rapariga,	A girl.
Hum amante,	A spark.
Huma amiga,	A miftrefs.
Huma criança, ou menino,	A child, a little child.
Hum rapaz,	A boy.
Hum rapazinho,	A little boy.
Huma menina,	A little girl.
Huma donzélla,	A maiden.
Huma virgem,	A virgin.
Amo,	A mafter.
Ama,	A miftrefs.
Criado,	A he fervant.
Criada,	A fhe fervant.
Cidadaõ,	A citizen.
Ruftico,	A countryman.
Hum eftrangèiro,	A ftranger.
Hum viuvo,	A widower.
Huma viuva,	A widow.
Hum herdeiro,	An heir.
Huma herdeira,	An heirefs.
Solteiro,	A bachelor.
Eftado de folteiro,	Bachelorfhip.

Homem

Homem casado,	A married man.
Molher casada,	A married woman.
Molher que está de parto,	A lying-in-woman.
Destro,	Dextrous.
Agudo,	Sharp.
Recatado,	Cautious.
Astuto, or *velhaco,*	Cunning, sly, crafty.
Esperto, or *vivo,*	Sprightly.
Doudo,	Mad.
Malicioso,	Malicious.
Timido,	Fearful.
Valeroso,	Brave.
Tonto,	Stupid.
Embusteiro,	Deceitful.
Grosseiro,	Clownish.
Bem criado,	Well-bred.
Cortez,	Courteous.
Justo,	Just.
Desavergonhado,	Impudent.
Impertinente,	Impertinent.
Importuno,	Troublesome.
Descuidado,	Careless.
Temerário,	Rash.
Constante,	Constant.
Devoto,	Devout.
Diligente,	Diligent.
Misericordioso, or *compassivo,*	Merciful.
Paciente,	Patient.
Ambicioso,	Ambitious.
Cobiçoso,	Covetous.
Soberbo,	Proud.
Cobarde,	Coward.
Lisonjeiro,	A flatterer.
Goloso,	Glutton.
Desleál,	Treacherous.
Desagradecido,	Ungrateful.
Inhumano,	Inhumane.
Insolente,	Insolent.
Luxuriôso,	Lewd.
Teimôso,	Positive, stubborn.
Preguiçôso,	Slothful.
Pródigo,	Prodigal.
Molherengo,	Given to women.
Atrevido,	Bold.
Alegre,	Merry.

Que

Que tem ciumes,	Jealous.
Adultero,	Adulterer.
Salteador,	A highwayman.
Matador,	A murderer.
Murmurador,	A cenfurer.
Calumniador,	A calumniator.
Feiticeiro,	A forcerer.
Trahidor,	A traitor.
Malvado,	Wicked.
Rebelde,	A rebel.
Perfido,	Perfidious.
Bobo,	A buffoon.
Mentirôſo,	A lyar.
Altivo,	Haughty.
Coxo,	Lame of the legs.
Eſtropeado das maõs,	Lame of the hands.
Cego,	Blind.
Mouco, or *ſurdo,*	Deaf.
Canhoto, or *eſquerdo,*	Left-handed.
Mudo,	Dumb.

Dos Moradores de huma Cidade.	*Of the Inhabitants of a City.*

Nobre,	A nobleman.
Fidalgo,	A gentleman.
Mecanico,	A mechanic.
Tendeiro,	A fhop-keeper.
Mercador, or *homem de nego-gocio,*	Merchant, *or* trader.
O vulgo, or *a plebe,*	The mob.
Canalha, or *a mais vil gente da plebe,*	The rabble.
Official,	A work-man, a man that labours with his hands.
Jornaleiro,	A journeyman.
Prateiro,	A filver-fmith.
Orives do ouro,	A gold-fmith.
Livreiro,	A book-feller.
Impreſſor,	A printer.
Barbeiro,	A barber.
Mercador de feda,	A mercer.
Mercador de panno.	A woollen-draper.

Mercador

Mercador de panno de linho, e roupas da India, or *fanqueiro,*	A linen-draper.
Alfayate,	A taylor.
Alfayate remendaõ,	Botcher.
Costureira,	A sempstress.
Sombreireiro,	A hatter.
Sapateiro,	Shoemaker.
Remendaõ (sapateiro),	A cobler.
Ferreiro,	A blacksmith.
Alveitar,	Farrier.
Cerralheyro,	A locksmith.
Parteira,	A midwife.
Medico,	A physician.
Charlataõ,	A quack.
Cirurgiam, or *surgiaõ*	A surgeon.
Sacamólas,	A tooth-drawer.
Selleiro,	A saddler.
Carpinteiro,	A carpenter.
Gastador (in an army),	A pioneer.
Padeiro,	A baker.
Carniceiro,	A butcher.
Fruteiro,	A fruiterer.
Molher que vende verduras, ou ortaliças,	An herb-woman.
Pasteleiro,	A pastry-cook.
Taverneiro, or *vendeiro,*	A vintner.
Cervejeiro, or *o que faz cerveja,*	A brewer.
Estalajadeiro,	A inn-keeper.
Bofarinheiro, or *mercader de mercearia.*	A pedlar.
Relogeiro,	A watch-maker.
Pregoeiro,	A crier.
Joyeiro, or *joyalheiro,*	A jeweller.
Boticario,	An apothecary.
Vidraceiro,	A glazier.
Carvoeiro,	A collier.
Jardineiro,	A gardener.
Letrado,	A lawyer.
Procurador,	A solicitor.
Advogado,	An advocate, *or* a pleader.
Juiz,	A judge.
Carcereiro,	A gaoler.
Verdugo, or *algôz,*	A hangman.
Puta,	A whore.

T

Alcoviteiro,

Alcoviteiro,	A pimp.
Mariola,	A porter.

Os cinco Sentidos.	*The five Senses.*
A vista,	The fight.
O ouvido,	The hearing.
O olfacto,	The smell.
O gosto,	The tafte.
O tacto,	The feeling.

As Partes do Corpo Humano.	*The Parts of the Human Body.*
Cabeça,	The head.
Miólos, or *cerebro*,	The brains.
Toutiço,	The hinder part of the head.
Tésta,	The forehead.
Molleira,	The mould of the head.
Fontes,	The temples.
Orelha,	The ear.
Cartilagem,	The griftle.
Timpano,	The drum of the ear.
Sobrancelha,	Eye-brow.
Palpebras, or *Capellas dos olhos*,	The eye-lid.
Pestanas,	The eye-lafhes.
Lagrimal,	The corner of the eye.
Alva do olho,	The white of the eye.
Meninas dos olhos,	The eye-balls.
Nariz,	The nofe.
Maçãa do rosto,	The ball of the cheeks.
Ventas,	The noftrils.
Septo, or *diaphragmo do nariz*,	The griftle of the nofe.
A ponta do nariz,	The tip of the nofe.
A boca,	The mouth.
Os dentes,	The teeth.
A gengiva,	The gum.
A lingoa,	Tongue.
Padar, paladar, or *ceo da boca*,	The roof, *or* palate of the mouth.
Queixada,	The jaw.
A barba,	The chin.
As barba,	The beard.

B *soles*

Bigodes,	Wiſkers.
O peſcoço,	The neck.
A nuca,	The nape of the neck.
A garganta,	The throat.
Gaſnate,	The gullet.
Seyo,	The boſom.
Teta,	The pap.
Peïto,	The breaſt.
Bico do peito,	The nipple.
Eſtomago,	The ſtomach.
Coſtelas,	The ribs.
Embigo,	The navel.
Barriga,	The belly.
Verilha,	The groin.
O braço,	The arm.
O cotovêlo,	The elbow.
Sobaco, or *ſovaco,*	The arm-pit.
A maõ,	The hand.
Munhéca,	The wriſt.
A palma da maõ,	The palm of the hand.
Os dedos,	The fingers.
O dedo polegar,	The thumb.
O dedo moſtrador,	The fore-finger.
Dedo do meyo,	The middle-finger.
Dedo annular,	The ring-finger.
Dedo meminho, or *minimo,*	The little-finger.
Pontas dos dedos,	The tips, *or* tops of the fingers.
Juntas, e nós dos dedos,	The joints, and knuckles of the fingers.
Dedo do pé,	A toe.
A unha,	The nail.
As coſtas,	The back.
Os ombros,	The ſhoulders.
Ilhargas,	The ſides.
As nádegas,	The buttocks.
Coxa,	The thigh.
Joelho,	The knee.
Barriga da perna,	The calf of the leg.
Eſpinhaço	The ridge-bone of the back.
Tornozelo,	The ancle.
O pé	The foot.
Sola do pé,	The ſole of the foot.
O coraçaõ,	The heart.
Os bofes,	The lungs.

O ſl-

O figado,	The liver.
O baço,	The spleen.
Os rins,	The kidneys.
A boca do estomago,	The pit of the stomach.
As tripas,	The guts.
O fel,	The gall.
A madre,	The womb.
Bexiga,	The bladder.
Sangue,	The blood.
Cuspo,	What's spit up.
Ourina,	Urine.
Excremento,	Dung.
Suòr,	Sweat.
Monco, or ranho,	Snot.
Lágrima,	Tear.
Carêpa, or caspa,	Scurf.

Dos Vestidos.   Of Cloaths.

Hum vestido,	A suit of cloaths.
Cabelleira,	A wig.
Cravàta,	A cravat, or neckcloth.
Chapéo,	A hat.
Abas do chapéo,	The brims.
Cordaõ, ou fita para o chapéo,	A hatband.
Barrete,	A cap.
Capa,	A cloak.
Gibaõ,	A doublet.
Véstià,	A waistcoat.
Camisa,	A shirt.
Casáca,	A close coat.
Casacaõ,	A great coat.
Calçoens,	Breeches.
Ceroulas,	Drawers.
Meas, or meyas,	Stockings.
Meyas de cabrestilho,	Stirrup-stockings.
Ligas,	Garters.
Sapatos,	Shoes.
Chinelas,	Slippers.
Bótas,	Boots.
Fivelas,	Buckles.
Espôras,	Spurs.
Punhos,	Ruffles.
Talim, or taly,	A shoulder-belt.

3   *Boldrié,*

Boldrié,	A waiſt-belt.
Eſpada,	A ſword.
Luvas,	Gloves.
Cinta,	A girdle.
Lenço,	Handkerchief.
Lenço para o peſcoço,	A neck handkerchief.
Samarra, or *pellote do campo,*	A ſhepherd's jerkin.

Para Molheres.	*For Women.*
Camiſa de molheres,	A ſhift, *or* ſmock.
Toucado,	A head-dreſs.
Saya,	A petticoat.
Mantilha,	A little cloak women wear on their heads.
Manto,	A mantle, a kind of cloak women wear in Portugal, covering their head and upper part of their body.
Avental,	An apron.
Braceletes,	Bracelets.
Anel,	Ring.
Arrecadas,	Ear rings.
Leque,	A fan.
Penteadôr,	A combing-cloth.
Toucadôr,	A toilet, a dreſsing-table.
Sinaes,	Patches to wear on one's face.
Eſpelho,	A looking-glaſs.
Regalo,	A muff.
Eſpartilho,	Stays.
Pente,	A comb.
Alfinetes,	Pins.
Teſoura,	A pair of ſciſſars.
Dedal,	A thimble.
Agulha,	A needle.
Fio,	Thread.
Fio de pérolas,	A necklace of pearls.
Polvilhos,	Powder.
Joyas,	Jewels.
Côr,	Paint.
Palito,	A tooth-pick.
Roca,	A diſtaff.
Fuſo,	The ſpindle.
Almofadinha para alfinetes,	Small pincuſhion.

Agulha de toucar,	Bodkin.
Fitas,	Ribbons.
Fichú, (forte de lenço para o peſcoço)	A neckatee.
Tenazinhas,	Nippers.
Pendentes,	Bob, *or* pendant.
Palatina,	Tippet.
Guarda-infante, or *Guardin-fante,*	Farthingale.
Véo,	Veil.
Renda,	Lace.
Bilros,	Bobbins.
Bilros feitos de oſſo,	Bones.
Agoa da rainha de Ungria,	Hungary water.
Agoa de cheiro,	Scented water.
Juſtilho,	Bodice.

Os doze Signos Celeſtes,	*The twelve Celeſtial Signs.*
Aries,	Aries, *or* the ram.
Touro,	The bull.
Gemini, or *Geminis,*	The twins.
Cancer,	The crab.
Leaõ,	The lion.
Virgem,	The virgin.
Libra,	The ballance.
Eſcorpiaã,	The ſcorpion.
Sagitario,	The archer.
Capricornio,	The goat.
Aquario,	The water-bearer.
Peixes,	The fiſhes.

De huma Caſa, e do que lhe pertence,	*Of a Houſe and all that belongs to it.*
Caſa,	A houſe.
Alicerſe,	Foundation.
Párede,	A wall.
Tabique,	A light brick wall.
Páteo, or *Patio,*	A court, *or* yard.
Andar, or *ſobrado,*	A floor.
Fachada,	The front.
Janella,	A window.

Abobada,

Abóbada,	A vault.
As escadas,	The stairs.
Degráos,	Steps.
Telhado,	A tiled roof.
Telhas,	Tiles.
Ladrilhos, or *tijoles,*	Bricks.
Aposento,	A room.
Antecamara,	Antichamber.
Sala,	A hall.
Tecto,	A roof.
Alcóva,	An alcove.
Balcaõ,	A balcony.
Gabinete,	Closet.
Almário,	A cupboard.
Guarda-roupa,	Wardrobe.
Adéga,	A cellar.
Cozinha,	A kitchen.
Despensa,	A pantry.
Cheminé,	A chimney.
Cavallariça,	The stable.
Gallinheiro, or *casa das gal-* *linhas,*	A hen-house.
Poleiro,	A hen-roost.
Jardim,	A garden.
Necessarias,	The necessary house.
Casa onde se janta,	A dining-room.
Camara, or *casa em que se* *dorme,*	Bed-chamber.
Sala de visitas nos baixos de *huma casa,*	A parlour.
Porta,	The door.
Postigo,	A wicket.
Liminar, or *lumiar,*	The threshold.
Vidraças que se poem no tecto *de huma casa para a alumiar,*	Sky-lights.
Algeróz,	The gutter.
Beiras, or *abas do telhado,*	The eaves.
A couceira da porta,	The hinges.
Fechadura,	A lock.
Cadeado,	A padlock.
Ferrolho,	The bolt.
Tranca da porta,	The bar of a door.
Cano da chave,	The pipe of a key.
Chave mestra,	A master-key.
Guardas da fechadura,	The wards of a lock.

T 4

Palhetaõ

Portuguese	English
Palhetaõ da chave,	Key-bit.
Vidraça,	The glafs of a window.
Efcada feita a caracol,	A winding ftair-cafe.
Efcada fecreta,	Back ftairs, a private ftair-cafe.
Viga,	A beam.
Parede meftra,	The main wall.
Paredes meyas,	The party-walls.
Arca,	Cheft.
Cama,	Bed.
Sobreceo da cama,	The bed's tefter.
Cortinas da cama,	Bed curtains.
Lençoes,	Sheets.
Cabeceira da cama,	The bed's-head.
Pés da cama,	Bed's-feet.
Colcha,	Counter-pane, a quilt.
Colchaõ,	A matrafs.
Cobertor,	A blanket.
Coberior de felpa,	A rug.
Catre, pés, taboas, &c. *de que fe compoem o leito,*	Bedftead.
Traveffeiro,	A pillow.
Tapete,	A carpet.
Tapeçaria,	Tapeftry.
Pederneira,	A flint.
Ifca,	Tinder.
Mecha,	Match.
Enxergaõ,	A ftraw-bed.
Efteira,	A mat.
Caens da cheminé,	Hand-irons.
Folles,	Bellows.
Tenazes,	Tongs.
Ferra,	A fhovel.
Abâno, or *abanador,*	Fire-fan.
Panella,	A pipkin.
Tefto,	The pot lid.
Aza da panella,	The ear of a pot, *or* pipkin.
Ferro para atiçar o lume,	A poker.
Efcumadeira,	A fkimmer.
Colher grande,	A ladle.
Caldeira,	A kettle.
Sertaã, or *frigideira,*	A frying-pan.
Coador,	A cullender; *or* ftrainer.
Grelhas,	Gridirons.
Ralo,	A grater.

Efpeto,

Espéto,	A spit.
Almofariz,	A mortar of metal wherein things are pounded.
Maõ do almofariz,	A pestle.
Redoma,	A vial.
Bolde,	A bucket, or pail.
Sabaõ,	Soap.
Rodilha,	A coarse cloth.
Esfregaõ	A dish-clout.
Forno,	Oven.
Pá do forno,	The peel of the oven.
Vasculho para alimparo forno,	A maukin, a coal-rake to make clean an oven.
Farinha,	Meal-flour.
Trinchante,	A carver.
Mordômo,	A steward.
Camareiro,	A valet de chambre.
Camareiro môr,	A chamberlain.
Escôva,	A brush.
Vassoura,	A broom.
Despenseiro,	A butler, a yeoman of the larder, a steward.
Pagem,	A page.
Lacayo,	Footman.
Cocheiro,	A coachman.
Cocheira,	A coach-house.
Maço dos cavallos, ou da estrebaria,	A groom.
Copeiro,	A cup-bearer.
Escudeiro de huma fidalga,	A lady's gentleman-usher.
Amo, ou senhor da casa,	Landlord.
Ama, ou senhora da casa,	Landlady.
Grimpa,	Weather-cock.

Côres.	Colours.
Branco,	White.
Azul,	Blue.
Azul celeste, or turqui,	Sky colour.
Azul ferrete,	Dark blue.
Azul claro,	Light blue.
Cor de camurça,	Light yellow.
Amarelo,	yellow.
Cor de rosa,	Rosy colour.
Cor de palha,	Straw colour.

Verde,

Verde,	Green.
Cor de verde mar, or *verde claro,*	Plunket colour, *or* sea-green.
Cor vermelha,	Red colour.
Cor vermelha muito viva, or *carmin,*	Carmine, a bright red colour.
Cor incarnada,	Carnation colour.
Cor de carne,	Flesh colour.
Cor carmesim,	Crimson red.
Cor negra, or *preta,*	Black colour.
Cor de mel,	A dark yellow.
Furta cores, or *cambiantes,*	A deep changeable colour.
Cor viva,	A lively and gay colour.
Cor triste,	A dull colour.
Cor escura,	A dark colour.
Cor carregada,	A deep colour.
Cor de fogo,	Fire colour.
Pardo,	Grey.
Cor de cinza,	Ash colour.
Escarlata,	Scarlet.
Leonado,	Tawney.
Cor de laranja,	Orange colour.
Cor de azeitona,	Olive colour.
Roxo,	Purple, violet.
Roxo, or *cor de aurora,*	Aurora colour.

Roxo sometimes signifies *red*, or *rosy colour*; particularly in poetry, as in *Camoens*, Canto I. Stanza 82.

> *Para que ao Portuguez se lhe tornasse*
> *Em* roxo *sangue a agoa, que bebesse.*

Bestas.	**Beasts.**
Besta domestica,	Tame beast.
Besta brava,	A wild beast.
Besta de carga,	A beast of burthen.
Besta de sella,	A beast for the saddle.
Gado,	Cattle.
Gado grosso,	Great cattle.
Gado miudo,	Small cattle.
Rebanho,	A flock.
Manada de gado grosso,	A herd of big cattle.
Touro,	A bull.
Bezerra,	Heifer.

Bezerro,

Bezerro,	A calf, a steer, a young bullock.
Boy,	An ox.
Burro,	An aſs.
Burra,	A ſhe aſs.
Porco,	A hog.
Porca,	A ſow.
Faca,	A young mare, alſo a nag.
Egoa,	A mare.
Cria,	A foal, a filly.
Potro.	A colt, or young horſe.
Cavallo,	A horſe.
Cavallo anaõ,	A nag.
Cavallo de poſta,	A poſt horſe.
Garanhaõ. or *cavallo de lançamento,*	A ſtaltion.
Cavallo de aluguel,	A hackney-horſe.
Cavallo de coche,	A coach-horſe.
Cavallo que anda de chouto,	A jolting-horſe.
Cavallo pequeno que ſerve para ſenhoras,	A palfrey.
Cavallo que toma o freio entre dentes,	A horſe that champs the bit.
Cavallo rijo da boca,	A hard-mouthed horſe.
Cavallo doce de freio,	A horſe of an eaſy reſt upon the hand.
Cavallo que tem boa boca,	A horſe that will eat any thing.
Cavallo que tropeſſa,	A ſtumbling horſe.
Cavallo eſpantadiço,	A ſtarting horſe.
Cavallo ardente, or *fogazo,*	A ſtately horſe.
Cavallo que morde e dá couces,	A biting and kicking horſe.
Cavallo rebellaõ,	An untamed horſe.
Cavallo que naõ ſoffre ancas,	A horſe that will not carry double.
Cavallo mal mandado,	A reſtive horſe.
Cavallo de albarda,	A pack horſe.
Cavallo de carro,	A cart-horſe
Cavallo de ſella,	A ſaddle-horſe.
Cavallo de correr,	A race-horſe.
Cavallo de guerra,	A war-horſe.
Cavallo ajaezado,	A horſe with all his furniture.
Cavallo de Barbaria,	A Moorîſh horſe, a barb.
Cavallo capado,	A gelding.
Cavallo ſem ſer capado,	A ſtone horſe.
Cavallo que dá aos folles,	A broken winded horſe.

Cavallo,

Cavallo quatralvo,	A horse that has four white feet.
Cavallo alazaõ,	A sorrel horse.
Cavallo baio,	A bay horse.
Cavallo castanho	A chesnut-coloured horse.
Cavallo baia e castanho,	A chesnut bay.
Cavallo rocim,	A worthless nag, a poor jade.
Cavallo remendado,	A dapple horse.
Cavallo ruaõ, or russo porcellana,	A dapple-grey horse.
Cavallo que soffre ancas,	A double horse.
Cavallo trotaõ,	A trotting horse.
Cavallo que serve para andar á caça,	A stalking horse.
Cavallo que anda de furtapasso,	A pad, an easy paced horse.
Caõ	A dog
Caõ de quinta,	A house dog.
Caõ de caça,	A hound.
Caõ de agoa,	A water spaniel.
Caõ de gado,	A shepherd's dog.
Caõ de mostra, podengo, or perdigueiro,	A setting dog.
Caõ de fila,	A great cur, a mastiff dog.
Caõ sacador,	A dog tumbler.
Caõ de busca,	A finder.
Alaõ,	A bull-dog.
Galgo,	A grey hound.
Caõ para caçar rapozas e lontras,	A tarrier.
Cachorrinha,	A little puppy, a whelp.
Cachorrinho de fralda,	A lap-dog.
Cachorro,	A little dog.
Mú, macho, or mulo,	A he mule.
Mula,	A she mule.
Corça,	A she deer, a doe.
Corça de tres annos,	A spade.
Corço de dous annos,	A priket.
Corço,	A wild buck.
Corço, ou corça, de hum anno,	A fawn.
Gamo,	A fallow deer.
Veado,	A stag.
Cabra montez,	A wild she-goat.
Veado grande, de cinco annos,	A hart
Doninha,	A weasel.
Teixugo, or texugo,	A badger.

Gate

Gato de algália,	A civet cat.
Doninha de rabo mui felpudo, a modo de rapofa,	A fquirrel.
Elephante,	An elephant.
Foinha, fuinha, or marta,	A marten, *or* martern.
Arminho,	An ermin.
Ouriço cacheyro,	An hedge-hog.
Arganáz,	A dormoufe.
Rato,	A rat.
Rapofa,	A fox.
Lobo,	A wolf.
Rato da India,	A rat of India of the bignefs of a cat.
Foraõ,	A ferret.
Toupeira,	A mole.
Leaõ,	A lion.
Leôa,	A lionefs.
Rato cheyrofo,	A mufk cat.
Leopardo,	A leopard.
Urfo,	A he bear.
Urfa,	A fhe bear.
Urfo pequeno,	A bear's cub.
Tigre,	A tyger.
Porco montez,	A wild boar.

Das Coufas do Campo,   *Of Country Affairs.*

Cafa do campo, or *quinta,*	A country-houfe.
Cafa de lavrador,	A farm houfe.
Quinteiro,	A husband-man, a farmer.
Boyeiro,	A herdfman, he that ploughs with oxen, *or* tends them.
Vaqueiro,	A cow-keeper.
Porqueiro,	A fwine herd.
Paftor,	A fhepherd.
Surraõ	A fcrip.
Cajado,	A fheep-hook.
Paftora,	A fhepherdefs, a rural lafs.
Herdade,	A great *or* large field, a wide arable ground.
Hortolaõ,	A gardner.
Hortaliça,	All forts of herbage.
Cavador,	A ditcher.
Vinhateiro,	A vine-dreffer.

Lavrador,

Lavrador,	A farmer, one who cultivates ground, whether his own or another's.
Paſtos,	Feeding ground, paſture, ſheep walk.
Arado,	A plough.
Ferro do arado,	The plough-ſhare.
Rabo do arado,	The plough handle.
Abegaõ, or *official que faz arados,*	A plough-wright.
Aguilhada,	A goad.
Enſinho,	A rake.
Grade,	A harrow.
Semeador,	A ſower.
Roçador,	A weeder.
Fouce roçadoura,	A weeding-hook.
Fouce,	A ſcythe, *or* ſickle.
Podaõ,	A pruning knife.
Segador,	A reaper, *or* mower, harveſt man.
Mangoal,	A flail.
Forcado,	A prong to caſt up ſheeves of corn with.
Caçador,	A huntſman.
Peſcador,	A fiſherman.
Rego,	A furrow.
Terra que fica levantada entre dous regos,	A balk, *or* ridge of land between two furrows.
Outeiro,	A hill.
Monte, or *montanha,*	A mountain.
Valle,	A valley.
Lagôa,	A moor, fen, *or* marſh, a ſtanding water, but ſometimes dry.
Lago,	A lake, *or* ſtanding pool, but always full of water.
Ribeiro,	A brook, a ſtream of water with a gentle *or* natural current.
Ribeirinho,	A rivulet, a ſtreamlet.
Plano, or *planicie,*	A plain.
Penha, or *rocha,*	A rock.
Penhaſco,	A great rock.
Deſerto,	A deſert, *or* wilderneſs.

Deſpenhadeiro,

Deſpenbadeiro,	A precipice.
Boſque,	A wood.
Boſque pequeno,	A grove, *or* thicket.
Pedaço de chaõ ſem arvores den-tro de hum boſque,	A glade in a wood.
Pomar, or *vergel,*	An orchard.
Prado,	A meadow.
Ramada,	A bower.
Fonte,	A fountain.
Trigo,	Wheat.
Trigo candial,	The beſt wheat.
Trigo bretanha,	Red wheat.
Centeo,	Rye.
Ferrãa,	Meſlin, mixed corn, as wheat and rye, &c.
Tremez,	The corn of three months growth.
Eſpélta,	Spelt.
Eſpiga,	Ear of corn.
Cabeça da eſpiga,	The little grain at the top of the ear of corn.
Bainha, donde ſahe a eſpiga depois de formada,	The cod, *or* huſk in which the ear of corn is lodged.
Legumes,	Pulſe.
Graõs,	Spaniſh peaſe.
Lentilha,	A lentil.
Tramoço, or *tremoço,*	A lupine.
Feijoens,	French-beans.
Feijaõ ſapata, or *bajes,*	Kidney-beans.
Feijao fradinho,	A ſort of ſmall French beans with a black ſpot.
Chicharo,	Chichlings.
Carreta,	A waggon.
Carro,	A cart.
Roda,	A wheel.
Caimbas,	The felloes of the wheel.
Eixo,	The axle-tree.
Rayo da roda,	The ſpoke of a wheel.
Curral de boys,	An ox-ſtall.
Curral de ovelhas,	A ſheep-fold.
Curral de cabras,	A houſe for goats.
Chiqueiro de porcos,	A hog's ſty.
Erva,	Graſs.
Trigo em erva,	Green corn.

Seara,

Seara,	Standing corn.
Tarro,	A milk-pail.
Cincho,	A cheese-vat, to make cheese in.
Enxada,	A mattock, a hoe.
Enxadaõ, or *alviaõ,*	A two forked tool, a prong to set plants with, or to dig up the ground with, and prepare it for planting.
Canga,	A yoke for oxen.
Cangalhos,	Two pieces of wood on both sides of the oxen's neck, to keep it fast under the yoke.
Sebe,	A hedge, *or* fence made round grounds, with prickly bushes.
O que faz sebes,	Hedger.
Fouce roçadoura de que uxaõ para fazer sebes,	Hedging-bill.
Tempo de tosquia e a festa que nelle fazem os rusticos.	The sheep shearing, the time of shearing sheep; the feast made when sheep are shorn.
Cantiga dos segadores despois de acabado o tempo da sega,	Harvest-home.
çarça,	A bramble.
Mata,	A thicket, a forest.
Mato,	A place where many shrubs grow.
Leira, or *taboleiro,*	A bed in a garden.
Chorro de agoa,	A water spout.
Vereda,	A path.
Rasto,	The track.
Césta,	A basket.
Cabáz,	A frail, a pannier.
Cabâna, or *choupana,*	A cottage, a hut.
Cabaço.	A dry hollow ground used by husbandmen to keep seeds.

Coufas pertencentes á Guerra,	*Things relating to War.*
Serviço, ou *vida militar,*	Warfare.
Militar, ou *servir na guerra,*	To go a warfaring.

Artilhari

θ,

Artilharia, artelharia, ou artilheria,	Artillery.
Canhaõ, ou peça de artilharia,	A cannon.
Canhaõ de ferro,	Iron cannon.
Canhaõ de bronze,	Brass cannon.
Alma do canhaõ,	The mouth of a cannon.
Fogaõ do canhaõ,	The touch-hole of a cannon.
Culatra do canhaõ,	The breech of a cannon.
Botaõ, ou extremidade da culatra,	The pummel.
Balas entadeadas,	Chainshots.
Bala de canhaõ,	A cannon bullet, cannon-ball, or cannon-shot.
Carreta do canhaõ,	The carriage of a cannon.
Pólvora,	Gun-powder.
Meyo canhaõ,	A demy-cannon.
Canhaõ debrada,	A double cannon.
Canhaõ para bater huma praça,	A cannon for battery.
Canhaõ de vinte e quatro,	A twenty-four pounder.
Calibre,	Caliber.
Carregar,	To load.
Escorvar,	To prime.
Fazer pontaria,	To level.
Petrechos, or municoens de guerra	Military stores.
Encravar huma peça,	To nail up a gun.
Descavalgar huma peça,	To dismount a gun.
Desparar,	To fire.
Tiro de peça,	A cannon shot.
Trem de artilharia,	The train of artillery.
Colubrina,	A culverin.
Falconete,	A falconet.
Petardo,	A petard.
Pedreiro,	A swivel gun, pederero, or paterero.
Bomba,	A bomb.
Bombarda,	A great gun, a bombard.
Morteiro,	A mortar-piece.
Granada,	A granade.
Espingarda,	A firelock.
Pistola,	A pistol.
Carabina,	A carabine.
Mosquete,	A musket.
Machadinha,	A battle-ax.
Lança,	A lance.

U   Alabárda,

Alabárda,	An halbert.
Partafána,	A partizan.
Pique,	A pike.
Calar os piques para refistir a cavalaria,	To prefent the pikes againſt the cavalry.
Alfange,	Scymetar.
Eſpada,	A ſword.
Deſembainhar a eſpada,	To unſheath the ſword.
Punho da eſpada,	The handle of a ſword.
Maçaã da eſpada,	The pommel of a ſword.
Guarnição da eſpada,	The hilt of a ſword.
Folha da eſpada,	The blade of à ſword.
Meter maõ a eſpada,	To clap one's hand on one's ſword.
Matar,	To kill.
Ferir,	To wound.
Deſbaratar,	To rout.
Saquear,	To ſack.
Punhal,	A poniard.
Bayoneta,	A bayonet.
Calar a bayoneta,	To fix the bayonet in the muſket.
Capacete,	A head-piece, or helmet.
Morriaõ,	A morrion.
Viſeira,	The vizor of an helmet.
Gorjal, or gola,	The gorget.
Peito de armas,	A breaſt-plate.
Couraça,	A cuiraſs.
Eſpaldár,	The back-plate.
Coſſolete,	A corſlet.
Broquel,	A buckler.
Eſcudo,	A ſhield.
Adaga,	Dagger, a ſhort ſword.
Saya de malha,	A coat of mail.
Rey de armas,	The king at arms, or king of heralds.
Arauto,	A Herald.
Generál,	A general.
Tenente general,	A lieutenant-general.
Sargento mor de batalha,	A major-general.
Sargento,	A ſerjeant.
Sargento mor,	Major.
Mariſcál, or mariſhál,	Marſhal.
Meſtre de campo general,	Maſter de camp general.
Coronel,	Colonel.

Meſtre

Mestre de campo,	Master de camp.
Coronel de infantaria,	Colonel of foot.
Official de guerra,	An officer.
Brigadeiro,	Brigadier.
Tenente coronel,	Lieutenant-colonel.
Ajudante de sargento mor,	Adjutant.
Ajudante de tenente de mestre de campo,	Aid de camp.
Capitaõ,	Captain.
Posto de capitaõ,	Captaincy, *or* captainship.
Tenente,	Lieutenant.
Corneta, —	Cornet.
Alferes,	Ensign.
Bandeiras,	Colours.
Estandarte,	Standard.
Alferes de cavalaria que traz o estandarte,	Standard-bearer.
Pagador,	Agent.
Provedor dos mantimentos de huma armada,	Purveyor.
Commissario,	Commissary.
Commissario geral,	Muster-master.
Engenheiro,	Engineer.
Apofentador do exercito,	Quarter-master.
Cabo de esquadra,	Corporal.
Tambor, ou caixa,	Drum.
Tambor, ou o que toca tambor,	A drummer.
Baguetas,	Drum-sticks.
Cordeis do tambor,	Drum-strings.
Toques do tambor,	The beats of a drum.
Tocar o tambor,	To beat the drum.
Alvorada, ou general,	The general, one of the beats of the drum.
Mostra,	Muster.
Passar mostra,	To muster, to review forces.
Trombeta, —	A trumpet.
Trombeteiro, ou Trombeta,	A trumpeter.
Pifano,	A fifer, *or* fife.
Soldo,	Wages, *or* pay for soldiers.
Soldado,	A soldier.
Soldado que esta de sentinella,	Soldier on duty.
Entrar de guarda,	To mount *or* go upon the guard.
Sentinella,	Duty, centinel.
Render a guarda, sentinellas, &c.	To relieve the guard, &c.

U 2 Blocar,

Blocar, or *bloquear*,	To block up.
Infante, or *soldado de pé*,	A foot soldier.
Granadeiro,	Grenadier.
Bigodes,	Whiskers.
Dragaõ,	Dragoon.
Soldado de cavallo,	Trooper, *or* cavalier.
Montar a cavallo,	To get on horseback.
Apear se,	To alight.
Guarda da pessoa real, or *ar-cheiro*,	Life-guard-man.
Cavalleiro armado de couraça,	Cuirassier.
Mosqueteiro,	Musketeer.
Soldado com espingarda,	Fuselier.
Alabardeiro,	Halberdier.
Genisero,	Janissary.
Soldado armado com lança,	A spearman.
Soldado que leva pique, or *pi-queiro*,	A pikeman.
Besteiro, ou *soldado que peleja com bésta*,	Cross-bow man.
Gastador,	A pioneer.
Mineiro, ou *minador*,	Miner.
Bombardeiro,	A bombardier.
O tiro da artilharia, ou *o es-paço que a bala disparada corre*,	Gunshot, *or* the space to which a shot can be thrown
Artilheiro,	Matross, also a gunner, *or* canoneer.
A arte da artilharia,	Gunnery.
General da artilharia,	General of the artillery.
Aventureiro,	A volunteer.
Recrutas,	Recruits.
Explorador, or *corredor de ex-ercito*,	Scout.
Espia,	Spy.
O que leva viveres ao exercito, ou *vivandeiro*,	Sutler.
Soldado que faz correrias,	A marauder, a soldier that goes a marauding.
Atabale,	Kettle-drum.
Infanteria,	The infantry.
Cavalaria,	Cavalry.
Cavalaria ligeira,	Light-horse.
Vanguarda,	The vanguard.
Corpo de batalha,	The main body of an army.

Reta-

Retaguarda,	The rear.
Corpo de reſerva,	The corps de reſerve.
Corpo da guarda,	The corps de guard.
Piquete,	The piquets of an army, *or* piquet-guard.
Ala,	The wing of an army.
Batalhaõ,	Battalion.
Deſtacamento,	Detachment.
Regimento,	Regiment.
Companhia,	A company.
Eſquadraõ,	A ſquadron.
Mochila,	Knapſack.
Bagagem, ou *bagage,*	Baggage.
Batedores do campo,	Diſcoverers.
Almazem, ou *armazem,*	Armory.
Muralhas,	Walls.
Amea, or *ameya,*	A battlement.
Parapeito,	The parapet.
Caſtello,	A caſtle.
Forte,	A fort.
Fortaleza,	A fortreſs.
Fortificaçao,	Fortification.
Torre,	A tower.
Citadella,	A citadel.
Baluarte,	Bulwark.
Fileira,	A file.
Cortina,	A curtin.
Meya lua,	Half-moon.
Troneira,	A loop-hole.
Terra-pleno,	A rampart.
Rebelim, ou *Revelim,*	A ravelin.
Contraſcarpa,	Counterſcarp.
Barreira,	A barrier.
Falſabraga,	A fauſsbraye.
Foſſo,	A ditch.
Guarita,	A centry-box.
Caſamata,	A caſemate.
Corredor, ou *eſtrada encoberta,*	The covert way.
Ceſtoens,	Gabions.
Eſtacada, ou *paliſſada,*	A paliſade.
Reduto,	A redoubt.
Atalaya,	A place to diſcover, a watch tower, *or* the perſon that ſtands to diſcover, *or* watch.

Manta, ou *Mantelete,*	A mantelet, *or* cover for men from the shot.
Faxina,	Fascines.
Mina,	A mine.
Contramina,	A countermine.
Fazer voar a mina,	To spring a mine.
Trincheira,	A trench.
Abrir as trincheiras,	To open the trenches.
Real,	Camp.
Viveres, ou *muniçoens de boca,*	Provisions.
Bisonho,	A new soldier.
Batalha,	A battle.
Dar batalha,	To give battle.
Escaramuça,	A skirmish.
Sitio,	A siege.
Quartel,	A quarter.
Encamisada,	A camisado.
Sortida,	A sally.
Bater,	To batter.
Brecha,	A breach.
Pontaõ,	A pontoon.
Escalada,	An escalade.
Assalto,	An assault.
Dar assalto,	To storm.
Tomar por assalto,	To take by storm.
Chamada,	The chamade.
Capitular,	To capitulate.
Capitulaçaõ,	Capitulation.
Tregoas,	Truce.
Guarniçaõ,	Garrison.
Prebóste,	A provost.
Prebóste general	A provost-marshal.
Leva,	Levy.
Levantar soldados, ou *fazer leva de gente,*	To raise men, to levy, *or* raise soldiers.
Levantar o sitio,	To raise the siege.
Levantar o campo,	To decamp.
Assentar o campo,	To pitch one's camp.
Campo volante,	A flying camp.
Campanha,	A campaign.
Meter-se em campanha,	To begin the campaign, to open the field.
Guerrear,	To war.
Peça de campanha,	A field-piece.
Forragem,	A forage.

4

Quar-

Quarteis de inverno,	Winter quarters.
Dar quartel,	To give quarter.
Aquartelar-se,	To take quarters.
Marchar,	To march.
Marchar com bandeiras despregadas,	To march with flying colours.
Tocar a recolher,	To found a retreat.
Entregar huma praça,	To surrender a place.

Navegação,	Navigation.
Navio,	A ship.
Náo,	A large ship.
Náo de guerra,	A man of war.
Náo de carga, ou mercantil,	A merchant-ship, a merchant-man.
Navio veleiro,	A very good sailer, or a ship that sails well.
Navio ronceiro,	A bad sailer.
Galé,	A galley.
Galeaça,	A galleass.
Galeaó,	A galleon.
Galeota, ou galeote,	A galliot, a small galley.
Comitre,	The boatswain of a galley.
Fragata,	A frigate.
Carraca,	A carrack.
Fusta,	A foist.
Pinaça,	A pinnace.
Barca de passagem,	A ferry-boat.
Barco,	A boat.
Barca,	A bark, a great boat.
Canôa,	A canoe.
Gôndola,	Gondola, a small boat much used in Venice.
Esquife,	A skiff.
Chalupa, ou balandra,	A sloop.
Chalupa pequena,	A shallop.
Bergantim,	A brigantine, or brig.
Balsa,	A float.
Capitâna,	The admiral's ship.
Almiranta,	The vice-admiral.
Armáda,	A fleet, a navy.
Frota,	A fleet of merchant ships.
Esquádra,	A squadron, part of a fleet.

U 4 *A bordo*

A bordo,	A-board.
Popa,	The poop, stern, *or* steerage.
Proa,	The p.ow, *or* head.
Peças de proa para dar caça ao inimigo,	Chase guns.
Tartána,	A tartan.
Brulote,	A fire-ship.
Patáxo,	A patache.
Falúa,	A felucca.
Batél, or bateira,	A small bark, a wherry.
Caravela,	A caravel.
Sorte de pataxo para serviço de huma não de guerra que he mayor delle,	A tender.
Navio de linha,	A capital ship, *or* line of battle-ship.
Guarda-costa,	A guard ship.
Galeota da qual se lançao as bombas.	Bomb-ketch.
Navio que serve para andar a corso,	A cruiser.
Navio preparado, e esquipado por armadores bata ir contra o inimigo,	A privateer.
Hyatte,	Yacht.
Navio de transporte,	A ransport.
Náo da India Oriental,	East-India man.
Náo da India Occidental,	West India ship.
Sorte de embarcaçaõ pequena Hollandeza de hum só masto,	A Dutch dogger.
Navio para levar carvaõ,	A collier.
Embarcaçoens pequenas,	Small craft.
Embarcaçaõ, ou barco grande que serve para levar fazendas a bordo,	A barge.
Embarcaçaõ grande, ou caravela, que serve para commerçear pella costa,	A fly boat, a large vessel used in the coasting trade.
Embarcaçaõ de avizo,	Advice-boat.
Paquete,	Packet-boat.
Barco de pescar,	A fishing-boat, *or* buss.
Lancha,	Cock-boat, a scull.
Remos,	Oars.
Pá do remo,	The blade of the oar.
Sentina,	The well.

Lastro,

Laftre, ou *lafto*,	Ballaft.
Laftar, ou *lançar laftro ao navio*,	To ballaft a fhip.
Mafto, or *arvore*,	A maft.
Mafto grande,	The main-maft.
Mafto de mezéna,	The mizen-maft.
Mafto do traquéte,	The fore-maft.
Mafto do gurapés,	The bowfprit, *or* boltfprit.
Gávea,	The round-top, main-top, *or* fcuttle of a maft.
Quilha,	The keel.
Verga, ou *entena*,	A yard.
Laiz, ou *extremidades das vergas*,	The yard-arms.
Pranchas, que cobrem os coftados do navio da parte de fóra,	Side-planks, *or* fide of a fhip.
Vela *,	A fail.
Vela meftra, or *a vela do mafto grande*,	The main fheet.
Vela da Gávea,	The main-top-fail.
Vela do joanete do mafto grande,	Main-top-gallant-fail.
Papafigos,	So they call the mizen and fore-fail.
Mezena,	Mizen-fail.
Gata, ou *vela de cima da mezena*,	Mizen-top-fail.
Traquete,	The fore-fail.
Velacho,	The fore-top-fail.
Joanete do traquete	The fore-top gallant-fail.
Cevadeira,	The fprit-fail.
Vela latina,	A fhoulder of mutton fail.
Fazer força de vela,	To crow the f il.
Maftaréos,	The top mafts, *or* top gallant-mafts.
Maftareos da mezena, ou *maftareos da gata*,	Mizen top maft.
Portinhola,	A port hole.
Bandeiras,	The colours.
Flammulas, ou *galbardetes*,	Streamers, pendants.
Agulha de marear,	The mariner's compafs.
Bitacola,	Bittacle.
Cofturas do navio,	The feams of a fhip.
Leme,	Helm, *or* rudder.

* By *vela* is oftentimes meant the fhip itfelf.

Cana do leme,	The whip, *or* whip-ftaff.
Cuberta,	Deck.
Cuberta corrida,	Flufh fore and aft.
Efcotilhas,	The hatches of a fhip, fcuttles.
Efcotilhaõ,	A room by the hatches, to keep the provifions.
Caftello de popa,	The hind caftle.
Caftello de proa,	The fore caftle.
Garrár a ancora,	To drive; that is, when an anchor does not hold faft, and the fhip drags it away.
Ancora	The anchor.
Meter a ancora na lancha, ou *bote depois de levantala,*	To boat the anchor.
Ancora de reboque,	A kedger.
Ancora da efperança,	Sheet anchor.
Unhas da ancora,	Flooks.
Argola da ancora,	The ring of an anchor.
Eftar a ancora a pique,	Is for the anchor to be a-peak.
Amarra,	A cable.
Picar, ou *cortar as amarras,*	To cut the cables,
Sonda, ou *prumo,*	Sounding lead.
Cutelos,	Studding fails.
Maré.	The tide.
Bofina,	A fpeaking trumpet,
Preparar hum navio de velas, cordas, &c,	To rig a fhip.
Piloto,	Pilot, *or* fteerfman,
Efcrivaõ,	A purfer.
Pilotagem,	Pilotage.
Carta de marear,	Sea-chart.
Capitaõ,	A captain.
Capitaõ tenente,	Firft lieutenant,
Contrameftre,	A boatfwain.
Marinheiro,	A failor.
Camarote,	A cabbin.
Marinheiro que he camarada, ou *pertence ao mefmo rancho,*	A meffmate,
Tormenta,	A tempeft.
Borrafca,	A ftorm.
Bonança,	Fair weather.
Calmaria,	Calm.
Vento em popa,	The wind full a-ftern, a fore-wind.

Navio

Navio arrafado em popa,	A fhip that fails before the wind.
Derrota,	The courfe, *or* way of a fhip.
Alar a bolina,	To fharp the main bowling, to haul up the bowling.
Ir pela bolina,	To tack upon a wind, fail upon a bowline.
Nó da bolina,	The bowling knot,
Barlavento,	Windward.
Ganhar o barlavento,	To get the wind.
Barlaventiar, ou *deitar a barlavento,*	To ply to windward.
Sotavento,	Leeward.
Efcovens,	Hawfers.
Efcotas,	Tacks.
Velame, cordas, e o mais que he neceffario para preparar hum navio,	Tackle, *or* tackling, the rigging of a fhip.
Corda,	A rope.
Enxarcias,	Shrowds.
Arribar,	To put into an harbour, to be driven into an harbour by ftrefs of weather; alfo to bear up, to bring the fhip more before the wind.
Bombordo,	Larboard.
Eftibordo,	Starboard.
Ló;	Loof.
Meter de ló,	To loof, or keep the fhip nearer the wind.
Bomba,	A pump.
Dar a bomba,	To pump.
Balde para deitar agoa na bomba,	Pump-can.
Efcuma que fabe da bomba depois de ter tirado a agoa,	Pump-fuck.
Navio, cuja agoa fe naõ pode tirar com a bomba,	A fhip that is ftoaked,
Manga de coûro por onde fabe a agoa da bomba,	Pump-dale.
Braço da bomba,	The pump-handle.
Faról,	Light, *or* lantern.
Vento,	Wind.

Rosa da Agulha, *ou dos* Ventos.	*The Fly of the Mariners Compass.*
Norte,	North.
Norte 4ª a nordéste,	N. by E.
Nor nordeste,	N. N. E.
Nordeste 4ª a norte,	N. E. by N.
Nordeste,	N. E.
Nordeste 4ª a léste,	N. E. by E.
Les nordeste,	E. N. E.
Léste 4ª a nordeste,	E. by N.
Léste,	East.
Léste 4ª a sueste,	E. by S.
Lés sueste,	E. S. E.
Sueste 4ª a leste,	S. E. by E.
Sueste,	S. E.
Sueste 4ª a sul,	S. E. by S.
Susueste,	S. S. E.
Sul 4ª a sueste,	S. by E.
Sul,	South.
Sul 4ª a sudoeste,	S. by W.
Susudoeste,	S. S. W.
Sudoéste 4ª a sul,	S. W. by S.
Sudoeste,	S. W.
Sudoeste 4ª a oeste,	S. W. by W.
Oés sudoeste,	W. S. W.
Oéste 4ª a sudoeste,	W. by S.
Oeste,	West.
Oeste 4ª a noroeste,	W. by N.
Oes noroeste,	W. N. W.
Noroeste 4ª a oeste,	N. W. by W.
Noroeste,	N. W.
Noroeste 4ª a norte,	N. W. by N.
Nor noroeste,	N. N. W.
Norte 4ª a noroeste,	N. by W.

Vento travessaõ, ou *travessia,*	Contrary wind.
Dar a embarcaçaõ a travez,	To hull, it is said of a ship with the helm *lashed a lee,* when the storm is so fierce, that she can bear no sail.
Pairar,	To ply to and again in one's station.

Esporaõ,

Esporaõ,	Beak.
Colher hum cabo,	To coil a cable.
Largar mais cabo,	To pay more cable.
Abrir agoa,	To leak, *or* spring a leak.
Fazer agoada,	To take in fresh water.
Arpaõ,	A grapnel.
Arpar hum navio,	To grapple a ship.
Fatexa,	Grapnel.
Pedaço de lona breada que se poem ao redor do masto e das bombas para que a agoa naõ penetre,	Coat.
Passador,	A fidd, *or* pin of iron to open the strands of ropes.
Corda cóm que se prende o bote, ou lancha á popa do navio,	Boat-rope, *or* gift-rope.
Apito,	A boatswain's call.
Abadernas,	Nippers.
Abita,	Bits.
Emproar,	To steer right forward, to turn the prow straight to any other ship *or* place.
Guinar o navio,	To yaw, *or* make yaws.
Parte superior, ou *mais alta* da popa de bum navio,	The tafferel.
Apagafanoes,	Leech-lines.
Arreigadas,	Puttocks.
Brioes,	Bunt-lines.
Barredouras,	Low-studding-sails.
Bartidouro,	Boat's skit.
Bastardos,	Parrels.
Bigota,	A dead-eye.
Botalós,	Studding-sail-booms.
Bracear,	To brace.
Braços,	Braces.
Bragueiro, *or* vergueiro,	The rudder's rope.
Brandaes,	Back-stays.
Buçardas,	Breast-hooks.
Cachólas,	Cheeks.
Cadaste,	Stand-post.
Cadernal,	A large block with more than one shive.
Cavernas,	The floor-timbers.
Colhedores,	Lines of the shrouds.

Com-

Compaffar hum navio,	To trim a ship.
Coffouros,	Trucks.
Craca,	The foulnefs in the ship's bottom.
Eftar hum navio lançado á banda,	Is for a ship to heel.
Cabreftante,	The capftan.
Dar caça,	To chafe.
Curvas,	The knees.
Mefas da guarniçaõ,	Chain-wales.
Defaftre,	Boat's fkit.
Embornaes,	Scupper-holes.
Poraõ,	The hold of a ship.
Maca,	Hammock.
Convez,	Deck, or quarter-deck.
Camarote do cirurgiaõ,	Cockpit.
Frete,	Freight.
Carga,	Cargo.
Ordem que o capitaõ recebe para dar a vela, ou carta de ordens,	Sailing orders.
A acçaõ de imbarcar-fe,	Embarkation.
Defembarque,	Difembarking.
Embargo,	Embargo.
Ancoragem,	Anchorage.
Batalha naval,	Sea-fight.
Caravela mexeriqueira, ou de efpia,	A ship for efpial.
Arriar, ou arrear,	To veer.
Arrear as velas,	To ftrike fail.
Arrear bandeira,	To ftrike the flag.
Levantar ferro, levar ancoras, levar ferro, levar-fe, ou levar,	To weigh anchor.
Leva,	The action of weighing, or taking up the anchor.
Bolear a peça,	To move a gun towards ftarboard, or larboard.
Peça de leva,	The fignal gun.
Rebocar, ou levar de reboque,	To tow.
Fazer cofturas,	To fplice.
Paffagem,	Paffage.
Paffageiro,	Paffenger.
Viagem,	Voyage.
Navio cujo capitaõ tem cartas de repre alias,	Letters of mark.

Que-

Querenar hum navio,	To careen a ship.
Brear as costuras do navio,	To pay the seams of a ship.
Dar á costa,	To run a ground, *or* on shore.
Soluçar a náo,	Is for a ship to roll, *or* to float in rough water.
Naufragar,	To suffer a wreck, to be wrecked.
Naufragio,	Shipwreck.
Patraõ, ou *mestre da náo,*	Ship master.
Carpenteiro de navios,	Shipwright.
Estaleiro,	Stock.
Embarcar,	To ship.
Embarcar,	To go aboard ship, to take shipping.
Grumete,	The meanest sort of sailor, *or* a servant to the sailors.
Rapaz que serve como moço do navio,	Shipboy.
Rapaz que serve ao capitaõ,	A cabbin-boy.
Calafate,	A calker.
Calafetar hum navio,	To calk a ship.
Calafeto,	Oakam.
Arsenal, ou *ribeira das náos,*	An arsenal, a store-house, *or* magazine.
Emmastear,	To fit a ship, *or* vessel with masts.
Remar,	To row.
Remador,	Rower.
Forçado,	Galley-slave.
Despenseiro,	Steward.
Marinheiros, e toda a outra gente, que pertence ao navio,	The crew of a ship.
Chusma,	Crew of galley-slaves.
Guarniçaõ da náo,	Marines, soldiers who serve on board of ship.
O sobrecarga do navio,	Supercargo.
Balestilha,	Cross-staff.
Quadrante,	Quadrant.
Outante,	Hadley's quadrant.
De ré,	Aft.
Paravánte,	Fore.
Situaçaõ de huma costa, ilha, &c. a respeito de qualquer outro lugar,	The bearing.
Quarentena,	Quarantine.

Baliza,

Baliza,	Sea-mark.
Larga,	Large.
Amarar,	To bear off.
Caçar a vela,	To turn the fail to the wind fide.
Cacear hum navio,	It is faid of a fhip that is hurried away from her courfe by ftrong winds, tides, &c.
Lançar hum navio ao mar,	To launch a fhip.
Fugir,	To bear away.
Entrar com vento frefco, e bom no porto,	To bear in with the harbour.
Bordo,	Tack.
Bordo, ou *banda,*	Broadfide.
Navio de alto bordo,	Firft rate man of war.
Caça,	Chace.
Prefa, ou *tomadia,*	Prize, *or* capture.
Eftar de vergadalto,	To ftand for the offing.
Ventos de monçaõ, ou *geraes,*	Trade winds.
Andar de conferva,	To keep company together, to fail under a convoy.
Dar, ou *fazer hum bordo,*	To tack the fhip, to tack about, *or* to bring her head about.
Eftar á capa, ou *por-fe á capa,*	To lie by at fea, to back the fails.

Do Commercio, e do que lhe pertence,	Of Trade, and of Things relating to it.
Conta,	Account.
Conta de venda,	Account of fales.
Fazer huma conta,	To caft up an account.
Pedir contas,	To call to an account.
Dar á conta,	To pay on account.
Conta corrente,	Account current.
Dinheiro de contado,	Ready money.
Acçaõ,	Stock.
O que negocea em comprar e vender acçoens,	Jobber.
Ballanço,	Ballance.
Fardo,	Bale.
Banco,	Bank.
Banqueiro,	Banker.

Quebra

Quebra,	Bankruptcy.
Falido, ou quebrado,	Bankrupt.
Ajufle, on concerto,	Bargain.
Troca,	Barter.
Portador,	Bearer.
Lançador,	Bidder.
O que lança mais,	Out-bidder.
Letra de cambio,	Bill of exchange, a draught.
Negociar huma letra de cambio,	To negotiate a bill of exchange.
Conta,	Bill.
Partida,	Parcel.
Conhecimento,	Bill of lading.
Escritura de obrigaçaõ,	Bond, engagement.
Guarda livros, ou o que em huma casa de negocio tem a seu cargo os livros,	Book-keeper.
Occupaçaõ, or negocio,	Busineſs.
Comprador,	Buyer.
Dinheiro,	Caſh.
Porte, ou carreto,	Carriage.
Caxeiro, ou o que guarda a caixa,	A caſhier, or caſh-keeper.
Cento,	Cent.
Certidaõ,	Certificate.
Cambio,	Change, exchange.
Freguez,	Chap, chapman, or cuſtomer.
Gaſtos,	Charges.
Barato,	Cheap.
Caro,	Dear.
Recibo da alfandega,	Clearance, or cocket.
Commiſſaõ,	Commiſſion.
Mercancia,	Commodity.
Compromiſſo,	Compromiſe.
Conſignaçaõ,	Conſignment.
Conſumo,	Conſumption.
Conteudo,	Contents.
Contrato,	Contract.
Correſpondencia,	Correſpondence.
Correſpondente,	Correſpondent.
Preço,	Price, rate.
Alfandega,	Cuſtom-houſe.
Guardas d'alfandega,	Cuſtom-houſe officers.
Guardas que eſtaõ vigiando até que os navios eſtejaõ deſcarregados,	Tideſmen, or tidewaiters.

Feitoría,	Factory, settlement.
Escritório,	Counting-house.
Crédito,	Credit.
Acredor,	Creditor.
Corrente,	Current.
Costume,	Custom.
Data,	Date.
Contratador,	Dealer.
Trafego, ou negocio,	Dealing, traffick.
Divida,	Debt.
Devedor,	Debtor.
Dinheiro desembolçado,	Disbursement.
Desconto,	Discount.
Extracto, ou copia,	Docket.
Depósito,	Deposite.
Desconto nos pagamentos que se fazem a dinheiro de contado, ou por qualquer outra razaõ,	Draw-back.
Acredor importuno,	Dun.
Copia,	Duplicate.
Corretor,	A broker.
Corretor de letras de cambio,	Money-changer, or exchange-broker.
Assegurador, ou segurador,	Insurer, or under-writer.
Endósso,	Endorsement.
Endossador,	Endorser.
Abarcador,	Engrosser.
Levantamento de preço,	Enhancement.
Assento no registo,	Entry.
Equivalente,	Equivalent.
Exigencia,	Exigency.
Despeza,	Expence.
Extraccaõ,	Export, or exportation.
Extorsaõ	Extortion.
Feitor,	Factor.
Feira,	Fair.
Fio, ou arame no qual se enfiaõ os papeis num escritorio,	File for papers.
Quatro, cinco, &c. por cento,	Four, five, &c. per. cent.
Fretar,	To freight a ship.
Frete,	Freight.
O que freta hum navio,	A freighter.
Cabedal, ou quantia de dinheiro destinado para alguma cousa,	Fund.

8

Ganho,

Ganho,	Gain, or profit.
O que ganha,	Gainer.
Fazendas, ou effeitos,	Goods, effects.
Estrea,	Handsel.
Escritura,	Hand-writing.
Entrada,	A custom for imported commodities.
Negociante que introduz fazendas numa praça ou reyno,	Importer.
Renda,	Income.
Interesse,	Interest.
Communicação, ou commercio,	Intercourse.
Inventario,	Inventory.
Insufficiencia, ou falta de meyos para pagar,	Insolvency.
Factura,	Invoice.
Arras,	Jointure.
Escritura de arrendamento,	Lease.
Arrendador,	Lessee.
Livro da razaõ,	Ledger-book.
Emprestimo,	Loan.
Dinheiro emprestado,	Money lent.
Carta,	Letter.
Sobrescrito da carta,	The direction of a letter.
Fechar huma carta,	To make, or close up a letter.
Fechar huma carta com sinete,	To make and seal up a letter.
Mala em que o correo traz as cartas,	Mail.
Hypotheca,	Mortgage.
Acredor hypothecario,	Mortgagee.
O que hypotheca,	Mortgager.
Fiador,	Bail.
Pagamento,	Payment.
Falta de pagamento,	Nonpayment.
Escrito de divida,	Note, or promissory note.
Dono,	Owner.
Fardo pequeno,	Pack, a truss.
Serapilheyra,	Packcloth, wrapper.
Brabante,	Packthread.
Maço de cartas,	Packet of letters.
Companheyro de alguem no negocio, ou socio,	Partner.
Sociedade, ou companhia no negocio,	Partnership.
Penhor,	Pawn, or pledge.

X 2

Contrato

Contrato do seguro das mercancias,	Policy of insurance.
Seguro,	Insurance.
Segurar,	To insure.
Protestar huma letra,	To protest a bill.
Aceitar huma letra,	To accept a bill.
Protesto,	Protest.
Sacár huma letra,	To draw a bill.
Correo aonde se lançaõ as cartas,	Post-office.
Correo que leva cartas,	Postman, or letter-carrier.
Porte de cartas,	Postage.
Premio, ou dinheiro que se paga aos seguradores,	Premium.
Dinheiro que se paga aos marinheiros por terem carregado o navio,	Primage.
Capital,	Principal, or capital.
Perdas e danos,	Losses and damages.
Importancia,	Proceed.
Importancia liquida,	Neat proceed.
Promessa,	Promise.
Bens,	Property.
Pontualidade,	Punctuality.
Compra,	Purchase.
Recibo,	Receipt.
Recambio,	Re-exchange.
Arbitro, ou louvado,	Referee, or umpire.
Louvamento, ou arbitrio,	Reference.
Regataõ,	Regrater.
Quitaçaõ,	Release.
Remessa,	Remittance.
Venda das cousas por miudo, como fazem os mercadores de retalho,	Retail.
Mercador de retalho, ou trapeyro,	Retailer.
Riquezas,	Riches, wealth.
Venda,	Sale, or vent.
Padraõ,	A pattern.
Amostra,	Sample.
Sinete,	Seal.
Lacre,	Sealing-wax.
Ajustamento de contas,	Settlement of accounts.
Loja,	Shop.
Mercador que tem loja,	Shop-keeper.

Livre

Livro em que o mercador de loja tem suas contas,	Shop-book.
O que faz contrabando,	Smuggler.
Fazenda de contrabando,	Contraband, *or* prohibited goods, goods smuggled, *or* run.
Fazer contrabando,	To run, to smuggle prohibited goods.
Modélo, ou fiel dos pezos e medidas publicas,	Standard meafure.
Almazem,	Ware-houfe.
Sobrescrevente,	Subfcriber.
Sobscripçaõ,	Subfcription.
Tára,	Tare and trett.
Fazenda roim,	Trafh of goods.
Risco,	Rifk.
Juros,	Intereft.
Uso,	Ufance.
Ufureiro,	Ufurer.
Ufura,	Ufury.
Obrêa,	Wafer.
Mercancias,	Wares.
Valor,	Worth.
Avaria,	Average.
Direitos,	Duties, *or* cuftom.
Tributo, ou *contribuiçaõ,*	Cefs, tribute.
Taxa,	A fet rate, affize.
Sifa,	Excife.
Sifeiro,	Excifeman.
Cáes,	Wharf.
Direito que se paga por defembarcar fazendas no caes,	Wharfage.
Colléctor do mefmo direito, ou *tributo,*	Wharfinger.
Dizimos,	Tenths, *or* tithes.
Dizimador, ou *dizimeiro,*	Tithe-gatherer.
Louça vidrada, fem fer da China,	Dutch-ware.
Mercador de fobrado,	Wholefale dealer.
Venda que fe faz por partidas,	Wholefale.

X 3 *De*

Da Moeda, *ou* Dinheiro Por-   *Of the Portuguese Coin.*
    tugez.

This mark * is prefixed to the imaginary money.

Real,	A ree, equal to $\frac{24}{100}d.$
Dez reis,	10 rees, $\frac{7}{8}d.$
Vintem,	A vintin, $1\frac{7}{10}d.$
Toſtaõ, ou 5 *ventens,*	A teſtoon, $6\frac{3}{4}d.$
4 *Toſtoens,* ou *hum cruſado,*	A cruſade, 2 s. 3 d.
Cruſado novo, ou 24 *vintens,*	A new cruſade, 2 s. $8\frac{2}{3}d.$
8 *Toſtoens,*	8 teſtoons, 4 s. 6 d.
Hum quarto de ouro, ou 12 *teſtoens,*	12 teſtoons, 6 s. 9 d.
Milreis, ou 10 *toſtoens,*	A milree, 5 s. $7\frac{1}{2}d.$
16 *Toſtoens,*	16 teſtoons, 9 s.
Meya moeda de ouro,	Half moidore, 13 s. 6 d.
3200, ou 32 *toſtoens,*	32 teſtoons, 18 s.
Moeda de ouro de 4800,	A moidore, 1 l. 7 s.
Meya dobra, ou 6400,	Joaneſe, 1 l. 16 s.
Dobra, ou 12800.	128 teſtoons, 3 l. 12 s.

COLLECÇAÕ

A

COLLECTION

D E

O F

Adagios Portuguezes.   Portugueſe Proverbs.

A Agoa o da, a agoa o leva.   WHAT is got over the devil's back will be ſpent under his belly; alſo, lightly come, lightly go.

Na agoa envolta peſca o peſca-dor,   To fiſh in troubled waters (to make a benefit of pub-lick troubles).

Eſtá como o peixe n'agoa,   He lives in clover.

Trazer a agoa para o moinho,   To bring griſt into the mill.

                        Levar

Levar agoa ao mar,	To carry coals to Newcaſtle.
As agoas eſtaõ baixas,	He, *or* ſhe is at a low ebb.
O que naõ pode al ſer, deves ſoffrer,	What can't be cured muſt be endured.
Come como hum alarve,	He eats like a threſher.
Meter a palha na albarda,	To cheat, to impoſe upon.
Alazaõ taſtado antes morto que cançado,	A dark ſorrel horſe will die before he'll jade.
Huma diſgraça alcança a outra,	One miſchief draws on another.
Eſtar na aldea, e naõ ver as caſas,	We ſay: you can't ſee wood for trees; *or* to be like the butcher, that looked for his knife when he had it in his mouth.
Quem trabalha, tem alfaya,	He that works has furniture.
Fallo-lhe em alhos, reſponde-me em bugalhos,	I talk of chalk and you of cheeſe.
Em tempo nevado o alho vale hum cavallo,	Garlick in the foggy weather is as good as a horſe: it means that garlick is a good defence for travellers a-againſt dampneſs and cold weather.
Tezo como hum alho,	As ſtiff as garlick; that is, a healthy ſtrong robuſt perſon.
Sua alma, ſua palma,	As you brew, even ſo bake.
Na almoeda tem a barba queda,	At a ſale keep your beard on your chin ſtill; that is, let not your beard wag too faſt in bidding, leſt you over-bid and repent.
Pagar os altos de vaſio,	To have but little *or* no ſenſe at all.
Quem ama a beltraõ, ama o ſeu caõ,	Love me, love my dog.
Cada qual ama ſeu ſemelhante,	Like will to like, *or* like loves like.
Tambem os ameaçados comem paõ,	Threatned folks eat bread; we ſay, threatned folks live long.
Contas de perto, e amigos de longe,	Even reckonings make long friends.

Naõ

Naõ se deve perder a amizade por da cá a quella palha,
An inch breaks no squares.

Tam bom he Pedro como seu amo,
Like master, like man.

Furtar o carneiro, e dar os pés pello amor de Deos,
We say, to steal a goose and give the giblets in alms.

Nem hum dado faz maõ, nem huma andorinha veraõ,
One swallow does not make summer. *Una hirundo non facit ver*, says *Horace*.

Levar palbas, e aralbos,
To sweep stakes.

Na arca aberta o justo pecca,
That is, it is opportunity makes the thief.

De hum argueiro, fazer hum cavalleiro,
We say, to make mountains of mole-hills.

Com arte, e com engano se vive meye anno; com engano, e com arte se vive a outra parte,
That is, all a man's life is a cheat.

Quem a boa arvore se chega boa sombra o cobre,
That is, he that relies on good worthy people, reaps a benefit.

Asno morto, cevada ao rabo,
A day after the fair, or, after meat, mustard.

Asno, que tem fome, cardos come,
We say, hungry dogs will eat dirty pudding.

Sopa de mel naõ se fez para a boca do asno,
Good things are not fit for fools; or a turd is as good for a sow as a pancake.

Mais quero asno, que me leve, que cavallo, que me derrube,
Better be an old man's darling, than a young man's warling.

Mais val má avença que boa sentença,
It is better to agree at any rate, than to go to law.

Quem naõ se aventura, naõ anda a cavallo, nem em mula,
Nothing venture, nothing have.

Naõ deites azeite no fogo,
Do not throw oil into the fire.

Boca naõ admitte fiador,
The belly has no ears.

Da maõ á boca se perde a sopa,
Much falls between the cup and the lip.

Em boca cerrada naõ entra mosca,
A close mouth catches no flies.

Quem tem boca vai a Roma,
That is, a man may go any where if he has language to speak for himself and ask his way.

Pella

Pella boca morre o peixe,	Much talking brings much woe.
Cada bofarinheiro louva feus alfinetes,	Every man thinks his own geefe fwans.
Quem tem quatro, e gafta cinco, naõ ha mifter bolfa nem bolfinho,	He that hath four and fpends five has no need of a purfe.
Cabra vai pella vinha por onde vai a may, vai a filha.	Like father like fon.
Matar dous coelbos de buma cajadada,	We fay, to kill two birds with one ftone.
Quem canta feus males efpanta,	The perfon who fings makes eafy his misfortunes; that is, finging caufes him not to reflect on it fo much as he otherwife would.
Deitar a capa ao touro,	To throw one's cloak at the bull; that is, to venture all a man has to fave his life.
Viva el rey, e da cá a capa,	Let the king live, and give me the cloak; that is fpoken of perfons who, under a pretence of authority, rob and plunder other people, and at the fame time pretend they are doing juftice to the power repofed in their hands.
Andar de capa cahida,	To be behind-hand in the world.
O caõ cem raiva de feu dono trava,	A mad dog bites his own mafter: there is no trufting to madmen, *or* people in a rage.
Quem com caens fe lança, com pulgos fe levanta,	We fay, lie with beggars and you'll be loufy.
A carne de lobo dente de caõ,	That is, to return railing for railing; *or* as our modern proverb fays, give him a Rowland for his Oliver: the Latins fay, *par pari referre.*
Quem faz cafa na praça, huns dizem que he alta, outros que he bayxa,	That is, a man in public bufinefs can't pleafe every body; or as *Solon* fays: 'tis rare that

that statesman can all parties please.

A cavallo dado naõ olhes o dente, — Never look in the mouth of a gift horse.

Quem quer cavallo sem tacha, sem elle se acha, — 'Tis a good horse that never stumbles.

Na terra dos cegos, o torto he rey, — In a country of blindmen he that has one eye is the king.

Cobra boa fama, e deita-te a dormir, — When your name is up, you may lie a-bed till noon.

Fazer as contas sem a hóspeda, — To reckon without the hostess, *or as we say,* the host.

Do contado come o lobo, — The wolf eats of what is counted; that is, thieves will steal, though they know it will be missed, much more if they think it will not.

Em casa de ladraõ naõ falles em corda, — You should not mention a halter to any whose relations or friends have suffer'd by it; that is, no man should be hit in the teeth of his disgrace

Do couro lhe sabem as correas, — The thongs come out of his skin; that is, he pays for it.

Cortar o vestido conforme o panno, — To cut one's coat according to the cloth.

Criay o corvo tirarvos-ha o olho, — It is said of a person that being recieved in distress defrauds or grows too great for him that entertained him.

Tanta culpa tem o ladraõ como o consentidor, — The receiver is as bad as the thief.

Dadivas quebrantaõ penhas, — Gifts break rocks; that is, kindness overcomes the hardest hearts, and bribes *or* presents corrupt the most resolved.

Melhor he fazer de balde que estar debalde, — It is better work for nothing, than be lazy and do nothing at all.

Deitar azeite no fogo, — To make bad worse. *Horace* says, *Oleum addere camino* *Naõ*

Naõ he o demo tam feo como o pintaõ,	We say, the lion is not so fierce as his picture.
Primeiro faõ dentes, que parentes,	We say, near is my coat, but nearer is my skin, &c. Terence says, *Heus proximus sum egomet mihi.*
Lá vai a lingoa, onde o dente grita,	To scratch where it itches.
Quando cuidas meter o dente em seguro toparáz o duro,	Harm watch, harm catch. *Horace says,* — *et fragili quærens illidere dentem,* *Offendet solido* ——
Dar com a lingoa nos dentes,	To contradict one's self, to belie.
Quem naõ falla naõ o ouve Deos,	A man may hold his tongue in an ill time; also, spare to speak, and spare to speed.
Ventura te dé Deos, filho; que saber pouco te basta,	God give you good luck, child, for a little learning will serve your turn; because it is fortune that raises men more than merit.
Cada qual por si, e Deos por todos,	Every one for himself, and God for all.
Em bons dias, boas obras,	The better days the better deed.
Para dia de saõ cerejo,	We say, when two Sundays come together, that is never.
Tudo pode o dinheiro,	Money governs the world.
O homem propoem, e Deos dispoem,	Man proposes and God disposes.
Dorme como hum arganaz,	He sleeps like a dormouse.
A bom entendedor poucas palavras,	A word to the wise is enough.
Gato escaldado da agoa fria ha medo,	We say a burnt child dreads the fire.
No escudellar verás quem te quer bem, ou mal,	That is, people's affections are discovered by their liberality.
Esmolou saõ Mattheus, esmolou para os seus,	Charity begins at home.
Naõ ha melhor espelho que o amigo velho,	There is no better looking-glass, than an old friend; that

that is such a one will not flatter a man, but tell him the truth.

Nem eſtopa com tiçoens, nem molher com varoens,
That is, converſation of women is dangerous; it is not good jeſting with edged tools.

Fallar ſem cuidar, he atirar ſem afrontar,
To let one's tongue run without reflecting on what one ſays, is like ſhooting at random.

Falla pouco e bem terte baō por alguem,
Talk little and well, and you'll be counted ſomebody; that is, you'll be eſteemed.

Quem a fama tem perdida, morto anda neſta vida,
He who has loſt his reputation, is as good as dead whilſt living : we ſay, one had as good be banged as have an ill name.

A quem má fama tem, nem accompanhes, nem digas bem,
Do not keep company with, nor be fond of one that has an ill name.

Aproveitador de farelos, eſperdiçador de farinha,
That is, one that ſaves at the ſpiggot and lets it run out at the bung; alſo, penny wiſe and pound fooliſh.

Naō fazem boa farinha,
They can't ſet their horſes together.

Quem ma a faz nella jaz,
Self do, ſelf harm.

Agora dá paō, e mel, e depois dará paō e fel,
After ſweet meat comes ſour ſauce.

Lingoa doce como mel, e coraçaō amargoſo como fel,
An honey tongue, an heart of gall,

Bater o ferro quando eſtá quente,
To beat the iron whilſt it is hot, or, to make hay whilſt the ſun ſhines.

Quem com ferro mata, a ferro morre,
He who kills by the ſword, dies by the ſword.

Carregado de ferro, carregado de medo.
He who is loaded with iron, is loaded with fear; that is, he who loads himſelf with armour and weapons againſt danger, diſcovers he is much afraid.

Quem

Quem te faz feſla, naõ ſoendo fazer, ou te quer enganar, ou te ha miſter,

He that makes more of you than he wont to do, either deſigns to cheat you, or ſtands in need of you.

Naõ fies, nem profies, nem ar-rendes, vivirás entre as gen-tes,

Do not truſt, nor contend, nor hire, and you'll live among men; that is, you'll live peaceably.

Mijar claro, dar huma figa ao medico,

Tell the truth and ſhame the devil.

Se naõ bebe na taverna, folga nella,

We ſay he does not ſmoke but ſmocks.

Achou forma para o ſeu ſapato,

He has found a laſt to his ſhoe; that is, he has met with his match.

Naõ ſejaes forneira ſe tendes a cabeça de manteiga,

Do not undertake to be a baker if your head is made of butter; that is, do not take upon you any buſineſs you are unfit for.

Ao homem ouſado a fortuna lhe dá a maõ,

Fortune ſavours the bold.

Roupa de francezes,

Things left at random, or expos'd to be pillaged.

Cabir da frigideira nas braſas,

To fall out of the frying-pan into the fire.

Dizem os filhos ao ſoalheiro, o que ouvem dizer a ſeus pays ao fumeiro,

Little pitchers have great ears.

Perto vai o fumo da chama,

We ſay, there is no ſmoke without ſome fire.

Quem huma vez furta, fiel nunca,

He who once ſteals is never truſty, or once a thief, al-ways a thief.

Mal vai ao fuſo quando a bar-ba naõ anda em cima,

Alas for the ſpindle when the beard is not over it. By the ſpindle is meant the woman, and by the beard the man.

Cada terra com ſeu uſo, cada roca com ſeu fuſo,

So many countries, ſo many cuſtoms.

Quantas cabeças, tantas cara-puças,

Several men, ſeveral minds.

Quem lhe doer a cabeça que a aperte,

We ſay, if any fool finds the cap fit him, let him put it on.

I

Se

Sé queres saber quem he o vil-laõ, metelhe a vara na maõ, — Set a beggar on horse-back, and he will ride to the devil.

Naõ ha rosa sem espinhos, — There is no rose without thorns, there is no sweet without some sweat.

Andar, andar, vir morrer á beira, — To eat an whole ox and faint at the tail. This proverb is spoke, when any body falls short of a thing, after having used all endeavours.

Quem naõ deve, naõ teme, — Out of debt, out of danger.

Quem, quando pode, naõ quer, quando quer, naõ pode, — It is good to make hay while the sun shines.

Homem honrado naõ ha mister gabádo, — We say, a good face needs no band.

Homem grande, bésta de páo, — This proverb intimates, that things are not to be valued by their bulk, but according to their intrinsic worth and value; and so we say, a lark is better than a kite.

Debaixo de má capa jaz bom bebedor, — A tattered cloak may cover a good drinker; that is, men are not to be judged by outward appearance.

Quem muyto abraça, pouco a-perta, — All grasp, all lose; or, covet all, and lose all.

No açougue, quem mal falla, mal ouve. — He that speaks lavishly, shall hear knavishly. *Terence* says, *Qui pergit ea, quæ vult, dicere, ea, quæ non vult, audiet.*

Quem em mais alto nada, mais presto se afoga, — That is, the highest charges are the more liable and nearer to the downfall.

Hospede com sól, há honor, — First come, first served.

Hospeda formosa, dano fáz á bolsa, — A beautiful hostess, or land-lady, is bad for the purse.

O hóspede e o peixe aos tres dias fede, — Fresh fish, and new-come guests, smell when they are three days old.

Hórta

Hórta sem agoa, casa sem tel-bádo, molher sem amôr, ma-rido sem cuidado, de graça he caro,

That is, a garden without water, a house untiled, a wife without love, and a careless husband, are all alike, being all stark naught.

Honra ao bom paraque te hon-re, e ao máo paraque te naõ e sb onre,

Honour a good man, that he may honour you; and an ill man, that he may not dishonour you.

Honra he dos amos e que se fáz aos criados,

The honour done to servants, redounds to their masters.

Officio de confelho, honra sem proveito,

An office in the council is honour without profit; that is, to be of the council of a town, by which nothing is got in Portugal.

Homem apercebido, meyo com-batido,

A man that is prepared, has half the battle over.

DIALOGOS FAMILIARES.

FAMILIAR DIALOGUES.

TENHA vm. muyto bons dias,	GOOD morrow, fir.
Como está vm. ? ou como páfa vm. ?	How do you do, fir?
Bem, naõ muyto bem, vou pafsando,	Well; not very well ; fo, fo
Muyto bem para fervir a vm.	Very well to ferve you.
A's ordens de vm.	At your fervice.
Fico-lhe muyto obrigado,	I am obliged to you.
Vm. muytos annos,	I thank you.
Como está, ou páffa o fenhor feu irmaõ ?	How does your brother do ?
Muyto bem, naõ muyto bem,	He is very well; not very well.
Elle terá gosto de ver a vm.	He will be glad to fee you.
Naõ terei tempo para hir a velo hoje,	I fhall have no time to fee him to day.
Faça favor de affentar-fe,	Be pleafed to fit down.
Dá huma cadeira ao fenhor,	Give a chair to the gentleman.
Naõ he neceffaria,	There's no occafion.
Tenho que hir a fazer huma vifita aqui nesta vifinhança,	I muft go make a vifit in the neighbourhood.
Vm. tem préffa,	You are in hafte.
Eu logo voltarei,	I'll be back, or return prefently.
Adeos meu fenhor,	Farewell, fir.
Fólgo de ver a vm. com boa faude,	I am glad to fee you in good health.
Beijo as maõs de vm.	I kifs your hand.
Sou criado de vm.	I am your fervant.
Sou muyto feu criado,	Your moft humble fervant.

DIA-

DIALOGO II.

Para fazer huma Visita de Manhaã.

ONDE *está teu amo?*
Ainda dorme?
Naõ, *senhor, elle está acordado.*
Está elle ja levantado?
Naõ, *senhor, elle ainda está na cama.*
Que vergonha de estar ainda na cama a estas horas!
Ontem á noite fui para a cama taõ tarde, que naõ me pude levantar cedo esta manhaã,
Que fizeraõ vm^ces depois de céa?
Dançámos, cantámos, rimos, e jugámos,
A que jogo?
Aos centos.
Quanto me peza de o naõ ter sabido!
Quem ganhou? quem perdeo?
Eu ganhei dez moedas.
Até que horas jugaraõ vm^ces?
Até duas horas despois da meya noite.
A que horas foi vm. para a cama?
A's três, ás três horas e meya.

Naõ me admiro que vm. se levante taõ tarde.
Que horas saõ?
Que horas lhe parece a vm. que sejaõ?
Pareceme que apénas saõ oito.
Sim! oito! ja deraõ déz.

Entaõ he preciso que me levante quanto mais depressa puder.

DIALOGUE II.

To visit in the Morning.

WHERE is your master?
Is he asleep still?
No, sir, he is awake.
Is he up?
No, sir, he is still a-bed.

What a shame 'tis to be a-bed at this time a-day!
I went to bed so late last night, I cou'd not rise early this morning.
What did you do after supper?
We danced, we sung, we laugh'd, we play'd.
At what game?
We play'd at piquet.
How grieved am I, I did not know it!
Who won? who lost?
I won ten moidores.
Till what hour did you play?
Till two in the morning.
At what o'clock did you go to bed?
At three, half an hour after three.

I don't wonder at your rising so late.
What's o'clock?
What do you think it is?

Scarce eight, I believe yet.
How! eight! it has struck ten.
Then I must rise with all speed.

Y　　　DIA-

DIALOGO III.

Para veſtir-ſe.

QUEM eſtá ahi?
Que quer vm.?

Deſpaxa-te, acende o lume, e
veſte-me.
Há muyto bem lume.
Da-me a minha camiſa.
Eila aqui eſtá, ſenhor,
Naõ eſtá quente, eſtá muyto fria,
Eu a aquentarei, ſe vm. quizér,
Naõ, naõ; traze me as min-
has meyas de ſeda,
Huma dellas eſtá róta,
Da lhe bum ponto, concerta-a,
Dei-a ao que as concerta,

Fizeſte bem,
Onde eſtaõ as minhas chinélas?
Onde eſtá a minha roupa de-
chambre?
Pentea-me,
Procura outro pente,
Da me o meu lenço,
Eis-aqui hum lavado,
Da-me o que eſtá na minha al-
gibeira,
Dei-o á lavandeira, elle eſtava
ſujo,
Trouxe ella ja a minha roupa?
Sim, ſenhor, e naõ falta nada.
Traze-me os meus calçoens,
Que veſtido quer vm. para ho-
je?
O meſmo de ontem,
O alfaiate ha de trazer logo o
ſeu veſtido,
Batem á porta, vé la quem hé,

Quem he?
He o alfaiate,
Deixa-o entrar,

DIALOGUE III.

To dreſs one's ſelf.

WHO is there?
What will you pleaſe
to have?

Be quick, make a fire, dreſs
me.
There is a fine fire.
Give me my ſhirt.
Here it is, ſir.
'Tis not warm,'tis quite cold.
If you pleaſe, I'll warm it.
No, no; bring me my ſilk
ſtockings.
One of them is torn.
Stitch it a little, mend it.
I have given it to the ſtock-
ing mender.
You have done right.
Where are my ſlippers?
Where is my night-gown?

Comb my head.
Look for another comb.
Give me my handkerchief.
Here is a clean one.
Give me that which is in my
pocket.
I gave it to the waſher-wo-
man, it was foul.
Has ſhe brought my linen?
Yes, there wants nothing.
Bring me my breeches.
What clothes will you wear
to-day?
Thoſe I wore yeſterday.
The taylor will bring your
cloth-ſuit preſently.
Somebody knocks, ſee who it
is.
Who is it?
It is the taylor.
Let him come in.

DIA.

DIALOGO IV.

O Senhor e o Alfaiate.

DIALOGUE IV.

The Gentleman and the Taylor.

TRAZEIS o meu vestido?

DO you bring my suit of cloaths?

Sim, senhor, eilo aqui.

Yes, sir, here 'tis.

Há muyto tempo que estou esperando por elle,

You make me wait a great while.

Naõ pude vir até agora,

I cou'd not come sooner.

Naõ estava acabado,

It was not finished.

Ainda naõ estava forrado,

The lining was not sewed.

Quer vm vestir a casaca para ver se lhe está bem?

Will you please to try the close coat on?

Vejamos se está bem feita.

Let us see whether it be well made.

Tenho para mim que lhe húja de agradar.

I believe it will please you.

Parece-me muyto comprida,

It seems to me to be very long.

He costume agora de traze-las compridas,

They wear them long now.

Abotoai-a,

Button me.

He muyto apertada,

It is too close.

Assim deve ser para que lhe esteja bem ao corpo,

To fit properly, it ought to be close.

Naõ saõ as mangas demasiadamente largas?

Are not the sleeves too wide?

Naõ, senhor, estaõ-lhe admiravelmente,

No, sir, they fit very well.

Os calçoens saõ muyto apertados?

The breeches are very narrow.

Esta he a moda de agora,

That is the fashion.

Este vestido está-lhe bizarramente,

This suit becomes you mighty well.

He muyto curto, muyto comprido, muyto grande, muyto pequeno,

'Tis too short, too long, too big, too little.

Tendes feito a vossa conta?

Have you made your bill?

Naõ, senhor, naõ tive tempo,

No, sir, I had no time.

Trazei a amanhaã, e pagarvos hei.

Bring it tomorrow, I'll pay you.

DIALOGO V. DIALOGUE V.

Para almoçar. *To breakfaſt.*

TRAZE-*nos alguma couſa* BRING us ſomething for
para almoçar, breakfaſt.

Sim, ſenhor, ha linguiças e Yes, ſir, there are ſome ſau-
paſtelinhos, ſages and petty-patees.

Góſta vm. de preſunto? Do you chuſe the gammon
of bacon?

Sim, traze-o; comeremos huma Yes, bring it; we will eat.
talhada delle, Cut a ſlice of it.

Eſtende hum guardanapo ſobre Lay a napkin on that table.
aquella meſa,

Da-nos pratos, facas, e garfos, Give us plates, knives, and
forks.

Lava os cópos, Rinſe the glaſſes.

Dá huma cadeira ao ſenhor, Reach the gentleman a chair.

Aſſente-ſe vm. aſſente-ſe ao pé do Sit down, ſir; ſit by the fire.
lume,

Naõ tenho frio, aqui ficarei I am not cold, I ſhall be very
muyto bem, well here.

Vejamos ſe o vinho he bom, Let us ſee whether the wine
be good.

Da cá aquella garráfa com Give me that bottle and a
aquelle cópo, glaſs.

Faça favor de provar aquelle Taſte that wine, pray.
vinho,

Como lhe agrada? que diz vm. How do you like it? what
delle? ſay you to it?

Naõ he máo, he muyto bom, It is not bad, It is very good.

Eis aqui as linguiças, tira Here are the ſauſages, take
aquelle prato, away this plate.

Cóma vm. linguiças, Eat ſome ſauſages, ſir.

Ja comi algumas, ellas ſaõ muy- I have eat ſome, they are
to boas, very good.

Da-me de beber, Give me ſome drink.

A' ſaude de vm. Your health, ſir.

Bom proveito faça a vm. Much good may it do you.

Dá de beber ao ſenhor, Give the gentleman ſome
drink.

Eu bebi ainda agora, I drank but juſt now.

Os paſtelinhos eraõ bem bons, The petty-patees were very
good.

Eſtavaõ hum pouco mais cozidos They were baked a little too
do que deviaõ eſtar, much.

Vm.

Vm. naõ come,	You do not eat.
Tenho comido tanto, que naõ poderei jantar,	I have eat too much, I shall not be able to eat any dinner.
Vm, eſtá zombando, vm. naõ tem comido nada,	You only jeſt, you have eat nothing at all.
Tenho comido com muyto goſto, tanto das linguiças como do Preſunto,	I have eat very heartily both of ſauſages and gammon of bacon.

DIALOGO VI.

Para fallar Portuguez.

DIALOGUE. VI

To ſpeak Portugueſe.

COMO vai vm. com o ſeu Portuguez?	HOW goes on your Portugueſe?
Eſtá vm. ja muyto adiantado nelle?	Are you much improved in it now?
Ainda me falta muyto; naõ ſei quaſi nada,	Far from it; I know nothing almoſt.
Dizem porem que vm. o falla muyto bem,	It is ſaid, however, you ſpeak it very well.
Prouvéra a Deos que aſſim foſſe!	Wou'd to God it were true!
Os que dizem iſſo, eſtaõ muyto enganados,	Thoſe that ſay ſo are much miſtaken.
Eſteja vm. na certeza que aſſim mo diſſeraõ,	I aſſure you I was told ſo.
Poſſo fallar algumas palavras que aprendi de cór,	I can ſay a few words which I have learnt by heart.
E unicamente o que he neceſſario para começar a fallar,	And ſo much as is neceſſary to begin to ſpeak.
O começar naõ he baſtante, he preciſo que vm acabe,	The beginning is not all, you muſt make an end.
Falle vm. ſempre ou bem, ou mal.	Be always ſpeaking, whether well, or ill.
Tenho medo de dar erros,	I am afraid committing blunders.
Naõ tenha vm. medo; a lingua Portugueza naõ he difficil,	Never fear; the Portugueſe language is not hard.
Conheço iſſo, e tambem que ella he muyto engraçada,	I know it; and that it has abundance of graces.
Que felicidade ſeria a minha ſe eu a ſoubeſſe bem!	How happy ſhou'd I be, if I were maſter of it!

Y 3   *A ap-*

A applicaçaõ he o unico meyo para aprende-la,	Application is the only way of learning it.
Qanto tempo há que vm. aprende?	How long have you been learning?
Apenas há hum méz,	Scarce a month yet.
Como se chama seu mestre?	What is your master's name?
Chama se ——	His name is ——
Há muyto tempo que o conheço,	I have known him a great while.
Elle tem ensinado a muytos dos meus amigos,	He has taught several friends of mine.
Naõ lhe diz elle ser preciso que falle sempre Portuguez?	Does not he tell you that you must constantly talk Portuguese?
Sim, senhor, assim me diz muytas vezes,	Yes, sir, he often tells me so.
Pois, porque naõ falla vm.?	Why do not you talk then?
Com quem quér vm. que eu falle?	Who will you have me talk with?
Com os que fallarem com vm.	With those that shall talk to you.
Eu quizéra fallar, mas naõ me atrevo,	I would fain talk, but dare not.
He preciso que vm. naõ tenha medo nem se peje dos que o ouvirem fallar,	You must not be afraid, you must be bold.

DIALOGO VII.
Do tempo,

DIALOGUE VII.
Of the Weather.

QUE tempo faz?	WHAT sort of weather is it?
O tempo está admiravel,	It is fine weather.
O tempo está roim.	It is bad weather.
Faz frio? faz calma?	Is it cold? Is it hot?
Naõ faz frio, naõ faz calma,	It is not cold, it is not hot.
Chove? naõ chove?	Does it rain? does it not rain?
Naõ o creyo,	I do not believe it.
O vento está mudado,	The wind is changed.
Teremos chuva,	We shall have rain.
Hoje naõ há de chover,	It will not rain to day.
Chove, chove a cantaros,	It rains, it pours.
Está nevando,	It snows.
Troveja,	It thunders.

3

Cabe

Cahe pedra,	It hails.
Relampaguea,	It lightens.
Faz muyta calma,	It is very hot.
Geou a noite paſſada?	Has it freez'd to night?
Naõ, ſenhor, mas agora eſtá geando,	No, ſir, but it freezes now.
Parece-me que há nevoeiro,	It appears to me to be a great fog.
Vm. naõ ſe engana, aſſim he,	You are not miſtaken, it is true.
Vm. tem hum grande catarre; ou eſtillicidio,	You have caught a violent cold,
Há quinze dias que o tenho,	I have had it this fort-night.
Que horas ſaõ?	What's-o'clock?
He cedo, naõ he tarde,	Tis early, 'tis not late.
He tempo de almoçar,	Is it breakfaſt time?
Peuco falta para ſerem horas de jantar,	'Twill be dinner-time immediately.
Que farémos depois de jantar?	What ſhall we do after dinner?
Daremos hum paſſeyo, ou iremos paſſear,	We'll take a walk,
Vamos dár huma vólta,	Let us take a turn now.
Naõ vamos fóra com eſte tempo,	We muſt not go abroad this weather.

DIALOGO VIII.   DIALOGUE VIII.

Para perguntar que novas ha,   *To enquire after News.*

QUE vai de novo? ou que novas ha?	WHAT news is ſtirring?
Sabe vm. alguma couſa de novo? ou ſabe vm. algumas?	Do you know any?
Naõ tenho ouvido nada de novo,	I have heard none,
De que ſe falla pella cidade?	What's the talk of the town?
Naõ ſe falla de nada,	There's no talk of any thing.
Naõ tendes ouvido fallar de guérra,	Have you heard no talk of war?
Naõ ouço fallar nada diſſo,	I heard nothing of it.
Porem falla-ſe de hum cerco,	There's a talk however of a ſiege.
Fallou-ſe niſſo, mas naõ he verdade,	Theie was ſuch a diſcourſe, but it is not true.

Y 4   Ante s

Antes pello contrario falla-se de páz,	On the contrary, there's talk of peace.
Assim o creyo,	I believe fo.
Que se diz na corte?	What fay they at court?
Falla-se de huma viagem.	They talk of a voyage.
Quando vos pareçe que el rey partirá?	When do you think the king will fet out?
Naõ se sabe. Naõ se diz quando.	'Tis not known, they do not fay when.
Onde, ou para onde se diz que elle hirá?	Where do they fay he'll go?
Huns dizem que hirá para Flandres, e outros para Alemanha.	Some fay into Flanders, others into Germany.
E que diz a Gazeta?	And what fays the gazette?
Eu naõ a li.	I have not read it.
He verdade o que se diz do Sr. ——?	Is it true what's reported of Mr ——?
Pois que se diz delle?	What of him?
Dizem que está ferido mortalmente,	They fay he is mortally wounded.
Muyto me pesariâ disso; elle he hum homem de bem.	I fhou'd be forry for that, he's an honeft man.
Quem o ferio?	Who wounded him?
Dous marôtos que o inveftiraõ,	Two rogues that fet upon him.
Sabe-se o porque?	Is it known upon what account?
A noticia que corre he, que deu num delles hum cofcorraõ,	The report is that he gave one of them a box on the ear.
Eu naõ creyo isso; nem eu tão pouco,	I don't believe it. Nor I neither.
Eilo vai, cedo faberemos a verdade,	However, we fhall foon know the truth.

DIALÓGO IX.

Para efcrever.

DIALOGUE IX.

To write.

DAI-ME huma folha de papél, huma penna, e huma pouca de tinta,	GIVE me a fheet of paper, a pen, and a little ink.
Ide ao meu quarto, e achareis em cima da mefa tudo o que vos for precifo,	Step to my clofet, you'll find on the table whatever you want. *Naõ*

Naõ ha pennas,	There are no pens.
Há grande quantidade dellas na escrivaninha,	There are a great many in the standish.
Naõ prestaõ para nada,	They are good for nothing.
Lá há outras,	There are some others.
Naõ estaõ aparádas,	They are not made.
Onde está o vosso canivéte?	Where is your pen-knife?
Sabeis vós aparár pennas?	Can you make pens?
Eu aparo-as a meu modo,	I make them my own way.
Esta naõ está má,	This is not bad.
Em quanto acabo esta carta, fazeime o favor de fechar as outras, e fazer hum maço dellas,	While I make an end of this letter, do me the favour to make a packet of the rest.
Que sello quer vm. que eu lhe ponha?	What seal will you have me put to it?
Sella-o com o meu sinète, ou com as minhas armas,	Seal it with my cypher, or coat of arms.
Com que lacre quer vm. que as feche?	What wax shall I put to it?
Fechai-as com o vermelho ou com o prêto; seja qual for, naõ importa,	Put either red, or black, no matter which.
Tem vm. pôsto a data?	Have you put the date?
Parece-me que sim, mas ainda naõ a assinei,	I believe I have, but I have not signed it.
A quantos estamos hoje do méz?	What day of the month is this?
A outo, a déz, a quinze, a vinte,	The eighth, the tenth, fifteenth, twentieth.
Ponde o sobrescrito?	Put the superscription.
Onde está a arêa?	Where is the powder?
Vós nunca tendes area,	You never have powder or sand.
Ahi há alguma no areeiro,	There's some in the sand-box.
Ahi está o seu criado; quer vm. que elle leve as cartas ao correo,	There's your servant, will you let him carry the letters to the post-house?
Léva as minhas cartas ao correo, e naõ te esqueças de pagar o porte,	Carry my letters to the post-office, and don't forget to pay postage.
Naõ tenho dinheiro,	I have no money.
Ahi está huma moeda de ouro,	There's a moidore.
Vai depréssa, e vem logo,	Go quickly, and return as soon as possible.

DIALOGO X.
Para comprar.

QUE quer vm. ?

Quero hum bom panno fino para hum vestido,

Tenha vm. a bondade de entrár, e verá o mais belo panno que há 'em Londres,

Deixe-me ver o melhor que vm. tem,

Aqui tem vm. hum excellente, que agora se costuma trazer,

He hum bom panno, mas a côr naõ me agrada,

Ahi tem vm. outra peça que tem a côr mais clara,

Agradame a côr, mas o panno naõ he forte, naõ tem corpo,

Veja esta peça; vm. naõ achará em nenhuma parte outra taõ boa como ella,

Quanto péde vm. por cada ana delle ?

O seu justo preço he ———

Sr. naõ he meu costume por-me a regatear; faça-me favor de dizer-me o ultimo preço,

Já disse a vm. que aquelle he o seu justo preço,

He muyto caro, dar lhe hei a vm. ———

Naõ posso dar nada de abate, ou naõ posso abater hum ceitil,

Vm. naõ o há de vender por esse preço,

Vm. quiz saber o ultimo preço, e eu disse-lho,

DIALOGUE X.
To buy.

WHAT do you want, sir? What would you please to have?

I want a good fine cloth to make me a suit of clothes.

Be pleased to walk in, sir, you'll see the finest in London.

Shew me the best you have.

There's a very fine one, and what's worn at present.

'Tis a good cloth, but I don't like the colour.

There's another lighter piece.

I like that colour well, but the cloth is not strong, 'tis too thin.

Look upon this piece here, sir, you'll not find the like any where else.

What do you ask for it an ell?

Without exacting, it is worth ———

Sir, I am not used to stand haggling; pray tell me your lowest price.

I have told you, sir, 'tis worth that.

'Tis too dear, I'll give you———

I can't bate a farthing.

You shall not have what you ask.

You asked me the lowest price, and I have told you.

Here

Hora vamos, córte vm. lá du- *as anas delle,*	Come, come, cut off two ells of it.
Affeguro-lhe a vm. como homem *de bem que fou, que naõ* *ganho nada com vm.*	I proteſt, on the word of an honeſt man, I don't get any thing by you.
Ahi tem vm. cinco moedas de *ouro, de-me a demaſia,*	There's five moidores, give me the change.
Tenha a bondade de dar-me ou- *tra em lugar diſta, por que* *naõ he de pezo,*	Be pleaſed, ſir, to let me have another for this, it wants weight.
Ahi eſtá outra,	There's another.
A Deos, criado de vm.	Farewel; ſir, your ſervant.

DIALOGO XI.

Para huma jornada,

DIALOGUE XI.

For a journey.

QUANTAS legoas ha da- *qui a N.?*	HOW many leagues is it from this place to N?
Ha outo legoas,	It is eight leagues.
Nos naõ poderemos chegar la hoje, *he muyto tarde,*	We ſhall not be able to get thither to day, it is too late.
Naõ he fenaõ meyo dia, vmces *ainda tem baſtante tempo,*	It is not more than twelve o'clock, you have time enough yet.
Hé a eſtrúda boa?	Is the road good?
Naõ he muyto boa, paſſaõ ſe *boſques e rios,*	So, ſo; there are woods and rivers to paſs.
Há algum perigo nella?	Is there any danger upon that road?
Naõ há noticias diſſo; he eſtra- *da real em que ſe encontra* *gente a cada paſſo,*	There's no talk of it, it is a high-way, where you meet people every moment.
Pois naõ dizem que há ladroens *nos boſques?*	Do not they ſay there are rob- bers in the woods?
Naõ há de que ter medo, nem *de dia, nem de noite,*	There's nothing to be feared either by day, or night.
Por onde ſe vai?	Which way muſt one take?
Quando vmces chegarem ao pé *do outeiro, he preciſo que* *tomem á maõ direita,*	When you come near the hill, you muſt take to the right hand.
Pois naõ he neceſſario fubir hum *outeiro?*	Is it not neceſſary to aſcend a hill then?

Naõ

Naõ Sr. naõ há outro outeiro, senaõ huma pequena ladeira, (ou defcida) no bofque,

No, fir, there is no other hill but a little declivity in the wood.

Cufta a atinár com o caminho pello meyo dos bofques?

Is it a difficult way through the woods?

Vmces naõ podem errá-lo,

You can't lofe your way.

Logo que vmces fahirem do bofque, lembrem-fe de tomár á maõ efquerda,

As foon as you are out of the wood, remember to keep to the left hand.

Vmce muytos annos, fico-lhe muyto obrigado,

I thank you, fir, and am very much obliged to you.

Vamos, vamos, fenhores, tomemos hum cavallo,

Come, come, gentlemen, let's take a horfe.

Onde eftá o marquéz?

Where's the marquis?

Elle foi adiante,

He is gone before.

Elle há de eftár esperando por vós logo alí fora da cidade,

He'll wait for you juft out of town.

Por que eftá vmce agora esperando? hora, vamo-nos daqui, acabemos,

What do you ftay for now? come, come, let's be gone, let's have done.

Fiquem-fe embora, fenhores, a deos,

Farewel, gentlemen, farewell.

Façaõ vmces muyto boa jornada,

I wifh you a very good journey.

DIALOGO XII.

Da Cea e da Poufada,

DIALOGUE XII.

Of the fupper and lodging.

COM QUE affim eftamos chegados a eftalagem,

SO, we are arrived at the inn.

Apeemo-nos, fenhores,

Let's alight, gentlemen.

Pega nos cavallos deftes fenhores, e trata delles,

Take thefe gentlemen's horfes, and take care of them.

Vejamos agora o que vm. nos há de dár para ceár,

Now let's fee what you'll give us for fupper.

Hum capaõ, meya duzia de pombos, huma falada, feis codornizes, e huma duzia de calhandras,

A capon, half dozen of pigeons, a fallad, fix quails, and a dozen of larks.

Querem vmces mais alguma coufa?

Will you have nothing elfe?

Ifto he baftante, dai-nos algum vinho que feja bom, e huma fobremefa,

That's enough, give us fome good wine, and a deffert.

7 *Deixem*

Deixem vmces iſſo por minha Conta, eu lhes prometo que fiquem bem ſervidos,	Let me alone, I'll pleaſe you, I warrant you.
Alumia aos ſenhores.	Light the gentlemen.
Dai-nos de ceár o mais depréſſa que for poſſivel,	Let's have our ſupper as ſoon as poſſible.
Antes que vmces tenhaõ deſcalçado as bótas, eſtará a cea na meſa,	Before you have pulled your boots off, ſupper ſhall be upon the table.
Tende cuidado que tragaõ para cima as noſſas malas e piſtólas,	Let our portmanteaus and piſtols be carried up ſtairs.
Deſcalcai-me as bótas, e deſpois ireis ver ſe tem dado algum feno aos cavallos,	Pull off my boots, and then you ſhall go ſee whether they have given the horſes any hay.
Levai-os ao rio, e tende cuidado que lhes dem alguma avéa,	You ſhall carry them to the river, and take care they give them ſome oats.
Eu terei cuidado de tudo, eſtejaõ vmces deſcançados,	I'll take care of every thing, don't trouble yourſelf.
Senhores, a cea eſtá prompta, eſtá na meſa,	Gentlemen, ſupper is ready, it is upon the table.
Nós vamos ja,	We'll come preſently.
Vamos ceár, ſenhores, para nos hirmos deitar cedo,	Let's go to ſupper, gentlemen, that we may go to-bed in good time.
Dai-nos agoa para lavár as mãos,	Give us water to waſh our hands.
Sentemo-nos, ſenhores, ſentemonos á meſa,	Let us ſit down, gentlemen, let's ſit down at table.
Dai-nos de beber,	Give us ſome drink.
A Saude de vmces meus ſenhores,	To your health, gentlemen.
He bom o vinho?	Is the wine good?
Naõ he máo,	It is not bad.
O capaõ naõ eſtá bem aſſado,	The capon is not done enough.
Dai-nos humas poucas de laranjas, e huma pouca de pimenta,	Give us ſome o anges with a little peppe.
Porque naõ cóme vmce deſtes pombos?	Why don't you eat of theſe pigeons?
Eu tenho comido hum pombo, e tres calhandras,	I have eaten one pigeon and three larks.
Dize ao eſtalajadeiro que lhe queremos fallar,	Tell the landlord we want to ſpeak with him.

D I A.

DIALOGO XIII.
Do faltar e do correr,

DIALOGUE XIII.
Of jumping and running.

HORA vamos, quer vm. faltar,

COME, will you go to jumping?

Naõ he bom faltar logo defpois de comer,

It is not good to jump immediately after dinner.

De que modo de faltar gofta vm. mais ?

What leaping do you like beft ?

O mais commum he a pés juntos,

The moft ufual is with one foot clofe to the other.

Quer vm. que faltemos fó com hum pé ?

Shall we hop with one leg ?

Como vm. quizer,

As you pleafe.

Efte he hum falto muyto grande,

This is a very great leap.

Quantos pés faltou vm. ?

How many feet have you leap'd?

Mais de quatro,

More than four.

Apófto que falto pır cima daquelle barranca,

I lay I leap clearly over that ditch.

Vm. falta com hum pao comprido,

You jump with a long ftick.

Demos huma carreira,

Let us run races.

Quer vm. que corramos a pé ou a cavallo,

Shall we run on foot or horfeback ?

De huma e outra forte,

Both ways.

Diga vm. donde fe há de começar, e onde fe ha de acabar,

Appoint the race.

Começaremos a correr daqui,

This will be the ftarting-place.

Correremos ate chegar a éfta arvore,

This tree fhall be the goal.

Tenho corrido trés vezes defde o lugar offinalado até a arvore,

I have run three times from the ftarting-place to the tree.

Vm. naõ efperou pello final para principıar a correr,

You did not ftay for the fignal to ftart.

Aquélle cavallo correo muyto bem,

That horfe has run his race very well.

Quantas carreiras tem elle dado ?

How many heats has he run ?

Três ou quatro,

Three or four.

Vm. tem ganhado,

You have won the plate.

DIALOGO XIV.
Para nadar.

DIALOGUE XIV.
To swim.

HOJE faz muyta calma,
Naõ ha que reparar niſ-
ſo, eſtamos no S. Joaõ,
Vamos nadar,
Eu naõ goſto de nadar,
Eu antes quero eſtar vendo, do
que nadar,
Nada elle bem?
Elle nada como hum peixe,
Elle tambem nada de coſtas,
He muyto perigôſo o nadar com
bexigas,
Porque ellas podem arrebentar,
Eſtive ontem quaſi affogado,

Eu tremo quando cuido niſſo,
Vm. hè muyto medrôſo,
Vm. tem medo da ſua propria
ſombra,

IT is very hot.
  No wonder, it is now
midſummer.
Let us go a ſwimming.
I do not like water.
I would rather look on than
ſwim my ſelf.
Does he ſwim well?
He ſwims like a fiſh.
He ſwims alſo on his back.
It is dangerous to ſwim with
bladders.
Becauſe they may burſt.
Yeſterday I had like to have
been drowned.
I tremble to think on it.
You are very fearful.
You are afraid of your ſha-
dow.

A NEW

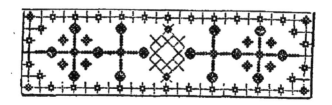

A NEW
PORTUGUESE
GRAMMAR.

****

PART IV.

CONTAINING

Several useful and entertaining Passages, whereof the greatest Part is collected from the best Portuguese *Writers, such as* Andrade, Barros, Camoens, Lobo, *&c.*

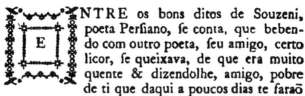

ENTRE os bons ditos de Souzeni, poeta Persiano, se conta, que bebendo com outro poeta, seu amigo, certo licor, se queixava, de que era muito quente & dizendolhe, amigo, pobre de ti que daqui a poucos dias te farão beber no inferno agoas sulfureas, & ardentes, que te abrazarão as entranhas; naõ importa, replicou Souzeni; baftará que me lembre algum dos teus verfos, que ellas se farão mais frias, que neve.

Catha-

Catharina Parthenay fobrinha da celebre *Anna Parthenay*, deu efta bella refpofta a *Henrique* lV. *faiba voffa magde que eu fou muito pobre para fer fua conforte; e que no mefmo tempo defcendo de huma familia muito illuftre, para fer fua dama.*

Huma Princeza Catholica, e de rara virtude vendo reduzido o Marichal de Saxonia ás agonias da morte, diffe, que era para fentir o naõ fe poder rezar hum *De profundis* pella alma de hum que tinha feito cantar tantos *Te Deum*.

A Dom *Chriftovaõ de Moura*, Marquez de Caftello Rodrigo, e Vice Rey de Portugal por Dom Philipe Terceiro, hindo por huma fala do Paço, de Lifboa, hum foldado honrado, que tinha bem fervido na India, lhe dava hum memorial, e pedia, que fe lembraffe dos feus papeis, porque havia largo tempo, que andava pretendendo. Refpondeo-lhe o Marquez, que havia muyta *Gente* para defpachar, e naõ fe podiaõ defpachar todos com brevidade; o foldado adiantando o paffo fe atraveffou diante fem defcompofiçaõ, e fazendo parar o Vice Rey lhe diffe com grande confiança; *fenhor Dom Chriftovaõ defpache Vs. os homens, e deixe a Gente.* O Marquez aceitou o memorial, e o defpachou no mefmo dia.

Mandando hum Fidalgo em Lifboa abrir em huma rua os Alicerces para fe fazerem huãs cafas, fem licença da camera, paffando por alli o procurador da cidade, poz pena aos officiaes, que naõ trabalhaffem na obra fem licença dos Vereadores; e os officiaes dizendo-o ao Fidalgo mandou-lhes elle que naõ deyxaffem de trabalhar, e que naõ fizeffem cafo do que dizia aquelle villaõ ruim; tornando o procurador da cidade por alli e achando os officiaes trabalhando mandou que deffem com elles no tronco; e naõ faltando quem lhe contaffe o que o Fidalgo differa, teve-o em olho; e no tempo que el-

Z le

le hia atraveſſando peſlo Rocio para ſua caſa, ſahio-
lhe ao caminho a cavallo, e com huma lança que
levava, dando na ſua ſombra, lhe diſſe : porque o
que diſſeſtes, foy em minha auſencia, dou em voſſa ſombra, ſe mo tiveſſeis dito no roſto, dera na voſſa peſſoa.

Abou Hamifab, o mais celebre doutor dos Muſ-
ſulmanes tendo recébido huma bofetada, diſſe ao
que o tinha inſultado : eu poderia vingarme, pa-
gandovos na meſma moeda ; mas naõ o quero fazer.
Poderia accuſarvos ao calife ; mas naõ quero ſer ac-
cuſador. Poderia nas minhas oraçoens queixarme a
Deos deſta affronta ; mas nem iſſo quero fazer. Por
fim poderia pedir a Deos, que ſe quer no dia do juizo
vos caſtigaſſe ; porem o meſmo ſenhor me livre de
ſemelhante penſamento ; mas antes, ſe ſuccedeſſe
que neſte inſtante chegaſſe aquelle formidavel dia ;
e ſe a minha interceſſaõ tiveſſe alguma efficacia para
com Deos, naõ quizera por companheiro ſe naõ a
vos para entrar no Paraiſo. Que admiravel exemplo para os Chriſtaõs aprenderem a perdoar as injurias !

Da Peregrinaçam.

Paſſadas que ſe daõ peregrinando, ſaõ degraos para
a caſa do deſengano. Das ſuas fontes ſahem os rios
muito pequenos, e creſcem correndo, e levaõ mares
ao mar. Homens, que da ſua terra naõ ſahem, ſaõ
navios, que acabaõ no eſtaleiro. A ſabedoria como
vinda do ceo, anda neſte globo terreſtre peregrina,
naõ he facil achala ſenaõ peregrinando ; errando por
eſte mundo, ſe apprende a naõ commetter erros.
Vapores, que na terra eram lodo, apartados della ſe
fazem eſtrellas. Aos homens que querem luzir,
deve a patria ſervir, como aos planetas o horizõte,
de berço, para enſayo do ſeu luzimento, longe do
ponto ortivo, e remontados á mais alta regiaõ, apuraõ
as influencias, e duplicaõ as luzes. Que nome teriaõ
hoje

hoje no mundo *Socrates*, *Pithagoras*, e *Plataõ*, e outros fabios da antiguidade, fe a modo de cepos, ou troncos, que aonde nafceraõ fazem rais, e no feu primeiro chaõ apodrecem, naõ bufcáraõ fora da Patria as noticias, que lhes faltavaõ. Naõ fe ornára *Hercules* com os defpojos dos Môftros, que domou, fe os naõ fora bufcar pelo mundo; á fua dilatada viagem devem os Argonautas a conquifta do vello de ouro; Se naõ corréra *Ulyffes* remotos climas, fora a Aldea de *Ithaca* de toda a fua gloria o theatro. Homens perpetuamente cafeiros, faõ gallos, que fó fabem do feu poleiro. Sabios peregrinos, imitaõ no feu curfo as fontes, que paffando por veas de prata, ouro, efmeraldas, e faffiras, tomaõ, e comfigo levaõ a flor de fuas preciofas qualidades. Zombe embora *Plutarco* dos que louvaõ a peregrinacaõ, e diga, que fe parecem com os que julgaõ as eftrellas errantes mais nobres, e felices, que as fixas. Naõ ha.efcola mais util para a vida, que as muitas vidas ou modos de viver, que na variedade das Naçoens fe obferva. Vem-fe muitas coufas nunca viftas; aprendem-fe muitas, que fe naõ fabiaõ, faz fe o homem capaz de toda a cafta de negocios, e folga de ver efte mundo, antes de fair delle. Até para os principes, que das fuas cortes fazem na terra o feu paraifo, bom he que peregrinem, para conhecerem o mundo, que elles governaõ. Os commodos, as delicias, os obfequios dos fubditos, podem dar a conhecer a hum homem, que nafceo foberano, mas com efte conhecimento, naõ o fazem digno da foberania: fe naõ fahira *Alexandre* da fua *Macedonia*, naõ paffara dos limites de regulo e naõ chegára a avaffallar o mundo.

Do Tempo futuro.

Trate o homem do prefente, e naõ queira penetrar no futuro; quem de taõ longe póem a mira, naõ pode dar no alvo. Muitas vezes bom hé ignorar o que ha de fucceder; por que fe for bem, a.di-

laçaõ

laçaõ he tormento; e se for máo, o trabalho he sem proveito. Para futuros, naõ ha segurança. Ao Embaixador, que na guerra movida por Luiz XI. Rey de França, a Carlos Duque de Borgonha, procurava attrahir ao Emperador Federico, com promessa de se repartirem com elle os despojos, e os estados, respondeo o dito Emperador com este apologo : tres caçadores com a esperança de apanharem hum urso, se comprometteraõ na repartiçaõ delle. Chegados á boca da caverna, sahio a fera com taõ grande impeto, que hum dos caçadores botou a fugir, outro, subio a hũa arvore, e o outro se estendeo no chaõ, fingindo-se morto; chegouse o urso a elle, poz-lhe o focinho no nariz, e nos ouvidos, e naõ lhe conhecendo fôlego, nem sinal de vida, o deixou por morto. O que estava na avore, disse ao companheiro: homem, que te disse o urso, quando te fallou á puridade, com o focinho nos ouvidos? Disseme que era mal feito, dispor da pelle, e carne do urso, antes de o verem morto. Com isto o Emperador deu a entender ao Embaixador, que era preciso apanhar primeiro ao Duque de Borgonha, e que depois se trataria da repartiçaõ dos seus estados. Dos successos do tempo futuro, só Deos tem certeza.

Dos Ricos.

Os Antigos Patriarchas eraõ ricos só em gado. Os Banqueiros saõ ricos em dinheiro. Os Principes saõ ricos em terras, & Senhorios. Em lugares estereis, sem hervas, nem plantas produz a natureza o ouro, para mostrar que os amadores das riquezas naõ tem fé, nem honra. Os ricos facinorosos, que ainda que celebrados nas historias, saõ o opprobrio da sua posteridade, poderiaõ ter boa fama, se lhes naõ facilitára este metãl a execuçaõ de seus danados intentos. Em todas as idades foraõ as riquezas antagonistas da virtude; ellas inventaraõ os mais enormes delitos; ellas ensináraõ os filhos a tirar a seus pays a vida ; enfináraō os podérofos a opprimir os innócentes, arruinar as familias, faquear os templos, & defpir os altares ; ellas induziraō os amigos a que faltaffem á fé, incitáraō os vaffallos a negar a os principes a obediencia, a os libidinofos deraō meyos para violar a pudicicia das donzellas, e eftragar a honra dos maridos ; finalmente ellas ainda que boas para a vida civil, faō caufa de todos os males ; e pofto que os fabios fe fouberaō aproveitar dellas, a cobiça, e o mao ufo das mefmas, enchêraō o mundo todo de criminofos. Homens ricos ordinariamente fe perdem, por terem muito, e faberem pouco ; defprezaō o faber, porques lhes parece, que para todo o genero de vida, lhes bafta o ter. A Ariftippo perguntou Dionyfio, porque razaō os filofofos frequentavaō as cazas dos ricos, e naō os ricos as dos filofofos. Refpondeo Ariftippo, que os filofofos conhecem o que lhes falta, e os ricos ignoraō o de que neceffitaō. Senhores ricos, e filofofos pobres, naō pódem fazer coufas grandes, porque a eftes lhes falta dinheiro, e áquelles efpirito. Dizia Diogenes, que muitos ricos faō como as plantas, que nafcem em defertos, e defpenhadeiros, porque dos frutos, que ellas daō, naō comem os homens, mas corvos, bilhafres, e feras ; tambem as riquezas de muitos naō faō para fugeitos benemeritos, mas para chocarreyros, efpadachins, rufiões, e meretrizes.

Da Liberalidade.

A liberalidade he huma virtude moral que fabe difpender as riquezas em bom ufo. Ariftotles diz, que he virtude, que com o dinheiro, e fazenda fe moftra benefica a os homens. Segundo a definicaō dos filofofos modernos, he virtude moderada do affecto humano no dar, e no receber riquezas humanas, unicamente pelo motivo do honefto. Na liberalidade naō faō actos incompativeis o dar e o receber, nem o liberal fe ha de envergonhar de receber ; por-

que

que dar sempre, e nunca receber, he caminho certo para em breves espaços naõ ter mais que dar.
Brevemente se secariaõ os rios, se o mar dando sempre do seu, naõ recebesse do alheyo, mas dando,
e recebendo, se faz o circulo do perpetuo movimento, com que se sustenta o mar e se fertiliza a
terra.　O liberal naõ da para receber, mas recebendo
para dar, da no mesmo tempo que recebe, recebendo
de huns com a maõ, e dando aos outros com a tençaõ.　Pintaraõ os antigos a liberalidade em figura
de molher, com a cornucopia em huma maõ, e hum
compasso na outra.　Na cornucopia significavaõ a
inclinaçaõ em dar ; e no compasso denotavaõ as medidas, que a prudencia ha de guardar nas dadivas.
Dar em excesso, he extinguir a liberalidade ; o
muito oleo apaga a luz ; conserva-se esta virtude
com effusaõ moderada ; dar pouco a pouco, e em
diversos tempos, he saborear o gosto de dar ; quem
dá com attençaõ, está com animo de dar mais.　Naõ
he bem fechar a arca de sorte que se naõ possa abrir ;
nem convem abrilla de maneira, que se naõ torne a
fechar.　Chuvas de ouro saõ larguezas de Deoses ;
ainda assim andou Jupiter moderado nesta preciosa
profuzaõ ; porque naõ cahe de pancada a agua da
chuva mas a gota, e gota se distribue.　Porem ao
rigor desta ley naõ estaõ obrigados os Principes,
que tem muyto que dar ; porque o seu melhor the-
souro he o coraçaõ dos subditos : tanto mais se aug-
menta este erario, quanto mais o da fazenda real se
despeja.　Repartindo Alexandre com os Macedo-
nios os seus dominios, se abrio caminho para con-
quistar o mundo.　Principalmente com litteratos, e
homens doutos foy liberalissimo.　A Aristoteles em
remuneraçaõ do trabalho que tomou em indagar a
natureza, e propriedades dos animaes, deo de hũ
jacto o valor de quatrocentos e oitenta mil escudos.
De Cyro, cognominado o Grande, escreve Atheneo,
que a Pythareo, seu domestico, fizera hum donati-
vo de sete cidades.　De Julio Cezar escreve Seneca,

que

que das suas victorias naõ queria outro proveito, que
o poder, e o gosto de distribuir com os seus soldados os despojos. Em nenhuma cousa mais se parecem os monarcas com Deos, que em dar; celebra
Cassiodoro a liberalidade de hum Principe, que para alegrar o povo, naõ reparava em fazer gastos ex-
orbitantes. Este genero da larguezas naõ arruina o
estado, porque alivia o povo. Nem estas devem
ser festas de todos os dias, porque o festejo chegaria a
ser estrago : só Deos, cujos thesouros saõ inexhaus-
tos, pode dar sempre, e a todos. Entre os antigos Romanos era inviolavel a ley, que mandava que ninguem gastasse em festa publica, sem prover do necessario os pobres do seu bayrro; tomavaõ por a-
fronta, que andassem hũs homens por portas, quando estavaõ outros brindando nas mesas. A este
proposito dizia Plataõ, que na cidade em que muito
pobre mendiga, ha muito ladraõ que furta. Mas
para que he dar regras, e ajuntar documentos, para
huma virtude, que a mofina, ou a cobiça desterrou
do mundo. Hoje a liberalidade he como aquelles
rios que sumidos na terra, nunca mais saõ vistos.

Da Liberdade.

A liberdade he hum estado natural, no qual tem o
homem todos os movimentos da sua vontade independentes, e livres. Esta he a liberdade da alma, a
que nem as influencias dos astros, nem a presciencia
divina, nem os divinos decretos, nem os ameaços dos
tirannos necessitaõ a querer, ou naõ querer; porque
Deos a deo ao homem, com livre alvedrio, e poder
absoluto, para observar, ou quebrantar sua divina
ley. O corpo pelo contrario he sugeito a todo o genero de cativeiros. Forma se na prisaõ do ventre
materno, apenas nascido, fica envolto, e preso nas
faxas ; livre desta escravidaõ cahe na da puericia
sugeito aos açoutes; nos confins da adolescencia,
esperaõ por elle tirannicas payxões, e crueis appetites

para

para o defpojar do refto da liberdade; cada arte, **ou** cada fciencia a que fe applica, he huma carga de **re-gras**, huma oppreffaõ de preceitos. Em idade mayor, achaques, e doenças o encravaõ na cama, donde cahe para a cova, em hum cativeiro que naõ tem refgate. Ainda affim, no meyo de todas as penfões, e prifões da fua trifte vida, logra o homem no feu trato huma certa liberdade, da qual ninguem fe quer privar, por naõ viver violentado. Até os animáes, as feras, e os mais vis infectos, procuraõ defender, e confervar a liberdade, que lhes deo a natureza; finalmente os elementos, ainda que infenfiveis, fe esforçaõ para vencer os obftaculos, que os cativaõ; voará o fogo hum monte, por naõ ficar conftipado na mina; indignada do freyo de hum dique trefbordará a agua, e alagará huma provincia; impaciente de claufura de lugares fubterraneos, abalará o ar hum reyno, e com horriveis tremores abrirá a cidades inteiras profundas fepulturas. Naõ he logo maravilha, que façaõ os homens tantos extremos para confervarem a liberdade propria do feu eftado. Diogenes aquelle famofo defprezador de quanto cubiça a ambiçaõ dos homens, para fe ver livre das fugeições defte mundo, fe revolvia no feu dolio, como planeta de differente esfera, e tendo valor para recufar a graça de Alexandre, naõ teve animo para fe fugeitar ao jugo da Corte. Naõ queremos fenhor, por brando que elle feja, (dizia Demofthenes) receofo da dominaçaõ de Antipater. A liberdade he hum bem que fe naõ deve perder fe naõ com o fangue. Naõ he fenhor de fi, quem a outrem fugeitou a lingua. Hum fó homem, que queira, e faiba fallar a tempo, faz callar, e tremer a muitos; pode fer caufa da confervacaõ de hum reyno, que o filencio perderia. Nefte perigo efteve o imperio Romano, reinando Tiberio, tempo em que (fegundo efcreve Tacito) o fallar era delito. Naõ tem outro açoute as culpas dos grandes, que o de huma lingua, generofamente folta. Abftenhafe de obrar mal,

quem

quem quizer que fe falle bem. A verdade muda
introduz a tirannia. Teve graça huma moça, filha
de certo homem rico de Lisboa, a qual perguntada,
porque naõ queria cafar com hum fugeito, que a
pedia a feu pay fem dote; diffe que por naõ perder
a liberdarde, que as outras mulheres tem, quando
tendo differenças com feus maridos, podem com
razaõ dizer, que os compráraõ com o que ellas lhes
deraõ em cafamento.

Das Demandas.

Litigios faõ chagas do eftado, e minas das familias.
Qualquer demanda he huma furia infernal, que
tudo defcompoem, e tira a todos do feu lugar. Da
cultura da terra tira ao lavrador, do commercio
ao mercador, do altar ao facerdote. Litigios faõ os
filhos do Chaos e da noite, tudo nelles faõ con-
fusões, e trevas. Saõ hum funefto compofto de
todos os males; tem na ira incendios, no rancor
veneno, no dolo ciladas, na vingança rayos. Diante
das demandas anda o dezejo da fazenda alheya; aos
lados a falfidade, o engano, a mentira, a perfidia;
vem atráz o arrependimento, e a pobreza, com pés
de chumbo fe ha de entrar em litigios, e fugir delles
com azas de aguia, fempre procuraõ os bons politicos atalhar os litigios, e abafallos no feu nafcimento.
Com efte intento fizeraõ os Cyrenios huma ley, pela
qual os homens litigiofos e demandiftas eraõ chamados para diante dos Juizes, chamados Ephoros,
e eftes depois de os multar, os declaravaõ infames.
Dizia Cataõ, que para bem fe haviaõ encher as au-
diencias, de eftrepes, e abrolhos, para as partes naõ
irem pleitear 'fem perigo de quebrar as pernas. Os
antigos Romanos levantaraõ na fua mayor audiencia
a eftatua de Marfyas, com huma corda na maõ dando a entender, que quem fem razaõ moveffe demanda
a alguem, encorreria na mefma pena que o dito
Marfyas, a quem por contender com Apollo teme-
rariamente

rariamente fobre as ventagens da mufica, os juizes
mandáraō dar garrote. Antigamente os juizes dei-
xavaō pendurados em hum prégo todos os pleitos
problematicos, ou feitos, em que havia razões para
julgar pro e contra. Por iffo Claudio Henrique,
julgador Parifiente, em huma das fuas orações foren-
fes traz o cazo da mulher de Smyrna, que por haver
dado peçonha a feu marido, os Areopagitas, feus
juizes, a abfolvéraō para cem annos, por quanto
efte mefmo feu marido havia morto hum filho do
primeiro cafamento da dita mulher, e na caufa
intentada havia compenfaçaō de delito. Toda a
peffoa, que fe poem a litigar, fe engolfa em hum
mar de provas, futilezas, e trapaças, que tem por
praya, e porto, a pobreza, e a morte. O peyor he,
que nefte conflicto, o gafto he das partes, e o proveito dos advogados. Em quanto com as raās pelejaō
os ratos, vem o minhoto, e papa tudo. A rapoza que
vio o leão, e o urfo canfados de pelejar fobre o logro
de huma preza, ainda que naturalmente muito timida,
fe foy chegando, e levou comfigo a materia da contenda. As ruinas de dous enriquecem o terceiro.

Da Lifonja.

A lifonja he huma nimia complacencia, e affectada
fineza em louvar as prendas, obras, ou palavras
alheyas. Mal fuave, doce veneno, vicio cortefaō,
brando verdugo da verdade, efcandalo dos animos
generofos, e fo de efpiritos humildes indigna eftimaçaō O boy, ruftico quadrupede, permitte que o
enfeitem; o leaō, generofa fera facode de fi os enfei-
tes da cama. Compoz Ariftobulo hum livro, cheyo
de lifonjas, fobre a victoria que Alexandre alcançára
del rey Poro; tomou o magnanimo principe o livro,
e lançando-o ao mar, diffe; merece o authòr feme-
lhante Caftigo Tambem da fua corte lançou Alexandre ao famofo efcultor Staficrates, que fe offere-
cêra a fazerlhe de todo o monte Athos hūa eftatua.
Notavel artifice he o lifonjeiro, para todas as caras

tem carêtas, e calçados para todos os pés; mas todas
as suas obras saõ postiças, e todo o seu artificio
fingimento. A sua mayor destreza está em conformar o som da sua lyra com a picada da Tarantula.
Com esta assonancia, ou consonancia se fez Sejano
taõ absoluto senhor da vontade de Tiberio, que
sendo este Principe para todos dissimulado, só era
facil, e sincero para Sejano. O Lisonjeiro, para viver
a sombra do seu Principe, se faz do seu Principe sombra, que assim como a sombra he o bugio do corpo,
anda com elle, e com elle para; com elle se deita,
e se levanta; se tem corcova, se encurva; e se coxea,
claudica; assim para o lisonjeiro he perfeicaõ arremedar até os defeitos do principe. Na corte de Antigono, que tinha o collo torto, os cortesãos se fizeraõ
torcicollos. Esta depravada imitaçaõ do Principe he
ruina da monarchia, porque he veneno da verdade.
Naõ tem esta mayor inimigo, que o falsete do interesse, que ordinariamente faz o compasso na musica
do palacianos. Pinta-se a lisonja em figura de mulher tocando huma frauta, com hum veado aos pés,
adormecido ao som deste instrumento; no veado se
representa o Principe, que vencido da suavidade da
lisonja, fecha os olhos a verdade. Com cem olhos
guardava Argos a Io, convertida em vacca, começou
Mercurio a tocar tam suavemente, que os cem olhos
de Argos se fecháraõ e teve Mercurio poder para lhe
tirar com a vacca a vida. A's falsas adulaçoës dos
Aulicos de Vitellio attribue a historia a cegueira do
orgulho, e crueldade deste Principe. Era Vespasiano de natural brando, e benigno, com lisonjeiras
falsidades o induziraõ seus cortesãos a carregar de
tributos o povo. Finalmente muitas vezes mayores
danos faz a lingua do lisonjeio, que a espada do
inimigo.

Da Vingança.

Toda a vingança particular, e privada he usurpaçaõ do poder, e da justiça publica, e divina. Desprezão

prezão nobres animos as injurias de fogeitos vulgares. Naõ fez Achilles cafo das calumnias de Therfites; Filippe de Macedonia, e Cefar foraõ infenfiveis aos tiros da maledicencia. Zombou a Aguia de Efopo da peça, que lhe fez o rato; pareceolhe indigno da fua ira, bicho nojento. O vingarfe naõ he reftaurar o credito, he confirmarfe defacreditado. Com feridas alheyas naõ fe curaõ as proprias, com fangue naõ fe efmaltaõ injurias. Enfurecerfe aos defacatos de hum furiofo, he fazerfe efpelho da fua braveza; rebater calumnias, he fazerfe ecco de aggravos. Se a cada bataria de ondas refpondera o penhafco com huma pedra, brevemente fe deftruiria o penhafco. Anelar vinganças, he ter aberta, e frefca huma ferida, a qual efquecida, eftaria encourada. Injurias lembradas fe perpetuaõ, porque fe fazem hereditarias. ellas faõ a unica coufa, que nefte mundo o tempo naõ gafta; enterradas renafcem, femelhantes aos rios, que depois de correr debaixo da terra, tornaõ a inundar os campos. Os que com moftras de amifade disfarçaõ o dezejo de fe vingar, faõ como a nuvem, que vio o profeta Ezequiel; era cercada de hum circulo de ouro, mas trazia dentro em fi rayos, e tormentas. A mais nobre vingança he moftrar o offendido, que fe póde vingar do offenfor; o naõ vingarfe, he moftrar, que naõ fentio a offenfa; e naõ fentilla, he prova de animo invulneravel. A impaffibilidade he attributo divino. As mulheres faõ vingativas, porque faõ frageis; a fua fenfibilidade he demoftraçaõ da fua fraqueza.

Da Loquacidade.

Ha homens, que naõ vivendo de ar, como o camalçonte, continuamente tem a boca aberta, e della cahe hum diluvio de palavras, que inunda os ouvidos, e affoga a gente. Quando ha trovoadas, emmudecem as rãas; eftes faõ rãas, que em charcos de pantanofas parlendas atroaõ o mundo. Huns metidos a politicos, tudo reduzem a razoens de eftado;

chovem

chovem da fua boca Democracias, Ariftocracias, Oligarchias, Ochlocracias, Capitolios, e Areopagos, Triumviratos, e Dictaturas, Plebifcitos, e Senatus-confultos, Leys Municipaes, e Caftrenfes; comparaõ o governo dos Cefares com o dos noffos Principes, as modernas com as antigas republicas, os coftumes de hoje com os dos antepaffados, e com infructuofa navegaçaõ correndo mares de fabedoria, ventilaõ queftões, fem dar fundo as materias. Outros prefumidos de geographos, fem tropeçar correm (como diz o vulgo) as fete partidas do mundo; puxaõ por zonas, e remotos climas, acarretaõ ifthmos, e peninfulas, terras arcticas, antarcticas, e auftraes incognitas, e quando parece que poem fim, pegaõ em longitudes, e com latitudes fe eftendem. Que diremos do poeta loquaz, mimofo das Mufas, e fanfarraõ do Parnaffo? A qualquer phrafe poetica, fente cócegas nos ouvidos, e naõ ouve fallar em verfos, que logo os naõ traga todos a baila: Hexametros, e Pentametros, Iambos, Saphicos, Adonicos, Choriambicos; da regras, e preceitos para Coplas Reaes, e Redondilhas, para Sonetos, encadeados, e retrogrados; allega com poetas nacionaes e eftranhos; amontoa todos os termos da Epica, Lyrica, Dramatica, Dithyrambica; a ouvillo bebe de hum gole toda a Hipocrene, e procura efgotar de hum jacto a Caballina fonte. Compara Plutarco aos loquazes com vafos vafios, que foaõ mais que os cheyos. A hum grande fallador, que depois de huma larga pratica pedio a Ariftoteles, que lhe perdoaffe a moleftia, refpondeo o filofofo: naõ tenho que perdoar, que eu naõ tomei fentido no que difeftes. Careon, homem loquaz, pedindo a Ifocrates, que lhe enfinaffe Rhetorica, pedio Ifocrates dobrado falario: e perguntando Careon a razaõ das duas pagas, refpondeo Ifocrates: quero huma para enfinarte a fallar, e quero outra, para enfinarte a callar. Grandes falladores faõ befpas, que todo o dia eftaõ zunindo, e naõ fazem mel nem cera. Homem

mem loquaz (dizia Solon) he cidade fem muros,
cafa fem porta, navio fem piloto, e cavallo fem freyo. Em cavallo defbocado ninguem fe poem fem
medo, fempre fe deve temer boca defenfreada. Foi
tomada a cidade de Athenas, e deftruida por Silla,
porque na loja de hum barbeiro os efpias defte
general ouviraõ praticar na parte mais fraca da dita
cidade.

Da Maledicencia.

O dizer mal, he proprio dos que naõ podem fazer
mal. De todos diz mal Pafquinho, que naõ tem
pés nem mãos, e ainda que eftivera inteiriço, por
fer eftatua, e figura immovel, naõ pode fazer mal.
Dizem que o Papa Adriano VI. lhe mandara dizer, que o faria lançar ..o rio Tybre; refpondeo
Pafquinho: Tambem debaixo da agua canta a
raã. Nem eftá fóra de razaõ, chamarfe raã o maldizente, porque fempre a fua voz he o rouço fom
de hum charco; e affim como as raãs, que infeftaraõ
a corte de Pharaó, fujáraõ a prata, o ouro, e as mais
ricas alfayas de palacio, affim fe pegaõ os maldi-
zentes á coroa, e tiaras. No proximo naõ enxergaõ
os olhos do maldizente fe naõ defeitos. O alvo dos
feus intentos he denigrir, procura ter fama, infa-
mando, funda em detracção o feu augmento, e
de vituperios efpera louvor. O. maldizente he o
tigre da republica; naõ fofre armonias de encomios
alheyos; a fua lingua he cauda de efcorpiaõ, fempre em acto de picar; fabe achar cicatriz, aonde
naõ houve chaga; naõ poupa vivos, nem mortos,
nem a amigos, muito menos a inimigos; he verdugo da reputaçaõ, e homicida do credito; femea
confufoens, e colhe difcordias. Notavel defeito he
efte da lingua humana, para os applaufos muda,
para vituperios eloquente. Toda a antiguidade
nos deo fó tres, ou quatro bons panegyricos, todas
as fatiras pareceraõ excellentes. Aos feus piques
deve

deve Tacito a fuà eftimaçaō ; muito mais agrada, quando moteja de Tiberio, do que quando celebra a Germanico ; finalmente todos o gabaō, porque nunca gabou a ninguem. Mas a virtude, ainda que perfeguida de maledicos, naō defconfia. Nenhum homem grande, quando calumniado, fe reputa pequeno. Tres grandes Emperadores, Theodoflo, Arcadio, e Honorio, pay, filho, e neto, fizeraō huma ley, aqual manda, que os que cegos da paixaō dizem mal, Sejaō perdoados, porque a fua maledicencia, fe procedeo de pouco juizo, merece defculpa; fe de furor, piedade; fe de malinidade, efquecimento e defprezo.

Prologo de Jacinto Freyre de Andrade.

Saō os prologos hum anticipado remedio aos a-chaques dos livros, porque andaō fempre de companhia os erros, e as defculpas. Eu por hora me defvio do caminho trilhado, nam quero pedir per-daō de nada: quem achar que dizer, naō me perdoe, (nem ferá neceffario encomendalo.) Se me notarem o livro de roim, naō negaráō que he breve, e efcrito em lingoa Portuguefa, que tantos engenhos modernos, ou temem ou defprezaō, como filhos ingratos ao primeiro leite, fervindo-fe de vozes eftrangeiras, por onde paffaraō como hofpedes, fem refpeito áquellas veneraveis Cans, e ancianidade madura de noffa linguagem antiga. Efcrevi efta hiftoria com verdade de memorias fieis, fem que a penna, ou o affecto alteraffe o menor accidente. Antes que efte papel fahiffe dos borroens, fey que muitos o taxaraō de efcaffo, dizendo, que houvera de dilatar a hiftoria com allufoens, e paffos da efcritura, que o fizeffem mais crecido; eftes compram os livros pello pezo, nam pello feitio: de mais que nam permittem tam licencioza penna as leys da hiftoria. Outros queriam que me valeffe do eftrepito de vozes novas, a que chamam cultura, deixando

a ef-

a eſtrada limpa por caminhos fragozos, e trocando
com eſtimaçao̅ pueril, o que he melhor, pello que
mais ſe uſa. Mas como nam determinei liſongear
a goſtos eſtragados, quis antes com a ſingeleza da
verdade ſervir ao aplauſo dos melhores, que á fama
popular, e errada.

*Prologo do Conde da Ericeira ao ſeu Portugal Reſtau-
rado.*

Eſta ceremonia, leytor, de eſcrever Prologo,
mais por eſcuſar a cenſura de que falto á ley de dar
principio com elle a huma hiſtoria tao̅ grave, que
por me parecer a ley preciſa, me reſolvo a obſer-
vála : porque diſcurſado o fim com que ſe eſtabe-
leceo, avalio por inutil eſte trabalho, entendendo
que na eſcolha da hiſtoria, e no acerto de eſcrevella
conſiſte toda a fortuna dos authores, Porque nem
a amizade dos leytores póde encobrir os defeitos do
eſcritor, nem eſcurecerlhe os acertos o odio ; e entre
eſtes dous extremos (ordinariamente vicioſos) ſe levanta o tribunal da juſtiça dos deſintereſſados, por
independentes, ou por nao̅ conhecidos, que coſtu-
mao̅ dar o louvor por premio aos benemeritos, e a
cenſura por caſtigo aos culpados.

Huma das mayores emprezas do mundo he a re-
ſoluçao̅ de eſcrever huma hiſtoria : porque além de
innumeravel multidao̅ de inconvenientes, que he
neceſſario que ſe vençao̅, e de hum trabalho ex-
ceſſivo, que he preciſo, que ſe ſuppere ; no meſmo
tempo em que ſe pretende lograr o fructo de tantas
diligencias, tendo-ſe vencido formar o intento, vencer a liçao, aſſentar o eſtilo, colher as noticias, lançar os borradores, tiralos em limpo, coñferilos, e a-
puralos, quando quem eſcreve ſe anima na emprenſa
do livro que eſcreveo ao pompoſo titulo de author,
entao̅ começa a ſer réo, e réo julgado com tao̅ ex-
ceſſiva tirannia, que tendo lingua para fallar de tantas peſſoas, como ſao̅ as que comprehende qualquer
volume

volume, a naõ pode ter para deixar de fer condem-
nado fem fer ouvido. Julgo por muito errada a
opiniaõ commua, que affenta, que a hiftoria he pa-
ralelo da pintura : porque he tanto mais privilegiado
o pintor que o efcritor, que teve lugar Apelles, pondo em publico huma figura que havia pintado, de
lhe emendar a roupa, que hum artifice della lhe
condemnou por imperfeita, e de caftigar a ouzadia
de outro, que naõ fendo pintor fe attreveo a ar-
guirlhe o perfil da figura. Naõ he concedida aos
efcritores tanta liberdade : porque no mefmo ponto
que os finetes do prelo acabaraõ de fellar a hiftoria
que efcreveraõ, logo perderaõ toda a acçaõ de emen-
dála, e na difficuldade de fatisfazer a hum mundo de
juizos diverfos, fica provado o defengano, de que
naõ pode haver hiftoria bem avaliada de todos. O
fol por que coftuma taõ repetidamente offerecerfe do
berço do oriente ao tumulo do occafo aos olhos do
univerfo, fe expoem á cenfura dos que fem penetrar
a mageftade do feu refplandor, e a utilidade dos feus
rayos, fugeitando a razaõ ao appetite, huns o con-
demnaõ de claro quando a calma os aperta, outros
de efcuro quando o frio os afflige, fem reparar que
os latidos do caõ celefte, que amedrentaõ na cani-
cula os vapores, de que as nuvens no inverno fe for-
maõ, faõ, e naõ o fol, culpados no rigor da calma, como
as nuvens na afpereza do frio. Que importa, que a
verdade da hiftoria, e pureza do eftilo a formem como
o fol perfeita, fe os leytores pretendem avaliala como
querem, e naõ como merece.

A eftas, e outras muitas difficuldades fe fujeita
quem fe refolve a efcrever huma hiftoria que pela
opiniaõ commua dos hiftoriadores coftuma fer de
feculos paffados, em que mais defaffogados os animos entraõ a defcubrir a verdade dos fucceffos. Po-
rêm quaes feraõ os inconvenientes, quaes os perigos
quafi invenciveis, a que fe arroja quem tomou a
temeraria refoluçaõ de imprimir em fua vida a
hiftoria do feu tempo. Em verdade que até imagi-

A a   nado

nado faz horror efte intento: porque oppoftas, e
incompativeis as obrigaçoens forçofas aos rifcos ma-
nifeftos, naõ parece poffivel, apurados, deftilarem
hum compofto perfeito; pois faltar á verdade fica
fendo infamia do author, defcóbrilla nas acçoens
defacertadas, cahe em defcredito dos comprehendi-
dos. Encarecer os benemeritos, ferá inveja dos in-
dignos: louvar os viciofos, opprobrio dos benemeritos: contar todos os fucceffos, he empenho inven-
civel: callar alguns póde fer queixa dos intereffados.
Nos cafos grandes, e aindá nos inferiores ajuftaremfe
todos em que faõ verdadeiramente contados, difficul-
tofamente fe poderá confeguir: porque eu experi-
mentei, achando-me em quatro batalhas, e em
outros encontros, com muitos mil homens, naõ fe
defcobrirem dous que concordaffem no mefmo facto;
e tenho alcançado que a razaõ defta variedade vem
a fer, que como hum fó homem naõ he poffivel affiftir a todos os fucceffos de hum conflicto, entendendo erradamente que cahe no defcredito de naõ ter
parte em tantas acçoens diverfas, todas as que naõ
póde alcançar com a vifta defacredita por fabulofas.
Se pois me naõ foi poffivel contar fem contradiçaõ
em varias converfaçoens hum fó fucceffo na prefença
dos que fe acharaõ nelle; como poderei confeguir
facilmente efcrevendo tantas batalhas, fitios, intre
prezas, e encontros fuccedidos á valerofa naçaõ
Portugueza por efpaço de vinte e oito annos nas
quatro partes do mundo, julgarem todos a narraçaõ
das victorias por verdadeiras, e por certos os motivos
das emprezas militares, e politicas, feguindofe ordinariamente defte erro de difcurfos, e falta de noticias
huma queixa perpetua contra quem efcreve, e em
alguns hum odio eterno, que muitas vezes fe def-
affoga pelos caminhos do delirio. A efte, pois, la-
biryntho de eftradas confufas, a efte encanto de fan-
tafmas disformes me perfuadio a arrojarme o entran-
havel amor da minha patria, de que fe compoz com
o fangue a natureza, fundado no jufto temor de que

naõ

naõ occultaffem mortaes, as urnas do efquecimento, as acçoens gloriofas de tantos heroes excellenteş: accrefcentandofe a eftas razoens outro mayor eftimulo, que foi avaliar como obrigaçaõ precifa defcobrir os motivos do principio, e remate defta hiftoria de Portugal reftaurado, que me animei a efcrever, pois como Alpha, e Omega, divino fymbolo dos Gregos, foraõ verdadeiramente os dous polos (fe unidos pela natureza, pelos accidentes diverfos) que me perfuadiraõ a abraçar efte grande empenho, pretendendo moftrar claramente ao mundo, affim a juftiça com que o Sereniffimo Rey D. Joaõ IV. de immortal memoria fe reftituio á Coroa de Portugal, como a jufta razaõ com que o excellente Principe D. Pedro, fegundo Tito, delicia dos homens, fem mais caufa, que a defenfa, confervaçaõ, e fegurança defte reyno, tomou fobre feus generofos hombros o governo delle, julgando-o por menos pezado que a coroa, que com tanta admiraçaõ dos meftres da politica, defpreza. Naõ me obrigando fó o zelo da honra da patria a defcobrir os fundamentos de taõ grandes fucceffos, fe naõ tambem a fegurança da minha opiniaõ que amei fempre mais que a propria vida; porque como logrei a fortuna de ter na guerra parte nas mayores victorias, que fe confeguiraõ nefte reyno, era neceffario moftrar que a guerra foi jufta, para que as acçoens fe julgaffem por virtuofas. E como da mefma forte me fuccedeo fer hum dos que affiftiraõ ás heroicas refoluçoens do Principe D. Pedro, era precifo manifeftar, que foraõ juftificadas, para me livrar da calumnia dos que fem noticias verdadeiras difcurfaffem a fatalidade del rey D. Affonfo VI. fem entenderem que foi depofto pelos tres eftados do reyno por incapaz do governo delle, e por inutil para a fuccefaõ da coroa.

Além deftas taõ urgentes caufas, naõ foraõ menos poderofas para me levar a efte intento, affim a magoa (como ja referi) de ver que infenfivelmente hia o tempo confumindo a noticia de tantas acçoens

heroicas,

heroicas, por faltar quem fe refolveffe a efcrevellas?
porque fó até o anno de 1644. que efcreveo com
erradas noticias Joaõ Bautifta Viraugua Veneziano os
fucceffos defte reyno, e o conde Mayolino nas fuas
guerras civis, fe acha memoria delles. Como a pena da pouca verdade com que todos os authores
Caftelhanos, que fe animaraõ a fallar na guerra
fuccedida entre as duas coroas a referiraõ: porque
naõ fó trataraõ de encobrir com ficçoens a grandeza
das noffas victorias, fenaõ que cahiraõ na ignoran-
cia de errar os tempos das campanhas, preferindo
as fucceffivas ás antecedentes, os nomes aos fitios
das provincias onde aconteceraõ, e aos cabos, e
officiaes que fe acharaõ nellas, feguindo o mefmo
delicto que condenaraõ a hum author Francez, que
imprimindo hum livro, em que affirmava, que Fran-
cifco I. Rey de França naõ fora prezo na batalha de
Pavia. E perguntandolhe a razaõ porque calumni-
ava a fua verdade, lançando ao mundo aquella mentira, refpondeo, que nos feculos futuros quem leffe
a fua hiftoria, e a dos Caftelhanos, daria credito a
opiniaõ a que fe affeiçoaffe. Eftes foraõ os motivos
que me perfuadiraõ a taõ difficultofo empenho, ani-
mandome juntamenté a tomallo por minha conta as
muitas circunftancias, que me habilitaraõ: porque
além de herdar de antigos, e valerofos avôs fer a
verdade alma da vida, como he da hiftoria, tive a
fortuna de me criar no paço com o foberano, e
efclarecido Principe D. Theodofio, affiftindolhe continuamente de idade de fete até quinze annos, e
igualmente aprendendo com elle a primeira gra-
matica e a liçaõ das hiftorias. Nefte tempo fiz memoria das primeiras politicas com que el Rey D.
Joaõ deo principio ao governo defte reyno.

De quinze annos comecei a fervir na guerra, em
que paffei por todos os poftos taõ vagarofamente
como qualquer foldado da fortuna, e cheguei ao
mayor emprego de governador das armas. Acheime
em todas as occafioens grandes da provincia deAlen-

tejo.

tejo do anno de 1650. até a batalha de Montes
Claros, e fui voto em todos os negocios de mayor
confideraçaõ. A guerra das provincias aonde naõ
affifti, e a das conquiftas conferi com os cabos e
officiaes que fe acharaõ em todas as emprezas, depois de examinar os papeis mais intimos em que a
curiofidade de varias peffoas fe havia exercitado.

As negoceaçoens fora do reyno, que tocaraõ a dif-
ferentes fugeitos, efcrevo por informaçaõ de cada
hum delles, e pelos livros em que os embaixadores
lançaraõ as embaixadas. Os mais negocios pelos
documentos das fecretarias de eftado, e guerra, buf-
cando em todos, alem deftas noticias, a fegurança
de teftimunhas defintereffadas, que tiveraõ fem de-
pendencia parte em todos os fucceffos politicos, e
militares.

Dez annos de trabalho me levou efte primeiro
volume: no difcurfo defte tempo naõ houve peffoa
douta ou intelligente que fe animaffe a examinal-
lo, a quem o naõ entregaffe, fugeitando-me a qualquer cenfura que fe me apontava, e emendando o
que fe me advertia, ainda que foffe contra o proprio entendimento, entendendo, que como efta hiftoria naõ ha de fer fó fatisfaçaõ do meu juizo, fe
naõ dos alheyos, ficó melhor livrado em ter por de-
fenfores os que a emendarem. He documento, que
felicemente devo ao fobre todos prudentiffimo difcurfo do Principe noffo fenhor. Antes que come-
çaffe a efcrevella paffei por efpaço de dous annos as
hiftorias mais feletas antigas, e modernas, conhecendo, que era neceffario affentar o eftylo: porque
naõ tendo feguido mais efcolas, que as militares, que
naõ coftumaõ deixar á liçaõ dos livros muitas horas
de exercicio, haviaõ levado a inclinaçaõ a equivocos,
e termos poeticos, frafe de que os primeiros annos
mais continuamente fe alimentaraõ, e de que me
fez apartar o mais que me foi poffivel a doutrina
dos meftres da hiftoria, e a dos preceitos hiftoricos de
Mafcarde Italiano, e do padre Mene Francez, que

A a 3 nefta

nefta idade com grande elegancia fe empregaraõ nefte affumpto. Nos ultimos dous annos padeci mayor trabalho: porque tocandome nelles a occupaçaõ de Védor da Fazenda da Repartiçaõ da India, que coftuma deixar poucas horas livres, as que me ficavaõ de defcanço, empregava nefte exercicio, conhecendo, que paffar dia fem lançar linha, he perder do tempo a melhor joya, que atégora naõ tem havido milagre que foffe poderofo para reftauralla.

Huma das mayores fatisfaçoens que tenho alcançado nefte meu emprego, he imprimirfe quafi juntamente com efte livro, os que com tanto louvor proprio, e com tanta honra da naçaõ Portugeza efcreveo o moderno Livio Manoel de Faria e Souza ; e como em todos chegaõ os fucceffos, que refere nas quatro partes do mundo, da fundaçao de Portugal até o anno de 1640. fica com a minha hiftoria enfiada a de Portugal até a paz celebrada entre efta coroa, e a de Caftella, que he o affumpto que comprehendem eftes dous volumes.

Agora, leytor, ou pio, ou malevolo, ou defintereffado, he neceffario affiar o difcurfo, e eu feguro que muito menos ha de cuftar aos leytores arguir, do que a mim me tem cuftado o efcrever. E fe alguma fatisfaçao fe entender que mereço pelo meu trabalho, naõ quero mayor recompenfa que o reconhecimento, de que atégora naõ fahio ao mundo hiftoria mais verdadeira: pois fem affeiçaõ, odio, efperança, ou temor, naõ perdoei a requifito algum neceffario para a hiftoria, que me ficaffe por efcrever, parecendome fó efcuzado relatar defeitos particulares, tendo por opiniaõ, que os que fe arrojaraõ a defcobrillos merecem mais o titulo de fatyricos que de hiftoriadores, exceptuando aquelles que referiraõ vicios, de que depende a narraçao da fua hiftoria, como he neceffario que me aconteça quando chegar a referir os fucceffos da vida del Rey D. Affonfo VI.

8   Naõ

Naõ podia Tito Livio eximirſe de contar os ex-
ceſſos de Tarquino, originando-ſe da ſua laciva a
mudança de Reys á Republica no Imperio Romano:
mas pudéra Quinto Curcio encobrir os vicios de
Alexandre Magno, que naõ lhe embaraçaraõ as victorias da Aſia. Preciſo foi a Joaõ de Mariana relatar
a cegueira de Henrique VIII. de Inglaterra na indigna affeiçaõ de Anna Bolena, ſendo eſte deſatino
a primeira cauſa de paſſar de Defenſor da Igreja Catholica a cabeça da perfidia heretica: mas pudera
Henrique Caterino de Avila diſſimular os diverti-
mentos de Henrique III. de França, que naõ per-
tenceraõ ao governo da ſua monarquia, Faminiano
Eſtrada os deſconcertos de Chapim Vitello, e o
Cardeal Bentivoglio nas ſuas memorias hiſtoricas os
vicios de alguns Cardeaes do ſacro collegio, e outros
muitos que uſaraõ deſta indigna liberdade. Deſco-
briremſe os defeitos que naõ prejudicaraõ a inter-
eſſes publicos, muitas vezes ſervem aos leytores mais
de eſtimulo, que de emenda, uſando dos exempla-
res para deſculpa dos vicios que pretendem ſeguir,
e he Deos verdadeira teſtimunha de que o meu principal intento, he atalhar todos os que podem offender a ſua divina mageſtade, e ſer prejudiciaes á gloria deſta monarquia.

*Ao muito poderoſo e Chriſtianiſſimo Principe el Rey Dom
Joaõ noſſo ſenhor, deſte nome o terceiro de Portugal.
Prologo de Joaõ de Barros, em as primeiras quatro
Decadas da ſua Aſia.*

Todalas couſas, muito poderoſo Rey e ſenhor
noſſo, tem tanto amor á conſervaçaõ de ſeu proprio
ſer: que quanto lhe he poſſivel, trabalhaõ em ſeu
modo por ſe fazerem perpetuas. As naturaes em
que ſomente obra a natureza, e naõ a induſtria humana, cadahuã dellas em ſi meſma tem huma virtude generativa, que quando devinamente ſaõ deſpoſ-
tas, ainda que periguem em ſua corrupçaõ: eſſa

meſma

eſſa meſma natureza as torna renovar em nôvo ſer, com que ficaõ vivas e conſervadas em ſua propria eſpecie. E as outras couſas que naõ ſaõ obras da natureza, mas feitos e actos humanos, eſtas porque naõ tinhaõ virtude animada de gérar outras ſemelhantes a ſi, e por a brevidade da vida do homem, acabavaõ com ſeu autor: os meſmos homens por conſervar ſeu nome em a memoria dellas, buſcaraõ hum divino artificio, que repreſentaſſe em futuro, o que elles obravaõ em preſente. O qual artificio, peró que a invençao delle ſe dê a diverſos autores : maes parece per Deos inſpirado, que inventado per algum humano entendimento. E que bem como lhe aprouue que mediante o pádar, lingua, dentes, e beiços, hum reſpiro de ar mouido dos bofes cauſado de huma potencia, a que os Latinos chamaõ *affatus*, ſe formaſſe em palavras ſignificativas, pera que os ouvidos ſeu natural objecto, repreſentaſſem ao intendimento diverſos ſignificados e conceptos, ſegundo a diſpoſiçaõ dellas : aſſi quiz que mediante os characteres das letras, de que uſamos, diſpoſtas na ordem ſignificativa da valia que cada naçaõ deu ao ſeu alfabeto, a viſta objecto receptivo deſtes characteres, mediante elles, formaſſe a eſſencia das couſas, e os racionaes conceptos, ao modo de como a fala em ſeu officio os denuncia. E ainda quiz que eſte modo de elocuçaõ artificial de letras, per beneficio de perpetuidade precedeſſe ao natural da fala. Porque eſta, ſendo animada, naõ tem maes vida que o inſtante de ſua pronunciaçaõ, e paſſa á ſemelhança do tempo, que naõ tem regreſſo : e as letras ſendo huns characteres mortos, e naõ animados, conthem em ſi eſpirito de vida, pois a daõ acerca de nós á todalas couſas. Cá ellas ſaõ huns elementos, que lhe daõ aſſiſtencia : e as fazem paſſar em futuro com ſua multiplicaçaõ de annos em annos, per modo maes excellente, do que faz a natureza. Pois vemos que eſta natureza pera gerar algũa couſa, corrompe e altera os elementos, de que he compoſta, e as letras ſendo

elementos,

elementos, de que se compoem e forma a significa-
çaõ das cousas, nem o entendimento (posto que seja
passivo na intelligencia dellas pelo modo de como
vem a elle:) mas vaõse multiplicando na parte me-
morativa per uso de frequentaçaõ, taõ espiritual em
habito de perpetuidade, que per meyo dellas no fim
do mundo, taõ presentes seraõ áquelles que entaõ
forem, nossas pessoas, feitos, e dittos; como hoje
per esta custodia literal, he vivo o que fezeraõ e dis-
seram os primeiros, que foraõ no principio delle. E
porque o fructo destes actos humanos, he mui differente do fructo natural, que se produze da semente
das cousas, por este natural fenecer no mesmo homem, pera cujo uso todas foraõ criadas, e o fructo
das obras delles he eterno, pois procede do entendimento e vontade, onde se fabricaõ e aceptaõ todas,
que por serem partes espirituaes, as fazem eternas:
fica daqui a cadahũ de nós huma natural e justa obrigaçaõ, que assi devemos ser diligentes e solicitos em
guardar em futuro nossas obras, pera com ellas apro-
veitarmos em bom exemplo, como prōtos e con-
stantes na operaçaõ presente dellas, pera commum e
temporal proveito de nossos naturaes. E vendo eu
que nesta diligencia de encomendar as cousas á
custodia das letras (conservadoras de todalas obras) a
naçaõ Portugues he taõ descuidada de si, quaõ
pronta e diligente em os feitos que lhe competem per
milicia, e que maes se preza de fazer, que dizer:
quiz nesta parte, usar ante do officio de estrangeiro,
que da condiçaõ de natural; despoendome a escrever o que elles fezeraõ no descobrimento e conquista
do Oriente, por se naõ perderem da memoria dos ho-
mẽs, que vierem despois de nos, taõ gloriosos feitos,
como vemos serem perdidos de vossos progenitores,
mayores em louuor do que lemos em suas chronicas
(segundo mostraõ algũs fragmentos de particulares es-
cripturas). E na aceptaçaõ deste trabalho e perigo
a que me despus, ante quero ser tido por taõ ousado
como foi o derradeiro dos trinta e tantos escriptores
que escreveraõ a passagem e expediçaõ que Alexandre

dre fez em Afia, o qual temeo pouco o que delle
podiaõ dizer, tendo tantos ante fi : que imitar
o defcuido de muitos, a quem efte meu trabalho per
officio e profiſſaõ competia.   Pois avendo cento
e vinte annos (porque de tantos tracta efta efcriptura) que voſſas armas e padroẽs de victorias tem tomado poſſe, naõ fômente de toda a terra
maritima de Africa e Afia, mas ainda de outros
mayores mundos, do que Alexandre lamentava, por
naõ ter noticia delles : naõ ouue alguem que fe an-
tremeteſſe a fer primeiro nefte meu trabalho, fômente Gomez Eanes de Zurara Chronifta mór deftes
reynos em as coufas do tempo do Infante Dom Henrique (do qual nós confeſſamos tomar a mayor parte
dos feus fundamẽtos, por naõ roubar o feu a cujo
he.)   No cometer do qual trabalho, vendo eu a
mageftade e grandeza da obra, naõ fui taõ atrevido
que logo como ifto defejei, puſeſſe maõs a ella ; ante
tomei por cautella defte cometimento, uzar do modo
que tem os architectores.   Os quais primeiro que
ponhaõ maõ na obra a traçaõ e debuxaõ, e de fi
aprefentaõ eftes deliniamentos de fua imaginaçaõ,
ao fenhor de cujo hade fer o edificio.   Porque efta
materia, de que eu queria tractar, era dos trium-
phos defte reyno, dos quaes naõ fe podia falar fem
licença do autor delles, que naquelle tempo defte
meu propofito era el Rey voſſo padre de gloriofa
memoria : eftando fua Alteza em Evora o anno de
quinhentos e vinte, lhe aprefentei hum debuxo feito
em nome de voſſa Alteza, porque com efte titulo
ante ella foſſe acepto.   O qual debuxo naõ era alguma vatrachomiomachia, guerra de raãs e ratos,
como fez Homero por exercitar feu engenho, ante
que efcreveſſe a guerra dos Gregos e Troyanos :
mas foi huma pintura metaphorica de exercitos, e
vitorias humanas, nefta figura racional do Emperador Clarimundo, titulo da traça (conforme a idade
que eu entaõ tinha) a fim de aparar o eftilo de minha poſſibilidade pera efta voſſa Afia.   A qual pintura

tura, por fer em nome de voffa Alteza, affi conten-
tou a el rey voffo padre, defpois que foube fer ima-
gem defta que ora tracto, que logo me pagou meu
trabalho : dizendo aver dias que defejava eftas coufas
das partes do oriente ferem poftas em efcriptura,
mas que nunca achara peffoa de que o confiaffe, que
fe me eu atrevia a efta obra, (como o debuxo mof-
trava) o meu trabalho naõ feria ante elle perdido.
Por a qual confiança lhe beijei a maõ per ante peffoas que hoje faõ vivas : por a pratica fer hum pouco alta lendolhe eu hum ou dous capitulos da moftra e debuxo.   E eftando pera abrir os aliceces defte
grande edificio, com o fervor da idade e favor das
palavras de confiança que fe de mi tinha : aprouve
a Deos levar a el Rey voffo padre áquelle celeftial
affento, que fe dá aos Catholicos e Chriftianiffimos
Principes, com que fiquei fufpenfo defta empreza.

Socedendo tambem logo proverme voffa Alteza dos
officios de thefoureiro da cafa da India e Mina, e
defpois de feitor das mefmas cafas, carregos que com
feu pezo fazem acuruar a vida, pois levaõ todolos dias
della, e com a occupaçaõ e negocio de fuas armadas
e commercios, afogaõ e cattivaõ todo liberal engenho.
Mas parece que affi eftava ordenado de cima, que
naõ fómente me coubeffe per forte da vida, os tra-
balhos de feitorizar os commercios de Africa e Afia:
mas ainda efcrever os feitos, que voffos vaffallos na
milicia e conquifta dellas fezeraõ.   Porque correndo
o tempo, e achando eu entre alguãs cartas que el
rey voffo padre ante da minha offerta, tinha efcripto.
a Dom Frãcifco d'Almeida, e a Affonfo d'Albo-
querque, que conquiftaraõ e governaraõ a India,
encomendandolhe que meudamente lhe efcreveffem
as coufas e feitos daquellas partes, com tençaõ de
as mandar poer em efcripto, e que voffa Alteza
com a mefma tençaõ o anno de quinhentos e trinta
e hum, tambem o efcreveo a Nuno d'Acunha, que
naquelle tempo a governava, mandandolhe fobre
ifto regimentos feitos per Lourenço de Caceres, a
quem

quem tinha encomendado a escriptura destas partes, o que naõ ouve effeito, e seria per ventura por elle falecer: determinei, por se naõ dilatar este dezejo que vossa Alteza tinha, e eu pagar a confiança que el Rey vosso padre de mim teve, repartir o tempo da vida, dando os dias ao officio, e parte das noites a esta escritura da vossa Asia: e assi compri com o regimento do officio, e com o dezejo que sempre tive desta empreza. E como os homens pela mayor parte saõ maes prontos em dar de si fructos voluntarios, que os encomendados, imitando nisto a terra sua madre, a qual he maes viva em dar as sementes que nella jazem per natureza, que as que lhe encomendamos per agricultura: parece que me obrigou ella a que patrizasse, e que per diligencia prevalecesse maes em mim a natureza que della tenho, que quanto outros tem recebido per obrigaçaõ de officio, profissaõ de vida, e agricultura de beneficios. Pois naõ tendo eu outra cousa maes viva pera tomar esta empreza, que hum zelo da gloria que se deve a vossas armas, e farha a meus naturaes, que militando nellas, verteraõ seu sangue e vida: fui o primeiro que brotei este fructo de escriptura desta vossa Asia, se he licito, por ser de arvore agreste, rustica, e naõ agricultada, poder merecer este nome de fructo ante vossa real magestade.

Prologo na Chronica del Rei Dom Emanuel, dirigida por Damiaõ de Goes abo serenissimo Principe Dom Henrique, Infante de Portugal.

Muitos, e graves authores nos principios de suas chronicas trabalaram em louvar ha historia, da qual tudo ho que dixeram foi sempre muito menos do que se devia dizer, porque assi quomo ella he infinita, assi seus louvores naõ tem fim, nem termo a que se possam reduzir, e pois tudo ho trattado nesta parte, he quasi nada em comparaçam do que deve ser voltarei daqui ha vela, pera poer ha proa nesta:

4   na

ña qual por çerto naõ oufara, nem devera de tocar, fe me naõ fora mandado per V. A. por fer de quali- dade, que dipois dalgũas pefloas ha terem começa- da el Rei dom Joam voflo irmaõ que fanĉta gloria haja, lhes mandou tomar ho que ja tinhaõ fcripto, pera fe acabar per outros, de cujas habilidades tinha mor opiniaõ, em maõs dos quaıs ficou atte feu fa- leçimento. E confyderando V. A. que pois eftas pefloas, de que fe tanto fperava, nam tinham feito em tempo de trinta e fette annos, que há que el Rei Dom Emanuel voflo pai faleçeo, coufa que re- fpondefle ao mereçimento de tal negoçio, fem fe lembrar de quaõ fraco eu devo fer pera hum taman- ho pefo, me mandou nefte anno do Senhor de M.D.LVIII. que daquillo em que muitos, quomo em coufa defefperada, fe nam atreveraõ poer ha maõ, tomafle eu ho cuidado, ho que fiz com mór oufadia do que a meu fraco juizo convinha, movido com tudo por fós dous refpeitos, ho hum por eu fer feĉtura do dito fenhor Rei voflo pai, criado em fua cafa, e em feu fervico, defde idade de nove annos, ho outro por me parecer que fe nam movera V. A. a me mandar coufa em que confiftiam todolos feitos, e louuores, defte feliçiffimo rei, e daquelles que ho ferviram na guerra, e na paz, fenam por confiar de mĩ ho mais fubftançial que no fcrever dás chronicas fe requere, que hé com verdade dar a cada hũ ho louuor ou reprehenfam que mereçe. Pelas quaes razoẽs matrevi a tomar efte trabalho, ho qual tal qual he, me pareçeo que naõ devia, nẽ era bem que dedicafle fe nam a V. A. quomo a prinçipal author de ha fama, e gloria del Rei feu pai fairem em luz, e nam pereçer a lembrança das coufas notaveis que aconteçeram ahos Portuguefes per todo ho difcurfo de feu regnado.)

De Francisco Rodriguez Lobo no seu Pastor Peregrino.

Chegaraõ as serranas ao pé da fonte com esta alegria, e saudaraõ ao peregrino, que com inveja da quella liberdade as estava olhando, e em quanto (lavando os cantaros) com graciosas perguntas importunaraõ a fonte, o velho pegureiro se veyo assentar junto delle, e perguntandolhe donde era, e o que alli buscava, vieraõ a travar pratica, da qual Lereno entendeo que o serrano era homem singelo, e taõ de vidro, que se lhe via pello rosto o coraçaõ, e pello amor com que elle tratava a gente daquella condiçaõ, lhe foi de hum lanço em outro, perguntando da vida, e do cuidado que tinha na serra, pois naquella companhia o via tam contente, ao que o velho respondeo desta maneira: ha mais de sessenta annos que naci detraz daquelle penedo que daqui apparece no alto da serra, e de entaõ ate agora, nem vi mais terra que a que delle se descobre, nem desejei outra, de quantas ouvi gabar a meus naturaes, nunca tive de meu outro bem mayor, que naõ desejar os alheos, nem outro mal que me desse mais cuidado, que as occasioens que o tempo me ofereceo de poder possuir o que os homens estimaõ, e sentem tanto perder, como saõ enganos; sou taõ pobre do que a fortuna reparte, que cada hora que me quiser tomar conta de tantos annos, lhe naõ ficarei devendo, nem hum desejo; vivo de guardar gado doutros donos, sou fiel em o tratar, diligente no pasto, e remedio delle, rico com a parte que me cabe da sua laã, e do seu leite, porque della me visto, e delle me sustento, nem quando os frutos saõ poucos me lastimo, nem quando as novidades saõ mayores me alvoroço: contentame o bem, naõ me çoçobra o mal; tenho huma cabana em que vivo, feita por minha propria maõ das arvores destas brenhas, naõ acharas dentro cousa que deva direitos á ísdade, tudo saõ instrumentos necessarios ao meu

officio

officio de guardador, e fe algũa coufa fobeja, ferá das que ainda faõ mais importantes pera a vida, da qui me alevanto contente, e aqui me recolho defcançado, porque nem acordo com os penfamentos na ventura, nem adormeço com elles repartidos em bens que enganaõ, e em males que os homens efcolhem de feu grado : de noite qualquer eftrella que vejo, he a minha, porque todas favorecem o meu eftado, de dia fempre o fol me apparece de hũa cor, porque o vejo com os olhos livres. Tenho efte inftrumento, a cujo fom canto, quando he bem me alegro, porque canto pera me alegrar, e quando pello contrario me naõ peza muito, porque o naõ faço por alegrar outrem, quando ha frio, e neve na ferra, tambem ha lenha neftes montes, e fogo neftas pedras com que me deffendo, quando a calma he grande, com o abrigo deftas arvores, e a vefinhança das fontes me recreo, affim faõ os meus manjares, como he a minha vida, nem ella me pede os que lhe façaõ dano, nem eu os tenho, o meu veftido he fempre defta cor, porque em qualquer coufa (ainda de menos contia) he a mudança perigofa. O mayor trabalho que tenho, hé os paftores com que trato, porque cada hũ tem hũa vontade, e hum entendimento, e eu me hei de fervir fó do meu pera com todos; porem de tal maneira ufo delle, que me naõ dá do fuceffo que pode acontecer; ao avarento naõ lhe peço nada, nem lhe aconfelho que dé a outrem, nem lhe louvo o naõ dar nada a ninguem, e affim nem lhe minto, nem o molefto. Ao foberbo, nem me faço grande por naõ ficar com elle em contenda, nem aòs outros pequenos, porque com elles fe naõ alevante mais. Ao ingrato, ou o naõ firvo, porque me naõ magoe, ou quando o firvo, lembrome que a fua má natureza naõ pode tirar o preço a obra, que de fi he boa. Ao fallador, calome: ao calado, defcubrome com tento. Ao doudo, naõ lhe atalho a furia: ao nefcio, naõ trabalho por lhe dar razaõ; ao pobre naõ lhe devo;

ao rico naõ lhe peço; ao vaõ, naõ o gabo; nem o reprendo; ao lifonjeiro naõ no creo e defte modo com todos eftou bem, e nenhum me faz mal. Naõ digo verdades que amarguem, nem tenho amizades que me profanem : naõ adquiro fazendas que outros me invejem, porque nefte tempo, das melhores tres coufas delle, nacem as mais danofas que ha no mundo : da verdade, odio, da converfaçaõ defprefo : da profperidade, inveja; fou qual me ves, e qual te eu digo, naõ quero parecer outro, nem fer mais do que pareço : venho muitas vezes a efta fonte, que me pegou a fua condiçao, falla verdade a todos, e com nenhum tem differença; cuftumeime a eftas fuas agoas, que ainda que faõ amargofas, faõ faudaveis, apagaõ peçonha, desfazem feitiços, e valem contra mordiduras de bicha. Se nifto que me ouvifte achas alguma coufa que te contente, e queres hir comigo, pois já he tarde, te hofpedarei na minha cabana, na qual podes entrar fem temor, dormir fem perigo, e fahir fem faudade; comeras do leite, ouviras dos contos, e partiras quando quizeres. Em quanto o velho pegureiro ifto dizia, eftava o paftor lançando contas a fua vida, com grande inveja do que aquelle lhe contava da fua, e no cabo lhe refpondeo com hũ fufpiro. Ah ditofo ferrano, as eftrellas te confervem nefte eftado, pera que nunca conheças a differença delle : tu fó vives, tu fó deves ao ceo eftar izento das leis da ventura, mais he pera invejar tua pobreza, que a mayor vaidade do mundo, mais pera eftimar a tua cabana, que os mais luftrofos edificios delle, mais pera fe dezejar a tua liberdade, que os mandos e fenhorios, com que os homens fe cativaõ, e engrandecem, e mais pera fe bufcar a tua companhia, que o mayor thefouro, eu naõ quero mais della por agora, que partirme chorando pello que te ouvi. A efte tempo fe partiaõ ja as ferranas, que o chamaraõ, elle fe defpedio do peregrino, dandolhe hũ pequeno vafo de cortiça que levaffe daquella agoa, e tocando a fua

rabeca

rabeca fe apartou, e o paftor ficou em batalha com males proprios, que á vifta dos bens alheos tomaraõ força contra hum fujeito, que elles já tinhaõ de todo defbaratado.

Naõ pareceo a Lereno o Lugar acommodado pera paffar nelle a noite, e quafi arrependido de naõ aceitar o offerecimento do ferrano, tomou outro caminho que hia mais polla fralda da ferra, imaginando que perto averia alguma aldea, em que fe recolhefe, e andando por elle o que ficava do dia, lhe veyo a faltar na entrada de hum valle, que por huma parte eftava cheo de arvores altas, e efpeffas, que apertadas de dous outeiros que as affombravaõ, e com a claridade das eftrellas que por entre os ramos as feria, fe moviaõ vagarofamente fobre huma lagoa, feita de hum ribeiro que decia do monte; na qual a fombra e movimento dos ramos, a luz que por entre elles lhe vinha, moftrando o efcuro das agoas, e algũs arrebatados faltos das roucas rans, fazendo hum temerofo ecco nos ouvidos, e na vifta, hum medrofo pavor, com trifteza, e receo conftrangiaõ o coraçaõ do defterrado paftor. E vendo que dalli pera diante lhe ficava outra vez o caminho da ferra, fe abrigou a hum tronco que tinha as coftas no ribeiro, que com o murmuro da agoa lhe podia ajudar a grangear o fono, e alli laneado entre as hervas, e os ramos naõ podendo adormecer, cantava defta maneira.

Entre eftes arvores triftes
Que a fombra da noite cobre
E com manfo movimento
Triftes penfamentos movem.

Ao longo defte ribeiro
Que por entre as pedras corre
Fazendo hum doce rugido
Que o mudo filencio rompe.

B b   De

Debaixo defte arvoredo
Que dos carregados montes
Tomando a cor, vai perdendo
Vifta, graça, fombra, e cores.

Perguntar quero a meus males
Pois fei que os males refpondem
Se exprimentei quanto cuftaō
Que me digaō quanto podem.

Se podem matar, que efperaō?
Se dar vida, qual efcolhem?
Pois a que entre elles padeço
He vida que fempre morre.

Mil annos há que a fuftento
E inda que mil annos conte
He porque em pezares crecem
Como pera os goftos fogem.

Conjuraraō fe contra ella
Dous cegos que eftaō conformes
Contra a razaō, e o dezejo,
Que he hum amor, outro a forte.

Mandaraō me defterrado,
E eu vou fem faber aonde,
So fei que ambos vaō comigo
E que fe eu ando, elles correm.

Males, fe aveis de acabarme,
Pera que faō tantos golpes?
Que o menor delles pedia
Hum fofrimento de bronze?

Contra mi vós, e a ventura
E eu fem outros valedores,
Mais que fo meus penfamentos
Pera que me faço forte?

Se quereis viver comigo,
Porque temeis voffa morte?
Que os males naō duraō mais,
Que em quanto hum trifte os efconde. Def-

Defcubrime algum remedio
De efperanças, que eſſas podem
Suſtentarme, e fuſtentarvos
Neſte valle, e noutros montes.

Porque inda que fam veneno
Que vai matando de lonje,
Crioufe com elle a vida
Que lhe tem poſto outro nome.

Que he iſto! naõ refpondeis?
Mas outrem por vós refponde,
Que aos males pedir razaõ
He pedir firmeza a forte.

Do Camoens.

Eſtavas linda Inez poſta em foſſego,
De teus annos colhendo o doce fruto,
Naquelle engano da alma, ledo, e cego,
Que a fortuna naõ deixa durar muito:
Nos faudofos campos do mondego,
De teus formofos olhos nunca enxuto,
Aos montes enfinando, e as ervinhas.
O nome, que no peito efcrito tinhas.

Do teu principe alli te refpondiaõ
As lembranças, que na alma lhe moravaõ,
Que fempre ante feus olhos te traziaõ,
Quando dos teus fermofos fa apartavaõ :
De noite em doces fonhos, que mentiaõ,
De dia em penfamentos, que voavaõ:
E quanto em fim cuidava, e quanto via,
Eraõ tudo memorias da alegria.

D'outras bellas fenhoras, e princezas,
Os dezejados talamos engeita,
Que tudo em fim, tu puro amor defprezas,
Quando hum geſto fuave te fugeita :
Vendo eſtas namoradas eſtranhezas,
O velho pay fefudo, que refpeita,
O murmurar do povo e fantafia
Do filho, que cafarfe naõ queria.

Tirar

Tirar Inez ao mundo determina,
 Por lhe tirar o filho, que tem prefo,
 Crendo co fangue fó da morte indina,
 Matar do firme amor o fogo acefo :
 Que furor confentio, que a efpada fina,
 Que pode fuftentar ò grande pefo
 Do furor Mauro, foffe levantada,
 Contra huma fraca dama delicada ?

Traziaōna os horriferos algozes
 Ante o Rey, ja movido a piedade,
 Mas o povo com falfas, e ferozes
 Razoens, á morte crua o perfuade :
 Ella com triftes e piedofas vozes,
 Sahidas fó de magoa e faudade
 Do feu Principe e filhos que deixava,
 Que mais que a propria morte a magoava.

Para o ceo criftalino levantando
 Com lagrimas os olhos piedofos,
 Os olhos, porque as maōs lhe eftava atando
 Hum dos duros miniftros rigurofos :
 E depois nos meninos atentando,
 Que taō queridos tinha, e taō mimofos,
 Cuja orfandade como māy temia,
 Para o avô cruel affi dizia.

Se ja nas brutas feras, cuja mente
 Natura fez cruel de nafcimento :
 E nas aves agreftes, que fómente
 Nas rapinas aerias tem o intento,
 Com pequenas crianças vio a gente,
 Terem piedofo fentimento,
 Como coa māy de Nino ja moftraraō,
 E cos Irmaōs, que Roma edificaraō.

O'tu que tens de humano o gefto, e peito,
 Se de humano he matar huma donzella
 Fraca, e fem força fo por ter fugeito
 O coraçaō, a quem foube vencella
 A eftas criancinhas tem refpeito
 Pois o naō tens á morte efcura della,

Movate a piedade fua, e minha,
Pois te naõ move a culpa, que naõ tinha.

E fe vencendo a Maura refiftencia,
A morte fabes dar com fogo, e ferro,
Sabe tambem dar vida com clemencia,
A quem para perdella naõ fez erro:
Mas fe to affi merece efta innocencia,
Poemme em perpetuo e mifero defterro,
Na Scythia fria, ou lá na Libia ardente,
Onde em lagrimas viva eternamente.

Poemme onde fe ufe toda a feridade,
Entre leoens, tigres, e verei
Se nelles achar poffo a piedade,
Que entre peitos humanos naõ achei;
Alli co amor intrinfeco, e vontade,
Naquelle por quem morro, criarei
Eftas reliquias fuas, que a qui vifte,
Que refrigerio fejaõ da mãy trifte.

Queria perdoarlhe o rey benino,
Movido das palavras, que o magoaõ,
Mas o pertinaz povo, e feu deftino,
(Que defta forte o quiz) lhe naõ perdoaõ;
Arrancaõ das efpadas de aço fino,
Os que por bom tal feito alli pregoaõ,
Contra huma dama, o peitos carniceiros,
Ferozes vos moftraes, e cavalleiros.

Qual contra a linda moça Policena,
Confolaçaõ extrema da mãy velha,
Porque a fombra de Achiles a condena,
Co ferro o duro Pirro fe aparelha:
Mas ella os olhos, com que o ar ferena
(Bem como paciente, e manfa ovelha)
Na mifera mãy poftos, que endoudece,
Ao duro facrificio fe offerece.

Taes contra Inez os brutos matadores,
No collo de alabaftro, que foftinha
As obras, cõ que amor matou de amores
A'quelle

A'quelle, que depois a fez rainha:
As espadas banhando, e as brancas flores,
Que ella dos olhos seus regadas tinha,
Se incarniçavaõ servidos, e irosos,
No futuro castigo naõ cuidosos.

Bem puderas, o sol, da vista destes,
Teus rayos apartar aquelle dia,
Como da seva mesa de Thyestes
Quando os filhos por maõ de Atreu comia:
Vos o concavos valles que pudestes,
A voz extrema ouvir da boca fria,
O nome do seu Pedro, que lhe ouvistes,
Por muito grande espaço repetistes.

Assi como a bonina, que cortada
Antes do tempo foi, candida, e bella,
Sendo das maõs lascivas mal tratada,
Da menina, que a trouxe na capella,
O cheiro traz perdido, e a cor murchada,
Tal está morta a pallida donzella,
Secas do rosto as rosas, e perdida
A branca, e viva cor, co a doce vida.

As filhas do Mondego a morte escura,
Longo tempo chorando memorâraõ,
E por memoria eterna em fonte pura,
As lagrimas choradas transformâraõ:
O nome lhe puzeraõ, que inda dura,
Dos amores de Inez, que alli passâraõ;
Vede, que fresca fonte rega as flores,
Que lagrimas saõ a agoa, e o nome amores.

Do Mesmo.

Porem ja cincos soes eraõ passados,
Que dalli nos partiramos, cortando
Os mares nunca de outrem navegados,
Prosperamente os ventos assoprando:
Quando hũa noite estando descuidados,
Na cortadora proa vigiando,
Huma nuve que os ares escurece,
Sobre nossas cabeças apparece.

Tam

Tam temorofa vinha, e carregadà,
  Que poz nos coraçoens hum grande medo,
  Bramindo o negro mar de longe brada,
  Como fe deífe em vaõ nalgum rochedo :
  O poteftade, diffe, fublimada,
  Que ameaço divino, ou que fegredo
  Efte clima, e efte mar nos aprefenta,
  Que mór coufa parece, que tormenta ?

Naõ acabava, quando huma figura
  Se nos moftra no ar, robufta, e valida,
  De disforme, e grandiffima eftatura,
  O rofto carregado, a barba efquallida :
  Os olhos encovados, e a poftura
  Medonha, e má, e a cor terrena, e pallida,
  A boca negra, os dentes amarellos.

Tam grande era de membros, que bem poffo
  Certificarte, que efte era o fegundo,
  De Rhodes eftranhiffimo Coloffo,
  Que hum dos fete milagres foi do mundo :
  Cũ tõ de voz nos falla horrendo, e groffo,
  Que pareceo fahir do mar profundo,
  Arrepiaõfe as carnes, e o cabello,
  A mi, e a todos, fó de ouvilo, e velo.

Do Cofta.

  Logo o poldro de generofa cafta,
Nos campos anda mais alto, e foberbo,
E poem a tempo as dobradieas pernas.
E primeyro fe atreve ir o caminho,
E tentar os arrebatados rios,
E arremeçarfe ao mar naõ conhecido ;
Nem dos eftrondos vaõs fe teme, e efpanta ;
O pefcoeo tem alto e tem pequena
A cabeça, e a barriga breve, e curta ;
As coftas tem muy gordas, e carnudas,
E com as polpas o animofo peyto
Se moftra proporcionadamente gordo.
Os mais fermofos faõ caftanhos claros,
Eos que tem de cor verde-mar os olhos ;

A mais

A mais má cor tem alvos, e melados ;
O genorofo naõ fabe eftar quedo ;
Se algumas armas deraõ fom de longe,
As orelhas levanta, e abayxa, e treme.
Cos membros todos, e nas ventas vo've
Hum recolhido fogo, reprimindo-o :
A coma tem efpeffa, a qual defcança
Sendo lançada no direito quarto ;
Mas pellos lombos paffa a larga efpinha,
Rapando cava a terra, e grandemente
A unha, que he de corno duro, foa.

Da Suadade.

Quinta effencia da dor, noyte temida,
  Em cuja fombra he monftro a claridade,
  Mortes, inftantes figlos, que a vontade
  Com a pena do temor mede atrevida.

De bens perdidos Argos homicida,
  Felice pompa da infelicidade,
  Alma da pena, *Trifte Saudade,*
  Vivo morret de huma defunta vida.

Abraços cos tormentos, que padeço
  Por quem a mefma pena a gloria tenho
  Com vofco animo triftes penfamentos.

A voffos males devo o que mereço
  Que a pezar da ventura a tirar venho
  Da auzencia fé, da dor merecimentos.

FINIS.

www.ingramcontent.com/pod-product-compliance
Lightning Source LLC
LaVergne TN
LVHW021946150425
808567LV00038B/52